Charles Lewis Hutchins

Sunday-School Hymnal

Containing also Hymns suited for other Occasions

Charles Lewis Hutchins

Sunday-School Hymnal
Containing also Hymns suited for other Occasions

ISBN/EAN: 9783337340865

Printed in Europe, USA, Canada, Australia, Japan

Cover: Foto ©Paul-Georg Meister /pixelio.de

More available books at **www.hansebooks.com**

THE
SUNDAY-SCHOOL
HYMNAL

CONTAINING ALSO HYMNS SUITED FOR OTHER OCCASIONS

Compiled and Edited by the

REV. CHARLES L. HUTCHINS

Edition C

BOSTON
CONGREGATIONAL PUBLISHING SOCIETY
CONGREGATIONAL HOUSE
BEACON STREET

Prefatory Note.

This edition of the Sunday-School Hymnal has been prepared at the request of some ministers and laymen of different religious communions. Deeply grateful for the honour and privilege conveyed in this request, the editor sends the book forth with the single desire that it may meet the requirements of those who may use it, and be found helpful in the special work for which it is designed.

MEDFORD, MASS., April 1, 1881.

Contents.

	NUMBERS
PSALMS AND CANTICLES.	
FROM THE OLD TESTAMENT	1–136
FROM THE NEW TESTAMENT	137–148
DOXOLOGIES, ETC., FROM THE APOCALYPSE	149–159
GLORIA IN EXCELSIS	160
TE DEUM LAUDAMUS	161–168
A SHORT CHORAL SERVICE	169–170
HYMNS.	
MORNING	171–178
EVENING	179–193
THE LORD'S DAY	194–201
THE SEASONS	202–205
OUR LORD JESUS CHRIST	206–268
HIS ADVENT	206–210
HIS NATIVITY: CHRISTMAS	211–225
HIS CHILDHOOD	226–229
HIS MANIFESTATION	229–232
HIS SELF-SACRIFICE	233–237
HIS TRIUMPHAL ENTRY	238–242
HIS DEATH	243–246
HIS BURIAL	247
HIS RESURRECTION	248–256
HIS ASCENSION	257–259
THE HOLY SPIRIT	260–265
THE BLESSED TRINITY	266–268
APOSTLES AND SAINTS	269–273

	NUMBERS
THE CHURCH: HER ORDINANCES AND OFFICES	274–283
BURIAL	284
MISSIONS	285–291
OFFERINGS	292–294
THANKSGIVING AND HARVEST HOME	295–297
NATIONAL FESTIVALS	298
SCHOOL FESTIVALS	299–301
GENERAL HYMNS	302–454
THE HOLY SCRIPTURES	302–305
REDEMPTION	306–309
FAITH	310–312
PRAYER	313–317
PRAISE	318–342
CONSECRATION	343
TRUST	344–353
HOPE	354–356
LOVE	357–370
COURAGE	371–373
ACTION	374–376
HEAVEN	377–391
MISCELLANEOUS	392–454
RESPONSIVE PRAYERS	455–458
GENERAL FESTIVAL HYMNS	459–473
CAROLS	474–524
CHRISTMAS	474–506
EASTER	507–523
PENTECOST	524

Copyright, 1871 and 1881, by
CHARLES L. HUTCHINS.

NOTES ON CHANTING.

I.—CHANTING may be defined as "*the recitation of words to a short piece of music.*" Good chanting is simply correct musical reading. Due regard, therefore, should be paid to emphasis, distinctness, and expression.

II.—CHANTS are ordinarily of two kinds, SINGLE and DOUBLE. A SINGLE CHANT contains seven bars of music, divided by five single bars and two double bars: each bar has two minims or their value. The first half of the chant has three, the second four bars. The first half is called the *mediation*, the second the *cadence*.

The following is an example of a single chant:

1.   HENLEY.

My heart rejoiceth | in the | Lord: mine horn is ex - | alt - ed | in the Lord.

The notes of the *first* and *fourth* bars are called *reciting* notes, because to them the principal portion of each verse is sung. This reciting note may be extended in time value, in order to allow many words to be sung to it, according to the *pointing* of the verses. These words should be deliberately recited, without either hurrying, or drawling. Musical time begins only with the first bar.

III.—The POINTING is the division of each verse of the Psalm or Canticle, to correspond with the division of the chant: the small bars between words or syllables corresponding with the single bars of the chant, and the colon with the double bar at the end of the mediation.

IV.—A SINGLE CHANT is intended to fit one verse of the Psalms or Canticles; a DOUBLE CHANT, which is twice the length of a single chant, is intended for two verses.

V.—The following is an example of a double chant:

3.   WESLEY.

In use, two verses of the Psalm or Canticle, would be sung to this chant.
Single chants are more used at the present time than double chants.

VI.—In the following arrangement of chants with Psalms and Canticles, all marks not essential to the singer, and all unnecessary stops, have been avoided.

The half-bar (') is placed between words and syllables, only when their division would otherwise be doubtful. Whenever thus used, it indicates that the words or syllables immediately preceding or following it, are to be sung to one note of the music.

Lines placed horizontally (' ═) show that the preceding syllable must be continued for the space indicated.

VII.—Care must be taken to avoid the habit of pausing on some inappropriate syllable in the recitation. No accents are given, as these interfere seriously with smoothness in chanting, and often give it a strained and unnatural effect. If the last syllable but one in the recitation will bear to be sustained, it makes a verse easier to chant: otherwise there must be no syllable so treated. *The last syllable but one, or none at all.* A little practice on the part of singers will show, much better than an arbitrary system of accents, what syllables can be so sustained.

VIII.—*Whenever a comma occurs in the recitation*, it is to be observed, for it is the mark for "taking breath." When no comma occurs, breath is not to be taken till after the colon. The bars in a chant are not intended, any more than in hymn tunes, as resting places. No verse should be begun without previously taking a *full breath*. The neglect of this rule is fatal to good chanting.

IX.—When, after the recitation, a word of more than one syllable is appointed to one note, time must be taken for its proper pronunciation; and, if necessary, the pace of the music must yield to this. It is a neglect of this rule which leads to the too common fault of "gabbling."

X.—The effect of chanting is greatly heightened by *antiphonal* singing, that is, the alternate singing of the verses by two sides of a choir, a school, or a congregation. Each verse should be taken up immediately after the preceding one, producing a continuous effect, as if, indeed (to a listener), the whole Psalm were one long verse.

XI.—An observance of these few rules, will, it is believed, greatly promote the effectiveness and enjoyment of this beautiful and impressive form of Church Music.

PSALMS AND CANTICLES.

I. FROM THE OLD TESTAMENT.

First.

1. HENLEY.
2. Five Voices. MIDGLEY.
3. WESLEY.
4. BODDINGTON.

I SAMUEL II. 1–10.

F **MY** heart rejoiceth | in the | Lord: mine horn is ex | alt-ed | in the | Lord:

2 My mouth is enlarged | over · mine | enemies: because I re- | joice in | Thy sal- | vation.

mf 3 There is none holy | as the | Lord: for | there is | none be- | side Thee.

4 For the Lord is a | God of | knowledge: and | by Him | actions · are | weighed.

5 The Lord killeth, and | maketh · a | live: He bringeth down to the | grave and | bring-eth | up.

6 The Lord maketh poor, and | maketh | rich: He bringeth | low, and | lifteth up.

7 He raiseth up the poor | out · of the | dust: and lifteth the | beg-gar | from the | dunghill.

8 To set them a- | mong · = | princes: and to make them in- | herit · the | throne of | glory.

9 For the pillars of the earth | are · the | Lord's: He hath | set the | world up- | on them.

10 He will keep the feet of His saints, *dim.* and the wicked shall be | silent · in | darkness: for by | strength shall | no · man pre- | vail.

11 The adversaries of the Lord shall be | broken · to | pieces: out of heaven shall He | thunder · up | on · = | them.

12 The Lord shall judge the | ends · of the | earth: (*cr.*) and He shall give strength unto His king, and exalt the | horn of | His an- | ointed.

F Glory be to the Father, | and · to the | Son: and | to the | Holy | Ghost:

As it was in the beginning, is now, and | ever | shall be: world without | end · = | A · = | men.

Second.

5. Russell.

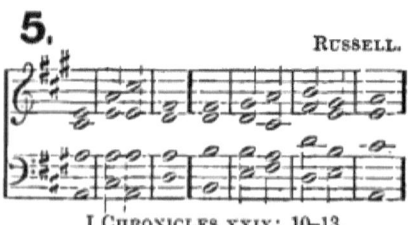

I CHRONICLES XXIX: 10–13.

F BLESSED be Thou, Lord God of | Israel ˙ our | Father: for | ev ˙ = | er and | ever.

2 Thine, O Lord, is the greatness, | and the | power, and the glory, and the | vic-tory, | and the | majesty;

3 For all that is | in the | heaven: and | in the | earth is | Thine;

4 Thine is the | kingdom ˙ O | Lord: and Thou art ex- | alted ˙ as | head ˙ above | all.

5 Both riches and honour | come of | Thee: and Thou | reign-est | o-ver | all;

6 And in Thine hand is | power ˙ and | might: and in Thine hand it is to make great, and to give | strength ˙ = | un-to | all.

7 Now therefore our God we |

6. Turton.

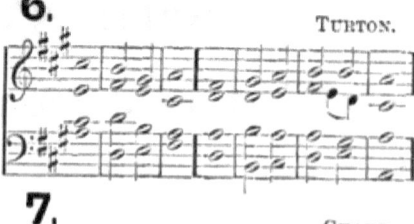

7. Chard.

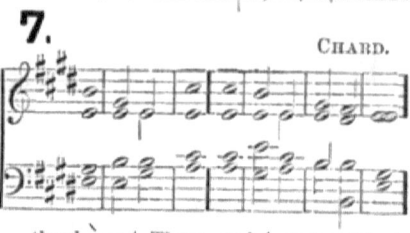

thank ˙ = | Thee: and | praise Thy | glo-rious | Name.

F Glory be to the Father | and ˙ to the | Son: and | to the | Holy | Ghost;

As it was in the beginning, is now, and | ever | shall be: world without | end ˙ = | A ˙ = | men.

Third.

8. Farrant.

PSALM I.

MF BLESSED is the man that walketh not in the counsel of the ungodly, nor standeth in the | way of | sinners: nor sitteth in the | seat ˙ = | of the | scornful.

2 But his delight is in the law | of the | Lord: and in His law doth he | medi-tate | day and | night.

3 And he shall be like a tree planted by the | rivers ˙ of | water: that bringeth forth his | fruit ˙ = | in his | season.

4 His leaf also | shall not | wither: and whatsoever he | do-eth | it shall | prosper.

5 The ungodly | are not | so: but are like the chaff which the | wind ˙ = | driveth ˙ a | way.

6 Therefore the ungodly shall not stand | in the | judgment: nor sinners

9. Monk.

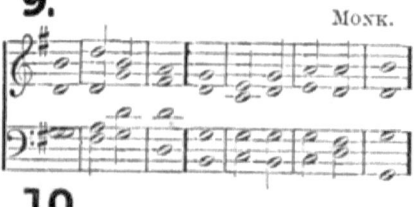

10. Frost.

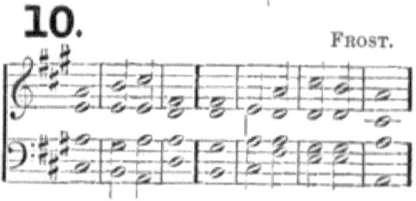

in the congregation | of the | righ ˙ = | teous.

7 But the Lord knoweth the | way ˙ of the | righteous: (*dim.*) but the way of the un- | godly ˙ shall | per ˙ = | ish.

F Glory be to the Father, | and ˙ to the | Son: and | to the | Holy | Ghost;

As it was in the beginning, is now, and | ever | shall be: world without end ˙ = | A ˙ = | men.

Fourth.

11. ANON. **12.** HAYES.

Psalm VIII.

F O LORD our Lord, how excellent is Thy Name in | all the | earth: who hast set Thy | glory ' a | bove the | heavens.

2 Out of the mouth of babes and sucklings hast Thou ordained strength, because of Thine | en-e- | mies: that Thou mightest still the enemy | and ' the a - | ven ' = | ger.

3 When I consider Thy heavens, the | work of ' Thy | fingers: the moon and the stars | which Thou | hast or- | dained.

p 4 What is man, that Thou art | mindful ' of | him: and the son of man, | that Thou | visit ' est | him?

5 For Thou hast made him a little lower | than the | angels: (cr) and hast | crown'd him ' with | glory ' and | honour.

6 Thou madest him to have dominion over the | works of ' Thy | hands: Thou hast put | all things | under ' his | feet;

7 All | sheep and | oxen: yea, and the | beasts ' = | of the | field;

8 The fowl of the air, and the fish | of the | sea: and whatsoever passeth through the | paths ' = | of the | seas.

full. 9 O | Lord our | Lord: how excellent is Thy | Name in | all the | earth!

F Glory be to the Father, | and ' to the | Son: and | to the | Holy | Ghost;
As it was in the beginning, is now, and | ever | shall be: world without | end ' = | A ' = | men.

Fifth.

13. DUPUIS.

Psalm XVI.

MF PRESERVE me | O ' = | God: for in Thee | do I | put my | trust.

2 O my soul, thou hast said unto the Lord, Thou | art my | Lord: my goodness ex- | tend-eth | not to | Thee.

3 But to the saints that are | in the | earth: and to the excellent in | whom is | all my ' de- | light.

4 Their sorrows shall be | mul-ti plied: that hasten | after ' an | oth-er | god.

5 Their drink offerings will | I not | offer; nor take up their | names in | to my | lips.

f 6 The Lord is the portion of my inheritance, and | of my | cup: Thou | dost main | tain my | lot.

7 The lines are fallen unto me in | pleasant | places: yea I | have a | goodly | heritage.

8 I will bless the Lord who hath | given ' me | counsel: my reins also instruct me | in the | night ' = | season.

9 I have set the Lord | always ' be | fore me: because He is at my right hand |

14. PURCELL.

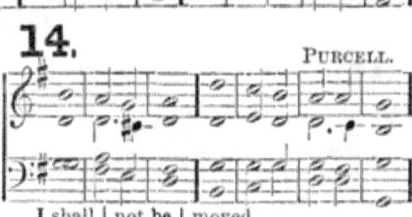

I shall | not be | moved.

10 Therefore my heart is glad, and my | glory ' re- | joiceth: my flesh | also ' shall | rest in | hope.

11 For Thou wilt not leave my | soul in | hell: neither wilt Thou suffer Thine Holy One to | see cor- | rup ' = | tion.

12 Thou shalt show me the path of life, in Thy presence is | fulness ' of | joy: at Thy right hand are | pleasures ' for | ever | more.

F Glory be to the Father, | and ' to the | Son: and | to the | Holy | Ghost;
As it was in the beginning, is now, and | ever | shall be: world without | end ' = | A ' = | men.

Sixth.

15. SMITH.

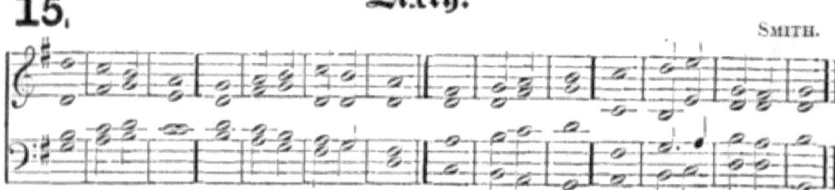

Psalm XIX.

F THE heavens declare the | glory · of | God: and the firmament | showeth · His | hand-y | work.

2 Day **unto day** | utter-eth | speech: and night **unto** | night · = | show-eth | knowledge.

3 There is **no** | speech nor | language: where their | voice · = | is not | heard.

4 Their line is gone out through | all the | earth: and their words to the | end · = | of the | world.

5 In them hath He set a tabernacle | **for** the | sun: which is as a bridegroom coming out of his chamber, and rejoiceth as a strong | man to | run a | race.

6 His going forth is from the end of **the heaven, and its circuit unto** the | **ends of** | **it: and there is nothing** hid | **from the** | heat there- | **of.**

7 The law **of the** Lord **is** perfect, con- | verting · **the** | soul: the testimony of the Lord is sure, | mak-ing | wise the | simple.

8 The statutes **of the Lord** are right, re | joicing the | heart; the commandment of the Lord is pure, en- | light-en- | ing the | eyes.

dim 9 The fear of the Lord is clean, en- | during · for | ever: the judgments of the Lord are true, **ard** | righ-teous | al-to- | gether.

10 More to be desired are they than gold, yea, than | much fine | gold: sweeter also than honey, | and the | hon-ey | comb.

11 Moreover, **by them is** Thy | ser-vant | warned: and in **keeping** of them | there is | great re- | **ward.**

p 12 Who can under- | stand his | errors; cleanse Thou me | from · = | se-cret | faults.

13 Keep back Thy servant also from presumptuous sins, let them not have dominion | o-ver | me: then shall I be upright, and I shall be innocent from the | great trans- | gress · = | ion.

14 Let the words of my mouth, and the meditation | of my | heart: be acceptable in Thy sight, O Lord, my | strength and | my Re- | deemer.

F Glory be the Father, | and · to the | Son: and | to the | Holy | Ghost:
As it **was** in the beginning, is now, and | ever | shall be: world without | end · = | A · = | men.

Seventh.

16. DUPUIS.   **17.** STATHAM.

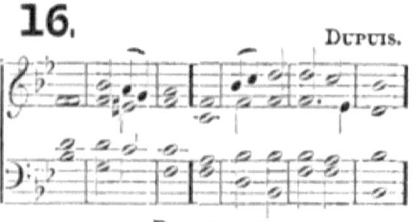 

Psalm XXIII.

MP THE Lord | is my | shepherd: I | shall · = | not · = | want.

2 He maketh me to lie down | in green | pastures: He leadeth me be- | side the | still · = | waters.

3 He re- | storeth · my | soul: He leadeth me in the paths of righteousness | for His | Name's · = | sake.

4 Yea, though I walk through the valley of the shadow of death, I will | fear no | evil: for Thou art with me, Thy rod and Thy | staff they | com-fort | me.

5 Thou preparest a table before me in the presence | of mine | enemies: Thou anointest my head with oil, my | cup · = | run-neth | over.

6 Surely goodness and mercy shall follow me all the | days of · my | life: and I will dwell in the **house** | of the | Lord for | ever.

F Glory be to the Father, | and · to the | Son: and | to the | Holy | Ghost:
As it **was** in the beginning, is now, and | ever | shall be: world without | end · = | A · = | men.

18. FUSSELL. **19.** TURLE.

 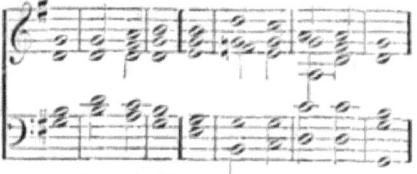

PSALM XXIV.

F THE earth is the Lord's, and the | ful-ness · there- | of : the world, and | they that | dwell there- | in.

2 For He hath founded it up- | on the | seas: and established | it up- | on the | floods.

p 3 Who shall ascend into the hill | of the | Lord: or who shall stand | in His | ho-ly | place?

4 He that hath clean hands, and a | pure · = | heart: who hath not lifted up his soul unto vanity, nor | sworn de- | ceit-ful- | ly

5 He shall receive the blessing | from the | Lord: and righteousness from the | God of | his sal- | vation.

6 This is the generation of | them that | seek Him: that | seek thy | face O | Jacob.

full. 7 Lift up your heads, **O ye gates, and** be ye lift up, ye ever- | last-ing | doors: and the King of | glo-ry | shall come | in.

p 8 Who is this | King of | glory: the Lord strong and mighty, **the** | **Lord** · = | mighty · in | battle.

full. 9 Lift up your heads O ye gates, even lift them up, ye ever- | last-ing | doors: and the King of | glo-ry | shall come | in.

p 10 Who is this | King of | glory: the **Lord** of hosts, | He is · the | King of | glory.

F GLORY BE, &c.

20. Ninth. LANGDON.

FROM PSALM XXVII.

MF THE Lord is my light and my salvation, whom | shall I | fear: the Lord is the strength of my life, of whom | shall I | be a- | fraid ?

2 When the wicked, even mine enemies and my foes, came upon me to eat | up my | flesh: they | stum-bled | and · = | fell.

3 Though a host should en- | camp a- | gainst me: my | heart · = | shall not | fear;

4 Though **war** should | rise a- | gainst me: in | this will | **I be** | confident.

5 One thing **have** I desired ; of the | **Lord**: and | that will | **I** seek | after:

6 That I may dwell in the house of the Lord all the | days · of my | life : to behold the beauty of the Lord, and to en- | quire · = | in His | temple.

7 For in the time of trouble He shall hide me in | His pa- | vilion: in the secret of His tabernacle shall He hide me, He shall | set me · up- | on a | rock.

8 Therefore will I offer in His tabernacle sacri- | fices of ! joy; I will sing, yea, I will sing | prai-ses | unto · the Lord.

p 9 Hear O Lord, when I | cry · with my | voice: have mercy also up- | on me and | ans-wer | me.

10 When Thou saidst, seek | ye my | face: my heart said unto Thee, Thy | face Lord | will I | seek.

p 11 Hide not Thy | face far | from me: put not Thy | servant · a- | way in | anger;

cr 12 Thou hast | been my | help: (p) leave me not neither forsake me O | God of | my sal- | vation.

13 When my father and my | mother · for | sake me: then the | Lord will | take me | up.

14 Teach me Thy | way O | Lord: and lead me in a plain path, be- | cause of · mine | en-e | mies.

15 I had fainted unless I | had be- | lieved: to see the goodness of the Lord in the | land · of the | liv · = | ing.

p 16 Wait on the Lord, (cr) be of good courage, and He shall | strengthen · thine heart: wait I | say up- | on the | Lord.

F GLORY BE, &c.

Tenth.

21. CROTCH.

22. ANON.

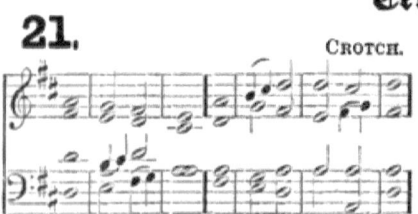

From Psalm XXXIV.

MF I WILL bless the Lord | at all | times:
His praise shall con- | tinual-ly | be ·
in my | mouth.

2 My soul shall make her | boast · in
the | Lord: the humble shall hear there- |
of · = | and be | glad.

3 O magnify the | Lord with | me and
let us ex- | alt His | Name to- | gether.

dim 4 I sought the Lord, | and He | heard
me: and delivered | me from | all my |
fears.

5 They looked unto Him, | and were |
lightened: and their | faces · were | not
a- | shamed.

p 6 This poor man cried, and the Lord |
heard · = | him: and saved him | out
of | all his | troubles.

7 The angel of the Lord encampeth
round about | them that | fear Him.
and | = · de | liver · eth | them.

cr 8 O taste and see that the | Lord is |
good: blessed is the | man that | trust-
eth · in | Him.

9 O fear the Lord, | ye His | saints:
for there is no want to | them that |
fear · = | Him.

10 The young lions do lack, and | suf-
fer | hunger: but they that seek the Lord
shall | not want | any · good | thing.

11 The righteous cry, and the |
Lord · = | heareth: and delivereth
them | out of | all their | troubles.

12 The Lord is nigh unto them that are
of a | bro-ken | heart: and saveth such
as be of a | con-trite | spir · = | it.

p 13 Many are the afflictions | of the |
righteous: (*cr*) but the Lord de- | liver-
eth · him | out · of them | all.

14 He keepeth | all his | bones: not |
one of | them is | broken.

15 Evil shall | slay the | wicked: and
they that hate the righteous | shall be |
de-so | late.

F GLORY BE, &c.

Eleventh.

23. ALCOCK.

24. STEPHENS.

Psalm XXXVI.

MF THE trangression of the wicked saith |
within · my | heart: that there is no
fear of | God be- | fore his | eyes.

2 For he flattereth himself in his
own · = | eyes: until his iniquity be
found · to be | hate · = | ful.

3 The words of his mouth are iniquity |
and de- | ceit: he hath left off to be
wise, | and to | do · = | good.

4 He deviseth mischief up- | on his |
bed: he setteth himself in a way that is
not good, he ab- | horreth · not | e · = |
vil.

f 5 Thy mercy, O Lord, is | in the |
heavens: and Thy faithfulness | reach-
eth | unto · the | clouds.

6 Thy righteousness is | like · the
great | mountains: Thy judgments are a
great deep O Lord, Thou pre- | serv-est |
man and | beast.

7 How excellent is Thy loving- | kind-
ness · O | God: therefore the children of
men put their trust under the | sha-
dow | of Thy | wings.

8 They shall be abundantly satisfied
with the fatness | of Thy | house: and
Thou shalt make them drink of the **riv-**

PSALMS AND CANTICLES.

er | of Thy | pleas ˙ = | ures.

9 For with Thee is the | fountain ˙ of | life: in Thy light | shall we | see ˙ = | light.

p 10 O continue Thy lovingkindness unto | them that | know Thee: and Thy righteousness | to the ˙ up- | right in | heart.

p 11 Let not the foot of pride | come a- | gainst me: and let not the hand of the | wicked ˙ re - | move ˙ = | me.

12 There are the workers of in- | iqui ˙ ty | fallen: they are cast down, and shall | not be | able ˙ to | rise.

F Glory be to the Father | and ˙ to the ˙ Son: and | to the | Holy | Ghost;

As it was in the beginning, is now, and | ever | shall be: world without | end ˙ = | A ˙ = | men.

Twelfth.

25. CROFT. **26.** WEBBE.

PSALM XXXIX.

P I SAID, I will take | heed to ˙ my | ways: that I | sin not | with my | tongue.

2 I will keep my | mouth with ˙ a | bridle: while the | wick-ed | is be- | fore me.

3 I was dumb with silence, I | held my | peace: even from good, | and my | sorrow ˙ was | stirred.

4 My heart was | hot with- | in me: while I was musing the fire burned, then | spake I | with my | tongue,

cr 5 Lord, make me to know mine end, and the measure of my days, | what it | is: that I may | know how | frail I | am.

p 6 Behold, Thou hast made my | days ˙ as a | handbreadth: and mine age is as nothing before Thee, verily every man at his best state is | al-to- | geth-er | vanity.

7 Surely every man walketh in a vain shew, surely they are dis- | quiet-ed in | vain: he heapeth up riches, and knoweth not | who shall | gath-er | them.

cr 8 And now Lord, what | wait I | for: my | hope ˙ = | is in | Thee.

9 Deliver me from | all ˙ my trans- | gressions: make me not the re- | proach ˙ = | of the | foolish.

p 10 I was dumb, I opened | not my | mouth: be- | cause ˙ = | Thou ˙ = | didst it.

11 Remove Thy stroke a- | way ˙ = | from me: I am consumed by the | blow ˙ = | of Thine | hand.

12 When Thou with rebukes dost correct man for iniquity, Thou makest his beauty to consume a | way ˙ like a | moth: surely | ev-er-y | man is | vanity.

cr 13 Hear my prayer, O Lord, and give ear | unto ˙ my | cry: hold not Thy | peace ˙ = | at my | tears.

p 14 For I am a | stranger ˙ with | Thee: and a sojourner, as | all my | fath-ers | were.

15 O spare me, that I may re | cov-er | strength: before I go hence, and | be ˙ = | no ˙ = | more.

F Glory be to the Father, | and ˙ to the | Son: and | to the | Holy | Ghost;

As it was in the beginning, is now, and | ever | shall be: world without | end ˙ = | A ˙ = | men.

Thirteenth.

27. HINE.

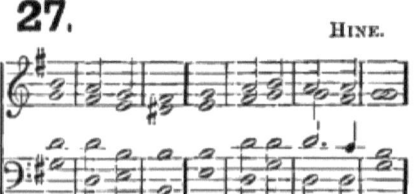

28. MONK.

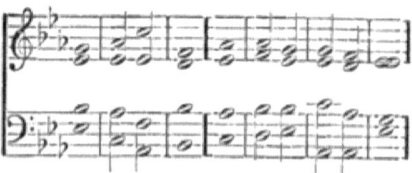

FROM PSALMS XLII AND XLIII.

MF AS the hart panteth after the | wa- ter | brooks; so panteth my soul | aft-er | Thee O | God.
  2 My soul thirsteth for God, for the | liv-ing | God: when shall I come and ap-| pear be-| fore ˙ = | God?
p 3 My tears have been my meat | day and | night: while they continually say unto me, | Where ˙ = | is thy | God?
  4 When I re- | member ˙ these | things: I | pour ˙ out my | soul with- | in me.
cr 5 For I had gone with the | mul-ti- | tude: I went with them | to the | house of | God.
f   6 With the voice of | joy and | praise: with a multitude | that kept | ho-ly | day.
p 7 Why art thou cast down | O my | soul: why art thou dis- | qui-et- | ed with-| in me?
full 8 Hope | thou in | God: for I shall yet praise Him for the | help of ˙ His | coun-te- | nance.
  9 Deep calleth unto deep at the noise of Thy | wa-ter- | spouts: all Thy ways and Thy | bil-lows | are gone | over me.
  10 Yet the Lord will command His lov-ing kindness | in the | day-time: and in the night His song shall be with me, and my prayer unto the | God ˙ = | of my | life.
mf 11 O send out Thy light and Thy truth, | let them | lead me: let them bring me unto Thy holy hill, and | to Thy | taber-na | cles.
  12 Then will I go unto the altar of God, unto God my ex- | ceed-ing | joy: yea upon the harp will I | praise ˙ Thee O | God my | God.
p 13 Why art thou cast down | O my | soul: and why art thou dis- | qui-et-| ed with- | in me?
full 14 Hope | thou in | God: for I shall yet praise Him who is the health of my | counte-nance | and my | God.

F Glory be to the Father, | and ˙ to the | Son: and | to the | Holy | Ghost;
  As it was in the beginning, is now, and | ever | shall be: world without | end ˙ = | A ˙ = | men.

Fourteenth.

29. From GOLDWIN.

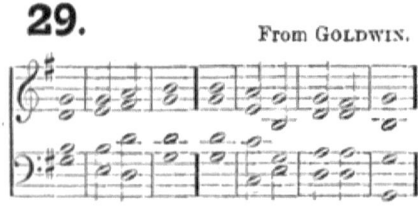

30. HOYTE.

PSALM XLVI.

F GOD is our | refuge ˙ and | strength: a very | present | help in | trouble.
  2 Therefore will not we fear, though the | earth be | removed: and though the mountains be carried into the | midst ˙ = | of the | sea.
  3 Though the waters thereof | roar and ˙ be | troubled: though the moun-tains | shake with ˙ the | swelling ˙ there- | of.
  4 There is a river, the streams whereof shall make glad the | city ˙ of | God: the holy place of the tabernacles | of the | Most ˙ = | High.

PSALMS AND CANTICLES. 13

5 God is in the midst of her, she shall | not be | moved: God shall help her, and | that right | ear · = | ly.

6 The heathen raged, the | kingdoms · were | moved: He uttered His voice, the | earth · = | melt · = | ed.

full 7 The Lord of | hosts is | with us: the God of | Ja-cob | is our | refuge.

8 Come, behold the | works · of the | Lord : what desolations He hath | made · = | in the | earth.

9 He maketh wars to cease unto the | end · of the | earth: He breaketh the bow and cutteth the spear in sunder, He burneth the | chari · ot | in the | fire.

p 10 Be still, and know that | I am | God (*cr.*) I will be exalted among the heathen, I will be ex- | alt-ed | in the | earth.

full 11. The Lord of | hosts is | with us: the God of | Ja-cob | is our | refuge.

F Glory be to the Father, | and · to the | Son: and | to the | Holy | Ghost;

As it was in the beginning, is now, and | ever | shall be : world without | end · = | A · = | men.

Fifteenth.

PSALM XLVII.

F O CLAP your hands, | all ye | people: shout unto God with the | voice of | tri · = | umph.

2 For the Lord most | high is | terrible: He is a great King | o-ver | all the | earth.

dim 3 He shall subdue the | peo-ple | under us: and the | na-tions | under · our | feet.

dim 4 He shall choose our in- | heri · tance | for us; the excellency of | Jacob | whom He | loved.

full 5 God is gone | up with · a | shout: the Lord | with the | sound of · a | trumpet.

6 Sing praises to | God, sing | praises: sing praises | unto · our | King, sing | praises.

7 For God is the King of | all the | earth: sing ye | praises · with | un-der | standing.

8 God reigneth | over · the | heathen: God sitteth upon the throne | of His | ho-li | ness.

9 The princes of the people are | gathered · to | gether: even the people of the | God of | A-bra- | ham.

10 For the shields of the earth be- | long · unto | God: He is | great · = | ly ex- | alted.

F Glory be to the Father, | and · to the | Son: and | to the | Holy | Ghost;

As it was in the beginning, is now, and | ever | shall be: world without | end · = | A · = | men.

Sixteenth.

34. OAKELEY. **35.** STEPHENS.

36. WHITFIELD.

PSALM XLVIII.

F GREAT is the Lord, and greatly | to be | praised: in the city of our God, in the | moun-tain | of His | holiness.

2 Beautiful for situation, the joy of the whole earth, | is Mount | Sion: on the sides of the north, the city of the great King, God is known in her | pala-ces | for a | refuge.

3 For lo, the | kings were · as- | sem-bled: they | pas-sed | by to- | gether.

4 They saw it, and | so they | marvel-led: (*dim.*) they were | troubled · and | hasted · a- | way.

p 5 Fear took hold up- | on them | there: and pain | as · of a | woman · in | travail.

6 Thou breakest the | ships of | Tar-shish: with | ═ · an | east · ═ | wind.

7 As we have heard | so have · we | seen: in the city | of the | Lord of | Hosts;

8 In the city | of our | God: God will es- | tab-lish | it for | ever.

f 9 We have thought of Thy loving-kindness | O · ═ | God: in the | midst · ═ | of Thy | temple.

10 According to Thy Name O God, so is Thy praise unto the ends | of the | earth: Thy right hand is | full of | righ-teous- | ness.

37. HINDLE.

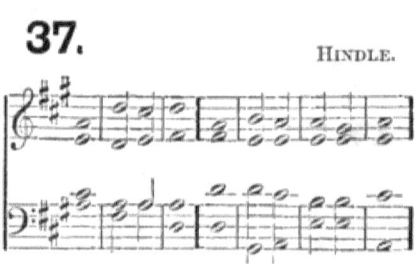

11 Let Mount | Sion · re | joice: let the daughters of Judah be glad be- | cause · ═ | of Thy | judgments.

12 Walk about Sion, and go | round a · bout | her: and | tell the | towers there- | of.

13 Mark ye well her bulwarks, con- | sider · her | palaces. that ye may tell it to the | gen-er- | a-tion | following.

14 For this God is our God for | ever · and | ever: He will be our | guide, · even | un-to | death.

F Glory be to the Father, | and · to the | Son: and | to the | Holy | Ghost ;

As it was in the beginning, is now, and | ever | shall be: world without | end · ═ | A · ═ | men.

PSALMS AND CANTICLES. 15

Seventeenth.

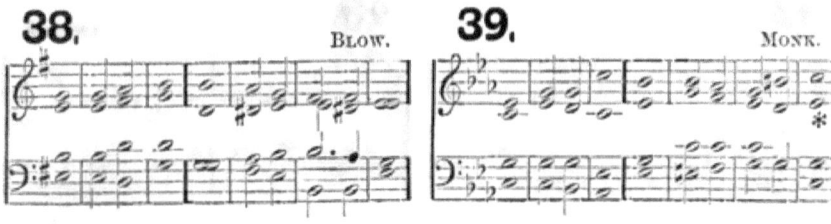

38. BLOW.

39. MONK.

40. FLINTOFF.

41. FELTON.

FROM PSALM LI.

P HAVE mercy up- | on · me, O | God: | according | to Thy | lov-ing | kind-ness.
2 According unto the mul-titude of Thy | ten-der | mercies: blot | out my | trans- · = | gressions.
3 Wash me thoroughly from mine in- | i-qui- | ty: and | cleanse me | from my | sin.
4 For I acknowledge | my trans- | gressions: and my | sin is | ever · be-| fore me.
5 Against Thee, 'Thee only, | have I | sinned: and done this | e-vil | in Thy | sight.
6 That Thou mightest be justified | when Thou | speakest: and be | clear · = | when Thou | judgest.
7 Behold, I was shapen in in- | i-qui- | ty: and in | sin did · my | mother · con- | ceive me.
8 Behold Thou desirest truth in the | in-ward | parts: and in the hidden part thou shalt | make · me to | know · = | wisdom.
9 Purge me with hyssop, and | I · shall be | clean: wash me, and | I · shall be | whiter · than | snow.
10 Make me to hear | joy and | gladness: that the bones which Thou hast | bro-ken | may re- | joice.
11 Hide Thy face | from my | sins: and blot out | all · mine in- | i-qui- | ties.
12 Create in me a clean | heart O | God: and re- | new · a right | spirit · with- | in me.

13 Cast me not away | from Thy | presence: and take not Thy | Ho-ly | Spirit | from me.
cr 14 Restore unto me the joy of | Thy sal- | vation: and uphold me | with Thy | free · = | Spirit.
15 Then will I teach trans- | gressors · Thy | ways: and sinners shall be con- | vert-ed | un-to | Thee.
16 O Lord, open | Thou my | lips: and my | mouth · shall show | forth Thy | praise.
17 For Thou desirest not sacrifice | else would · I | give it: Thou delightest not | in burnt | offer- | ings.
p 18 The sacrifices of God are a | broken | spirit: a broken and a contrite heart O God, | Thou wilt | not de- | spise.

F Glory be to the Father, | and · to the | Son: and | to the | Holy | Ghost;
As it was in the beginning, is now, and | ever | shall be: world without | end · = | A · = | men.

Eighteenth.

42. HOPKINS.

PSALM LVII.

MP BE merciful unto me, O God, be merciful unto me, for my soul | trusteth ᐧ in | Thee: yea, in the shadow of Thy wings will I make my refuge, until these calamities | be ᐧ = | o-ver- | past.

2 I will cry unto | God most | high: unto God that performeth | all things | for ᐧ = | me.

cr 3 He shall send from heaven, and save me from the reproach of him that would | swallow ᐧ me | up : God shall send forth His | mer-cy | and His | truth.

4 My soul is among lions, and I lie even among them that are set on fire, even the | sons of | men: whose teeth are spears and arrows, and their | tongue a | sharp ᐧ = | sword.

full 5 Be Thou exalted, O God, a- | bove the | heavens; let Thy glory be a- | bove ᐧ = | all the | earth.

43. OAKELEY.

p 6 They have prepared a net for my steps, my soul is | bow-ed | down, they have digged a pit before me, into the midst whereof | they are | fallen them- | selves.

f 7 My heart is fixed, O God, my | heart is | fixed: I will | sing and | give ᐧ = | praise.

8 Awake up my glory, awake | psaltery ᐧ and | harp: I myself | will a- | wake ᐧ = | early.

9 I will praise Thee O Lord, a- | mong the | people: I will sing unto | Thee a- | mong the | nations.

10 For Thy mercy is great | unto ᐧ the | heavens: and Thy | truth ᐧ = | unto ᐧ the | clouds.

full 11 Be Thou exalted O God, a- | bove the | heavens: let Thy glory be a- | bove ᐧ = | all the | earth.

F GLORY BE, &c.

Nineteenth.

44. CROTCH.

PSALM LXIII.

MF O GOD, Thou | art my | God: early | will I | seek ᐧ = | Thee.

2 My soul thirsteth for Thee, my flesh | longeth ᐧ for | Thee: in a dry and thirsty land, | where no | wa-ter | is.

3 To see Thy power | and Thy | glory: so as I have seen Thee | in the | sanctu- | ary.

4 Because Thy loving-kindness is | better ᐧ than | life: my | lips shall | praise ᐧ = | Thee.

5 Thus will I bless Thee | while I |

45. GOSS.

live: I will lift up my | hands in | Thy ᐧ = | Name.

6 My soul shall be satisfied as with | marrow ᐧ and | fatness: and my mouth shall | praise Thee ᐧ with | joy-ful | lips.

7 When I remember Thee up- | on my | bed : and meditate on Thee | in the | night ᐧ = | watches.

8 Because Thou hast | been my | help therefore in the shadow of Thy | wings will | I re- | joice.

9 My soul followeth | hard ᐧ after | Thee: Thy right | hand up- | hold-eth | me.

10 But those that seek my soul | to de- | stroy it: shall go into the | low-er | parts · of the | earth.
11 They shall | fall by · the | sword: they shall | be a | portion · for | foxes.
12 But the king shall rejoice in God, every one that sweareth by | Him shall | glory: but the mouth of them that speak | lies · = | shall be | stopped.
F Glory be to the Father, | and · to the | Son: and | to the | Holy | Ghost;
As it was in the beginning, is now, and | ever | shall be: world without | end · = | A · = | men.

Twentieth.

46. ROBINSON.
47. BANISTER.
48. TURNER.

PSALM LXV.

F PRAISE waiteth for Thee, O | God, in | Sion: and unto Thee shall the | vow · = | be per- | formed.
2 O Thou that | hear-est | prayer: unto | Thee shall | all flesh | come.
3 Blessed is the man | whom Thou | choosest: and causest to approach unto Thee, that | he may | dwell · in Thy | courts.
4 We shall be satisfied with the goodness | of Thy | house : even | of Thy | ho-ly | temple.
5 By terrible things in righteousness wilt Thou | an-swer | us: O | God of | our sal- | vation;
6 Who art the confidence of all the | ends · of the | earth: and of them that are afar | off up- | on the | sea.
7 Which by His strength setteth | fast the | mountains: being | gird · = | ed with | power;
p 8 Which stilleth the | noise · of the | seas: the noise of their waves, and the | tu-mult | of the | people.
9 They also that dwell in the uttermost parts are afraid | of Thy | tokens: Thou makest the out-goings of the morning and | eve-ning | to re- | joice.
f 10 Thou visitest the earth, and | wa-ter-est | it: Thou greatly enrichest it with the river of God, | which is | full of | water.
11 Thou pre- | parest · them | corn: when Thou hast | so pro- | vi-ded | for it.
12 Thou waterest the ridges thereof a- | bun-dant- | ly : Thou | settlest · the | furrows · there-| of.
13 Thou makest it | soft with | showers : Thou | blessest · the | spring-ing · there | of.
14 Thou crownest the year | with Thy | goodness: and Thy | paths drop | fat · = | ness.
15 They drop upon the pastures | of the | wilderness: and the little hills re- | joice on | ev-ery | side.
16 The pastures are | clothed · with | flocks: the valleys also are covered over with corn, they shout for | joy, they | al-so | sing.
F Glory be to the Father, | and · to the | Son: and | to the | Holy | Ghost;
As it was in the beginning, is now, and | ever | shall be: world without | end · = | A · = | men.

Twenty-First.

49. ALDRICH.

50. BARNBY.

51. OUSELEY.

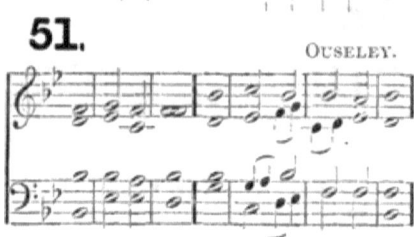

Psalm LXVII.

MP GOD be merciful unto | us, and | bless us: and cause His | face to | shine up- | on us.

2 That Thy way may be | known· upon | earth : Thy **saving** | health a- | mong all | nations.

full 3 Let the people | praise Thee · O | God: let |·all the | peo-ple | praise Thee.

4 O let the nations be glad and | sing for | joy: for Thou shalt judge the people righteously, and govern the | nations | up-on | earth.

full 5 Let the people | praise Thee · O | God: let | all the | peo-ple | praise Thee.

6 Then shall the earth [yield her | increase: and God, even | our own | God shall | bless us.

dim 7 God shall | bless · = | us: and all the ends of the | earth shall | fear · = | Him.

F GLORY BE, &c.

Twenty-Second.

52. HINDLE.

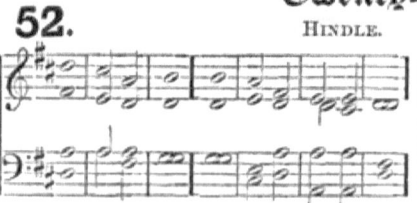

53. FELTON.

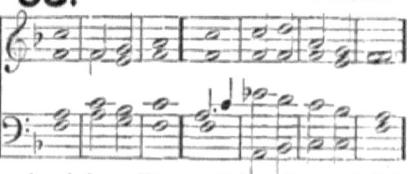

From Psalm LXXII.

MF GIVE the king Thy | judgments · O | God: and Thy righteousness | unto · the | king's · = | son.

2 He shall judge Thy people with right-eous- | ness: and Thy | poor with | judg · = | ment.

3 He shall judge the poor | of the | people: He shall save the children of the needy, and shall break in pieces | the op- | press · = | or.

4 He shall come down like rain upon the | mown · = | grass : as | showers · that | water · the | earth.

5 In **his** days shall the | right-eous | flourish: and abundance of peace so | long · as the | moon en- | dureth.

6 He shall have dominion also from | sea to | sea: and from the river | unto · the | ends · of the | earth.

7 They that dwell in the wilderness shall | bow be- | fore Him: and His | enemies · shall | lick the | dust.

8 Yea, **all** kings shall fall | down be- | fore Him : all | nations · shall | serve · = | Him.

dim 9 For He shall deliver the needy | when he | crieth: the poor also, and | him that | hath no | helper.

dim 10 He shall spare the | poor and | needy: and shall save the | souls · = | of the | needy.

dim 11 He shall redeem their soul from de- | ceit and | violence : and precious shall their | blood be | in His | sight.

cr 12 His Name shall endure for ever, His Name shall be continued as long | as the | sun: and men shall be blessed in Him, all | nations · shall | call Him | blessed.

13 Blessed be the Lord God, the | God of | Israel : who only | do-eth | wondrous | things.

f 14 And blessed be His glorious | Name for | ever: and let the whole earth be filled with His glory. A- | men · = | and A- | men.

F GLORY BE, &c.

Twenty-Third.

54. HAYES. **55.** MACFARREN.

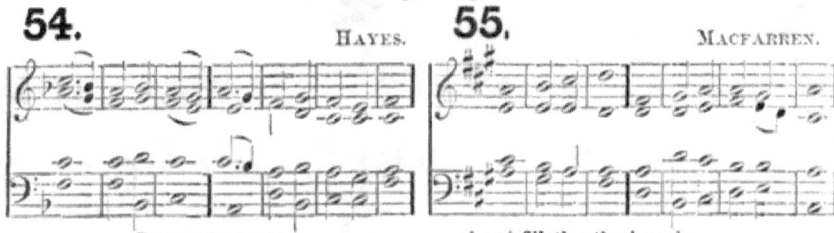

PSALM LXXXIV.

MF HOW amiable | are Thy | tabernacles:
O | Lord ' = | of ' = | hosts!
2 My soul longeth, yea, even fainteth for the | courts ' of the | Lord: my heart and my flesh crieth | out ' for the | living | God.
3 Yea, the sparrow hath found a house and the swallow a nest for herself, where she may | lay her | young: even Thine altars, O Lord of hosts, my | King ' = | and my | God.
4 Blessed are they that | dwell in ' Thy | house : they will be | still ' = | prais-ing | Thee.
5 Blessed is the man whose | strength ' is in | Thee: in whose heart | are the | ways of | them.
6 Who passing through the valley of Baca | make it ' a | well: and rain |

al-so | filleth ' the | pools.
7 They go from | strength to | strength: every one of them in Sion ap- | peareth ' be- | fore ' = | God.
p 8 O Lord God of hosts, | hear my | prayer: give | ear O | God of | Jacob.
9 Behold O | God our | shield : and look upon the | face of | Thine a- | nointed.
cr 10 For a day in Thy courts is better | than a | thousand : I had rather be a doorkeeper in the house of my God, than to | dwell ' in the | tents of | wickedness.
f 11 For the Lord God is a | sun and | shield the Lord will give grace and glory, no good thing will He withhold from | them that | walk up- | rightly.
12 O | Lord of | hosts: blessed is the | man that | trusteth ' in | Thee.
F GLORY BE, &c.

Twenty-Fourth.

56. SMITH. **57.** HAYES.

PSALM LXXXV.

MP LORD, Thou hast been favourable | unto ' Thy | land: Thou hast brought back the cap- | tiv-i- | ty of | Jacob.
2 Thou hast forgiven the iniquity | of Thy | people: Thou hast | cover-ed | all their | sin.
3 Thou hast taken away | all Thy | wrath: Thou hast turned Thyself from the | fierce-ness | of Thine | anger.
p 4 Turn us, O God of | our sal- | vation: and cause Thine | anger ' toward | us to | cease.
5 Wilt Thou be angry with | us for | ever: wilt Thou draw out Thine anger to | all ' = | gen-er- | ations.
cr 6 Wilt Thou not re- | vive ' us a- | gain: that Thy people | may re- | joice in | Thee.
7 Show us Thy | mercy ' O | Lord: and grant us | Thy sal- | vation.

8 I will hear what God the | Lord will | speak: for He will speak peace unto His people and to His saints, but let them not | turn a- | gain to | folly
cr 9 Surely His salvation is nigh | them that | fear Him: that | glory may | dwell in our | land.
10 Mercy and truth are | met to- | gether: righteousness and | peace have | kissed ' each | other.
11 Truth shall spring | out ' of the | earth : and righteousness | shall look | down from | heaven.
12 Yea, the Lord shall give | that ' which is | good: and our | land shall | yield her | increase.
13 Righteousness shall | go be- | fore Him: and shall set us | in the | way ' of His | steps.
F GLORY BE, &c.

Twenty=Fifth.

58. CROFT.

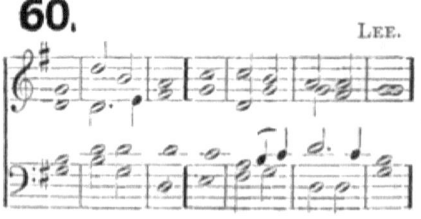

59. TOMLINSON.

FROM PSALM XC.

p LORD, Thou hast been our | dwelling | place: in | all · = | gen-er | ations.
2 Before the mountains were brought forth, or ever Thou hadst formed the | earth · and the | world: even from everlasting to ever | lasting | Thou art | God.
3 Thou turnest man | to de- | struction: and sayest, Re | turn, ye | children · of | men.
4 For a thousand years | in Thy | sight: are but as yesterday when it is past, and | as a | watch in · the | night.
5 Thou carriest them away as with a flood, they | are · as a | sleep: in the morning they are like | grass which | grow-eth | up.
6 In the morning it flourisheth, and | grow-eth | up: in the evening it is cut | down and | with-er- | eth.
dim 7 For we are consumed | by Thine | anger:

and by Thy | wrath · = | are we | troubled.
p 8 Thou hast set our iniquities be | fore · = | Thee: our secret sins in the | light · of Thy | coun-te | nance.
dim 9 For all our days are passed away | in Thy | wrath: we spend our years as a | tale · = | that is | told.
p 10 The days of our years are three-score years and ten, and if by reason of strength they be | four-score | years: yet is their strength labour and sorrow, for it is soon cut off, | and we | fly a- | way.
11 Who knoweth the power | of Thine | anger: even according to Thy | fear so | is Thy | wrath.
cr 12 So teach us to | number · our | days: that we may apply our hearts · = | un-to | wisdom.
F GLORY BE, &c.

Twenty=Sixth.

60. LEE.

61. ARNOLD.

PSALM XCI.

MF HE that dwelleth in the secret place of the | Most · = | High: shall abide under the | shadow · of | the Al- | mighty.
2 I will say of the Lord, He is my refuge | and my | fortress: my God, in | Him · = | will I | trust.
3 Surely He shall deliver thee from the | snare · of | the | fowler: and from the | noi-some | pes-ti- | lence.
4 He shall cover thee with His feathers, and under His wings | shalt thou | trust: His truth shall | be thy | shield and | buckler.
5 Thou shalt not be afraid for the | terror · by | night: nor for the | arrow · that | flieth · by | day.
6 Nor for the pestilence that | walketh · in | darkness: nor for the destruction that | wasteth · at | noon · = | day
p 7 A thousand shall fall at thy side, and ten thousand at | thy right | hand: but it | shall not | come nigh | thee.
p 8 Only with thine eyes shalt | thou be- | hold: and see the re- | ward · = | of the |

wicked.
f 9 Because thou hast made the Lord, which | is my | refuge: even the Most | High thy | hab-i- | tation.
10 There shall no | evil · be- | fall thee: neither shall any | plague come | nigh thy | dwelling.
cr 11 For He shall give His angels charge | o-ver | thee: to | keep · thee in | all thy | ways.
12 They shall bear thee up | in their | hands: lest thou dash thy | foot a- | gainst a | stone.
13 Thou shalt tread upon the | lion · and | adder: the young lion and the dragon shalt thou | tram-ple | un-der | feet.
14 Because he hath set his love upon me, therefore will I de | liv-er | him: I will set him on high, be- | cause he · hath | known my | Name.
15 He shall call upon me, and | I will · answer him: I will be with him in trouble, I will de | liv-er | him and | honour him.
16 With long life will I | satis-fy | him: and | shew him | my sal- | vation.
F GLORY BE, &c.

PSALMS AND CANTICLES. 21

Twenty Seventh.

62. ANON.

63. HINDLE.

PSALM XCII.

F IT is a good thing to give thanks |
unto · the | Lord: and to sing praises
unto Thy | Name · = | O Most | High.
2 To shew forth Thy lovingkindness |
in the | morning and Thy | faithful-
ness | eve-ry | night.
3 Upon an instrument of ten strings, |
and up- | on the | psaltery: upon the
harp | with a | sol-emn | sound.
4 For Thou, Lord, hast made me glad |
through Thy | works: I will triumph in
the | works · = | of Thy | hands.
full 5 O Lord, how great | are Thy | works:
and Thy | thoughts are | ve-ry | deep.
p 6 A brutish man | know-eth | not :
neither doth a fool | un-der | stand · = |
this.
p 7 When the wicked spring as the grass
and when all the workers of in- | iquity ·
do | flourish : it is that they shall | be
de- | stroyed for | ever.
8 But | Thou O | Lord : art most |
high for | ev-er | more.

9 For lo Thine | enemies · O | Lord:
for lo Thine | en-e- | mies shall | perish.
10 For | all the | workers: of in- | iqui-
ty | shall be | scattered.
11 But my horn shalt Thou exalt like
the | horn · of a | unicorn : I shall be
a- | noint-ed | with fresh | oil.
12 Mine eyes also shall see my desire |
on mine | enemies: and mine ears shall
hear my desire of the wicked | that
rise | up a- | gainst me.
f 13 The righteous shall flourish | like
the | palm tree: he shall grow | like a |
cedar · in | Lebanon.
14 Those that be planted in the
house | of the | Lord : shall flourish in
the | courts · = | of our | God.
15 They shall still bring forth fruit
in old | age: they shall be | fat and | flour-
ish- | ing.
16 To show that the | Lord is · up- |
right: He is my Rock, and there is no
un- | right-eous- | ness in | Him.
F GLORY BE, &c.

Twenty Eighth.

64. GOODSON.

65. CROTCH.

PSALM XCV.

F O COME, let us sing | unto · the |
Lord: let us make a joyful noise to
the | Rock of | our sal- | vation.
2 Let us come before His presence |
with thanks- | giving: and make a joy-
ful noise | un-to | Him with | psalms.
3 For the Lord is a | great · = | God: |
and a great | King a- | bove all | gods.
4 In his hand are the deep places | of
the | earth : the strength of the | hills
is | His · = | also.
5 The sea is His | and He | made it: and
His hands | formed the | dry · = | land.
full 6 O come, let us worship | and bow |
down: let us kneel be- | fore the | Lord
our | Maker.

cr 7 For | He is · our | God: (*dim*) and we
are the people of His pasture, and the |
sheep of | His · = | hand.
8 To-day if ye will hear His voice,
harden | not your | heart: as in the pro-
vocation, and as in the day of tempta -
tion | in the | wil-der | ness:
p 9 When your fathers | temp-ted | me:
proved | me and | saw my | work.
p 10 Forty years long was I grieved with
this gener- | ation · and | said : it is a
people that do err in their heart, and
they | have not | known my | ways.
11 Unto whom I | sware in · my |
wrath: that they should not | en-ter |
into · my | rest.
F GLORY BE, &c.

Twenty-Ninth.

66. Turle.

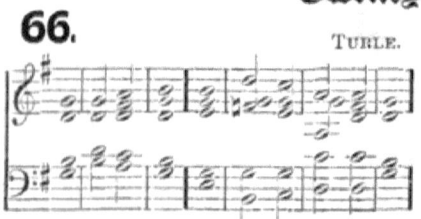

PSALM XCVI.

F O SING unto the Lord a | new · = | song: sing unto the | Lord · = | all the | earth.
  2 Sing unto the Lord, | bless His | Name : show forth His sal- | vation · from | day to | day.
  3 Declare His honour a- | mong the | heathen: His | wonders · a- | mong all | people.
  4 For the Lord is great, and greatly | to be | praised: He is to be | feared · a- | bove all | gods.
  5 For all the gods of the | nations · are | idols : but the | Lord · = | made the | heavens.
  6 Honour and majesty | are be- | fore Him: strength and | beauty · are | in His | sanctuary.
  7 Give unto the Lord O ye kin- dreds | of the | people: give unto the | Lord · = | glory · and | strength.

67. Bacon.

  8 Give unto the Lord the glory due | unto · His | Name : bring an offering and | come in- | to His | courts.
p 9 O worship the Lord in the | beauty · of | holiness: (cr) fear be- | fore Him | all the | earth.
  10 Say among the heathen that the | Lord · = | reigneth: the world also shall be established that it shall not be moved, He shall | judge the | peo-ple | right- eously.
cr 11 Let the heavens rejoice, and let the | earth be | glad. let the sea roar | and the | fulness · there- | of.
  12 Let the field be joyful, and all that | is there- | in: then shall all the trees of the wood re- | joice be- | fore the | Lord.
dim 13 For He cometh, He cometh to | judge the | earth : He shall judge the world with righteousness, and the | peo- ple | with His | truth.
F GLORY BE, &c.

Thirtieth.

68. Arnold.

PSALM XCVII.

F THE Lord reigneth, let the | earth re- | joice; let the multitude of | isles be | glad there- | of.
  2 Clouds and darkness are | round a- | bout Him : righteousness and judgment are the habi- | ta-tion | of His | throne.
  3 A fire | goeth · be- | fore Him: and burn- eth up His | ene=mies | round a- | bout.
  4 His lightnings en- | lightened · the | world: the | earth · = | saw and | trembled.
  5 The hills melted like wax at the pres- ence | of the | Lord : at the presence of the Lord | of the | whole · = | earth.
  6 The heavens declare His | righteous- | ness: and all the | peo-ple | see His | glory.
  7 Confounded be all they that serve graven images, that boast them- | selves of | idols :

69. Chard.

worship | Him · = | all ye | gods.
  8 Sion heard, | and was | glad : and the daughter of Judah rejoiced because of Thy | judgments | O · = | Lord.
  9 For Thou Lord, art high above | all the | earth: Thou art exalted | far a- | bove all | gods.
dim 10 Ye that love the Lord, | hate · = | evil : He preserveth the souls of His saints, He deliv- ereth them out of the | hand · = | of the | wicked.
cr 11 Light is sown | for the | righteous : and gladness | for the · up- | right in | heart.
full 12 Rejoice in the | Lord ye | righteous: and give thanks at the remembrance | of His | ho-li- | ness.
F GLORY BE, &c.

Thirty=First.

70. AYRTON.   **71.** RUSSELL.

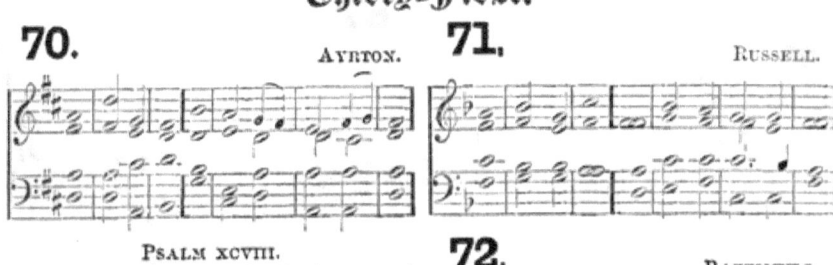

72. BATTISHILL.

PSALM XCVIII.

F O SING unto the Lord a | new ‧ = | song: for He hath | done ‧ = | mar vel ‧ lous | things.
 2 His right hand and His | ho-ly | arm: hath | got-ten | Him the | victory.
 3 The Lord hath made known | His sal- | vation: His righteousness hath He openly showed | in the | sight ‧ of the | heathen.
mf 4 He hath remembered His mercy and His truth toward the house of | Is-ra- | el: all the ends of the earth have seen the sal- | va-tion | of our | God.
f 5 Make a joyful noise unto the Lord | all the | earth : make a loud noise, and re- | joice and | sing ‧ = | praise.
 6 Sing unto the Lord | with the | harp: with the harp and the | voice ‧ = | of a | psalm.
 7 With trumpets and | sound of | cor- net: make a joyful noise be- | fore the | Lord, the | King.
 8 Let the sea roar, and the | fulness ‧ there- | of: the world, and | they that | dwell there- | in.
 9 Let the floods clap their hands, let the hills be joyful together be- | fore the | Lord: for He | cometh ‧ to | judge the earth.
dim 10 With righteousness shall He | judge the | world: and the | people ‧ with | e-qui- | ty.
F GLORY BE, &c.

Thirty=Second.

73. HAYES.   **74.** OUSELEY.

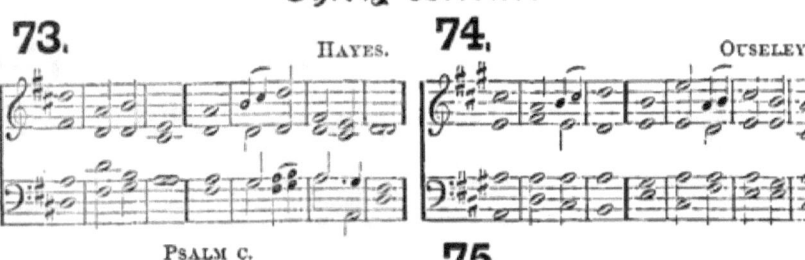

75. HOPKINS.

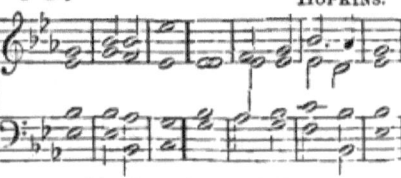

PSALM C.

F MAKE a joyful noise unto the Lord, | all ye | lands: serve the Lord with gladness, come before His | presence ‧ with | sing ‧ = | ing.
 2 Know ye that the Lord | He is | God: it is He that hath made us, and not we ourselves, (*dim*) we are His people, and the | sheep of ‧ His | pas ‧ = | ture.
 3 Enter into His gates with thanksgiv- ing, and into His | courts with | praise: be thankful unto Him, | and ‧ = | bless His | Name.
p 4 For the Lord is good, His mercy is | ev-er- | lasting: (*cr*) and His truth en- dureth to | all ‧ = | ge-ner- | ations.
F GLORY BE, &c.

Thirty=Third.

76. MORNINGTON.

77. GREENE. **78.** ANON.

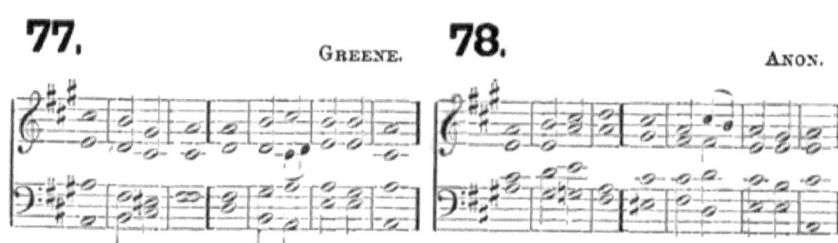

PSALM CIII.

F BLESS the Lord, | O my | soul: and all that is within me, | bless His | ho-ly | Name.

2 Bless the Lord | O my | soul: and for- | get not | all His | benefits.

3 Who forgiveth all | thine in- | iqui-ties: who | healeth · all | thy dis- | eases.

4 Who redeemeth thy life | from de- | struction: who crowneth thee with lov-ing- | kindness · and | ten-der | mercies.

5 Who satisfieth thy mouth | with good | things: so that thy youth is re- | new-ed | like the | eagle's.

6 The Lord executeth **righteousness** and | judg · = | ment: **for** | **all that** | **are** op- | pressed.

7 He made known His | ways · unto | Moses: His acts | unto · the | children of | Israel.

8 The Lord is merciful and | gra · = | cious: slow to anger and | plen-te- | ous in | mercy.

9 He will not | al-ways | chide: neither will He | keep His | anger · for | ever.

10 He hath not dealt with us | after · our | sins: nor rewarded us ac- | cord-ing · to | our in- | iquities.

11 For as the heaven is high a- | bove the | earth: so great is His mercy to-ward | them that | fear · = | Him.

12 As far as the east is | from the | west: so far hath He removed | our trans- | gres-sions | from us.

13 Like as a father | pitieth · his |

children: so the Lord | piti-eth | them that | fear Him.

dim 14 For He | knoweth · our | frame: He re- | membereth · that | we are | dust.

p 15 As for man, his | days · are as grass: as a flower of the field, | so he | flour-ish-| eth.

16 For the wind passeth over it, | and · it is | gone: and the place thereof shall | know · = | it no | more.

cr 17 But the mercy of the Lord is from everlasting to everlasting upon | them that | fear Him: and His righteousness | un-to | chil-dren's | children.

cr 18 To such as | keep His | **covenant**: and to those that remember | His com- | mandments · to | do them.

19 The Lord hath prepared His throne | in the | heavens: and His king-dom | ru-leth | o-ver | all.

ff 20 Bless the Lord, ye His angels, that ex- | cel in | strength: that **do** His com-mandments, hearkening | unto · the | voice of His | word.

21 Bless ye the Lord, all | ye His | hosts: ye ministers of His, that | do His | pleas · = | ure.

22 Bless the Lord, all His works in all places of | His do- | minion: bless the | Lord · = | O my | soul.

F Glory be to the Father, | and · to the | Son: and | to the | Holy | Ghost;

As it was in the beginning, is now, and | ever | shall be: world without | end · = | A · = | men.

Thirty=Fourth.

79. SOAPER.

80. BELLAMY.

FROM PSALM CIV.

F BLESS the Lord, | O my | soul : O Lord my God, Thou art very great, Thou art clothed with | honour ' and | ma-jes-| ty.

2 Who coverest Thyself with light as | with a | garment : who stretchest out the | hea-vens | like a | curtain.

3 Who layeth the beams of His chambers | in the | waters: who maketh the clouds His chariot, who walketh upon the | wings ' = | of the | wind.

4 Who maketh His | an-gels | spirits: His | ministers ' a | fla-ming | fire.

5 Who laid the foundations | of the | earth : that it should | not ' be re-| moved ' for | ever.

dim 6 Thou coveredst it with the deep as | with a | garment' the waters | stood a-| bove the | mountains.

7 At Thy re | buke they | fled: at the voice of Thy | thunder.' they | hasted ' a- | way.

8 He watereth the hills | from His | chambers : the earth is satisfied with the | fruit ' = | of Thy | works.

9 He causeth the grass to grow | for the | cattle: and herb | for the | service ' of | man.

10 He appointed the | moon for | seasons: the sun | knoweth ' his | go-ing | down.

cr 11 Man goeth forth | unto ' his | work: and to his | labour 'un-| til 'the | evening.

full 12 O Lord, how manifold | are Thy | works : in wisdom | hast Thou | made them | all.

13 The earth is | full of ' Thy | riches: so is this great and wide sea, wherein are things creeping innumerable, both | small and | great ' = | beasts.

14 There | go the | ships: there is that leviathan, whom Thou hast | made to | play there- | in.

cr 15 These wait | all ' upon | Thee: that Thou mayest give them their | meat ' = | in due | season.

mf 16 That Thou 'givest | them they | gather: Thou openest Thine hand, | they are | filled with | good.

dim 17 Thou hidest Thy face, | they are | troubled: Thou takest away their breath, they die, and re- | turn ' = | to their | dust.

cr 18 Thou sendest forth Thy spirit, | they are ' cre- | ated: and Thou renewest the | face ' = | of the | earth.

19 The glory of the Lord shall endure for | ever: the Lord | shall rejoice in ' His | works.

f 20 I will sing unto the Lord as long | as I | live: I will sing praise to my God | while I | have my | being.

21 My meditation of Him | shall be sweet: I will be | glad ' = | in the | Lord.

22 Let the sinners be consumed out of the earth, and let the wicked | be no | more: bless thou the Lord, O my soul, | praise ' = | ye the | Lord.

F Glory be to the Father, | and ' to the | Son: and | to the | Holy | Ghost;

As it was in the beginning, is now, and | ever | shall be: world without | end ' = | A ' = | men.

Thirty=Fifth.

81. JONES.
82. GADSBY.

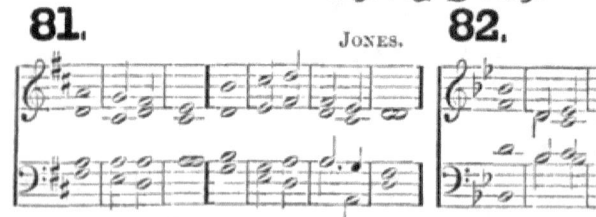

PSALM CXI.

F PRAISE | ye the | Lord: I will praise the | Lord with | my whole | heart.
2 In the assembly | of the | upright: and | in the | con-gre-| gation.
3 The works of the | Lord are | great: sought out of all them | that have | pleasure · there- | in.
4 His work is honourable and | glori- | ous : and His righteousness en- | dureth · for | e · = | ver.
5 He hath made His wonderful works to | be re-| membered : the Lord is | gracious · and | full of · com- | passion.
6 He hath given meat unto | them that | fear Him : He will ever be | mindful | of His | covenant.
7 He hath shewed His people the power | of His | works : that He may give them the | heri-tage | of the | heathen.
8 The works of His hands are | verity · and | judgment : all | His com | mandments · are | sure.
9 They stand fast for | ever · and | ever : and are | done in | truth · and up- | rightness.
10 He sent redemption | unto · His | people : He hath commanded His covenant for ever, holy and | rever- · end | is His | Name.
11 The fear | of the | Lord : is | the be- | ginning · of | wisdom.
12 A good understanding have all they that | do His · com- | mandments: His | praise en- | dureth · for | ever.

F GLORY BE, &c.

Thirty=Sixth.

83. LEE.
84. ELVEY.

 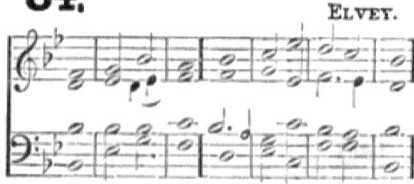

FROM PSALM CXV.

MF NOT unto us O Lord, not unto us, but unto Thy | Name give | glory : for Thy mercy and | for Thy | truth's · = | sake.
2 Wherefore should the | hea-then | say : Where | · = is | now their | God ?
3 But our God is | in the | heavens : He hath done whatso- | e-ver | He hath | pleased.
4 O Israel, trust thou | in the | Lord: He is their | help · = | and their | shield.
f 5 O house of Aaron, trust | in the | Lord : He is their | help · = | and their | shield.
6 Ye that fear the Lord, trust | in the | Lord : He is their | help · = | and their | shield.
7 The Lord hath been mindful of us, | He will | bless us : He will bless the house of Israel, He will | bless the | house of | Aaron.
8 He will bless them that | fear the | Lord : both | small · = | and · = | great.
9 The Lord shall increase you | more and | more; you |,and your | chil · = | dren.
10 Ye are blessed | of the | Lord : which | made · = | heaven and | earth.
11 The heaven, even the heavens | are the | Lord's : but the earth hath He given | to the | children · of | men.
p 12 The dead praise | not the | Lord : neither any that | go down | in-to | silence.
cr 13 But we will | bless the | Lord : from this time forth and evermore, | (*f*) praise = | = · the | Lord.

F GLORY BE, &c.

Thirty-Seventh.

85. *Moderate.* Verses 1 & 2. GAUNTLETT.

86. *Recit.* Verses 3 & 4.

PSALM CXVI.

MF 1 I | LOVE the | Lord: because He hath heard my voice | and my | sup-pli- | cations.

2 Because He hath inclined His ear | un-to | me: therefore will I call upon Him as | long ' = | as I | live.

p 3 The sorrows of death | com-passed | me: and the pains of | hell gat | hold up- | on me.

cr 4 I found | trouble 'and | sorrow: then called I up- | on the | Name of ' the | Lord.

87. *Plaintive.* Verse 5.

88. *Moderate.* Verses 6–10.

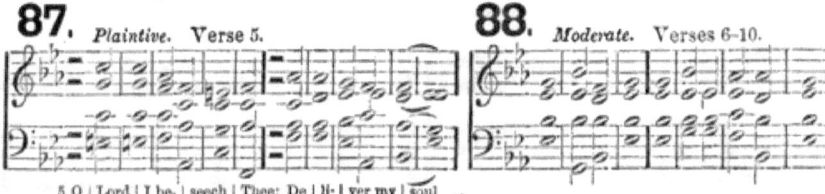

5 O | Lord | I be- | seech | Thee: De | li- | ver my | soul ..

p 6 Gracious is the | Lord, and | right-eous: yea our | God is | mer-ci- | ful.

p 7 The Lord pre- | serveth ' the | sim-ple: I was brought low, | and He | help-ed | me.

8 Return unto thy rest, | O my | soul: for the Lord hath dealt | boun-ti- | ful-ly | with thee.

9 For thou hast delivered my | soul from | death: mine eyes from tears, | and my | feet from | falling.

10 I will walk be- | fore the | Lord: in the | land ' = | of the | living.

89. *Recit.* Verses 11 & 12.

11 I believed therefore | have I | spoken: I was | great ' = | ly af- | flicted.

12 I said | in my | haste: All | = ' = | men are | liars.

90. *Joyful.* Verses 13–20.

13 What shall I render | unto ' the | Lord: for | all His | bene-fits | toward me?

14 I will take the cup | of sal- | vation: and call up- | on the | Name of ' the | Lord.

15 I will pay my vows | unto the | Lord: now in the | presence ' of | all His | people.

16 Precious in the sight | of the | Lord: is the | death ' = | of His | saints.

17 O Lord, truly | I am ' Thy | servant: I am Thy servant, and the son of Thine handmaid, | Thou hast | loosed my | bonds.

18 I will offer to Thee the sacrifice | of thanks- | giving: and will call upon the | Name ' = | of the | Lord.

cr 19 I will pay my vows | unto ' the | Lord: now in the | presence ' of | all His | people.

f 20 In the courts of the | Lord's ' = | house: in the midst of thee O Jerusa-lem, | praise ' = | = ' the | Lord.

F GLORY BE, &c.

Thirty-Eighth.

91. HENLEY.

92. MONK.   **93.** HAYES.

FROM PSALM CXVIII.

F O GIVE thanks unto the Lord, for | He is | good: because His | mercy · en- | dureth · for | ever.

2 Let | Israel · now | say: that His | mercy · en | dureth · for | ever.

3 Let the house of | Aaron · now | say: that His | mercy · en- | dureth · for | ever.

4 Let them now that | fear the · Lord | say: that His | mercy · en | dureth · for | ever.

5 I called upon the Lord | in dis- | tress: the Lord answered me, and | set me | in a · large | place.

6 The Lord is on my side, I | will not | fear: what can | man do | un-to | me.

7 It is better to | trust · in the | Lord: than to put | con-fi- | dence in | man.

8 It is better to | trust · in the | Lord: than to put | con-fi- | dence in | princes.

9 The Lord is my | strength and | song: and is be- | come · = | my sal- | vation.

10 The voice of rejoicing and salvation is in the tabernacles | of the | righteous: the right hand of the | Lord · = | do- eth | valiantly.

11 The right hand of the **Lord** | is ex- | alted: the right hand of **the** | Lord · = | do-eth | valiantly.

12 I shall not | die, but | live: and de- clare the | works · = | of the | Lord.

p 13 The **Lord** hath | chastened · me | sore: (*cr*) but He hath not given me |

o-ver | un-to | death.

mf 14 Open **to** me the gates of | right- eous- | ness: I will go into them, and | I will | praise the | Lord.

15 This gate | of the | Lord : into | which the | righteous · shall | enter.

16 I will praise Thee, for | Thou hast | **heard** me: and art be- | come · = | my sal- | vation.

17 The **stone** which the | builders · re- | fused: is become the | head stone | of the | corner.

18 This is the | **Lord's** · = | doing. it **is** | marvel-lous | in our | eyes.

19 This is the day which the | Lord hath | made: **we** will rejoice | and be | glad in | it.

20 Save **now** I beseech Thee, | O · = | Lord: O Lord, I be- | seech Thee · send | now pros- | perity.

21 Blessed be that cometh in the | Name of · the | Lord we have blessed you | out of · the | house of · the | Lord.

22 God **is** the Lord, which hath | shewed · **us** | light: bind the sacrifice with cords, **even** | unto · the | horns of · the | altar.

f 23 Thou art my God and | I will | praise Thee: **Thou art my** | God, I | will ex- | alt Thee.

24 O give thanks unto the Lord, for | He is | good: for His | mercy · en | dur- eth · for | ever.

F GLORY BE, &c.

Thirty-Ninth.

Psalm CXXI.

94. TRAVERS.

MF 1 I WILL lift up mine eyes | unto ‧ the | hills : from | whence ‧ = | cometh ‧ my | help.
2 My help cometh | from the | Lord : who | made both | heaven and | earth.
3 He will not suffer thy foot | to be | moved : He that | keepeth thee | will not | slumber.
4 Behold, He that | keep-eth | Israel : shall | nei-ther | slumber ‧ nor | sleep.
5 The Lord | is thy | keeper: the Lord is thy shade up- | on thy | right ‧ = | hand.
6 The sun shall not | smite thee ‧ by | 'day: nor | yet the | moon by | night.
7 The Lord shall preserve thee | from all | evil : He | shall pre- | serve thy | soul.
8 The Lord shall preserve thy going out and thy | com-ing | in: from this time forth, and | even ‧ for | e-ver- | more.
F Glory be to the Father, | and ‧ to the | Son: and | to the | Holy | Ghost;
As it was in the beginning, is now, and | ever | shall be: world without | end ‧ = | A ‧ = | men.

Psalm CXXII.

95. KELWAY.

F 1 I WAS glad when they said | un-to | me: let us go | into ‧ the | house of ‧ the | Lord.
2 Our | feet shall | stand: within thy | gates, ‧ = | O Je- | rusalem.
3 Jerusalem is builded | as a | city : that | is com- | pact to- | gether.
4 Whither the tribes go up, the tribes | of the | Lord : unto the testimony of Israel, to give thanks unto the | Name ‧ = | of the | Lord.
5 For there are set | thrones of | judgment the thrones | of the | house of | David.
p 6 Pray for the peace of Je- | ru-sa- | lem : (*cr*) they shall | pros-per | that love | thee.
p 7 Peace be with- | in thy | walls: (*cr*) and prosperity with- | in thy | pa-la- | ces.
8 For my brethren and com- | pan-ions' | sakes I will now say, | Peace ‧ = | be with- | in thee.
9 Because of the house of the | Lord our | God: I | will ‧ = | seek thy | good.
F Glory be to the Father, | and to the | Son: and | to the | Holy | Ghost;
As it was in the beginning, is now, and | ever | shall be: world without | end ‧ = | A ‧ = | men.

Psalm CXXV.

96. LESLIE.

MF 1 THEY that | trust in ‧ the | Lord: shall be as mount Sion which cannot be removed, | but a- | bideth ‧ for | ever.
2 As the mountains are round about Je- | ru-sa- | lem: so the Lord is round about His people from | hence-forth | even ‧ for | ever.
3 For the rod of the wicked shall not rest upon the lot | of the | righteous: lest the righteous put forth their hands | un-to i- | ni-qui- | ty.
dim 4 Do good, O Lord, unto | those that ‧ be | good: and to them that are | upright | in their | hearts.
5 As for such as turn aside unto their crooked ways, the Lord shall lead them forth with the workers | of i- | niquity: but | peace shall | be upon | Israel.
F Glory be to the Father, | and ‧ to the | Son: and | to the | Holy | Ghost;
As it was in the beginning, is now, and | ever | shall be: world without | end ‧ = | A ‧ = | men.

Fortieth.

97. FELTON.

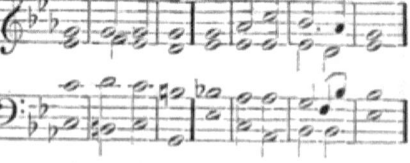

PSALM CXXX.

P O UT | of the | depths: have I cried | un-
to | Thee, O | Lord.

2 Lord, | hear my | voice: let Thine ears be attentive to the voice | of my | sup-pli- | cations.

3 If Thou Lord, shouldest | mark in- iquities; O | Lord, ‧ = | who shall | stand?

cr 4 But there is for- | giveness ‧ with Thee: that | Thou ‧ = | mayest ‧ be | feared.

p 5 I wait for the Lord, my | soul doth | wait: and in His | word ‧ = | do I | hope.

6 My soul waiteth | for the | Lord: more than they that | watch ‧ for the | morn ‧ = | ing.

7 I say, | more than | they: that | watch ‧ = | for the | morning.

cr 8 Let Israel hope in the Lord, for with the Lord | there is | mercy: and | with Him ‧ is | plenteous ‧ re- | demption.

cr 9 And He shall re- | deem ‧ = | Israel: from | all ‧ his in- | i-qui- | ties.

F GLORY BE, &c.

Forty-First.

98. WOODWARD.

PSALM CXXXII.

P LORD, re- | mem-ber | David: and | all ‧ = | his af- | flictions.

2 How he sware | unto ‧ the | Lord: and vowed **unto** the | migh-ty | God of | Jacob.

3 Surely **I will not come unto the** tabernacle | **of my** | **house:** nor | go **up** | **into** ‧ **my** | **bed.**

cr 4 **I will not** give sleep to mine eyes, nor slumber | to mine | eyelids: until I find out **a** place for the Lord, a habitation for the | migh-ty | God of | Jacob.

mf 5 Lo, we heard of it at | Eph-ra | tah: we found it | **in the** | fields of ‧ the | wood.

6 We will go | **into** ‧ His | tabernacles: we will | wor-ship | **at His** | footstool.

7 Arise O Lord, | into Thy | rest: **Thou**, | and the | ark of ‧ **Thy** | **strength**.

8 Let **Thy** priests be | clothed ‧ with | righteousness: and let Thy | saints ‧ = | shout for | **joy**.

9 For **Thy servant** | Da-vid's | sake : turn not **away** the | face of | Thine a- | nointed.

10 The Lord hath sworn in truth | un-to | David: He | will ‧ = | not turn | from it.

11 Of the fruit | of thy | body: will I | set up- | on thy | throne.

12 If thy children will keep my cove- nant and my testimony that | I shall | teach them: their children shall also sit upon thy | throne for | e-ver- | more.

13 For the Lord hath | cho-sen | Sion: **He** hath desired it | for His | ha-bi- | tation.

14 This **is my** | rest for | ever : here will I dwell, | **for I** | have de- | sired it.

15 I will abundantly | bless her ‧ pro- | vision: I will | satis-fy her | poor with | bread.

16 I will also clothe her priests | with sal- | vation: and her saints shall | shout a- | loud for | joy.

17 There will I make the horn of | David ‧ to | bud : I have ordained a | lamp for | mine a- | nointed.

18 His enemies will I | clothe with shame : but upon himself | shall his | crown ‧ = | flourish.

F GLORY BE, &c.

PSALMS AND CANTICLES. 31

Forty-Second.

99. Gregorian.   **100.** Havergal.

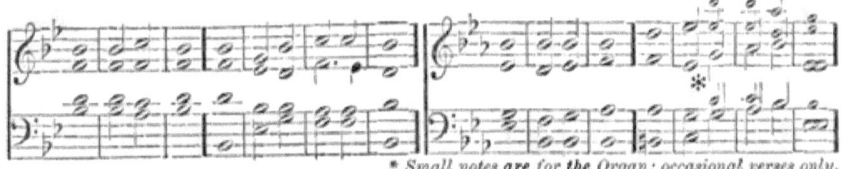

* Small notes are for the Organ; occasional verses only.

PSALM CXXXVI.

F O GIVE thanks unto the Lord, for | He is | good: for His | mercy ‧ en- | dureth ‧ for | ever.
2 O give thanks unto the | God of | gods: for His | mercy ‧ en- | dureth ‧ for | ever.
3 O give thanks to the | Lord of | lords: for His | mercy ‧ en- | dureth ‧ for | ever.
4 To Him who alone | doeth ‧ great | wonders: for His | mercy ‧ en- | dureth ‧ for | ever.
5 To Him that by wisdom | made the | heavens: for His | mercy ‧ en- | dureth ‧ for | ever.
6 To Him that stretched out the earth a- | bove the | waters: for His | mercy ‧ en- | dureth ‧ for | ever.

7 To Him that | made great | lights: for His | mercy ‧ en- | dureth ‧ for | ever.
8 The sun to | rule by | day: for His | mercy ‧ en- | dureth ‧ for | ever.
9 The moon and stars to | rule by | ‧ night: for His | mercy ‧ en- | dureth ‧ for | ever.
p 10 Who remembered us in our | low e- | state: (*cr*) for His | mercy ‧ en- | dureth ‧ for | ever.
mf 11 And hath redeemed us from our | en-e- | mies: for His | mercy ‧ en- | dureth ‧ for | ever.
12 Who giveth food to | all ‧ = | flesh: for His | mercy ‧ en- | dureth ‧ for | ever.
13 O give thanks unto the | God of | heaven: for His | mercy ‧ en- | dureth ‧ for | ever.

F GLORY BE, &c.

Forty-Third.

101. Barry.   **102.** Bradley.

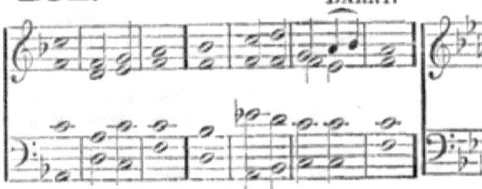 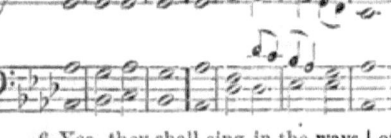

PSALM CXXXVIII.

F I WILL praise Thee | with my ‧ whole | heart: before the gods will I sing | praise ‧ = | un-to | Thee.
2 I will worship toward Thy | ho-ly | temple: and praise Thy Name | for Thy | lov-ing | kindness.
3 And | for Thy | truth: for Thou hast magnified Thy word a- | bove ‧ = | all Thy | Name.
4 In the day when I cried Thou | an-swer-edst | me: and strengthenedst me with | strength ‧ = | in my | soul.
5 All the kings of the earth shall | praise Thee ‧ O | Lord: when they | hear the | words of ‧ Thy | mouth.

6 Yea, they shall sing in the ways | of the | Lord: for great is the | glo-ry | of the | Lord.
dim 7 Though the Lord be high, yet hath He respect | unto ‧ the | lowly: but the proud He | knoweth a- | far ‧ = | off.
p 8 Though I walk in the | midst of | trouble: yet | Thou ‧ = | wilt re- | vive me.
9 Thou shalt stretch forth Thine hand against the wrath | of mine | enemies: and | Thy right | hand shall | save me.
cr 10 The Lord will perfect that which con- | cern-eth | me: Thy mercy O Lord endureth for ever, (*p*) forsake not the | works of | Thine own | hands.

F GLORY BE, &c.

Forty=Fourth.

103. HAYES.

104. From LANGDON.

105. LAHEE.

106. ARMES.

FROM PSALM CXXXIX.

MP O LORD, Thou hast | searched me and | known me: Thou knowest my downsitting and mine uprising, Thou understandest my | thought a- | far · = | off.

2 Thou compassest my path and my | ly-ing | down : and art ac- | quainted with | all my | ways.

p 3 For there is not a word | in my | tongue: but lo, O Lord, Thou | knowest · it | al-to- | gether.

4 Thou hast beset me behind | and be- | fore: and | laid Thine | hand up- | on me.

5 Such knowledge is too | wonder-ful | for me: it is high, I | cannot · at- | tain un- | to it.

p 6 Whither shall I go | from Thy | Spirit: (*cr*) or whither shall I | flee · = | from Thy | presence?

7 If I ascend up into heaven, | Thou art | there: if I make my bed in hell, be- | hold · = | Thou art | there.

8 If I take the | wings of · the | morn-ing : and dwell in the | utter-most | parts of · the | sea;

9 Even there shall | Thy hand | lead me : and | Thy right | hand shall | hold me.

10 If I say, surely the | darkness · shall | cover me: even the night | shall be | light a- | bout me.

11 Yea the darkness hideth | not from | Thee: the darkness and the light are | both a- | like to | Thee.

cr 12 How precious also are Thy thoughts unto | me O | God: how | great is · the | sum of | them.

13 If I should count them, they are more in number | than the | sand: when I awake, | I am | still with | Thee.

p 14 Search me, O God, and | know my | heart: try | me, and | know my | thoughts.

p 15 And see if there be any | wicked · way | in me: (*cr*) and **lead** me in the | way · = | e-ver- | lasting.

F Glory be to the Father, | and · to the | Son: and | to the | Holy | Ghost;

As it was in the beginning, is now, and *f* ever | shall be : world without | end · = | A · = | men.

Forty-Fifth.

107. WOODWARD.

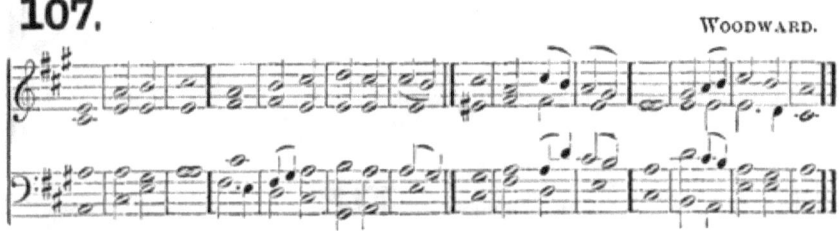

108. WOODWARD. **109.** THORNE.

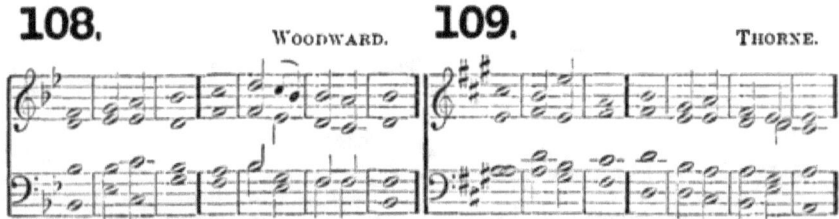

PSALM CXLV.

F I WILL extol Thee, my | God, O | King: and I will bless Thy | Name for | ever · and | ever.
  2 Every day | will I | bless Thee: and I will praise Thy | Name for | ever · and | ever.
  3 Great is the Lord, and greatly | to be | praised: and His | great-ness | is un- | searchable.
  4 One generation shall praise Thy works | to a- | nother: and shall de- | clare Thy | might-y | acts. *p*
  5 I will speak of the glorious honour | of Thy | majesty: and | of Thy | wondrous | works. *cr*
  6 And men shall speak of the might of Thy | terri-ble | acts: and | I · will de- | clare Thy | greatness.
  7 They shall abundantly utter the memory of | Thy great | goodness: and shall | sing of · Thy | right-eous- | ness.
  8 The Lord is gracious, and | full of · com-| passion: slow to anger, | and of | great · = | mercy
  9 The Lord is | good to | all: and His tender mercies are | o-ver | all His | works.
  10 All Thy works shall | praise Thee · O | Lord: and Thy | saints shall | bless · = | Thee.
  11 They shall speak of the glory | of Thy | kingdom: and | talk of | all Thy |

power.
  12 To make known to the sons of men His | mighty | acts: and the glorious | majes-ty | of His | kingdom.
  13 Thy kingdom is an ever- | last-ing | kingdom: and Thy dominion endureth through- | out all | ge-ne- | rations.
  14 The Lord upholdeth | all that | fall: and raiseth up all those | that be | bow-ed | down.
  15 The eyes of all | wait · upon | Thee: (*cr*) and Thou givest them their | meat in | due · = | season.
  16 Thou | openest · Thine | hand: and satisfiest the desire of | ev-ery | liv-ing | thing.
  17 The Lord is righteous in | all His | ways: and | holy · in | all His | works.
  18 The Lord is nigh unto all them that | call up- | on Him: to all that | call up- | on Him · in | truth.
  19 He will fulfil | the de- | sire: of | them that | fear · = | Him.
  20 He also will | hear their | cry: and | will de- | liv-er | them.
  21 The Lord preserveth all | them that | love Him: and let all flesh bless His holy | Name for | ever · and | ever. *ff*
F Glory be to the Father, | and · to the | Son: and | to the | Holy | Ghost;
  As it was in the beginning, is now, and | ever | shall be: world without | end · = | A · = | men.

PSALMS AND CANTICLES.

Forty-Sixth.

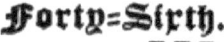

110. Walter.   **111.** Turpin.

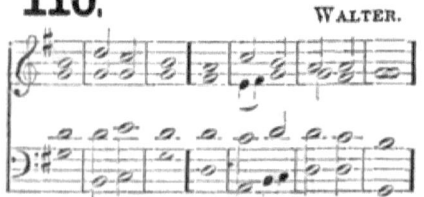

PSALM CXLVI.

F PRAISE | ye the | Lord: praise the | Lord ' = | O my | soul.
2 While I live will I | praise the | Lord: I will sing praises unto my God | while I | have ' any | being.
dim 3 Put not your | trust in | princes: nor in the son of man, in | whom there | is no | help.
dim 4 His breath goeth forth, he return-eth | to his | earth: (*p*) in that very | day his | thoughts ' = | perish.
cr 5 Happy is he that hath the God of Jacob | for his | help: whose hope is | in the | Lord his | God.
6 Who made heaven and earth, the sea, and all that | there-in | is: who | keep-eth | truth for | ever.
7 Who executeth judgment | for ' the op- | pressed: who giveth | food ' = | to the | hungry.
8 The Lord | looseth ' the | prisoners: the Lord | openeth ' the | eyes of ' the | blind.

112. Goss.

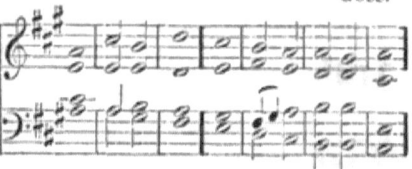

9 The Lord raiseth them that are | bow-ed | down: the | Lord ' = | loveth ' the | righteous.
10 The Lord pre- | serveth ' the | strangers: He relieveth the | fa-ther- | less and | widow.
11 But the way | of the | wicked: He | turn-eth | up-side | down.
f 12 The Lord shall | reign for | ever: even thy God, O Sion, unto all generations, | praise ' = | ye the | Lord.

F GLORY BE, &c.

Forty-Seventh.

113. Boyce.

FROM PSALM CXLVII.

F PRAISE ye the Lord, for it is good to sing praises | unto ' our | God: for it is pleasant, and | praise ' = | is ' = | comely.
2 The Lord doth build up Je- | rusa- | lem: He gathereth together the out | casts of | Is-ra- | el.
dim 3 He healeth the | broken ' in | heart: and | bind-eth | up their | wounds.
4 He telleth the number | of the | stars: He calleth them | all ' = | by their | names.
5 Great is our Lord, and | of great | power: His under- | standing ' is | in-fi- |

114. Monk.

nite.
6 The Lord lifteth | up the | meek: (*dim*) He casteth the wicked | down ' = | to the | ground.

cr 7 Sing unto the Lord | with thanks- | giving: sing praise upon the | harp ' = | unto ' our | God.

8 Who covereth the heaven with clouds, who prepareth rain | for the | earth: who maketh grass to | grow up- | on the | mountains.

9 He giveth to the | beast his | food: and | to the ' young | ravens ' which | cry.

f 10 Praise the Lord, O Je-| ru-sa- | lem: praise thy | God, O | Si ' = | on.

11 For He hath strengthened the bars | of thy | gates: He hath | blessed ' thy | children ' with- | in thee.

p 12 He maketh peace | in thy | borders: (*cr*) and filleth thee with the | fin-est | of the | wheat.

13 He sendeth forth His command- ment | up-on | earth: His word | run- neth | ve-ry | swiftly.

14 He giveth | snow like | wool: He scattereth the hoar | frost like | ash ' = | es.

15 He casteth forth His | ice like | morsels: who can | stand be- | fore His | cold.

16 He sendeth out His word and | melt-eth | them: He causeth His wind to blow, | and the | wa-ters | flow.

17 He sheweth His word | un-to | Jacob: His statutes and His | judg- ments | un-to | Israel.

dim 18 He hath not dealt so with | a-ny | nation: and as for His judgments, they have not known them, *f* | praise ' = | ye the | Lord.

F GLORY BE, &c.

Forty=Eighth.

PSALM CXLVIII.

F PRAISE ye the Lord | from the | heavens: praise | = ' Him | in the | heights.

2 Praise ye Him | all His | angels: praise | ye Him | all His | hosts.

3 Praise ye Him, | sun and | moon : praise Him, | all ye | stars of | light.

4 Praise Him, ye | heavens of | heav- ens: and ye waters that | be a- | bove the | heavens.

5 Let them praise the Name | of the | Lord: for He commanded, | and they | were cre- | ated.

6 He hath also stablished them for | ever ' and | ever: He hath made a de- | cree which | shall not | pass.

7 Praise the Lord | from the | earth: ye | dragons, | and all | deeps.

8 Fire, and hail, | snow, and | vapour: stormy | wind ful- | filling ' His | word.

9 Mountains, | and all | hills : fruit- ful | trees, and | all ' = | cedars.

10 Beasts, | and all | cattle: creeping | things, and | fly-ing | fowl.

11 Kings of the earth, | and all | people: princes, and all | judg-es | of the | earth.

12 Both young men and maidens, old men and children, let them praise the | Name ' of the | Lord: for His Name alone is excellent, His glory is a - | bove the | earth and | heaven.

13 He also exalteth the horn of His people, the praise of | all His | saints: even of the children of Israel, a people near unto Him, | praise ' = | ye the | Lord.

F GLORY BE, &c.

Forty-Ninth.

118. HUMPHREYS.

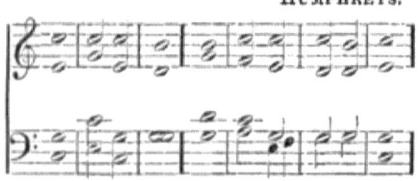

119. ELVEY.

PSALM CL.

F PRAISE God in His | sanc-tu- | ary:
praise Him in the | firma-ment | of
His | power.
2 Praise Him for His | migh-ty | acts:
praise Him according | to His | excel-
lent | greatness.
3 Praise Him with the sound | of the |
trumpet   praise Him with the | psal-
te- | ry and | harp.
4 Praise Him with the | timbrel ' and |
dance : praise Him with stringed | in-
stru- | ments and | organs.
5 Praise Him upon the | loud ' = |
cymbals   praise Him upon the |

120. TERRY.

high ' = | sound-ing | cymbals.
6 Let everything | that hath | breath:
praise | = ' = | = ' the | Lord.
MF GLORY BE, &c.

Fiftieth.

121. HANDEL.

ISAIAH XI: 1-10.

MF AND there shall come forth a rod out
of the | stem of | Jesse : and a
Branch shall | grow ' = | out of ' his |
roots.
mp 2 And the spirit of the Lord shall |
rest ' up- | on Him: the spirit of | wis-
dom ' and | un-der- | standing.
3 The spirit of | counsel ' and | might:
the spirit of knowledge and of the |
fear ' = | of the | Lord.
4 And righteousness shall be the gir-
dle | of His | loins : and faithfulness
the | gir-dle | of His | reins.
5 The wolf also shall | dwell ' with
the | lamb : and the leopard shall | lie
down | with the | kid.
6 And the calf and the fatling and the
young | lion ' to- | gether   and a | lit-
tle | child shall | lead them.

122. WEBBE.

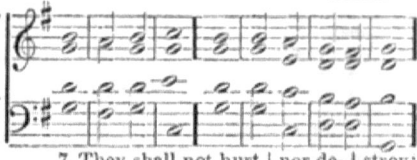

7 They shall not hurt | nor de- | stroy:
in | all my | ho-ly | mountain.
cr 8 For the earth shall be full of the
knowledge | of the | Lord : as the | wa-
ters | cover the | sea.
9 And in that day shall there be a |
root of | Jesse. which shall stand for an |
en-sign | of the | people.
10 To it shall the | Gen-tiles | seek:
and His | rest ' = | shall be | glorious.

F GLORY BE, &c.

PSALMS AND CANTICLES.

Fifty=First.

123. BATTISHILL. **124.** BROWNSMITH.

125. RIMBAULT.

FROM ISAIAH XXVI.

MF THOU wilt keep him in perfect peace, whose | mind is | stayed on | Thee. be- | cause he | trust-eth | in Thee.
2 Trust ye in the | Lord for- | ever: for in the Lord Jehovah is | ev-er | last-ing | strength.
dim 3 For He bringeth down them that | dwell on | high: the lofty | city • He | layeth · it | low.
p 4 He layeth it low even | to the | ground: He bringeth it ; e-ven | to the | dust.
5 The way of the just | is up- | rightness: Thou, most upright, dost | weigh the | path of • the | just.
6 Yea, in the way of Thy judgments, O Lord, have we | wait-ed | for Thee: the desire of our soul is to Thy Name, and | to the • re- | membrance | of Thee.
7 With my soul have I desired Thee | in the | night; yea, with my spirit within me | will I | seek Thee | early.
8 For when Thy judgments are | in the |

earth: the inhabitants of the | world will | learn • — | righteousness.
9 Lord Thou wilt or-dain | peace • — | for us: for Thou also hast | wrought all | our works | in us.
10 O Lord our God, other lords beside Thee have had do | min-ion | over us: but by Thee only will we make | men-tion | of Thy | Name.
F GLORY BE, &c.

Fifty=Second.

126. HIGGINS.

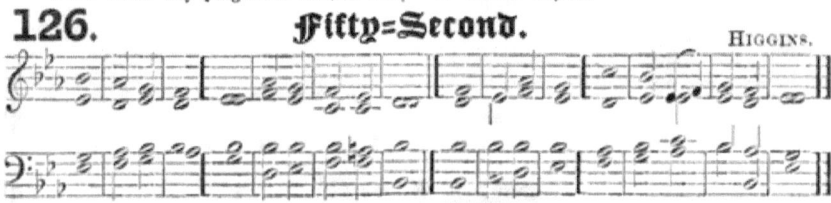

FROM ISAIAH XL.

MF COMFORT ye, comfort ye my peo- ple | saith your | God: speak ye comfortably | to Je- | ru-sa- | lem.
2 And cry unto her that her warfare | is ac- | complished: that her iniquity is pardoned, for she hath received of the Lord's hand | double • for | all her | sins.
cr 3 The voice of him that crieth in the | wil-der- | ness: pre- | pare • ye the | way of • the | Lord.
4 Make straight | in the | desert: a | high-way | for our | God.
5 Every valley shall | be ex- | alted: and every mountain and | hill shall | be made | low.
6 And the crooked shall | be made | straight: and the | rough • — | pla-ces | plain.
7 And the glory of the Lord shall | be re- | vealed: and all | flesh shall | see it | to- | gether.
8 For the mouth | of the | Lord: the mouth | of the | Lord hath | spoken it.
f 9 O Sion that bringest good tidings, get thee up into the | high • — | mountain: O Jerusalem that bringeth good tidings

127. MEDLEY.

lift | up thy | voice with | strength.
10 Lift it up, be | not a- | fraid: say unto the cities of | Judah, be- | hold your | God.
11 Behold, the Lord God will come with | strong • — | hand: and His | arm shall | rule • — | for Him.
12 Behold, His re- | ward is | with Him: and | — • His | work be- | fore Him.
dim 13 He shall feed His flock | like a | shepherd : He shall gather the | lambs • — | with His | arm.
p 14 And carry them | in His | bosom: and shall gently lead | those that | are with | young.
F GLORY BE, &c.

38 PSALMS AND CANTICLES.

Fifty-Third.

128. KETTLE.

129. ALDRICH.

130. KING.

ISAIAH LII: 7-10.

MF HOW beautiful up- | on the | moun- tains: are the feet of | him that | bringeth · good | tidings.
  2 That publisheth peace, that bringeth good | tidings · of | good : that publish- eth salvation, that saith unto | Si-on | thy God | reigneth.
  3 The watchmen shall lift | up the | voice: with the voice to- | ge-ther | shall they | sing.
  4 For they shall see | eye to | eye: when the | Lord shall | bring · again |

Sion.
  5 Break | forth · into | joy : sing to- gether ye waste pla-ces | of Je- | ru-sa- | lem.
  6 For the Lord hath | comforted · His | people: He hath re- | deemed · Je- | ru-sa- | lem.
  7 The Lord hath made bare His | ho-ly | arm: in the | eyes of | all the | nations.
  8 And all the ends | of the | earth: shall see the sal- | va-tion | of our | God.
F GLORY BE, &c.

Fifty-Fourth.

ISAIAH LII: 7-10.

131. SMITH.

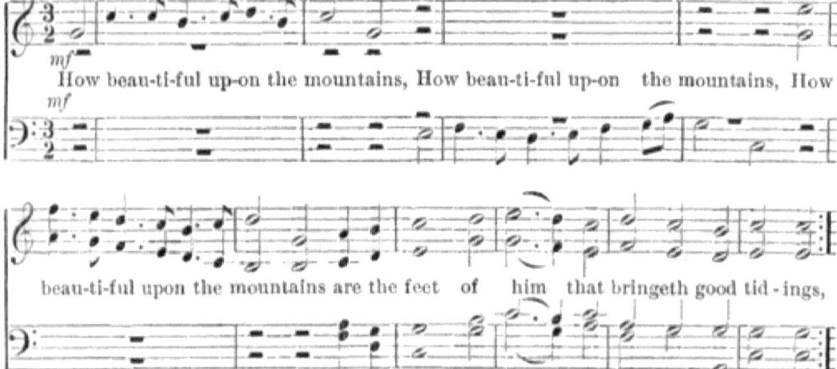

Andante moderato.
How beau-ti-ful up-on the mountains, How beau-ti-ful up-on the mountains, How beau-ti-ful upon the mountains are the feet of him that bringeth good tid-ings,

Fifty=Fifth.

132. MORLEY.

133. TURLE.   **134.** DOUGLAS.

From ISAIAH LIII.

MP HE is despised and re- | jected ᐧ of | men: a man of sorrows, | and ac- | quainted ᐧ with | grief.

2 And we hid as it were our | fa-ces | from Him: He was despised, and | we es- | teemed Him | not.

3 Surely He hath | borne our | griefs: and | car-ried | our ᐧ = | sorrows.

4 Yet we did es- | teem Him | stricken: smitten of | God ᐧ = | and af- | flicted.

5 But He was wounded for | our trans- | gressions : He was | bruised ᐧ for | our in- | iquities.

6 The chastisement of our peace | was up- | on Him: and with | His stripes | we are | healed.

7 All we like sheep have | gone a- | stray: we have turned every | one to | his own | way.

8 And the Lord hath | laid on | Him: the in- | iqui-ty | of us | all.

9 He was oppressed, and | He was ᐧ af- | flicted: yet He | open-ed | not His | mouth.

10 He is brought as a | lamb ᐧ to the | slaughter: and as a sheep before her shearers is dumb, so He | open-eth | not His | mouth.

11 He was taken from prison | and from | judgment and who shall de- | clare His | gen-er- | ation ?

12 For He was cut off out of the | land of ᐧ the | living: for the transgression of my | peo-ple | was He | stricken.

13 And He made His | grave ᐧ with the | wicked: and with the | rich ᐧ = | in His | death.

14 Because He had | done no | violence: neither was any de- | ceit ᐧ = | in His | mouth.

15 Yet it pleased the | Lord to | bruise Him ; yea | He hath | put Him ᐧ to | grief.

16 He shall see of the | travail ᐧ of His | soul: and | shall be | sat-is- | fied.

17 Because He hath poured out His | soul ᐧ unto | death: and He was | numbered | with the ᐧ trans- | gressors.

18 And He bare the | sin of | many: and made inter- | cession ᐧ for | the trans- | gressors.

F Glory be to the Father, | and ᐧ to the | Son: and | to the | Holy | Ghost;

As it was in the beginning, is now, and | ever | shall be : world without | end ᐧ = | A ᐧ = | men.

II. FROM THE NEW TESTAMENT.

Fifty-Sixth.

135. WEBBE.

136. CRESER.

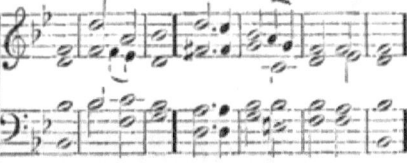

S. LUKE, 1: 46.

p MY soul doth magni | fy the | Lord:
and my spirit hath re | joiced ' in |
God my | Saviour.
mf 2 For He | hath re | garded: the low-
li | ness of | His hand | maiden.
3 For be | hold from | henceforth: all
gener | ations ' shall | call me | blessed.
4 For He that is mighty hath | mag-
ni ' fied | me: and | holy | is His | Name.
p 5 And His mercy is on | them that |
fear Him: through | out all | gener | a-
tions.
6 He hath showed strength | with
His | arm: He hath scattered the proud
in the imagin | ation | of their | hearts.
7 He hath put down the mighty | from
their | seat: and hath ex | alted ' the |
humble ' and | meek.

137. OUSELEY.

8 He hath filled the hungry with |
good ' = | things: and the rich He hath |
sent ' = | empty ' a | way.
p 9 He remembering His mercy, hath
holpen His servant | Isra | el: as He
promised to our forefathers, Abraham |
and his | seed for | ever.

F GLORY BE, &c.

Fifty-Seventh.

138. OUSELEY.

139. ALDRICH.

S. LUKE, 1: 68.

F BLESSED be the Lord God of | Isra |
el: for He hath visited | and re |
deemed ' His | people;
2 And hath raised up a mighty sal |
vation | for us: in the house | of His |
servant | David.
3 As He spake by the mouth of His |
holy | Prophets: which have been | since
the | world be | gan;
mf 4 That we should be saved | from
our | enemies: and from the hand of |
all that | hate ' = | us.
5 To perform the mercy promised | to
our | fathers: and to re- | member ' His |
ho-ly | covenant.
6 The oath which He sware to our |
fa-ther | Abraham: that He would grant
p unto us, that we being delivered out
of the hand of our enemies, might |

serve Him | with-out | fear.
p 7 In holiness and righteousness be- |
fore ' = | Him: all the | days of |
our ' = | life.
mf 8 And Thou Child, shalt be called the
Prophet | of the | Highest: for Thou
shalt go before the face of the Lord | to
pre- | pare His | ways.
9 To give knowledge of salvation |
unto ' His | people: by the re- | mission |
of their | sins.
10 Through the tender mercy | of
our | God: whereby the day-spring from
on | high hath | visit-ed | us.
11 To give light to them that | sit in |
darkness: and | in the | shadow ' of |
death.
p 12 To | guide our | feet: in- | to the |
way of | peace.

F GLORY BE, &c.

Fifty=Eighth.

140. Anon.

141. Blow.

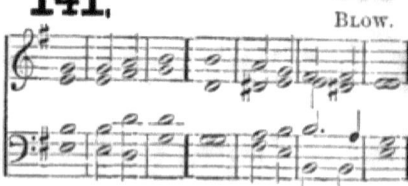

S. Luke, ii: 29.

MF LORD, now lettest Thou Thy servant
de | part in | peace: ac | cording | to
Thy | word.
  2 For mine | eyes have | seen: Thy |
= · sal | va · = | tion,
  3 Which Thou | hast pre | pared: before the | face of | all · = | people;
  4 To be a light to | lighten · the | Gentiles: and to be the glory of Thy | people |
Isra | el.
  F Glory be to the Father, | and · to the |
Son: and | to the | Holy | Ghost;

142. Medley.

As it was in the beginning, is now,
and | ever | shall be: world without |
end · = | A · = | men.

Fifty=Ninth.

143. Crotch.

1 Corinthians, v. &c.

F CHRIST our passover is | sacrificed |
for us: therefore | let us | keep the |
feast;
  2 Not with the old leaven, neither with
the leaven of | malice · and | wickedness:
but with the unleavened bread of sin |
ceri | ty and | truth. 1 *Cor* v. 7.
F CHRIST being raised from the dead |
dieth no | more: death hath no more
do | minion | over | Him.
  p 3 For in that He died, He died unto |
sin · = | once: (*f*) but in that He liveth,
He | liveth | unto | God.
  4 Likewise reckon ye also yourselves to
be dead in | deed · unto | sin: but alive
unto God through | Jesus | Christ our |
Lord   *Rom.* vi: 9.
F CHRIST is risen | from the | dead: and
become the first | fruits of | them
that | slept.

144. Fisher.

  p 5 For since by | man came | death: (*cr*)
by man came also the resur | rection | of
the | dead.
  p 6 For as in Adam | all · = | die: (*f*)
even so in Christ shall | all be | made a |
live. 1 *Cor.* xv: 20.
  F Glory be to the Father, | and · to the |
Son: and | to the | Holy | Ghost;
  As it was in the beginning, is now,
and | ever | shall be: world without |
end · = | A · = | men.

Sixtieth.

145. WESLEY.

146. MONK.

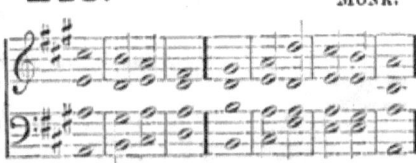

FROM 1 CORINTHIANS XV.

MF NOW is Christ risen | from the | dead: and become the first | fruits of | them that | slept.

2 For since by | man came | death: by man came also the resur | rec-tion | of the dead.

p 3 For as in Adam | all ‧ = | die: (*cr*) even so in Christ shall | all be | made a- | live.

4 But every man in his own order, | Christ the | first fruits: afterward they that are | Christ's ‧ = | at His | coming.

dim 5 Behold, I | show you ‧ a | mystery: we | shall not | all ‧ = | sleep.

p 6 But we shall | all be | changed: in a moment, in the twinkling of an eye | at the | last ‧ = | trump.

(*cr*) 7 For the | trumpet ‧ shall | sound: and the dead shall be raised incorruptible, and | we ‧ = | shall be | changed.

8 For this corruptible must put on | incor- | ruption: and this mortal must | put on | im-mor- | tality.

9 So when | this cor- | ruptible: shall have | put on | in-cor- | ruption,

10 And | this ‧ = | mortal: shall have | put on | im-mor | tality,

f 11 Then shall be brought to pass the saying | that is | written: death is | swallowed | up in | victory.

p 12 O death, | where is ‧ thy | sting: O Grave, | where ‧ = | is thy | victory.

p 13 The sting of | death is | sin: and the | strength of | sin ‧ is the | law.

cr 14 But | thanks ‧ be to | God: who giveth us the victory through | our Lord | Je-sus | Christ.

F GLORY BE, &c.

Sixty-First.

147. RICHARDSON. **148.** BATTISHILL.

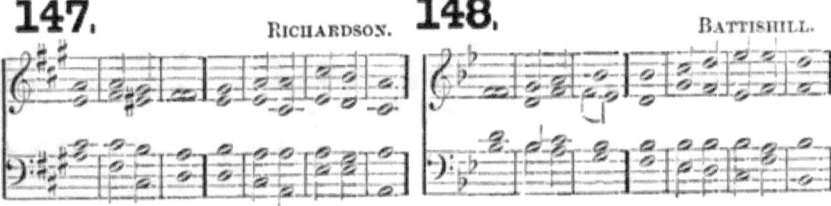

REVELATION I: 5-8.

F UNTO | Him that | loved us: and washed us from our | sins in | His own | blood,

2 And hath made us kings and priests unto | God ‧ and His | Father: to Him be glory and dominion for | ever ‧ and | ever ‧ A- | men.

3 Behold, He | cometh ‧ with | clouds: and | ev - ery | eye shall | see Him.

4 And they | also who | pierced Him: and all kindreds of the earth shall wail because of Him, | e - ven | so, A - | men.

5 I | am | Alpha ‧ and | Omega: the beginning and the | end - ing | saith the | Lord:

6 Who is | and who | was: and who is to come, | the ‧ = | Al ‧ = | mighty.

F GLORY BE, &c.

Doxologies, &c., from the Apocalypse.

Sanctus of the Cherubim.

149.

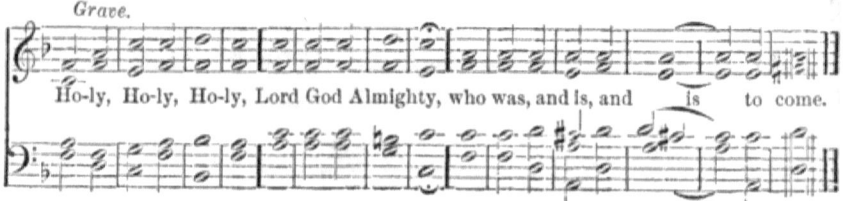

Ho-ly, Ho-ly, Ho-ly, Lord God Almighty, who was, and is, and is to come.

First Doxology of the Redeemed Church.

150.

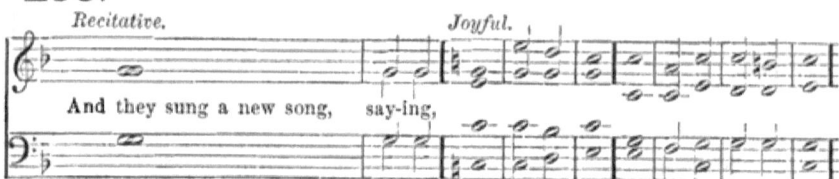

And they sung a new song, say-ing,

THOU art worthy to | take the | book: and to | open · the | seals there- | of.
2 For | Thou wast | slain: and hast redeemed us to | God by | Thine own | blood,
3 Out of every | kindred · and | tongue: out of | ev-ery | people · and | nation.
4 And hast made us unto our God | Kings and | Priests: and we shall | reign up- | on the | earth.

Second Doxology of the Redeemed Church.

151.

Thou art wor-thy, O Lord: to receive glo-ry and hon-our and power;

For Thou hast cre-a-ted all things: { and for Thy pleas-ure they } are, and were cre-a-ted.

PSALMS AND CANTICLES.

Doxology of the Holy Angels.

152.

1 Worthy .... is the Lamb: the Lamb ' = that was slain,
2 { To receive power, and riches, and } wisdom, and strength: and honour, and glory, and blessing.

First Doxology of the Universal Creation.

153.

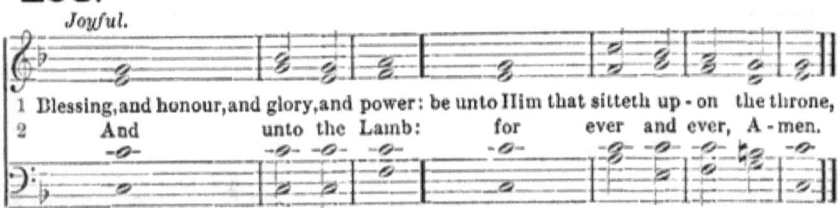

1 Blessing, and honour, and glory, and power: be unto Him that sitteth up‑on the throne,
2 And .... unto the Lamb: for ever and ever, A‑men.

Second Doxology of the Universal Creation.

154.

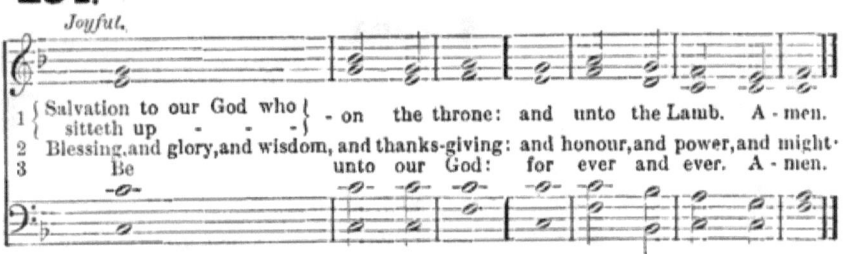

1 { Salvation to our God who sitteth up .... } ‑on the throne: and unto the Lamb. A‑men.
2 Blessing, and glory, and wisdom, and thanks‑giving: and honour, and power, and might‑
3 Be .... unto our God: for ever and ever. A‑men.

Songs of Victory.

Thanksgiving for Victory over Persecutors.

155.

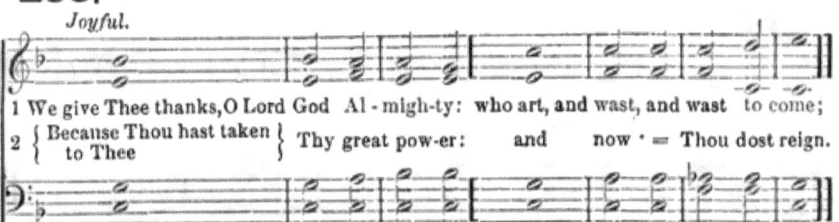

1 We give Thee thanks, O Lord God Al‑migh‑ty: who art, and wast, and wast to come;
2 { Because Thou hast taken to Thee } Thy great pow‑er: and now ' = Thou dost reign.

PSALMS AND CANTICLES.

THANKSGIVING FOR VICTORY OVER SATAN.

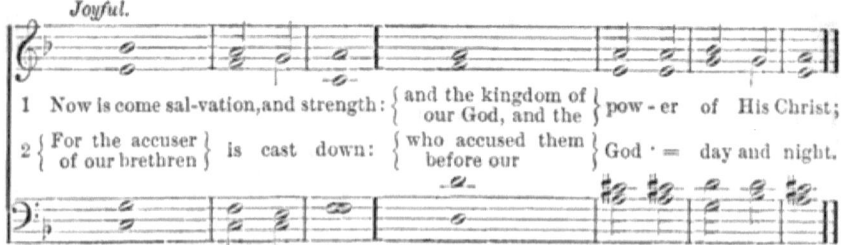

Alleluia.

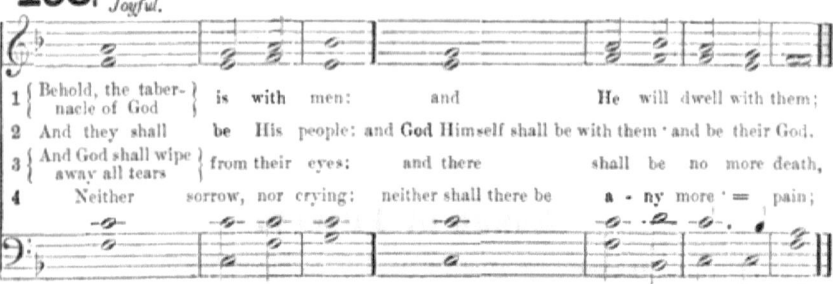

160. Gloria in Excelsis.

OLD CHANT.

GLORY be to | God on | high : and on earth, | peace, good | will towards | men.
We praise Thee, we bless Thee,

we | worship | Thee: we glorify Thee, we give thanks to | Thee for | Thy great | glory.

O Lord God, | Heavenly | King : God the | Father | Al ˙ = | mighty.

O Lord, the only begotten Son | Jesus | Christ : O Lord God, Lamb of | God, Son | of the | Father,

That takest away the | sins ˙ of the | world : have mercy | upon | us.
Thou that takest away the | sins ˙ of the | world : have mercy | upon | us.

Thou that takest away the | sins ˙ of the | world : re | ceive our | prayer.
Thou that sittest at the right hand of | God the | Father : have mercy | upon | us.

A - MEN.

For Thou only | art ˙ = | holy : Thou | only | art the | Lord.
Thou only, O Christ, with the | Holy |

Ghost : art most high in the | glory ˙ of | God the | Father.

Te Deum Laudamus.

161. BULLINGER.
162. GARDNER.
163. FOWLER.
164. HODGES.

NOTE.—*If more than one chant is used, the first change may be made at the words "WHEN THOU TOOKEST," &c., and the second change at the words "DAY BY DAY," &c.*

f WE praise | Thee, O | God: we acknowl- | edge | Thee to | be the | Lord.
2 All the earth doth | worship | Thee: the *p* Father | ever | last ･ ⸗ | ing.
3 To Thee all Angels | cry a | loud: the Heavens, and | all the | Powers there | in.
4 To Thee Cherubim, and | Sera | phim: con | tinually | do ･ ⸗ | cry.
5 (*full, slower*) Holy, | Holy, | Holy: Lord | God of | Saba | oth;
6 (*faster*) Heaven and earth are full | of the | Majesty: of | Thy ･ ⸗ | Glo ･ ⸗ | ry.
7 The glorious company | of ･ the A | postles: praise | ⸗ ･ ⸗ | ⸗ ･ ⸗ | Thee.
8 The goodly fellowship | of the | Prophets: praise | ⸗ ･ ⸗ | ⸗ ･ ⸗ | Thee.
9 The noble army | of ･ ⸗ | Martyrs: praise | ⸗ ･ ⸗ | ⸗ ･ ⸗ | Thee.
10 The holy Church throughout | all the | world: doth | ⸗ ･ ac | knowledge | Thee;
11 The | Fa ･ ⸗ | ther: of an | in finite | Majes | ty;
12 Thine a | dora ･ ble | true: and | on ･ ⸗ | ⸗ ･ ly | Son;
13 Also the | Holy | Ghost: the | Com ･ ⸗ | ⸗ ･ fort | er.
14 (*full*) Thou art the | King of | Glory: O | ⸗ ･ ⸗ | ⸗ ･ ⸗ | Christ.
15 Thou art the ever | lasting | Son: of | ⸗ ･ the | Fa ･ ⸗ | ther.
¶ 16 (*p*) When Thou tookest upon Thee to de | liver | man: Thou didst humble Thyself to be | born ･ ⸗ | of a | Virgin.
17 When Thou hadst overcome the | sharpness ･ of | death: (*cr*) Thou didst open the kingdom of Heaven to | all be | liev ･ ⸗ | ers.
f 18 Thou sittest at the right | hand of | God: in the glory | of the | Fa ･ ⸗ | ther.
19 We believe that | Thou shalt | come: to | be ･ ⸗ | our ･ ⸗ | Judge.
p 20 (*slower*) We therefore pray Thee | help Thy | servants: whom Thou hast redeemed | with Thy | pre ･ cious | blood.
21 (*faster*) Make them to be numbered | with Thy | Saints: in glory | ever | last ･ ⸗ | ing.
22 O Lord, | save Thy | people: and | bless Thine | herit | age.
23 Gov ･ ⸗ | ･ ern | them: and | lift them | up for | ever.
¶ *f* 24 (*full*) Day | by ･ ⸗ | day: we | magni | ･ fy ･ ⸗ | Thee;
p 25 (*full*) And we worship | Thy ･ ⸗ | Name: ever | world with | out ･ ⸗ | end.
26 Vouchsafe, | O ･ ⸗ | Lord: to keep us this | day with | out ･ ⸗ | sin.
27 O Lord, have | mer ･ cy up | on us: have | mer ･ cy up | on ･ ⸗ | us.
28 O Lord, let Thy mercy | be up | on us: as our | trust is | in ･ ⸗ | Thee.
cr 29 (*full*) O Lord, in Thee | have I | trusted: let me never | be con | found ･ ⸗ | ed.

A SHORT CHORAL SERVICE.

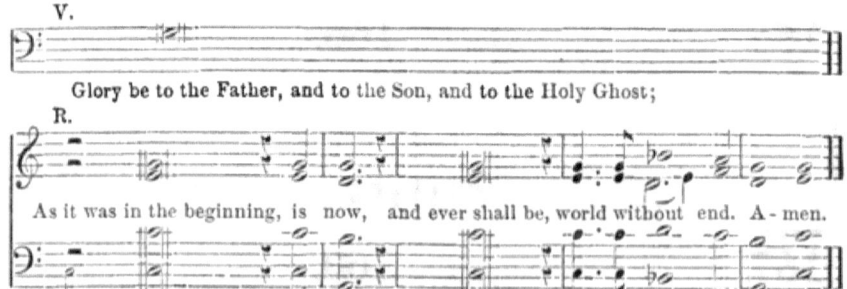

Glory be to the Father, and to the Son, and to the Holy Ghost; As it was in the beginning, is now, and ever shall be, world without end. A-men.

¶ *Then may follow the reading of Holy Scripture, or one of the preceding Psalms or Canticles may be sung.*

¶ *Then may follow, at the discretion of the Minister or Superintendent, any Prayers, the following Hymn, or any of the Hymns in the accompanying Hymnal.*

170.

Jesus, from Thy throne on high, Far above the bright blue sky, Look on us with loving eye. Hear us, Holy Jesus. A-MEN.

2 Little children need not fear,
When they know that Thou art near,
Thou dost love us, Saviour dear.
Hear us, Holy Jesus.

3 Little hearts may **love** Thee well,
Little lips Thy love may tell,
Little hymns Thy praises swell.
Hear us, Holy Jesus.

4 Little lives may be divine,
Little deeds of love may shine,
Little ones be wholly Thine.
Hear us, Holy Jesus.

5 Be Thou with us every day,
In our work and in our play,
When we learn, and when we **pray.**
Hear us, Holy Jesus.

6 Make us brave without a fear,
Make us happy, full of cheer,
Sure that Thou art always near.
Hear us, Holy Jesus.

7 May we prize our Christian name,
May we guard it free from blame,
Fearing all that causes shame.
Hear us, Holy Jesus.

8 May we grow from day to day
Glad to learn each holy way,
Ever ready to obey.
Hear us, Holy Jesus.

9 May we ever try to be
From our sinful tempers free,
Pure and gentle, Lord, like Thee.
Hear us, Holy Jesus.

10 May our thoughts be undefiled,
May our words be true and mild,
Make us each a holy child.
Hear us, Holy Jesus.

11 Jesus, whom we hope to see,
Calling us in heaven to be,
Happy evermore with Thee.
Hear us, Holy Jesus. AMEN.

Hymns and Carols.

Morning.

171.
Joyful.

MORNING HYMN.
L. M.

A-wake, my soul, and with the sun Thy dai-ly course of du-ty run: Shake off dull sloth, and ear-ly rise To pay thy morn-ing sac-ri-fice. A-MEN.

2 Let all thy converse be sincere,
Thy conscience as the noon-day clear;
Think how the all-seeing God, thy ways
And all thy secret thoughts surveys.

3 Wake, and lift up thyself, my heart,
And with the angels bear thy part;
Who all night long unwearied sing,
"Glory to Thee, eternal King."

4 Lord, I my vows to Thee renew;
Scatter my sins as morning dew;
Guard my first springs of thought and will,
And with Thyself my spirit fill.

5 Direct, control, suggest this day
All I design, or do, or say,
That all my powers, with all their might,
In Thy sole glory may unite.

6 Praise God, from whom all blessings flow,
Praise Him, all creatures here below;
Praise Him above, ye heavenly host;
Praise Father, Son, and Holy Ghost.

MORNING.

172.
Melcombe. L. M.

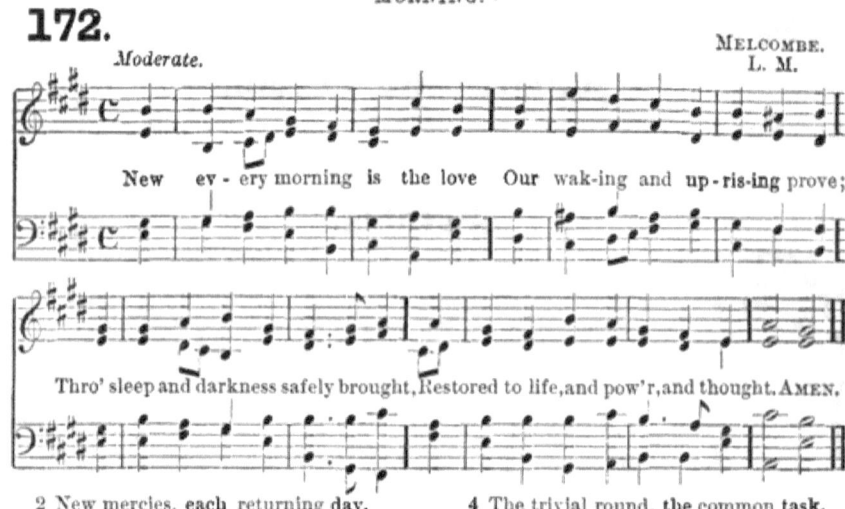

New every morning is the love Our waking and uprising prove;
Thro' sleep and darkness safely brought, Restored to life, and pow'r, and thought. Amen.

2 New mercies, each returning day,
Hover around us while we pray;
New perils past, new sins forgiven,
New thoughts of God, new hopes of heaven.

3 If on our daily course our mind
Be set to hallow all we find,
New treasures still of countless price,
God will provide for sacrifice.

4 The trivial round, the common task,
Will furnish all we ought to ask:
Room to deny ourselves: a road
To bring us daily nearer God.

5 Only, O Lord, in Thy dear love
Fit us for perfect rest above;
And help us this, and every day
To live more nearly as we pray.

173.
Smallwood. 7s.

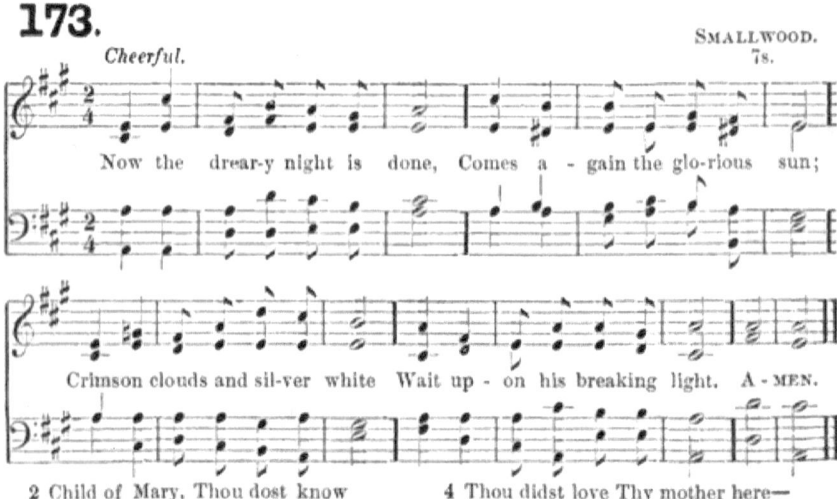

Now the dreary night is done, Comes again the glorious sun;
Crimson clouds and silver white Wait upon his breaking light. Amen.

2 Child of Mary, Thou dost know
What of danger, joy, or woe
Shall to-day my portion be,—
Let me meet it all in Thee.

3 Thou wast meek and undefiled—
Make me holy too, and mild;
Thou didst foil the tempter's power;
Help me in temptation's hour.

4 Thou didst love Thy mother here—
Make me gentle, kind, and dear;
Thou wast subject to her word—
Teach me to obey, O Lord.

5 Fretful feelings, passion, pride
Never did with Thee abide;
Make me watch myself to-day,
That they lead me not astray.

MORNING.

174.
THE MORNING BRIGHT.
P. M.

Cheerful.

The morning bright, With rosy light, Hath waked me from my sleep;
Father, I own Thy love alone Thy little one doth keep. A-MEN.

2 All through the day,
　I humbly pray,
Be Thou my Guard and Guide;
　My sins forgive,
　And let me live,
Blest Jesus, near Thy side.

3 Oh make Thy rest
　Within my breast,
Great Spirit of all grace;
　Make me like Thee,
　Then shall I be
Prepared to see Thy face.

175.
FERRIER.
7s.

Moderate.

Jesus, holy, undefiled, Listen to a little child;
Thou hast sent the glorious light, Chasing far the silent night. A-MEN.

2 Thou hast sent the sun to shine
O'er this glorious world of Thine;
Warmth to give, and pleasant glow,
On each tender flower below.

3 Now the little birds arise,
Chirping gaily in the skies;
Thee their tiny voices praise
In the early songs they raise.

4 Thou by whom the birds are fed,
Give to me my daily bread;
And Thy Holy Spirit give,
Without whom I cannot live.

5 Make me, Lord, obedient, mild,
As becomes a little child;
All day long, in every way,
Teach me what to do and say.

6 Make me, Lord, in work and play,
Thine more truly every day;
And when Thou at last shall come,
Take me to Thy heavenly home.

MORNING.

176.   Dawn.   C. M.

Moderate.

The breaking morn comes back to bless The earth from pole to pole;
So come, sweet Sun of Righteous-ness, And shine in-to my soul. A-MEN.

2 A silver mist along the lawn,
From every dewy sod,
Goes up to heaven; and so at dawn
I lift my thoughts to God.

3 I think how Thou didst wake, O Lord,
Before the break of day,
And seek the lonely mountain sward;
So teach my lips to pray.

4 I think how Thou didst sleep and rise,
So many nights and days,
A Child obedient, holy, wise,
And perfect in Thy ways.

5 The dawn of day, the dawn of life,
Were blest alike to Thee;
Thou know'st the danger and the strife;
Lord bless them both to me.

177.   S. Helen.   L. M.

Quietly.

O God, who, when the night was deep, Hast kept me safe and lent me sleep,
Now with Thy sun Thou bid'st me rise, And look around with older eyes. A-MEN.

2 Each happy morning Thou dost give,
I have one morning less to live;
O help me so this day to spend,
To make me fitter for the end.

3 O bid all wicked thoughts to fly;
The fretful word, the idle eye,
Help me to think in all I do,
"God sees me:—would He have it so?"

4 Make my first wish and thought to be
For others sooner than for me;
And let me pardon them, as I
Hope for God's pardon when I die.

5 Be with me when I work and play;
Be with me now and every day:
Be near me, when I pray Thee hear;
And when I pray not,—Lord! be near.

MORNING.

178.

AWAKE, AND AWAY.
6s. 5s. *with Chorus.*

Joyous.

The morning light fling-eth Its wak-en-ing ray; And as the day bringeth The work of the day, The hap-py heart singeth, A-wake, and a-way!

Chorus after each verse.

A-wake, and a-way! A-wake, and a-way! A-wake, a-wake, and a-way, a-way! Awake, awake, and a-way, a-way! The hap-py heart sing-eth, A-wake, and a-way! A-MEN.

2 No life can be dreary,
　When work is delight;
　Though evening be weary,
　Rest cometh at night,
　And all will be cheery,
　If faithful and right.
CHORUS.—Awake, and away, &c.

3 When duty is pleasure,
　And labour is joy,
　How sweet is the leisure
　Of ended employ!
　Then only can pleasure
　Be free from alloy.
CHORUS.—Awake, and away, &c.

179. Evening.

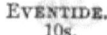
EVENTIDE.
10s.

(If preferred, the tune "Ellers" (No. 201) can be used for this hymn.)

Quietly.

A-bide with me: fast falls the e-ven-tide; The dark-ness deep-ens; Lord, with me a-bide; When oth-er help-ers fail, and comforts flee, Help of the helpless, O a-bide with me. A-MEN.

2 Swift to its close, ebbs out life's little day;
Earth's joys grow dim, its glories pass away;
Change and decay in all around I see;
O Thou, who changest not, abide with me.

3 I need Thy presence every passing hour;
What but Thy grace can foil the tempter's power?
Who like Thyself my guide and stay can be?
Through cloud and sunshine, Lord, abide with me.

4 I fear no foe, with Thee at hand to bless:
Ills have no weight, and tears no bitterness,
Where is death's sting? where, grave, thy victory?
I triumph still, if Thou abide with me.

5 Hold Thou Thy Cross before my closing eyes;
Shine through the gloom, and point me to the skies;
Heaven's morning breaks, and earth's vain shadows flee;
In life, in death, O Lord, abide with me.

(SECOND TUNE.)   TROYTE No. 1.

EVENING.

180.

HURSLEY.
L. M.

Moderate.

Sun of my soul, Thou Saviour dear, It is not night if Thou be near;
O may no earth-born cloud arise To hide Thee from Thy servant's eyes. A-MEN.

2 When the soft dews of kindly sleep
My weary eyelids gently steep,
Be my last thought, how sweet to rest
For ever on my Saviour's breast.

3 Abide with me from morn till eve,
For without Thee I cannot live;
Abide with me when night is nigh,
For without Thee I dare not die.

4 If some poor wandering child of Thine
Have spurn'd to-day the voice divine,
Now, Lord, the gracious work begin;
Let him no more lie down in sin.

5 Watch by the sick; enrich the poor
With blessings from Thy boundless store;
Be every mourner's sleep to-night,
Like infant slumbers, pure and light.

6 Come near and bless us when we wake,
Ere through the world our way we take,
Till in the ocean of Thy love
We lose ourselves in heaven above.

181.

DAY IS PAST.
P. M.

Moderate.

Day is past and gone; Darkness hastens on;
Blessed Lord, in mercy keep Angel-guards around Thy sheep. A-MEN.

2 Work again is past;
Rest has come at last;
Blessèd Lord, forgive, I pray,
All I have done wrong to-day.

3 Soon in silence deep
God will give me sleep:
Blessèd Lord, be Thou my light,
In the watches of the night.

4 When the night is o'er,
And I wake once more,
Blessèd Lord, who lovest me.
Make Thy child to follow Thee.

EVENING.

182. STELLA. Six 8s.

Sweet Saviour, bless us ere we go; Thy word into our minds instil:
And make our lukewarm hearts to glow With lowly love and fervent will.
Through life's long day and death's dark night, O gentle Jesus, be our light. A-MEN.

2 The day has gone, its hours have run,
    And Thou hast taken count of all,
The scanty triumphs grace hath won,
    The broken vow, the frequent fall.
Through life's long day and death's dark night,
    O gentle Jesus, be our light.

3 Grant us, dear Lord, from evil ways
    True absolution and release;
And bless us, more than in past days,
    With purity and inward peace.
Through life's long day and death's dark night,
    O gentle Jesus, be our light.

4 Labour is sweet, for Thou hast toil'd:
    And care is light, for Thou hast cared;
Ah! never! let our works be soil'd
    With strife, or by deceit ensnared.
Through life's long day and death's dark night,
    O gentle Jesus, be our light.

5 For all we love, the poor, the sad,
    The sinful, unto Thee we call;
O let Thy mercy make us glad;
    Thou art our Jesus, and our all.
Through life's long day and death's dark night,
    O gentle Jesus, be our light.

6 Sweet Saviour, bless us; night is come;
    Through night and darkness near us be,
Good angels watch about our home,
    And we are one day nearer Thee.
Through life's long day and death's dark night,
    O gentle Jesus, be our light.

EVENING.

TALLIS'S CANON.
L. M.

All praise to Thee, my God, this night, For all the blessings of the light:
Keep me, O keep me, King of kings, Un-der Thine own Al-might-y wings. A-MEN.

2 Forgive me, Lord, for Thy dear Son,
The ills that I this day have done;
That with the world, myself, and Thee,
I, ere I sleep, at peace may be.

3 Teach me to live, that I may dread
The grave as little as my bed;
Teach me to die, that so I may
Rise glorious at the awful day.

4 O may my soul on Thee repose,
And with sweet sleep mine eyelids close:
Sleep, that may me more vigorous make
To serve my God, when I awake.

5 When in the night I sleepless lie,
My soul with heavenly thoughts supply:
Let no ill dreams disturb my rest,
No powers of darkness me molest.

6 Praise God, from whom all blessings flow;
Praise Him, all creatures here below;
Praise Him above, ye heavenly host;
Praise Father, Son, and Holy Ghost.

184.

GERMAN EVENING HYMN.
7s.

Now the light has gone a-way. Sa-viour, lis-ten while I pray,
Ask-ing Thee to watch and keep, And to send me quiet sleep. A-MEN.

2 Jesus, Saviour, wash away,
All that has been wrong to-day;
Help me every day to be
Good and gentle, more like Thee.

3 Let my near and dear ones be,
Always near and dear to Thee;
O bring me and all I love
To Thy happy Home above.

4 Now my evening praise I give;
Thou didst die that I might live,
All my blessings come from Thee,
O how good Thou art to me!

5 Thou my best and kindest Friend,
Thou wilt love me to the end!
Let me love Thee more and more,
Always better than before.

EVENING.

185.

SOUTHGATE'S.
8s. 4s.

Moderate.

God, that madest earth and heaven, Dark-ness and light; Who the day for toil hast giv-en, For rest the night: May Thine an-gel guards de-fend us, Slumber sweet Thy mer-cy send us, Ho-ly dreams and hopes at-tend us, This live-long night. A-MEN.

Guard us waking, guard us sleeping,
　And, when we die,
May we in Thy mighty keeping,
　All peaceful lie:
When the last dread trump shall wake us,
Do not Thou, our Lord, forsake us,
But to reign in **glory** take **us**
　With Thee on high.

186.

S. ANATOLIUS.
P. M.

Quietly.

The day is past and o-ver; All thanks, O Lord, to Thee!

EVENING.

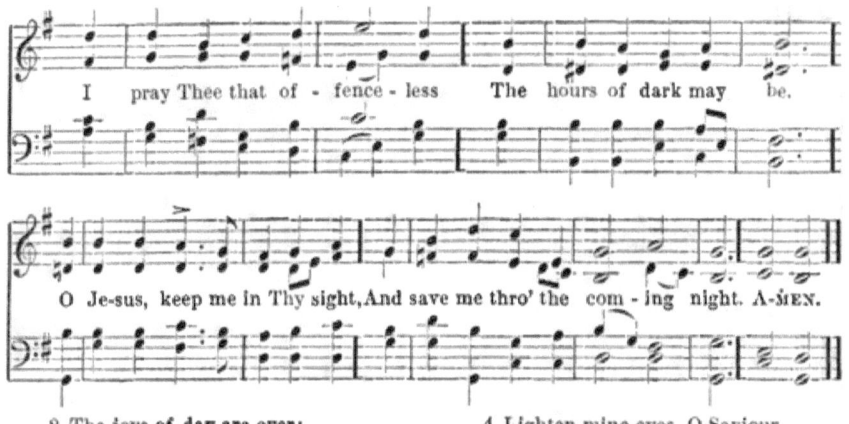

I pray Thee that of-fence-less The hours of dark may be.
O Je-sus, keep me in Thy sight, And save me thro' the com-ing night. A-MEN.

2 The joys of day are over;
   I lift my heart to Thee,
And call on Thee that sinless
   The hours of gloom may be.
O Jesus, make their darkness light,
And save me through the coming night.

3 The toils of day are over;
   I raise the hymn to Thee,
And ask that free from peril
   The hours of fear may be:
O Jesus, keep me in Thy sight,
And guard me through the coming night.

4 Lighten mine eyes, O Saviour,
   Or sleep in death shall I,
And he, my wakeful tempter,
   Triumphantly shall cry.
"Against him I have now prevailed:
Rejoice! the child of God has failed!"

5 Be Thou my soul's Preserver,
   O God! for Thou dost know,
How many are the perils
   Through which I have to go.
O loving Jesus, hear my call,
And guard and save me from them all!

187.

S. SYLVESTER.
8s. 7s.

Quietly.

Hear Thy children, gentle Je-sus, While we breathe our evening prayer;
Save us from all harm and dan-ger, Take us 'neath Thy sheltering care. A - MEN.

2 Save us from the wiles of Satan,
   'Mid the lone and silent night
Sweetly may bright guardian angels
   Keep us 'neath their watchful sight.

3 Gentle Jesus, look in pity
   From Thy great white throne above:

All the night Thy care is watchful;
   Never closed Thine eyes of love.

4 Shades of evening fast are falling,
   Day is fading into gloom;
When the shades of death fall round us,
   Lead Thy ransomed children home.

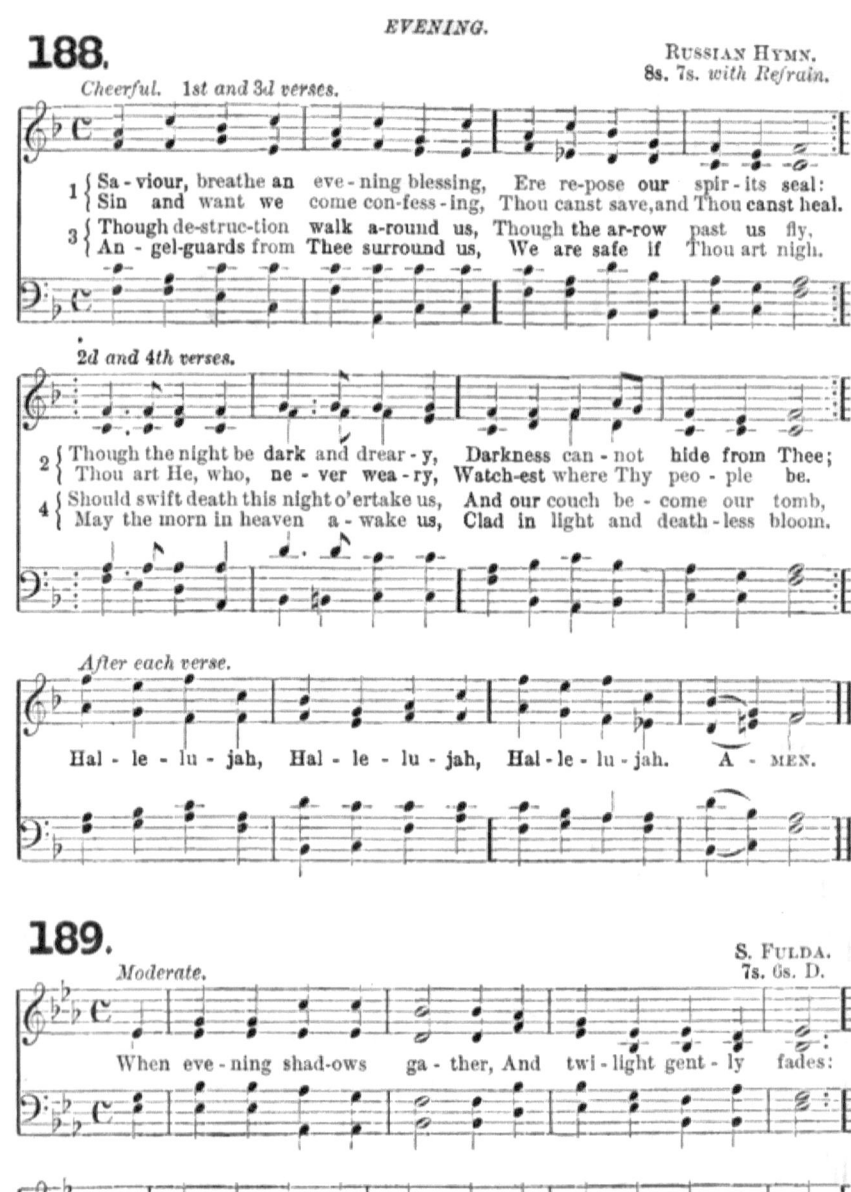

EVENING.

188. RUSSIAN HYMN. 8s. 7s. *with Refrain.*

Cheerful. 1st and 3d verses.

1. Sa - viour, breathe an eve - ning blessing, Ere re - pose our spir - its seal:
   Sin and want we come con - fess - ing, Thou canst save, and Thou canst heal.
3. Though de - struc - tion walk a - round us, Though the ar - row past us fly,
   An - gel-guards from Thee surround us, We are safe if Thou art nigh.

2d and 4th verses.

2. Though the night be dark and drear - y, Darkness can - not hide from Thee;
   Thou art He, who, ne - ver wea - ry, Watch-est where Thy peo - ple be.
4. Should swift death this night o'ertake us, And our couch be - come our tomb,
   May the morn in heaven a - wake us, Clad in light and death - less bloom.

After each verse.

Hal - le - lu - jah, Hal - le - lu - jah, Hal - le - lu - jah. A - MEN.

189. S. FULDA. 7s. 6s. D.

Moderate.

When eve - ning shad - ows ga - ther, And twi - light gent - ly fades:

When all is still and si - lent In mid-night's dark - er shades;

EVENING.

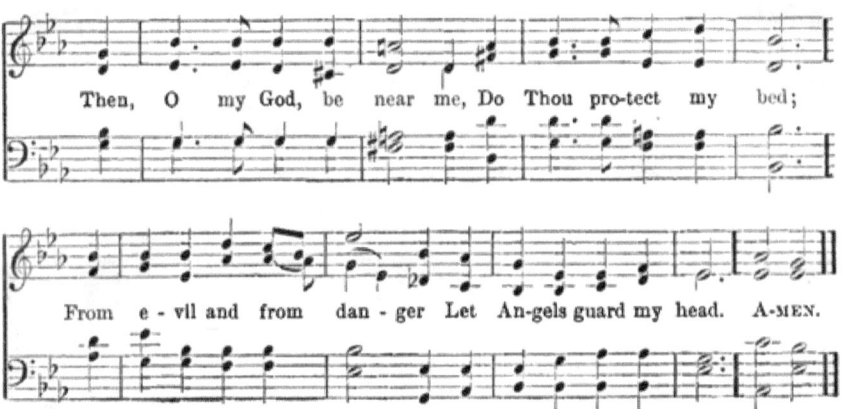

Then, O my God, be near me, Do Thou protect my bed;
From evil and from danger Let Angels guard my head. A-MEN.

2 We know not, when we slumber,
  That we shall e'er awake,
  To see another day begin,
  Another dawning break:
  But Thou art ever watching,
  Thou wilt our vigils keep,
  And, trusting in Thy mercy,
  We sink in peaceful sleep.

3 But, ere our eyelids closing,
  We humbly seek Thy face,
  And pray for Thy forgiveness,
  And Thy sustaining grace:
  For we are weak and erring,
  And need Thy mighty power;
  O Jesus, ever guard us
  In dark temptation's hour.

4 We pray for those who languish
  In sickness and distress,
  That Thou wilt soothe their anguish,
  And their afflictions bless:
  We pray for those in peril
  Upon the mighty sea;
  We pray for friends and loved ones;—
  Do Thou their Guardian be.

5 And now to Thee we render
  Our thanks for mercies past,
  With grateful hearts imploring
  Thy favour to the last.
  And at the great awakening
  May we be found above,—
  With saints and angels praising
  Thy providence and love.

190.

LANGTON.
S. M.
Moderate.

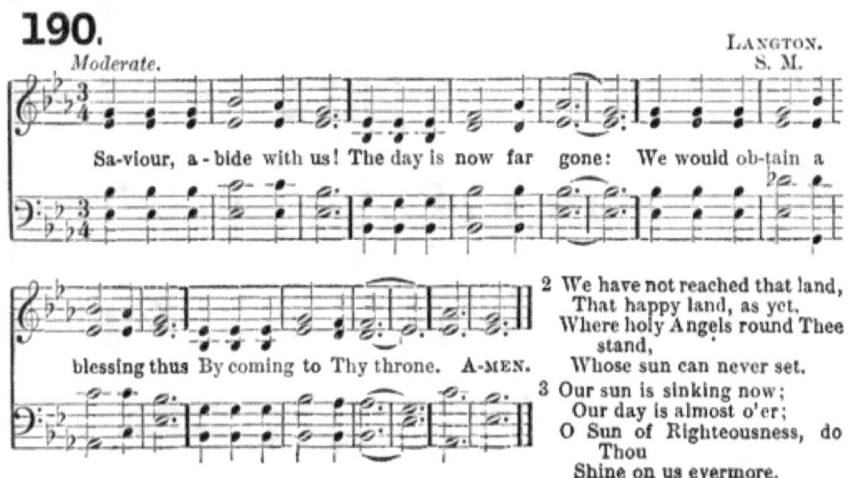

Saviour, abide with us! The day is now far gone: We would obtain a
blessing thus By coming to Thy throne. A-MEN.

2 We have not reached that land,
  That happy land, as yet,
  Where holy Angels round Thee
      stand,
  Whose sun can never set.

3 Our sun is sinking now;
  Our day is almost o'er;
  O Sun of Righteousness, do
      Thou
  Shine on us evermore.

EVENING.

191.

EUDOXIA.
6s. 5s.

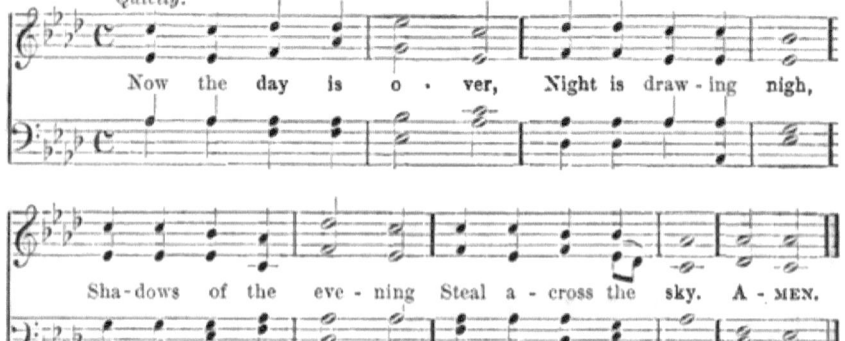

Now the day is over, Night is drawing nigh,
Shadows of the evening Steal across the sky. A-MEN.

2 Now the darkness gathers,
  Stars begin to peep,
  Birds, and beasts, and flowers
  Soon will be asleep.
3 Jesus, give the weary
  Calm and sweet repose,
  With Thy tenderest blessing
  May our eyelids close.
4 Through the long night watches
  May Thine Angels spread

Their white wings above me,
  Watching round my bed.
5 When the morning wakens,
  Then may I arise
  Pure and fresh and sinless
  In Thy holy eyes.
6 Glory to the Father,
  Glory to the Son,
  And to Thee, blest Spirit,
  Whilst all ages run.

192.

TENDER SHEPHERD.
8s. 7s.

Jesus, tender Shepherd, hear me; Bless Thy little lamb to-night,
Thro' the darkness be Thou near me: Keep me safe till morning light. A-MEN.

2 All this day Thy hand has led me,
  And I thank Thee for Thy care:
  Thou hast warmed me, clothed and fed me,
  Listen to my evening prayer.

3 Let my sins be all forgiven;
  Bless the friends I love so well;
  Take us all at last to heaven,
  Happy there with Thee to dwell.

193. *Moderate.*   EVENING.   EVENING PRAYER. 7s. 6s.

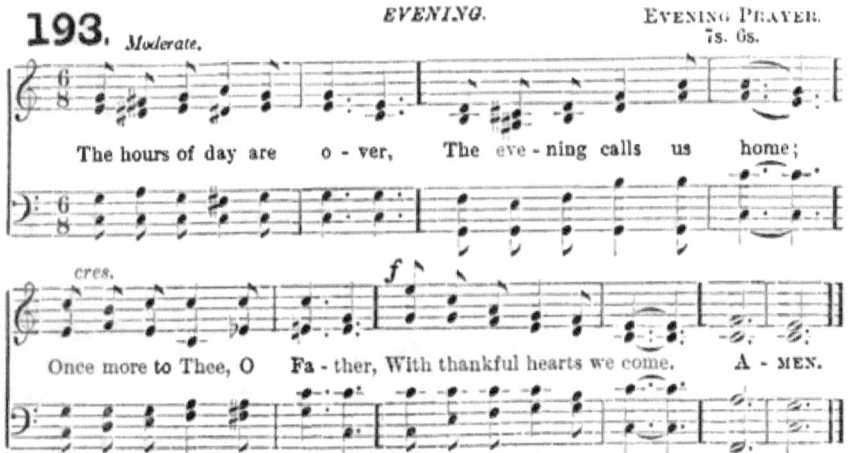

The hours of day are o-ver, The eve-ning calls us home; Once more to Thee, O Fa-ther, With thankful hearts we come. A-MEN.

2 For all Thy countless blessings
   We praise Thy holy Name,
   And own Thy love unchanging
   Through days and years the same.

3 For all the dear affection
   Of parents, brothers, friends,
   To Him our thanks we render
   Who these and all things sends.

4 But these, O Lord, can show us
   Thy goodness but in part;
   Thy love would lead us onward
   To know Thee as Thou art;

5 The Teacher ever present,
   The Friend for ever nigh,
   The Home prepared by Jesus
   For us above the sky.

6 Lord, gather all Thy children
   To meet Thee there at last,
   When earthly tasks are ended,
   And earthly days are past.

7 With all our dear ones round us
   In that eternal Home,
   Where death no more shall part us,
   And night shall never come.

194. The Lord's Day.   SWABIA. S. M.

This is the day of light; Let there be light to-day; O Day Spring, rise up-on our night, And chase its gloom a-way. A-MEN.

2 This is the day of rest:
   Our failing strength renew;
   On weary brain and troubled breast
   Shed Thou Thy freshening dew.

3 This is the day of peace:
   Thy peace our spirits fill;
   Bid Thou the blasts of discord cease,
   The waves of strife be still.

4 This is the day of prayer:
   Let earth to heaven draw near;
   Lift up our hearts to seek Thee there;
   Come down to meet us here.

5 This is the first of days:
   Send forth Thy quickening breath,
   And wake dead souls to love and praise,
   O Vanquisher of death!

THE LORD'S DAY.

195.
CLEETHORPES.
7s. 6s. D. with chorus.

Again the morn of gladness, The morn of light is here; And earth itself looks fairer, And heav'n itself more near: The bells, like angel voices, Speak peace to every breast, And all the land lies quiet To keep the day of rest. Glory be to Jesus, Let all the children say; He rose again, He rose again, On this glad day! A-MEN.

2 Again, O loving Saviour,
　The children of Thy grace
Prepare themselves to seek Thee
　Within Thy chosen place.
Our song shall rise to greet Thee,
　If Thou our hearts wilt raise;
If Thou our lips wilt open
　Our mouth shall shew Thy praise.
　　Glory be to Jesus, &c.

3 The shining choir of angels
　That rest not day or night,
The crowned and palm-decked martyrs,
　The saints arrayed in white,
The happy lambs of Jesus
　In pastures fair above,—
These all adore and praise Him
　Whom we too praise and love.
　　Glory be to Jesus, &c.

4 The Church on earth rejoices
　To join with these to-day;
In every tongue and nation
　She calls her sons to pray:
Across the Northern snow-fields,
　Beneath the Indian palms,
She makes the same " pure offering,"
　And sings the same sweet psalms.
　　Glory be to Jesus, &c.

5 Toll out, sweet bells, His praises!
　Sing, children, sing His Name!
Still louder and still farther
　His mighty deeds proclaim!
Till all whom He redeemèd
　Shall own Him Lord and King,
Till every knee shall worship,
　And every tongue shall sing!
　　Glory be to Jesus, &c.

196. THE LORD'S DAY.

ROTTERDAM.
7s. 6s. D.

O Day of rest and gladness, O day of joy and light,
O balm of care and sadness, Most beautiful, most bright,
On thee, the high and lowly, Through ages join'd in tune,
Sing, Holy, holy, holy, To the great God Tri-une. A-MEN.

2 On thee, at the Creation,
  The light first had its birth;
On thee for our salvation
  Christ rose from depths of earth;
On thee our Lord victorious
  The Spirit sent from heaven;
And thus on thee most glorious
  A triple light was given.

3 Thou art a port protected
  From storms that round us rise;
A garden intersected
  With streams of Paradise;
Thou art a cooling fountain
  In life's dry, dreary sand;
From thee, like Pisgah's mountain,
  We view our promised land.

4 To-day on weary nations
  The heavenly manna falls:
To holy convocations
  The silver trumpet calls;
Where gospel-light is glowing
  With pure and radiant beams:
And living water flowing
  With soul-refreshing streams.

5 New graces ever gaining
  From this our day of rest,
We reach the rest remaining
  To spirits of the blest;
To Holy Ghost be praises,
  To Father, and to Son;
The Church her voice upraises
  To Thee, blest Three in One.

197.

THE LORD'S DAY.

BARRY.
6s. 5s. D.

Moderate.

Hap-py, hap-py Sun-day! Day of rest and peace, Which from earthly la-bours Bringeth us re-lease; Day which tells of Je-sus Ris-ing from the dead, *Org.* Day on which His members With His grace are fed! A-MEN.

In the absence of tenors and basses, the two upper parts may be sung as a choral duet by trebles.

2 Jewish bondage ended,
　Jewish rites surpassed,
On this day we worship
　Christ, the First and Last;
Here in Christian freedom,
　Gladly we may sing
Hymns of praise and honour
　To our loving King.

3 Every week, in Jesus,
　Thus do we begin,
Who redeemed and called us,
　Saving us from sin;
And our week-day labours
　Are for ever blest,
By the gracious worship
　Of the Sunday Rest.

198.

GRANGE.
8s. 7s. 7s.

Joyous.

Al - le - lu - ia! Fair-est morn-ing! Fair-er than our words can say!

THE LORD'S DAY.

Down we lay the heavy burden Of life's toil and care to-day;
While this morn of joy and love Brings fresh vigour from above. A-MEN.

2 Sunday, full of holy glory!
  Sweetest rest-day of the soul!
Light upon a world of darkness
  From thy blessèd moments roll!
Holy, happy, heavenly day,
Thou canst charm our grief away.

3 In the gladness of His worship
  We will seek our joy to-day;
It is there we learn the fulness
  Of the grace for which we pray,
When the word of life is given,
Like the Saviour's voice from heaven.

4 Let the day with Thee be ended,
  As with Thee it has begun;
And Thy blessing, Lord, be granted,
  Till earth's days and weeks are done;
That at last Thy servants may
Keep eternal Sabbath-day.

199.

ABELARD.
S. M.

Moderate.

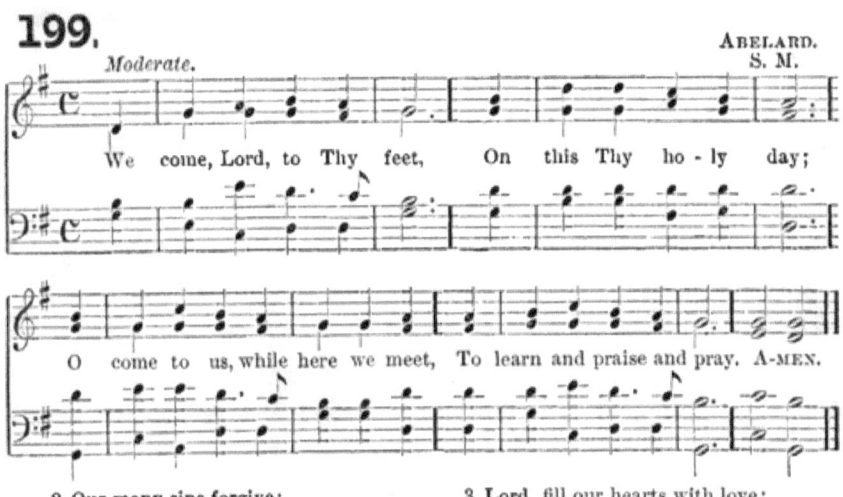

We come, Lord, to Thy feet, On this Thy holy day;
O come to us, while here we meet, To learn and praise and pray. A-MEN.

2 Our many sins forgive;
  The Holy Spirit send;
And teach us to begin to live
  The life that knows no end.

3 Lord, fill our hearts with love;
  Our teachers' labours own:
That we and they may meet above,
  To sing before Thy throne.

THE LORD'S DAY.

200. SABBATH BELLS. P. M.

2 The day we love best!
 The brightest and best of the seven,
 The pearl of the week, and the light of our way;
 We hold it a treasure, And count it a pleasure,
 To welcome its dawning, and praise Him to-day.

3 O sweet Sabbath rest!
 The gift of our Father in heaven;
 A herald sent down from the home far away,
 With peace for the weary, And joy for the dreary,
 Then, oh! let us thank Him, and praise Him to-day.

THE LORD'S DAY.

(At the close of service in the afternoon or evening.)

201. Ellers. 10s.

Saviour, again to Thy dear Name we raise
With one accord our parting hymn of praise;
We stand to bless Thee ere our worship cease,
Then, lowly kneeling, wait Thy word of peace. A-MEN.

2 Grant us Thy peace upon our homeward way;
With Thee began, with Thee shall end the day;
Guard Thou the lips from sin, the hearts from shame,
That in this house have called upon Thy Name.

3 Grant us Thy peace, Lord, through the coming night,
Turn Thou for us its darkness into light;
From harm and danger keep Thy children free,
For dark and light are both alike to Thee.

4 Grant us Thy peace throughout our earthly life,
Our balm in sorrow, and our stay in strife;
Then, when Thy voice shall bid our conflict cease,
Call us, O Lord, to Thine eternal peace.

The Seasons.

SPRING.

202. *Joyous.* — Lux Eoi. 8s. 7s. D.

All is bright and cheerful round us, All above is soft and blue; Spring at last hath come and found us, Spring and all its pleasures too; Ev-ery flower is full of gladness; Dew is bright and birds are gay; Earth, with all its sin and sad-ness, Seems a hap-py place to-day. A-MEN.

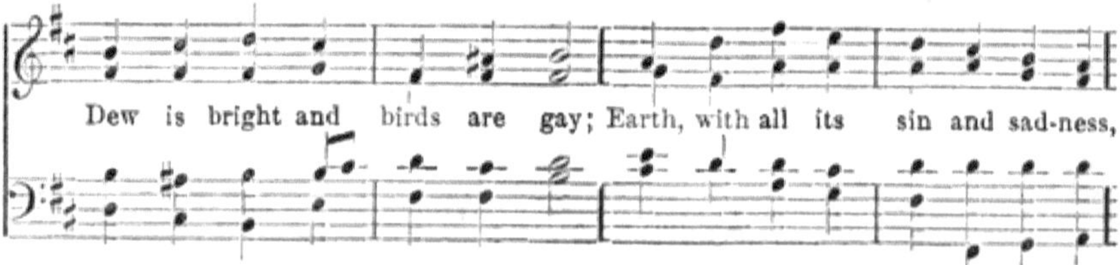

2 If the flowers, that fade so quickly,
If a day, that ends in night,
If the sky, that clouds so thickly
Often cover from our sight,—
If they all have so much beauty,
What must be God's Land of Rest,
Where His sons, that do their duty,
After many toils are blest?

3 *There* are leaves that never wither,
There are flowers that ne'er decay;
Nothing evil goeth thither,
Nothing good is kept away.
They that came from tribulation,
Washed their robes and made them white,
Out of every tongue and nation,
They have rest, and peace, and light.

SUMMER.

203. *Joyous.* — Ruth. 6s. 5s. D.

Summer suns are glowing O-ver land and sea, Hap-py light is flow-ing

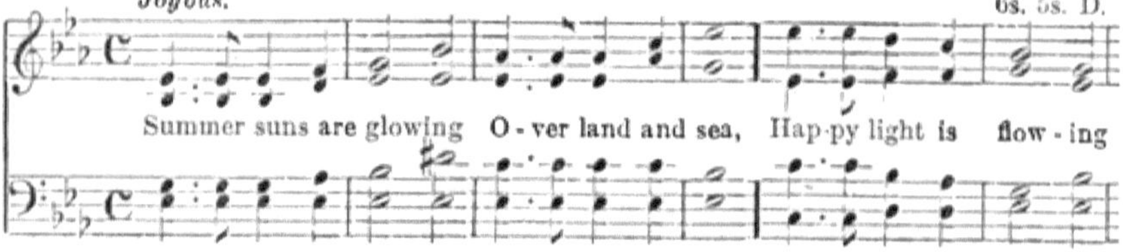

THE SEASONS.

Boun-ti-ful and free. Everything re-joi-ces In the mellow rays, All earth's thousand voi-ces Swell the psalm of praise. A-MEN.

2 God's free mercy streameth
  Over all the world,
And His banner gleameth
  Everywhere unfurled.
Broad and deep and glorious
  As the heaven above,
Shines in might victorious
  His eternal Love.

3 Lord, upon our blindness,
    Thy pure radiance pour;
  For Thy loving kindness
    Make us love Thee more.
  And when clouds are drifting
    Dark across our sky,
  Then, the veil uplifting,
    Father, be Thou nigh.

4 We will never doubt Thee,
    Though Thou veil Thy light;
  Life is dark, without Thee:
    Death with Thee is bright.
  Light of Light! shine o'er us
    On our pilgrim way,
  Go Thou still before us
    To the endless day.

AUTUMN.

204.

AUTUMNIA.
7s. 6s.

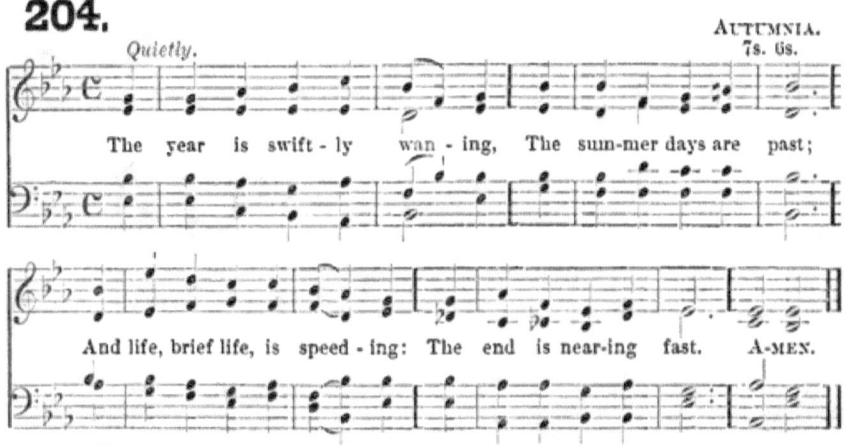

Quietly.
The year is swift-ly wan-ing, The sum-mer days are past; And life, brief life, is speed-ing: The end is near-ing fast. A-MEN.

2 The ever-changing seasons
    In silence come and go;
  But Thou, Eternal Father,
    No time or change canst know.

3 Oh! pour Thy grace upon us
    That we may worthier be,
  Each year that passes o'er us,
    To dwell in Heaven with Thee.

4 Behold, the bending orchards
    With bounteous fruit are crowned;
  Lord, in our hearts more richly
    Let heavenly fruits abound.

5 Oh! by each mercy sent us,
    And by each grief and pain,
  By blessings like the sunshine,
    And sorrows like the rain,

6 Our barren hearts make fruitful
    With every goodly grace,
  That we Thy Name may hallow,
    And see at last Thy Face.

THE SEASONS.

WINTER.

205.   BEDWYN. 7s.

Winter reigneth o'er the land, Freezing with its icy breath;
Dead and bare the tall trees stand; All is chill and drear as death.

5th and 6th verses.

5. But the sleeping earth shall wake, And the flow'rs shall burst in bloom,
And all Nature rising break Glorious from its wintry tomb. A-MEN.

2 Yet it seemeth but a day
   Since the summer flowers were here,
   Since they stacked the balmy hay,
   Since they reaped the golden ear.

3 Sunny days are past and gone:
   So the years go, speeding **fast,**
   Onward ever, each new one
   Swifter speeding than the last.

4 Life is waning; life is brief:
   Death, like winter, standeth nigh:
   Each one, like the falling leaf,
   Soon shall fade, and fall, and die.

5 But the sleeping earth shall wake,
   And the flowers shall burst in bloom,
   And all Nature rising break
   Glorious from its wintry tomb.

6 So, Lord, after slumber blest
   Comes a bright awakening,
   And our flesh in hope shall rest
   Of a never-fading Spring.

Our Lord Jesus Christ.

His Advent.

206.

IMMANUEL. 7s. 6s. 8.

Briskly.

Be-hold! be-hold He com-eth, Who doth sal-va-tion bring; Lift up your heads re-joic-ing, And wel-come Zi-on's King; With hymns of joy we praise the Lord, Ho-san-na to th' In-car-nate Word! A-MEN.

2 Hosanna to the Saviour,
  Who came on Christmas morn,
And, of a lowly Virgin,
  Was in a stable born;
Immanuel! Blessèd Jesus! come!
Within Thy children make Thy home.

3 Yea, come in love and meekness
  Our Saviour now to be;
Come to be formèd in us,
  And make us like to Thee,
Before the Day of Wrath draw near,
When, as our Judge, Thou shalt appear.

4 Soon shalt Thou sit in glory
  Upon "the great White Throne,"
And punish all the wicked,
  And recompense Thine own;
When every word and deed and thought
To righteous judgment shall be brought.

5 *Here*, good and bad are mingled;
  But on that Judgment Day
The Angels shall divide them,
  And take the bad away;
Grant, Lord, that we be faithful found
When the last trumpet-call shall sound!

* May be sung also as a two-part Chorus by Trebles, either with or without Accompaniment.

ADVENT.

207.
Joyful.
Goss.
S. M.

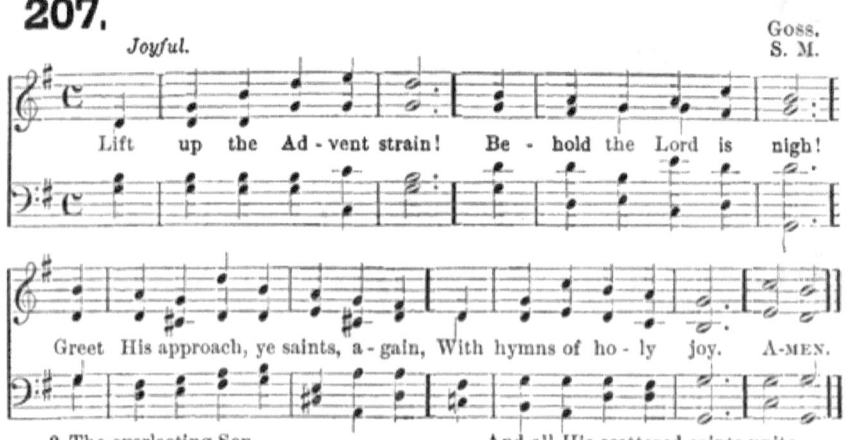

Lift up the Advent strain! Behold the Lord is nigh! Greet His approach, ye saints, again, With hymns of holy joy. A-MEN.

2 The everlasting Son,
  Incarnate deigns to be;
Our God the form of slave puts on,
  A race of slaves to free.
3 Daughter of Sion, rise
  To meet Thy lowly King,
Nor let the faithless heart despise
  The peace He comes to bring.
4 As Judge in clouds of light
  He shall come down again,
And all His scattered saints unite
  With Him in Heaven to reign.
5 Before that dreadful day
  May all our sins be gone,
The old man all be put away,
  The new man all put on.
6 Jesus, all praise to Thee,
  Our joy and endless rest;
We pray Thee here our Guide to be
  Our crown amid the blest.

208.*
Moderate.
JENNER.
6s.

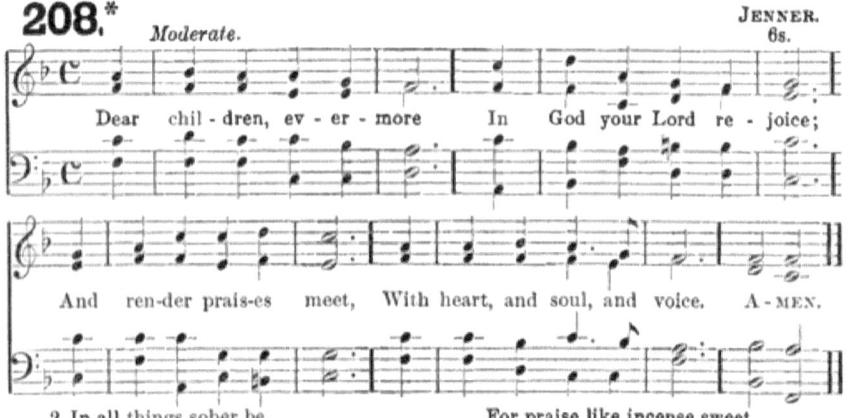

Dear children, evermore In God your Lord rejoice; And render praises meet, With heart, and soul, and voice. A-MEN.

2 In all things sober be,
  For Jesus is at hand;
So live that when He comes
  Accepted ye may stand.
3 Cast ye aside all care,
  And with glad heart alway,
Make known your every want;
  God loves to hear you pray.
4 With every meek request
  Let praises glad ascend,
For praise like incense sweet
  Should with petition blend.
5 A glad and thankful heart
  Wins blessings from the skies,
And is a sacrifice
  Most precious in God's eyes.
6 Then in the Lord alway,
  O children dear, rejoice;
And glorify His Name,
  With heart, and soul, and voice.

* May be used at other seasons.

ADVENT.

209.

IN CŒLIS.
P. M.

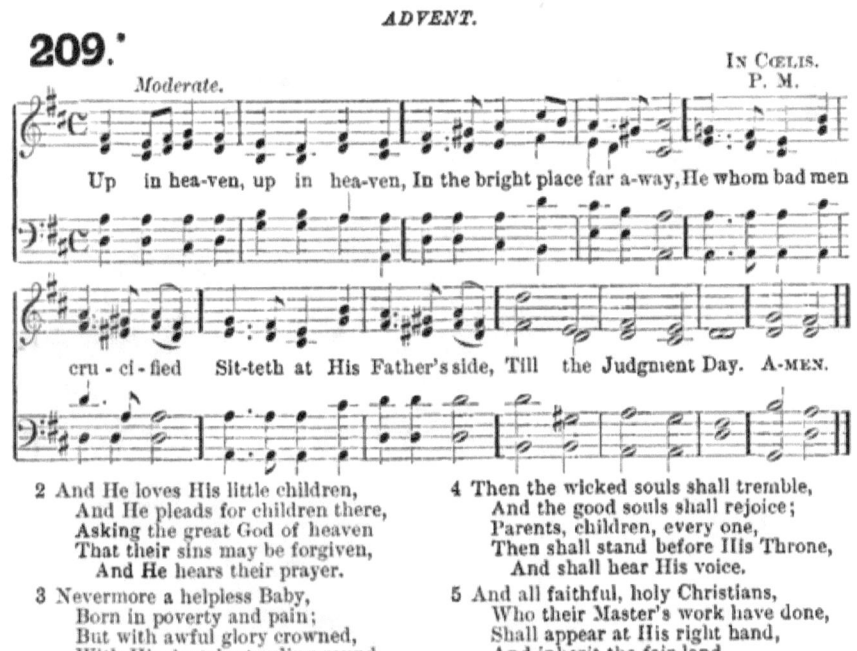

Up in heaven, up in heaven, In the bright place far away, He whom bad men cru-ci-fied Sit-teth at His Father's side, Till the Judgment Day. A-MEN.

2 And He loves His little children,
And He pleads for children there,
Asking the great God of heaven
That their sins may be forgiven,
And He hears their prayer.

3 Nevermore a helpless Baby,
Born in poverty and pain;
But with awful glory crowned,
With His Angels standing round,
He shall come again.

4 Then the wicked souls shall tremble,
And the good souls shall rejoice;
Parents, children, every one,
Then shall stand before His Throne,
And shall hear His voice.

5 And all faithful, holy Christians,
Who their Master's work have done,
Shall appear at His right hand,
And inherit the fair land
That His love has won.

210.

SALFORD.
C. M.

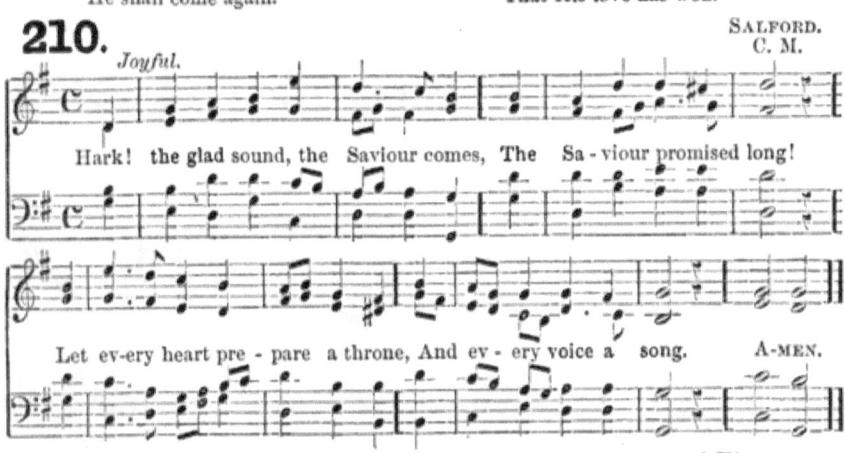

Hark! the glad sound, the Saviour comes, The Sa-viour promised long! Let ev-ery heart pre-pare a throne, And ev-ery voice a song. A-MEN.

2 He comes, the prisoners to release,
In Satan's bondage held;
The gates of brass before Him burst,
The iron fetters yield.

3 He comes, the broken heart to bind,
The bleeding soul to cure,

And with the treasures of His grace,
To enrich the humble poor.

4 Our glad Hosannas, Prince of Peace,
Thy welcome shall proclaim;
And heaven's eternal arches ring
With Thy beloved Name.

Also the following:
304. Holy Bible, Book divine.   **311.** Rock of ages, cleft for me.

* May be used at other seasons.

Christmas.
The Story of the Nativity.

211.

I.—THE HOLY CHILD.

Quietly.

Cradled in a man-ger, In a stable bare, Lies a lit-tle infant, Pure and fair.

O-ver him his mother Bends with loving eye, While an old man watches, Standing by.

3 Far from home, and friendless,
　Who so poor as they!
　From the crowded inn door
　　Turned away.
4 Wearied with the journey,
　And the hard world's scorn,
　Here the mother welcomes
　　Her first born.

5 Oxen share his shelter,
　Cold the night wind blows,
　Straw his bed, and rough his
　　Swaddling clothes.
6 Weak as other infants,
　Child of want and care,
　Claims he aught but pity,
　　Lying there?

II.—THE MIGHTY GOD.

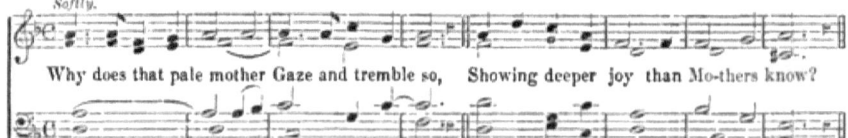

Softly.

Why does that pale mother Gaze and tremble so, Showing deeper joy than Mo-thers know?

2 Why, before her baby
　Does that mother kneel?
　Whence the holy light her
　　Eyes reveal?

Moderate.

Cra-dled in that man-ger Lies the E-ter-nal Son, Who is with the Fa-ther, E-ver One.

On that mother's bosom Sleeps in slumber still He who ru-leth all things By His will.

3 Mary's child the prophets
　Called Immanuel,—
　God, with us His creatures
　　Come to dwell.
4 And the name of Jesus
　God by Gabriel gave;
　For, from sin His people
　　He shall save.

5 Faith can see the Angels
　Watch around Him now,
　And, before the infant,
　　Humbly bow.
6 Faith can hear them singing
　Sweetest songs of praise,
　Faith can catch the meaning
　　Of their lays.

CHRISTMAS.
III.—THE SAVIOUR OF THE WORLD.

Holy Babe, we worship At Thy manger throne, And our Lord and Master Thee we own.

2 Oh! what love has led Thee
  To be born for us,
  All Thy power and glory
    Hidden thus!

3 Shall Thy love yet bring Thee
  Into deeper woe
  Than our coarser natures
    Ever know?

4 Shalt Thou long and labour
  Wandering souls to gain,
  Calling sinners to Thee,
    And in vain?

5 Shall those hands so tender,
  Feel the piercing nails,
  While Thy life in torment
    Sinks and fails?

6 Shall Thy form hang naked
  On the shameful tree—
  Friends all fled, and foes all
    Mocking Thee?

7 Yes, for this Thou camest
  From Thy throne on high,
  For us men to suffer,
    And to die.

8 On Thy path no sorrow
  Shall unlooked for fall,
  Thou, from the beginning
    Knowest all.

9 Yet, Thy joys are deeper
  Than Thy sorrows are,
  And Thy zeal to save us
    Stronger far.

10 Thou wouldst have us joyful,
   Even as Thou art,
   Though we keep Thy sorrow
     In our heart.

11 We may hail Thy coming,
   Saviour, Healer, Friend,
   And, with Thee, look forward
     To the end.

12 When in our frail nature
   Thou hast toiled and died,
   Thou shalt rise to heaven,
     Glorified.

13 Souls shall fill the mansions
   In the home above,
   Trophies of Thy sorrow
     And Thy love.

IV.—THE PRINCE OF PEACE.

Now the new Cre-a-tion Is in Thee be-gun, All that A-dam lost us More than won.

Thou art the In-car-nate, God with man made one, Giving man once more the Place of Son. A-MEN.

3 Thou art born to free us
  From the power of earth,
  Binding us to Thee in
    The New Birth.

4 Thou art born to save us
  From the power of sin,
  From the evil round us
    And within.

5 Thou art born to change us
  By Thy grace Divine,
  And to make our natures
    Like to Thine.

6 Thou hast left Thy glory,
  Far beyond the skies,
  That with Thee to heaven
    We may rise.

7 One with Thee, O Saviour,
  May our lives be blest,
  One with Thee O bring us
    To Thy rest.

8 While by faith we see Thee,
  May our hearts adore,
  Till our eyes behold Thee
    Evermore.

CHRISTMAS.

213.

MENDELSSOHN.
7s. D.

Hark! the herald angels sing Glory to the newborn King; Peace on earth, and mercy mild, God and sinners reconcil'd! Joyful all ye nations, rise, Join the triumph of the skies; With th' angelic host proclaim Christ is born in Bethlehem. Hark! the herald angels sing Glory to the newborn King. A-MEN.

Organ Pedal.

2 Christ, by highest heaven adored,
Christ, the Everlasting Lord,
Late in time behold Him come,
Offspring of the Virgin's womb.
Veiled in flesh the Godhead see;
Hail the Incarnate Deity,
Pleased as Man with men to dwell,
Jesus, our Emmanuel.
    Hark! the herald-angels sing
    Glory to the new-born King.

3 Risen with healing in His wings,
Light and life to all He brings.
Hail, the Sun of Righteousness;
Hail, the heaven-born Prince of Peace!
Holy Father; Holy Son,
Holy Spirit, Three in One!
Glory, as of old, to Thee,
Now and evermore shall be!
    Hark! the herald-angels sing
    Glory to the new-born King.

CHRISTMAS.

214. YORKSHIRE. Six 10s.

Christians, awake, salute the happy morn, Whereon the Saviour of mankind was born; Rise to adore the mystery of love, Which hosts of angels chanted from above; With them the joyful tidings first begun Of God Incarnate and the Virgin's Son. A-MEN.

2 Then to the watchful shepherds it was told,
Who heard the angelic herald's voice: "Behold
I bring good tidings of a Saviour's birth
To you and all the nations upon earth
This day hath God fulfill'd His promised word,
This day is born a Saviour, Christ the Lord."

3 He spake; and straightway the celestial choir
In hymns of joy, unknown before, conspire:
The praises of redeeming love they sang,
And heaven's whole arch with alleluias rang:
God's highest glory was their anthem still,
Peace upon earth, and unto men good-will.

4 To Bethlehem straight the happy shepherds ran
To see the wonder God had wrought for man:
And found with Joseph and the blessèd maid,
Her Son, the Saviour, in a manger laid;
Amazed, the wondrous story they proclaim,
The earliest heralds of the Saviour's Name.

5 Let us, like these good shepherds, then employ
Our grateful voices to proclaim the joy;
Trace we the Babe, who hath retrieved our loss,
From His poor manger to His bitter Cross;
Treading His steps, assisted by His grace,
Till man's first heavenly state again takes place.

6 Then may we hope, the angelic thrones among,
To sing, redeemed, a glad triumphal song;
He, that was born upon this joyful day
Around us all His glory shall display;
Saved by His love, incessant we shall sing,
Eternal praise to heaven's Almighty King.

215.

CAROL.
C. M. D.

It came upon the midnight clear, That glorious song of old, From angels bending near the earth, To touch their harps of gold: "Peace on the earth, good-will to men From heaven's all gracious King;" The world in solemn stillness lay To hear the angels sing. A-MEN.

2 Still through the cloven skies they come,
  With peaceful wings unfurl'd;
And still their heavenly music floats
  O'er all the weary world:
Above its sad and lowly plains
  They bend on hovering wing,
And ever o'er its Babel sounds
  The blessèd angels sing.

3 O ye beneath life's crushing load,
  Whose forms are bending low,
Who toil along the climbing way,
  With painful steps and slow!
Look now, for glad and golden hours
  Come swiftly on the wing;
O rest beside the weary road,
  And hear the angels sing.

4 For lo, the days are hastening on,
  By prophets seen of old,
When with the ever-circling years
  Shall come the time foretold,
When the new heaven and earth shall own
  The Prince of Peace their King,
And the whole world send back the song
  Which now the angels sing.

* *May be used at other seasons.*

216. CHRISTMAS. HEAVENLY SONG. P. M.

Cheerful.

Hark, the Heaven's sweet melo-dy Echoes now on earth, And the bands of those on high
Sing the Virgin-Birth; What mean ye, O ye passers-by, Share ye not their mirth? A-MEN.

2 Shepherds watch their flocks by night;
  Angel notes they hear;
Songs of glory in the height,
  Peace and love brought near;
To us they sing, through Love's dear might;
  Praise to CHRIST they bear.

3 Of His Birth the bright stars tell,
  Pouring floods of light;
Shepherds seek out Bethlehem's cell,
  All those stars in sight;
They find the King of Heaven where dwell
  Ox and ass of right.

4 There, within the manger laid,
  They their LORD descry:
We that Child of Mother-maid
  Sing with praises high;
With homage, LORD, thus duly paid
  We to Thee draw nigh.

217. HOLY VOICES. 8s. 7s.

Cheerful.

Hark! what mean those ho-ly voi-ces, Sweetly sounding thro' the skies?
Lo, th' angel-ic host re-joic-es, Heavenly Al-le-lu-ias rise. A-MEN.

2 Listen to the wondrous story,
  Which they chant in hymns of joy—
"Glory in the highest, glory!
  Glory be to God most high!

3 "Peace on earth, good-will from heaven,
  Reaching far as man is found:
Souls redeemed and sins forgiven,
  Loud our golden harps shall sound.

4 "Christ is born; the great Anointed!
  Heaven and earth His praises sing!
O receive whom God appointed
  For your Prophet, Priest, and King!

5 "Hasten, mortals, to adore Him;
  Learn His Name to magnify,
Till in heaven ye sing before Him,
  Glory be to God most high!"

CHRISTMAS.

218.
GABRIEL.
C. M. D.

Joyful.

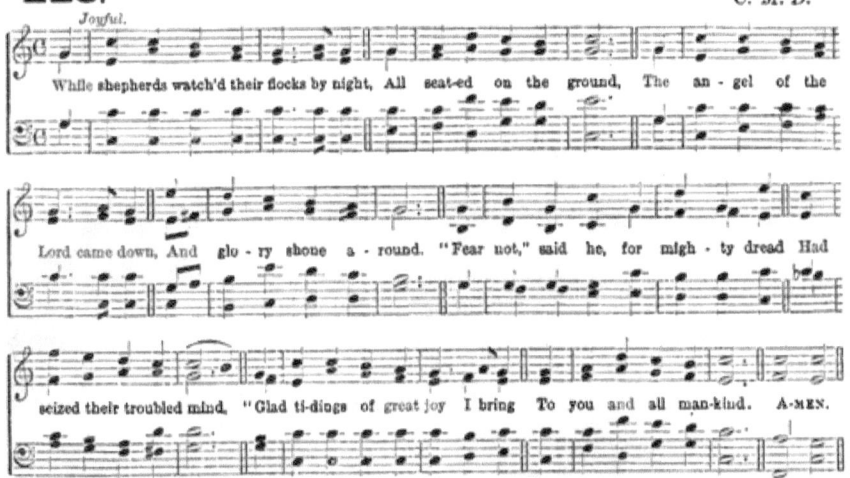

While shepherds watch'd their flocks by night, All seated on the ground, The angel of the Lord came down, And glory shone around. "Fear not," said he, for mighty dread Had seized their troubled mind. "Glad tidings of great joy I bring To you and all mankind. A-MEN.

2 "To you, in David's town this day
  Is born of David's line,
The Saviour, who is Christ the Lord,
  And this shall be the sign.
"The heavenly Babe you there shall find,
  To human view display'd,
All meanly wrapt in swathing bands,
  And in a manger laid."

3 Thus spake the seraph; and forthwith
  Appeared a shining throng
Of angels, praising God, who thus
  Address'd their joyful song:
"All glory be to God on high,
  And to the earth be peace;
Good-will henceforth from heaven to men
  Begin, and never cease."

219.
STUTGARD.
8s. 7s.

Joyful.

Hail! Thou long expected Jesus, Born to set Thy people free; From our fears and sins release us; Let us find our rest in Thee. A-MEN.

Israel's strength and consolation,
  Hope of all the earth Thou art;
Long desired of every nation,
  Joy of every waiting heart.

3 Born Thy people to deliver,
  Born a child, yet God our King,
Born to reign in us for ever,
  Now Thy gracious kingdom bring.

4 By Thine own eternal Spirit,
  Rule in all our hearts alone:
By Thine all-sufficient merit,
  Raise us to Thy glorious throne.

220. CHRISTMAS.

REGENT SQUARE.
8s. 7s. 4.

Joyful.

Angels from the realms of glory, Wing your flight o'er all the earth;
Ye who sang creation's story, Now proclaim Messiah's birth!
Come and worship, come and worship, Worship Christ the new-born King. A-MEN.

2 Shepherds in the field abiding,
  Watching o'er your flocks by night;
God with man is now residing,
  Yonder shines the infant-light:
    Come and worship,
  Worship Christ, the new-born King.

3 Sages, leave your contemplations;
  Brighter visions beam afar:
Seek the great Desire of nations,
  Ye have seen His natal star:
    Come and worship,
  Worship Christ, the new-born King.

4 Saints before the altar bending,
  Watching long in hope and fear,
Suddenly the Lord, descending,
  In His temple shall appear.
    Come and worship,
  Worship Christ, the new-born King.

221.

COLOGNE.
L. M.

Joyful.

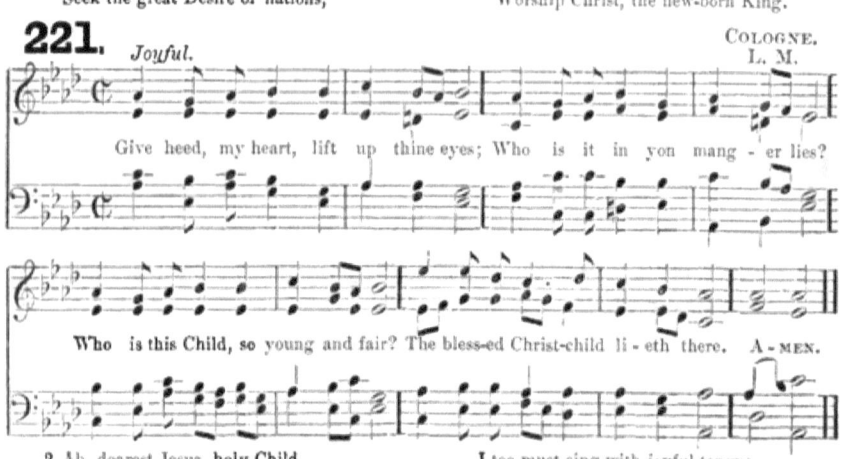

Give heed, my heart, lift up thine eyes; Who is it in yon manger lies?
Who is this Child, so young and fair? The blessed Christ-child lieth there. A-MEN.

2 Ah, dearest Jesus, holy Child,
  Make Thee a bed, soft, undefiled,
  Within my heart, that it may be
  A quiet chamber kept for Thee.

3 My heart for very joy doth leap,
  My lips no more can silence keep;
  I too must sing with joyful tongue,
  That sweetest ancient cradle-song:

4 Glory to God in highest heaven,
  Who unto man His Son hath given;
  While angels sing with pious mirth,
  A glad new year to all the earth.

CHRISTMAS.

222.

Cheerful.

REX INFANS.
8s. 7s. with Refrain.

Once in Bethlehem of Judah, Far away across the sea, There was laid a little Baby On a Virgin Mother's knee. O Saviour, gentle Saviour! Hear Thy little children sing, The God of our salvation, The Child that is our King. A-MEN.

2 It was not a stately palace
　Where that little Baby lay,
With His servants to attend Him,
　And with guards to keep the way.
　　　O Saviour, gentle Saviour, &c.

3 But the oxen stood around Him
　In a stable, low and dim:
In the world He had created
　There was not a room for Him!
　　　O Saviour, gentle Saviour, &c.

4 For He left His Father's glory,
　And the golden halls above,
And He took our human nature
　In the greatness of His love.
　　　O Saviour, gentle Saviour, &c.

5 Of His infinite compassion
　He can feel our want and woe;
For He suffered, He was tempted,
　When He lived our life below.
　　　O Saviour, gentle Saviour, &c.

6 Still His childhood's bright example
　Gives a light to our poor homes;
From the blood of His atoning
　Still our hope of pardon comes.
　　　O Saviour, gentle Saviour, &c.

7 Still He stands and pleads in heaven
　For us, weak and sin defiled,—
God, who is a man for ever,
　Jesus, who was once a Child!
　　　O Saviour, gentle Saviour, &c.

* May be used at other seasons.

CHRISTMAS.

223.
Moderate.

S. LOUIS.
P. M.

O lit-tle town of Beth-le-hem! How still we see thee lie, A-bove thy deep and dreamless sleep, The si-lent stars go by; Yet in thy dark streets shin-eth The ev-er-last-ing Light; The hopes and fears of all the years, Are met in thee to-night. A-MEN.

2 For Christ is born of Mary,
And gathered all above,
While mortals sleep the angels keep
Their watch of wondering love.
O morning stars together
Proclaim the holy birth!
And praises sing to God the King,
And peace to men on earth.

3 How silently, how silently,
The wondrous gift is given;
So God imparts to human hearts
The blessings of His heaven.
No ear may hear His coming,
But in this world of sin,
Where meek souls will receive Him still,
The dear Christ enters in.

4 O holy Child of Bethlehem!
Descend to us, we pray,
Cast out our sin and enter in,
Be born in us to-day.
We hear the Christmas angels,
The great glad tidings tell,
O, come to us, abide with us,
Our Lord Emmanuel!

224.
Cheerfully.

CHRISTMAS MORN.
7s.

Sing with joy, 'tis Christmas Morn, Un-to us a Child is born;

CHRISTMAS.

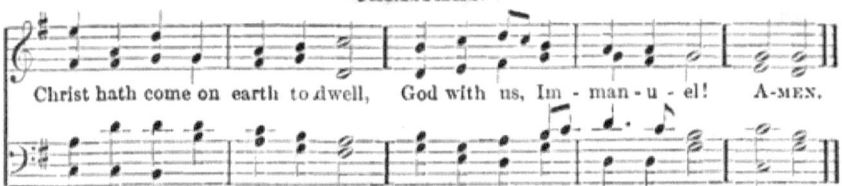

Christ hath come on earth to dwell, God with us, Im-man-u-el! A-MEN.

2 Shepherds, watching thro' the night,
Wondering at the dazzling light,
Hear the glorious Angel tell
Of the Hope of Israel.

3 Thousand thousand angels raise
Songs of glad triumphant praise;
Singing, through the starry sky,
"Glory be to God on High!"

4 Joyously the shepherds ran,
Knelt to Jesus—God and Man:
"Come," they bid us haste with them,
"See the Babe of Bethlehem"!

5 Jesus! whom we now adore,
May we love Thee more and more;
As by faith we, wondering, see
This Thy great humility!

225.* *Moderate.* CHRISTCHILD. 6s. 8s.
(May be sung unaccompanied.)

Be-hold a lit-tle Child Laid in a man-ger bed, The wintry blasts blow wild.... A-round His in-fant head; But who is this so low-ly laid? 'Tis He by whom the worlds were made. A-MEN.

2 Alas! in what poor state
The Son of God is seen;
Why doth the Lord so great
Choose out a home so mean?
That we may learn from pride to flee,
And follow His humility.

3 Where Joseph plies his trade,
Lo! Jesus labours too;
The hands that all things made
An earthly craft pursue,
That weary men on Him may rest,
And faithful toil in Him be blest.

4 Among the doctors see
The Boy so full of grace:
Say, wherefore taketh He
The scholar's lowly place?
That Christian boys with reverence meet
May sit and learn at Jesus' feet.

5 Christ! once Thyself a boy,
Our boyhood guard and guide;
Be Thou its light and joy,
And still with us abide;
That Thy dear love, so great, so free,
May draw us evermore to Thee.

Also the following:
337. Hosanna! loud Hosanna.
412. Once in royal David's city.
410. Sweet it is for child like me.
474—506. Christmas Carols.

* May be used at other seasons.

226. His Childhood.
Moderate. — S. BEES. 7s.

Je-sus! Name of won-drous love! Name all oth-er names a-bove!
Un-to which must ev-ery knee Bow in deep hu-mil-i-ty. A-MEN.

2 Jesus! Name decreed of old:
To the maiden mother told,
Kneeling in her lowly cell,
By the angel Gabriel.

3 Jesus! Name of priceless worth
To the fallen sons of earth,
For the promise that it gave—
"Jesus shall His people save."

4 Jesus! Name of mercy mild,
Given to the holy Child,
When the cup of human woe
First He tasted here below.

5 Jesus! only Name that's given
Under all the mighty heaven,
Whereby man, to sin enslaved,
Bursts his fetters, and is saved.

6 Jesus! Name of wondrous love!
Human name of God above;
Pleading only this we flee,
Helpless, O our God, to Thee.

227.
Moderate. — SPRINGHILL. 8s. 7s.

Chris-tian child-ren must be ho-ly, Serv-ing God from day to day,
Ne-ver is the time too ear-ly For a Christian to o-bey. A-MEN.

2 Jesus taught us in His childhood;
Only eight short days He saw
Ere He suffered circumcision
And obeyed His Father's law.

3 He who is our great Example,
Let no moment run to loss;
Not one precious hour He wasted
From the cradle to the Cross.

4 Soon He sorrowed, soon He suffered;
We must meek and gentle be,
Little pain and childish trial
Ever bearing patiently.

5 Soon He showed a Son's obedience;
We must early learn to do
Not our own will, but our Father's,
And be found obedient too.

Also the following:
320. All hail the power of Jesus' Name. 312. How sweet the Name of Jesus sounds.
330. There is no name so sweet on earth.

* May be used at other seasons.

228.

Moderate.

Chope.
7s.

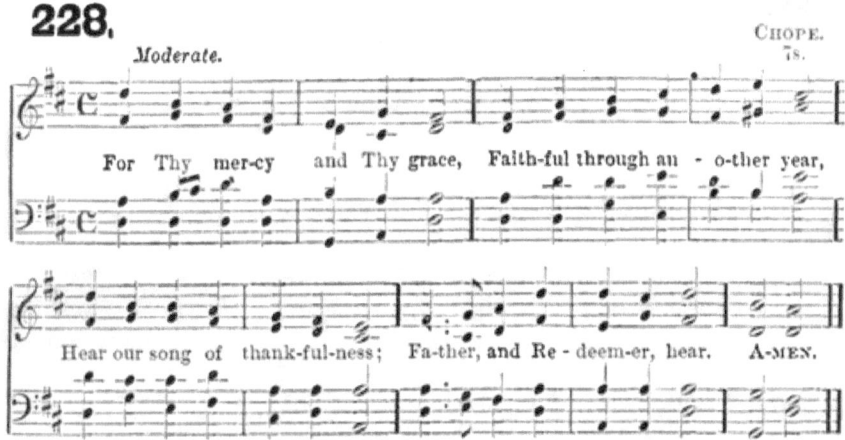

For Thy mer-cy and Thy grace, Faith-ful through an-o-ther year,
Hear our song of thank-ful-ness; Fa-ther, and Re-deem-er, hear. A-MEN.

2 In our weakness and distress,
  Rock of Strength, be Thou our Stay,
  In the pathless wilderness
  Be our true and living Way.

3 Who of us death's awful road,
  In the coming year shall tread;
  With Thy rod and staff, O God,
  Comfort Thou his dying head.

4 Make us faithful, keep us pure,
  Keep us evermore Thine own;
  Help, O help us to endure;
  Fit us for the promised crown.

5 So within Thy palace gate
  We shall praise, on golden strings,
  Thee, the only Potentate,
  Lord of lords, and King of kings.

229. His manifestation to the Gentiles.

Moderate.

S. Oswald.
8s. 7s.

Beth-le-hem! of no-blest cit-ies, None can once with thee com-pare;
Thou a-lone the Lord from Heaven Didst for us In-car-nate bear. A-MEN.

2 Fairer than the sun at morning;
  Was the star that told His birth;
  To the lands their God announcing,
  Hid beneath a form of earth.

3 By its radiant beauty guided,
  See, the Eastern kings appear!
  See them bend, their gifts to offer,
  Gifts of incense, gold, and myrrh.

4 Offerings of mystic meaning!
  Incense doth the God disclose;
  Gold a Royal Child proclaimeth,
  Myrrh the future tomb foreshows.

5 Holy Jesus! In Thy brightness
  To the Gentile world displayed,
  With the Father and the Spirit,
  Endless praise to Thee be paid.

HIS MANIFESTATION.

230.* *Joyful.* ZOAN. 7s. 6s. D.

Hail to the Lord's A-noint-ed, Great Da-vid's greater Son! Hail, in the time ap-point-ed, His reign on earth be-gun! He comes to break op-pres-sion, To set the cap-tive free; To take a-way trans-gres-sion, And rule in e-qui-ty. A-MEN.

2 He comes with succour speedy,
To those who suffer wrong,
To help the poor and needy,
And bid the weak be strong;
To give them songs for sighing,
Their darkness turn to light,
Whose souls, condemn'd and dying,
Were precious in His sight.

3 He shall descend like showers
Upon the fruitful earth;
And love and joy, like flowers,
Spring in His path to birth:
Before Him, on the mountains,
Shall peace, the herald, go;
And righteousness, in fountains,
From hill to valley flow.

4 To Him shall prayer unceasing,
And daily vows ascend:
His kingdom still increasing,
A kingdom without end
The tide of time shall never,
His covenant remove,
His Name shall stand forever;
That Name to us is Love.

* *May be used at other seasons.*

231. *Joyful.* WEBER. 11s. 10s.

Bright-est and best of the sons of the morn-ing, Dawn on our

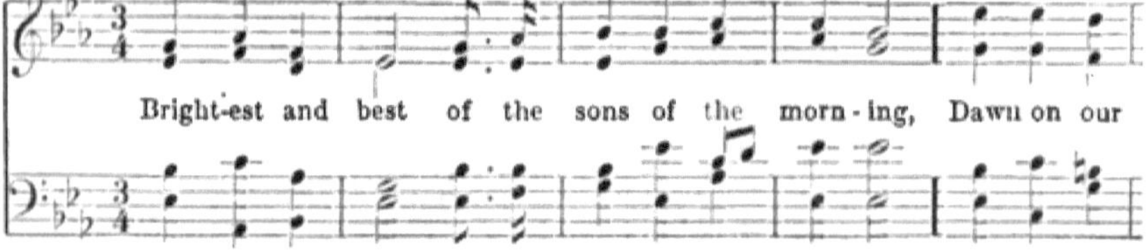

HIS MANIFESTATION.

2 Cold on His cradle the dew-drops are shining,
  Low lies His head with the beasts of the stall;
  Angels adore Him in slumber reclining,
  Maker and Monarch and Saviour of all.

3 Say, shall we yield Him in costly devotion,
  Odours of Edom, and offerings divine,
  Gems of the mountain, and pearls of the ocean,
  Myrrh from the forest, and gold from the mine?

4 Vainly we offer each ample oblation,
  Vainly with gifts would His favour secure;
  Richer by far is the heart's adoration,
  Dearer to God are the prayers of the poor.

5 Brightest and best of the sons of the morning,
  Dawn on our darkness, and lend us Thine aid:
  Star of the East, the horizon adorning,
  Guide where our infant Redeemer is laid.

232.

Dix. Six 7s.

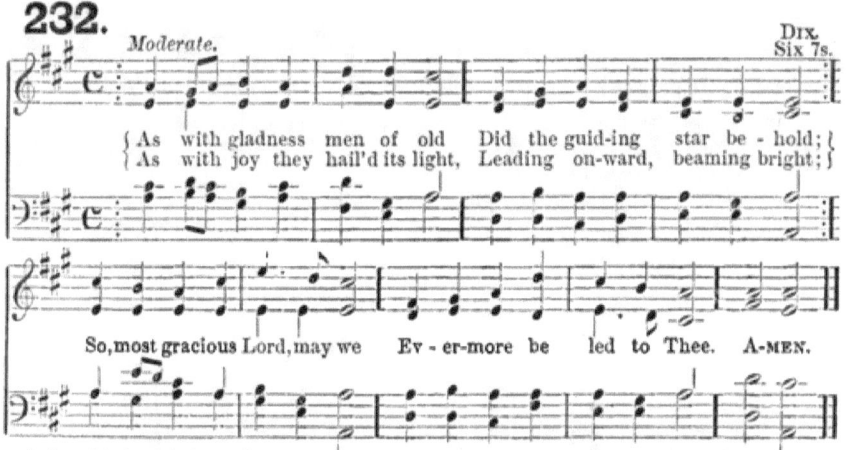

2 As with joyful steps they sped
  To that lowly manger-bed,
  There to bend the knee before
  Him whom Heaven and earth adore;
  So may we with willing feet
  Ever seek the mercy-seat.

3 As they offer'd gifts most rare
  At that manger rude and bare;
  So may we with holy joy,
  Pure and free from sin's alloy,
  All our costliest treasures bring.
  Christ, to Thee, our heavenly King.

4 Holy Jesus, every day
  Keep us in the narrow way;
  And, when earthly things are past,
  Bring our ransom'd souls at last
  Where they need no star to guide,
  Where no clouds Thy glory hide.

5 In the heavenly country bright
  Need they no created light;
  Thou its Light, its Joy, its Crown,
  Thou its Sun, which goes not down;
  There for ever may we sing
  Alleluias to our King.

Also the following.

286. Jesus shall reign where'er the sun.

His Example of Self-Sacrifice.
The Story of the Cross.

233.

I.—THE QUESTION.

Quietly. Voices in unison.

In His own raiment clad—With His Blood dyed; Women walk sorrow-ing By His side.

2 Heavy that Cross to Him—
Weary the weight—
One who will help Him waits
At the gate.

3 See! they are travelling
On the same road—
Simon is sharing with
Him the load.

4 Oh, whither wandering,
Bear they that tree?
He who first carries it—
Who is He?

II.—THE ANSWER.

Quietly.

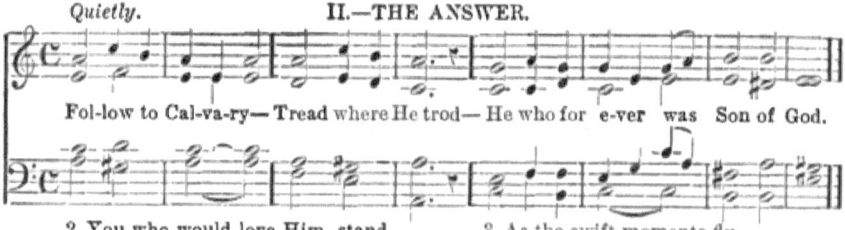

Fol-low to Cal-va-ry— Tread where He trod— He who for e-ver was Son of God.

2 You who would love Him, stand,
Gaze at His face;
Tarry awhile on your
Earthly race.

3 As the swift moments fly
Through the Blest Week,
Read the great story the
Cross will teach.

4 Is there no beauty to
You who pass by
In that lone figure which
Marks the sky?

III.—THE STORY.

Quietly.

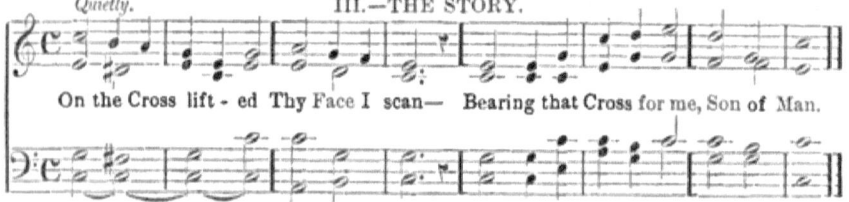

On the Cross lift - ed Thy Face I scan— Bearing that Cross for me, Son of Man.

2 Thorns form Thy diadem,
Rough wood Thy throne—
For us Thy Blood is shed—
Us alone.

3 No pillow under Thee
To rest Thy Head—
Only the splintered Cross
Is Thy bed.

4 Nails pierce Thy Hands and Feet,
Thy Side the Spear;
No voice is nigh, to say
Help is near.

5 Shadows of midnight fall,
Though it is day—
Thy friends and kinsfolk stand
Far away.

HIS SELF-SACRIFICE.

6 Loud is Thy bitter cry·
  Sunk on Thy breast
  Hangeth Thy bleeding Head
    Without rest.

7 Loud scoffs the dying thief,
  Who mocks at Thee—
  Can it, my Saviour, be
    All for me?

8 Gazing afar from Thee,
  Silent and lone,
  Stand those few weepers Thou
    Call'st Thine own.

9 I see Thy title, Lord,
  Inscribed above—
  " JESUS of Nazareth,"
    King of Love!

10 What, O my Saviour,
   Here didst Thou see,
  Which made Thee suffer and
    Die for me?

IV—THE APPEAL FROM THE CROSS.

Moderate.   Part IV should, if possible, be sung by a Tenor or Bass voice.

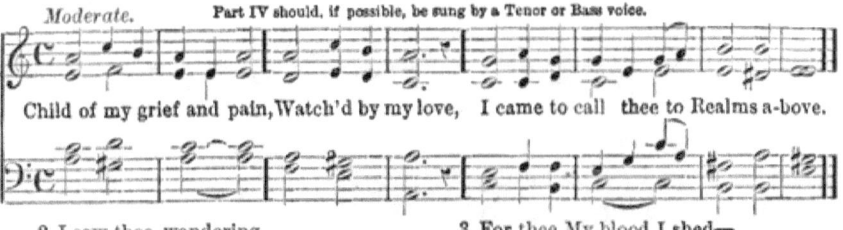

Child of my grief and pain, Watch'd by my love, I came to call thee to Realms a-bove.

2 I saw thee wandering
  Far off from me:
  In love I seek for thee—
    Do not flee.

3 For thee My blood I shed—
  For thee alone;
  I came to purchase thee—
    For Mine own.

4 Weep not for My grief,
  Child of my love—
  Strive to be with Me in
    Heaven above.

V.—THE CRY TO JESUS.

Cheerful.

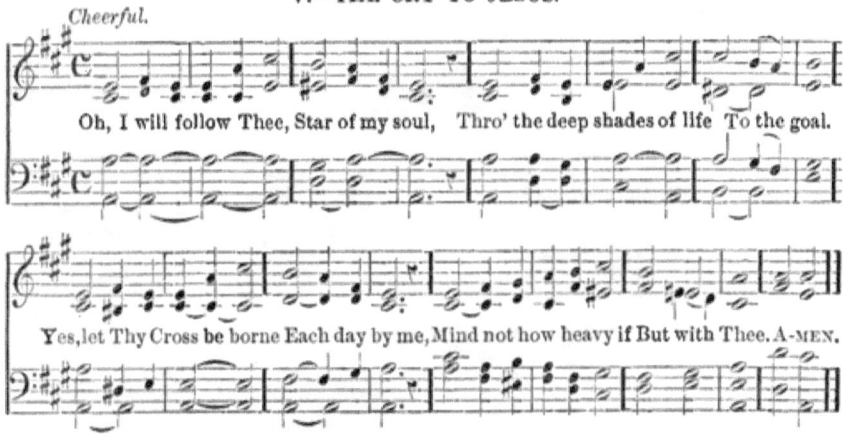

Oh, I will follow Thee, Star of my soul, Thro' the deep shades of life To the goal.

Yes, let Thy Cross be borne Each day by me, Mind not how heavy if But with Thee. A-MEN.

3 Lord, if Thou only wilt
  Make me Thine own,
  Give no companion, save
    Thee alone.

4 Grant through each day of life
  To stand by Thee;
  With Thee, when morning breaks,
    Ever to be.

HIS SELF-SACRIFICE.

234. SPANISH CHANT. 7s. D.

Saviour, when in dust to Thee, Low we bow th' adoring knee;
When, repentant, to the skies Scarce we lift our streaming eyes;
O, by all Thy pains and woe, Suffered once for man below,
Bending from Thy throne on high, Hear our solemn litany. A-MEN.

2 By Thy birth and early years,
By Thy human griefs and fears,
By Thy fasting and distress
In the lonely wilderness,
By Thy victory in the hour
Of the subtle tempter's power;
Jesus, look with pitying eye;
Hear our solemn litany.

3 By Thy conflict with despair,
By Thine agony of prayer,
By the purple robe of scorn,
By Thy wounds, Thy crown of thorn,
By Thy cross, Thy pangs, and cries,
By Thy perfect sacrifice;
Jesus, look with pitying eye;
Hear our solemn litany.

4 By Thy deep expiring groan,
By the seal'd sepulchral stone,
By Thy triumph o'er the grave,
By Thy power from death to save;
Mighty God, ascended Lord,
To Thy throne in heaven restored,
Prince and Saviour, hear our cry,
Hear our solemn litany.

* May be used at other seasons.

HIS SELF-SACRIFICE.

235.*
GRACE CHURCH.
L. M.

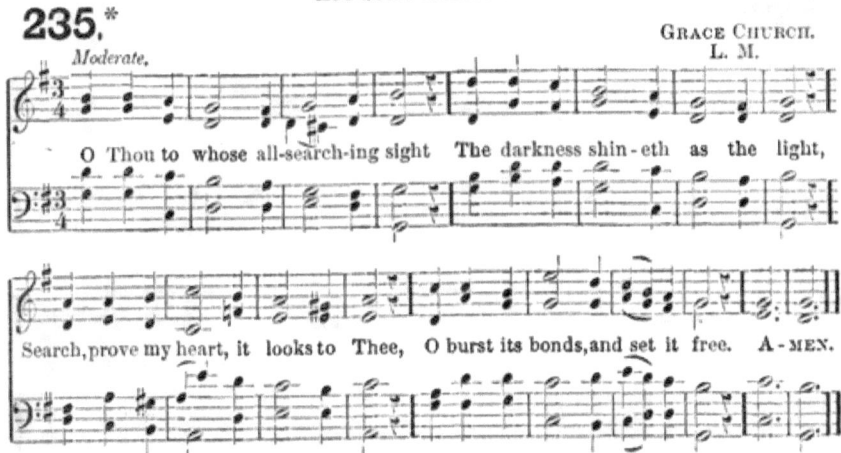

O Thou to whose all-searching sight The darkness shineth as the light, Search, prove my heart, it looks to Thee, O burst its bonds, and set it free. A-MEN.

2 Wash out its stains, remove its dross,
Bind my affections to the Cross;
Hallow each thought; let all within
Be clean, as Thou, my Lord, art clean.

3 If in this darksome wild I stray,
Be Thou my light, be Thou my way;
No foes, no violence I fear,
No harm, while Thou, my God, art near.

4 When rising floods my soul o'erflow,
When sinks my heart in waves of woe,
Jesus, Thy timely aid impart,
And raise my head, and cheer my heart.

5 Saviour, where'er Thy steps I see,
Dauntless, untired, I follow Thee:
O let Thy hand support me still,
And lead me to Thy holy hill.

236.*
S. PHILIP.
Three 7s.

Lord, in this Thy mercy's day, Ere the time shall pass away, On our knees we fall and pray. A-MEN.

2 Holy Jesus, grant us tears,
Fill us with heart-searching fears,
Ere the hour of doom appears.

3 Lord, on us Thy Spirit pour,
Kneeling lowly at Thy door,
Ere it close for evermore.

4 By Thy night of agony,
By Thy supplicating cry,
By Thy willingness to die,

5 By Thy tears of bitter woe
For Jerusalem below,
Let us not Thy love forego.

6 Judge and Saviour of our race,
When we see Thee face to face,
Grant us 'neath Thy wings a place.

7 On Thy love we rest alone,
And that love will then be known
By the pardon'd round Thy throne.

* *May be used at other seasons.*

HIS SELF-SACRIFICE.

237.*

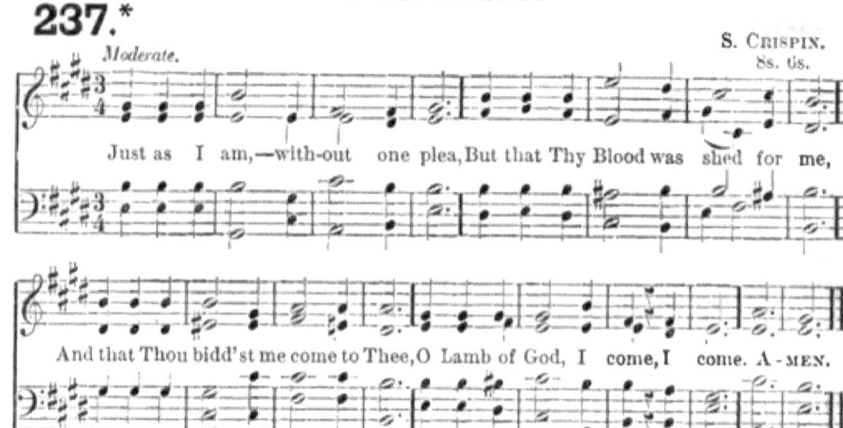

S. CRISPIN.
8s. 6s.

Just as I am,—without one plea, But that Thy Blood was shed for me, And that Thou bidd'st me come to Thee, O Lamb of God, I come, I come. A-MEN.

2 Just as I am,—though toss'd about,
  With many a conflict, many a doubt,
  Fightings and fears, within, without,
    O Lamb of God, I come.

3 Just as I am,—poor, wretched, blind—
  Sight, riches, healing of the mind,
  Yea, all I need, in Thee to find,
    O Lamb of God, I come.

4 Just as I am,—Thou wilt receive,
  Wilt welcome, pardon, cleanse, relieve;
  Because Thy promise I believe,
    O Lamb of God, I come.

5 Just as I am,—Thy love unknown
  Has broken every barrier down;
  Now to be Thine, yea, Thine alone,
    O Lamb of God, I come.

* May be used at other seasons.

His Triumphal Entry.

238.

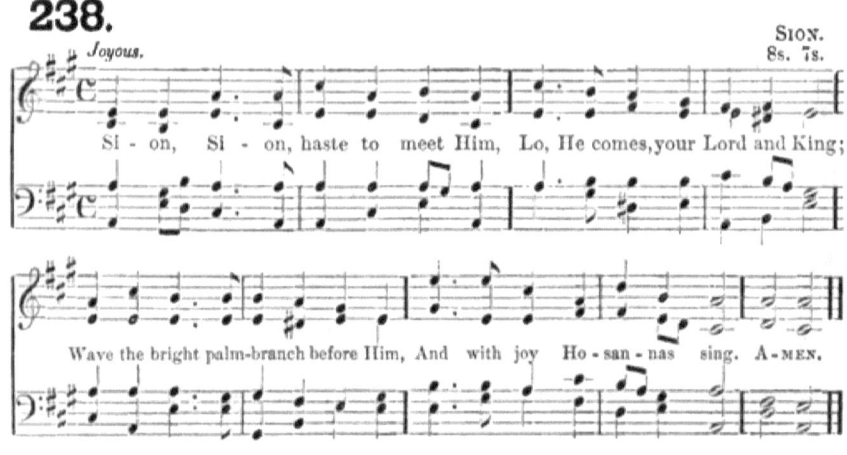

SION.
8s. 7s.

Si-on, Si-on, haste to meet Him, Lo, He comes, your Lord and King; Wave the bright palm-branch before Him, And with joy Hosannas sing. A-MEN.

2 See the eager crowd around Him
    Strew with garments fair His way,
  Honour to the Son of David,
    With glad voices hear them say.

3 Even little tender children,
    Haste their loving Lord to meet;
  Sing Hosannas with sweet voices,
    Strew palm-branches at His feet.

HIS TRIUMPHAL ENTRY.

239.

S. Theodulph.
7s. 6s. with Refrain.

All glo - ry, laud, and hon - our, To Thee, Re - deem - er, King!
To whom the lips of chil - dren, Made sweet Ho - san - nas ring.

Thou art the King of Is - rael, Thou Da - vid's roy - al Son,
Who in the Lord's Name com - est, The King and Bless - ed One.

All glo - ry, laud, and hon - our, To Thee, Re - deem - er, King!
To whom the lips of chil - dren, Made sweet Ho - san - nas ring. A - men.

3 The company of angels
   Are praising Thee on high;
   And mortal men and all things
   Created, make reply.
           All glory, &c.

4 The people of the Hebrews
   With palms before Thee went:
   Our praise and prayer and anthems
   Before Thee we present.
           All glory, &c.

5 To Thee before Thy passion
   They sang their hymns of praise:
   To Thee, now high exalted
   Our melody we raise.
           All glory, &c.

6 Thou didst accept their praises;
   Accept the prayers we bring,
   Who in all good delightest,
   Thou good and gracious King.
           All glory, &c.

240.

HIS TRIUMPHAL ENTRY.

BRADFORD.
7s. 6s. D.

Bold.

Hosanna! loud hosanna! The little children sang;
Through pillar'd court and temple The lovely anthem rang;
To Jesus, who had bless'd them, Close folded to His breast,
The children sang their praises, The simplest and the best. A-MEN.

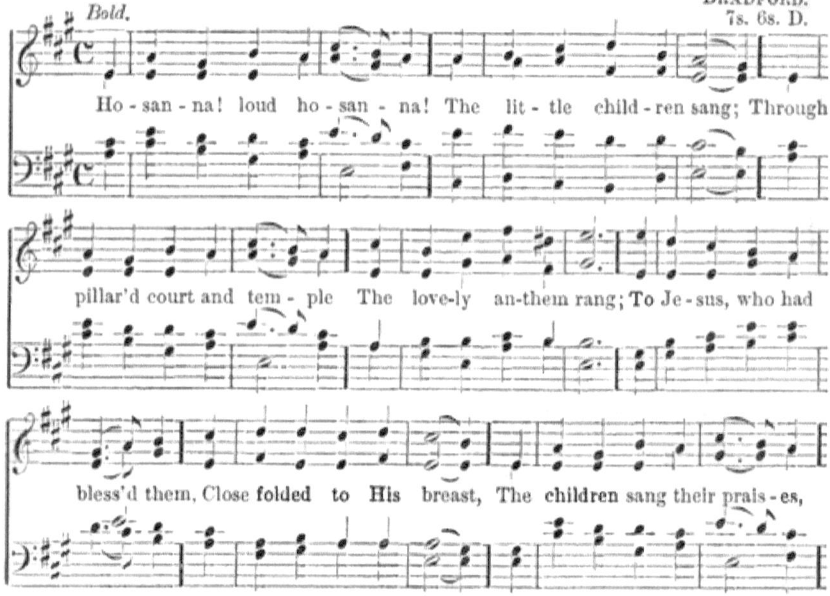

2 From Olivet they followed,
  'Midst an exultant crowd,
  Waving the victor palm branch,
  And shouting clear and loud;
  Bright angels joined the chorus,
  Beyond the cloudless sky—
  "Hosanna in the highest:
  Glory to God on high!"

3 Fair leaves of silvery olive
  They strewed upon the ground,
  Whilst Salem's circling mountains
  Echoed the joyful sound;
  The Lord of men and angels
  Rode on in lowly state,
  Nor scorned that little children
  Should on His bidding wait.

4 "Hosanna in the highest!"
  That ancient song we sing,
  For Christ is our Redeemer,
  The Lord of Heaven our King.
  Oh! may we ever praise Him,
  With heart, and life, and voice,
  And in His blissful presence
  Eternally rejoice!

* May be used at other seasons.

241.

ROYAL SAVIOUR.
6s. 5s. D.

Moderately slow.

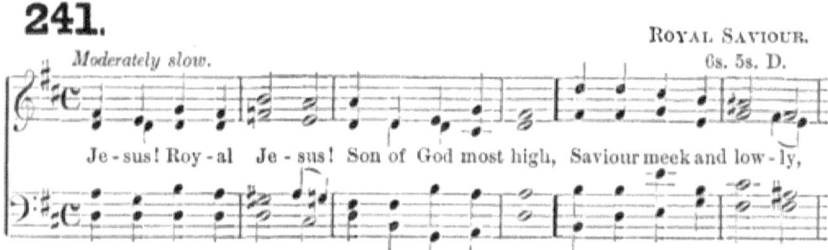

Jesus! Royal Jesus! Son of God most high, Saviour meek and lowly,

HIS TRIUMPHAL ENTRY.

Ri-ding forth to die! On a colt Thou sit - test, While the peo-ple sing, "Glo-ry in the High-est, Bless-ed be the King!" AMEN.

2 Tell we forth Thy praises,
  Palms in triumph wave;
  Blessing, with hosannas,
  Whom we hail to save.
  We with hearts and voices
  Honour Thee with them
  Who Thy footsteps welcomed
  To Jerusalem.

3 Soon will these, O Jesus!
  Raise the Cross on high,
  And the crowd, so faithless,
  Shout "Him crucify."
  Dearest Lord, increase us
  With Thy perfect love,
  That through all temptations,
  We may faithful prove.

4 Grant us Thee to follow,
  And Thy Cross to bear,
  So Thy Resurrection
  We at last may share;
  So that we may praise Thee
  On Thy Heavenly Throne,
  Who art, with the Father,
  And the Spirit, One!

242.*

SALEM.
8s. 7s. 4.

Earnestly.

Once was heard the song of chil-dren By the Sa-viour when on earth; Joy-ful in the sa-cred tem-ple Shouts of youthful praise had birth; And Ho-san-nas, And Ho-sannas Loud to David's Son broke forth. AMEN.

2 Palms of victory strewn around Him,
  Garments spread beneath His feet,
  Prophet of the Lord they crowned Him,
  In fair Salem's crowded street,
  While Hosannas
  From the lips of children greet.

3 God o'er all in heaven reigning,
  We this day Thy glory sing;
  Not with palms Thy pathway strewing,
  We would loftier tribute bring,—
  Glad Hosannas
  To our Prophet, Priest, and King.

4 O, though humble is our offering,
  Deign accept our grateful lays;
  Those from children once proceeding
  Thou didst deem "perfected praise."
  Now Hosannas,
  Saviour, Lord, to Thee we raise.

* *May be used at other seasons.*

243. His Death.

HORSLEY.
C. M.

Moderate.

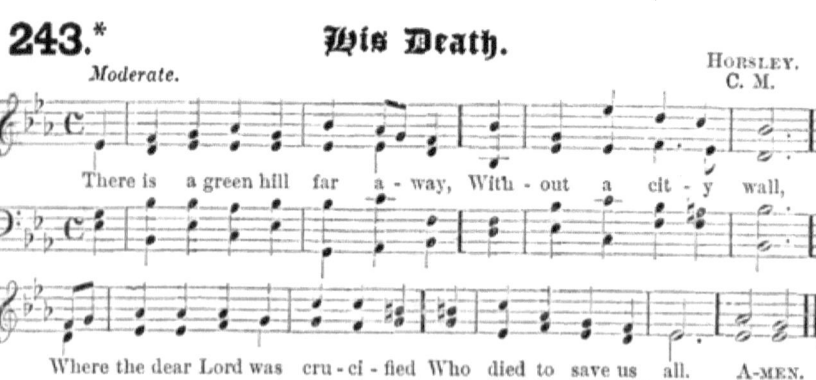

There is a green hill far away, Without a city wall,
Where the dear Lord was cru-ci-fied Who died to save us all. A-MEN.

2 We may not know, we cannot tell,
  What pains He had to bear,
  But we believe it was for us
  He hung and suffered there.
3 He died that we might be forgiven,
  He died to make us good,
  That we might go at last to heaven,
  Saved by His precious blood.

4 There was no other good enough
  To pay the price of sin,
  He only could unlock the gate
  Of heaven, and let us in.
5 Oh, dearly, dearly has He loved,
  And we must love Him too,
  And trust in His redeeming blood,
  And try His work to do.

244.

ROCKINGHAM.
L. M.

Moderate.

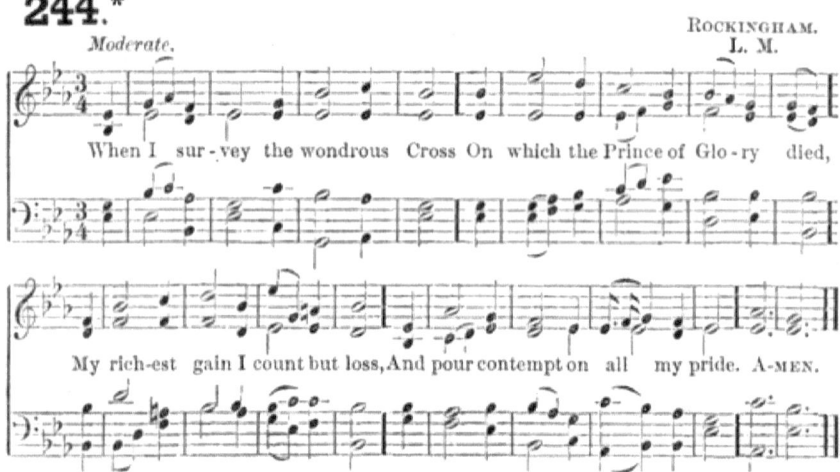

When I sur-vey the wondrous Cross On which the Prince of Glo-ry died,
My rich-est gain I count but loss, And pour contempt on all my pride. A-MEN.

2 Forbid it, Lord, that I should boast,
  Save in the Cross of Christ, my God;
  All the vain things that charm me most,
  I sacrifice them to Thy Blood.
3 See, from His head, His hands, His feet,
  Sorrow and love flow mingled down!
  Did e'er such love and sorrow meet?
  Or thorns compose a Saviour's crown?
4 Were the whole realm of nature mine,
  That were a tribute far too small;
  Love so amazing, so divine,
  Demands my soul, my life, my all.

* *May be used at other seasons.*

HIS DEATH.

245.*
Quietly. BATTY.
8s. 7s.

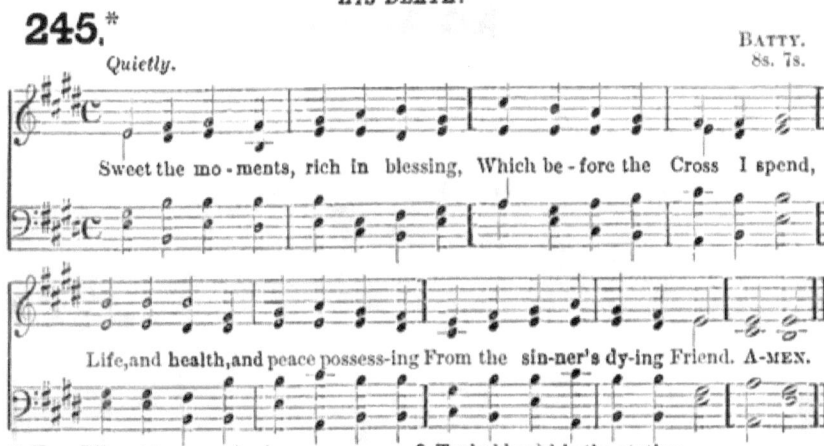

Sweet the moments, rich in blessing, Which before the Cross I spend,
Life, and health, and peace possessing From the sinner's dying Friend. A-MEN.

2 Here I'll rest forever viewing
  Mercy poured in streams of blood:
  Precious drops, my soul bedewing,
  Plead, and claim my peace with God.

3 Truly blessèd is the station,
  Low before His Cross to lie;
  Whilst I see divine compassion
  Beaming in His languid eye.

4 Lord, in ceaseless contemplation
  Fix my thankful heart on Thee,
  Till I taste Thy full salvation,
  And Thine unveil'd glory see.

246.*
Quietly. THURGAU.
8s. 7s.

Hear Thy children, gentle Jesus, Hear Thy children cry to Thee;
Self and sin no more shall please us; Hear our solemn Litany. A-MEN.

2 Thou didst suffer, gentle Jesus,
  Bitter shame and agony;
  From sin's bondage to release us,
  Thou didst hang upon the tree.

3 But our sins it was that stung Thee,
  Not the scourge, and nails and spear;
  'Twas our sins alone that hung Thee
  On the cross, O Saviour dear!

4 Thou wert pierced, O holy Jesus,
  Pierced that sinners might not die;
  Oh, let sin no longer please us,
  Make us Thine eternally.

5 Gentle Jesus, Thou hast won us
  By Thy Passion and Thy love;
  Gentle Jesus, deign to own us
  In the land of rest above.

Also the following.

310. Jesus, Lover of my soul.
349. My God, my Father, while I stray.
430. Lord, Thy children guide and keep.

* *May be used at other seasons.*

His Burial.

247.
Quietly. REDHEAD, 76. Six 7s.

Rest-ing from His work to-day, In the tomb the Sa-viour lay;
Still He slept, from Head to Feet, Shrouded in the wind-ing-sheet,
Ly-ing in the rock a-lone, Hid-den by the seal-ed stone. A-MEN.

2 Late at even there was seen
Watching long the Magdalene;
Early, ere the break of day,
Sorrowful she took her way
To the holy garden glade,
Where her buried Lord was laid.

3 So with Thee, till life shall end,
I would solemn vigil spend:
Let me hew Thee, Lord, a shrine
In this rocky heart of mine,
Where in pure embalmèd cell
None but Thou may ever dwell.

4 Myrrh and spices will I bring,
True affection's offering;
Close the door from sight and sound
Of the busy world around;
And in patient watch remain
Till my Lord appear again.

Easter.
The Story of the Resurrection.

I.—THE QUESTION.

248. *Not fast.*

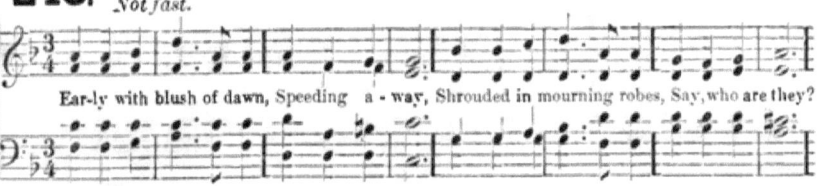

Ear-ly with blush of dawn, Speeding a-way, Shrouded in mourning robes, Say, who are they?

2 See, in their hands they bear
  Spices most sweet,
  Whom are they hastening
  Early to greet?

3 Whose is that garden-fold
  Eager they seek,
  Why that stone rolled away
  Baffling the weak?

4 Why are they pausing now,
  Close by the Cave?
  Whom are they seeking for
  In the dark grave?

II.—THE ANSWER.

Not fast.

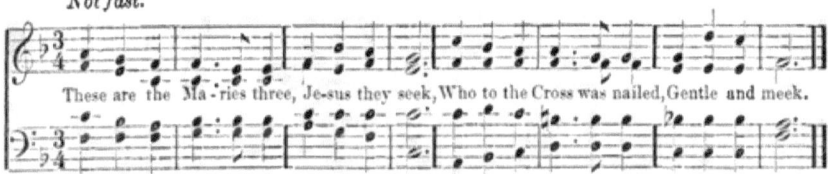

These are the Ma-ries three, Je-sus they seek, Who to the Cross was nailed, Gentle and meek.

2 This is the garden-fold
  Wherein they laid,
  Loving, His lifeless form,
  Bold, yet afraid.

3 Trembling, they now behold
  Where He had lain,
  Clothed in shining robes,
  Bright angels twain.

4 Hark! they are speaking now—
  "Fear not," they say;
  "Whom you are seeking here
  Is risen to-day!"

III.—THE STORY.

A little faster.

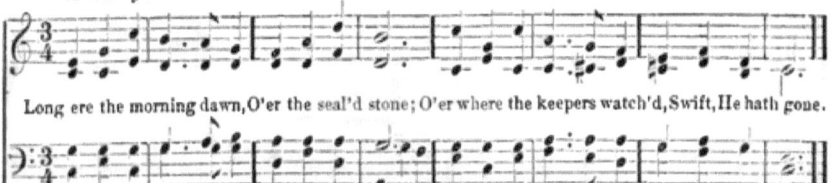

Long ere the morning dawn, O'er the seal'd stone; O'er where the keepers watch'd, Swift, He hath gone.

2 Lo! as with haste they came,
  Bringing their tale,
  Greeting, His voice was heard—
  "Children, all hail!"

3 When fell the eventide
  Through the closed door
  To His disciples came
  Jesus once more.

4 See, at His feet they kneel,
  Blessings to win,
  "Peace," He is whispering,
  "Pardon from sin."

5 "Peace," once again He breathes,
  "Bear it abroad,
  Peace to the contrite soul
  Thirsting for God!"

6 Thomas the eighth day come,
  Chiding, He bade
  Touch the deep scars and wounds
  The nails had made.

7 In the fair morning hour,
  Nigh to the sea
  Asked He of Jonas' son—
  "Lovest thou Me?"

8 "Feed this dear flock of Mine,
  Bought with My Blood,
  Preach ye, baptize, and win
  Souls to their God.

9 To your and My Father-God
  Now I ascend,
  Yet in My Church abide
  On to the end!"

10 Then on Ascension Day,
   By His own might,
   Jesus to Heaven went
   Up in their sight.

250.

EASTER.

WHITNEY.
7s.

Joyful.

Christ, the Lord, is risen to-day, Sons of men and an-gels say: Raise your joys and tri-umphs high, Sing, ye heav'ns; and earth, re-ply. A-MEN.

2 Love's redeeming work is done,
Fought the fight, the victory won;
Jesus' agony is o'er,
Darkness veils the earth no more.

3 Vain the stone, the watch, the seal,
Christ hath burst the gates of hell;
Death in vain forbids Him rise,
Christ hath open'd Paradise.

4 Soar we now where Christ hath led,
Following our exalted Head;
Made like Him, like Him we rise;
Ours the cross, the grave, the skies.

251.

ARIMATHEA.
P. M.

Joyful.

An-gels, roll the rock a-way! Death, yield up the might-y Prey! See, the Sa-viour quits the tomb, Glow-ing with im-mor-tal bloom. Al-le-lu-ia, Al-le-lu-ia, Christ the Lord is risen to-day. A-MEN.

2 Shout, ye seraphs; angels, raise
Your eternal song of praise:
Let the earth's remotest bound
Echo to the blissful sound.
Alleluia! alleluia!
Christ the Lord is risen to-day.

3 Holy Father, Holy Son,
Holy Spirit, Three in One,
Glory as of old to Thee,
Now and evermore shall be.
Alleluia! alleluia!
Christ the Lord is risen to-day.

252.

EASTER.

S. ALBINUS.
7s. 8s.

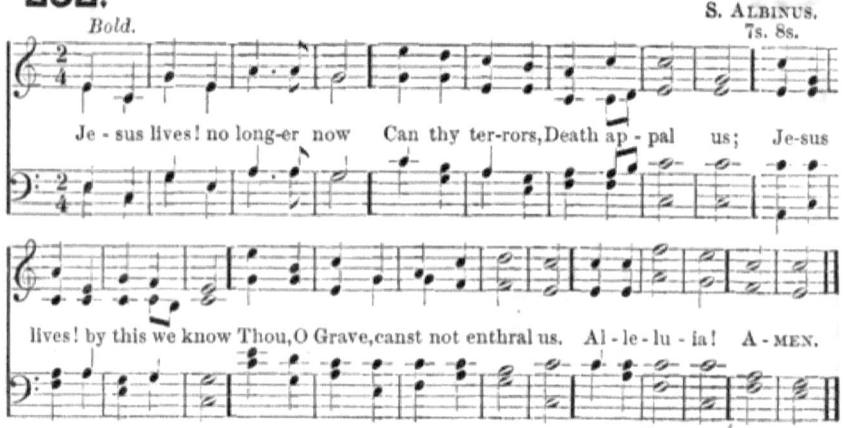

Jesus lives! no longer now Can thy terrors, Death appal us; Jesus lives! by this we know Thou, O Grave, canst not enthral us. Alleluia! Amen.

2 Jesus lives! henceforth is death
But the gate of life immortal;
This shall calm our trembling breath,
When we pass its gloomy portal.
Alleluia!

3 Jesus lives! for us He died;
Then, alone to Jesus living,
Pure in heart may we abide,
Glory to our Saviour giving.
Alleluia!

4 Jesus lives! our hearts know well
Nought from us His love shall sever;
Life, nor death, nor powers of hell
Tear us from His keeping ever.
Alleluia!

5 Jesus lives! to Him the Throne
Over all the world is given;
May we go where He is gone,
Rest and reign with Him in Heaven.
Alleluia!

253.*

EASTER DAWN.
P. M.

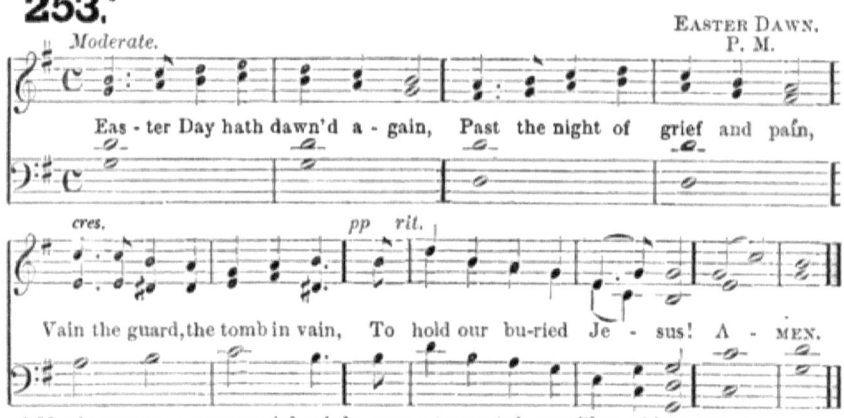

Easter Day hath dawn'd again, Past the night of grief and pain, Vain the guard, the tomb in vain, To hold our buried Jesus! Amen.

May be sung as an accompanied melody, or as a two-part chorus with or without accompaniment.

2 Faithful hearts their watch have kept,
Loving eyes have mourned and wept,
Where, it seemed, He lately slept,
So still and silent, Jesus!

3 Now, all tears have passed away
With the early morning ray;
From the grave, where once He lay,
There hath arisen Jesus!

4 On this blessèd Even-tide,
Two there were He walked beside,
And they prayed—"With us abide!"
Although they knew not Jesus!

5 Jesus, Lord! I pray to Thee,
Though Thy Face not yet I see,
Evermore abide with me—
My Lord—my God—my Jesus!

EASTER.

254.
Moderate. CRAMER. 7s. 6s. D.

The day of Re-sur-rec-tion! Earth, tell it out a-broad; The Pass-o-ver of glad-ness, The Pass-o-ver of God. From death to life e-ter-nal, From this world to the sky, Our Christ hath brought us o-ver, With hymns of vic-to-ry. A-MEN.

2 Our hearts be pure from evil,
  That **we may** see aright
The Lord in rays eternal
  Of resurrection-light,
And, listening to His accents,
  May hear so calm and plain
His own "All hail!" and hearing,
  May **raise** the victor-strain.

3 Now let the heavens be joyful!
  Let earth her song begin!
Let the round world keep triumph,
  And all that is therein
Invisible and visible
  Their notes let all things blend,
For Christ the Lord hath risen,
  Our joy that hath no end.

255.
Moderate. ALNWICK. 7s. 5s.

Rise, the ris-en Sa-viour saith! Rise to high-er things; Draw a-new thy quick-en'd breath, Use Thy new made wings! A-MEN.

2 Broken down thy prison **walls;**
  Sit no more forlorn;
Every chain and hindrance falls
  On glad Easter Morn.

3 Therefore sing thy glad new song,
  Live as children free;
Raise with voices loud and strong
  Shouts of Jubilee!

EASTER.

256.
Joyful.
S. KEVIN.
7s. 6. D.

Come ye faith-ful, raise the strain Of tri-um-phant glad-ness;
God hath brought His Is-ra-el In-to joy from sad-ness;
Loosed from Pha-raoh's bit-ter yoke Ja-cob's sons and daugh-ters;
Led them with un-moistened foot Through the Red Sea wa-ters. A-MEN.

2 'Tis the Spring of souls to-day:
  Christ hath burst His prison;
And from three days' sleep in death
  As a sun hath risen,
All the winter of our sins,
  Long and dark, is flying
From His light, to whom we **give**
  Laud and praise undying.

3 Now the Queen of Seasons, bright
  With the day of splendour,
With **the** royal Feast of feasts,
  Comes its joy **to** render;
Comes to glad Jerusalem,
  Who with true affection,
Welcomes in unwearied strains
  Jesus' Resurrection.

4 Alleluia now we cry
  To our King Immortal,
Who triumphant burst the bars
  Of the tomb's dark portal;
Alleluia, with the Son
  God the Father praising;
Alleluia **yet** again
  To the Spirit **raising.**

Also the following.

320. All hail the power of Jesus' Name.   **369.** The King of love my Shepherd is.
393. Thou art the Way;—to Thee alone.   **507—523.** EASTER CAROLS.

2 He who came to save us,
   He who bled and died,
   Now is crowned with glory
   At His Father's side;
   Never more to suffer;
   Never more to die;
   Jesus, King of glory,
   Is gone up on high.
      All His work is ended, &c.

3 Praying for His children
   In that blessed place,
   Calling them to glory,
   Sending them His grace;
   His bright home preparing,
   Little ones for you;
   Jesus ever liveth
   Ever loveth too.
      All His work is ended, &c.

258. ASCENSION.

Joyful.   ASCENSION. 7s. with Alleluia.

Hail the day that sees Him rise, Alleluia! To His throne above the skies; Alleluia! Christ the Lamb for sinners given, Alleluia! Enters now the highest heav'n. Alleluia! A-MEN.

2 There for Him high triumph waits, Alleluia!
 Lift your heads, eternal gates; Alleluia!
 He hath conquered death and sin, Alleluia!
 Take the King of glory in. Alleluia!

3 Lo, the heaven its LORD receives, Alleluia!
 Yet He loves the earth He leaves; Alleluia!
 Though returning to His throne, Alleluia!
 Still He calls mankind His own. Alleluia!

4 LORD, though parted from our sight, Alleluia!
 Far above the starry height, Alleluia!
 Grant our hearts may thither rise, Alleluia!
 Seeking Thee above the skies. Alleluia!

259.

Cheerfully.   OLIVET. 7s. 5s. 7.

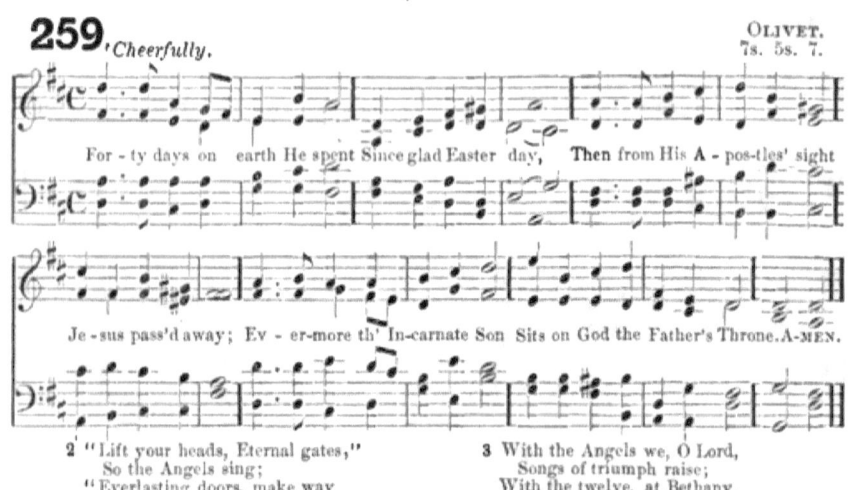

For-ty days on earth He spent Since glad Easter day, Then from His A-pos-tles' sight Je-sus pass'd away; Ev-ermore th' In-carnate Son Sits on God the Father's Throne. A-MEN.

2 "Lift your heads, Eternal gates,"
  So the Angels sing;
 "Everlasting doors, make way
  For the Glorious King!"
 Satan's power is overthrown,
 Christ the Victor reigns alone!

3 With the Angels we, O Lord,
  Songs of triumph raise;
 With the twelve, at Bethany,
  Up to Heaven we gaze;
 Soon Thou wilt return—may we
 Watch with joy to welcome Thee!

Also the following:
320. All hail the power of Jesus' Name.   328. Glory to the Blessed Jesus.
209. Up in heaven, up in heaven.

The Holy Spirit.

260. S. CUTHBERT. P. M.

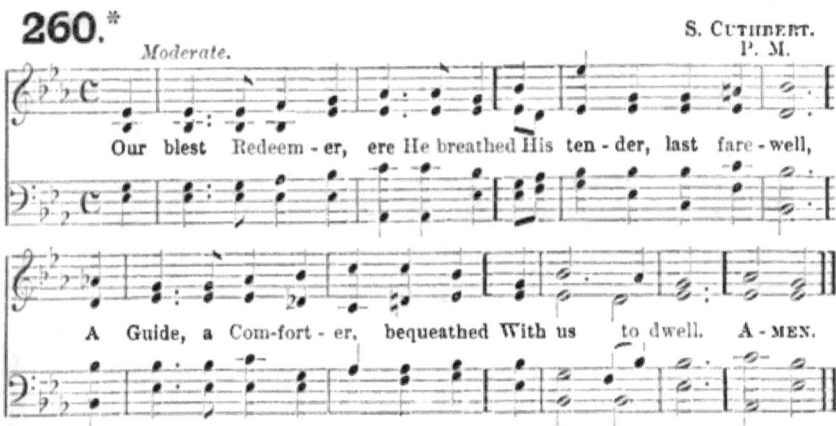

Our blest Redeemer, ere He breathed His tender, last farewell, A Guide, a Comforter, bequeathed With us to dwell. A-MEN.

2 He came in semblance of a Dove
  With sheltering wings outspread,
  The holy balm of peace and love
    On earth to shed.

3 He came sweet influence to impart,
  A gracious, willing guest,
  While He can find one humble heart
    Wherein to rest.

4 And His that gentle voice we hear,
  Soft as the breath of even,
  That checks each thought, that calms each
    And speaks of heaven.   [fear,

5 And every virtue we possess,
  And every victory won,
  And every thought of holiness
    Are His alone.

6 Spirit of purity and grace,
  Our weakness, pitying, see;
  O make our hearts Thy dwelling-place,
    And meet for Thee.

7 O praise the Father; praise the Son;
  Blest Spirit, praise to Thee;
  All praise to God, the Three in One,
    The One in Three.

261. FEDERAL STREET. L. M.

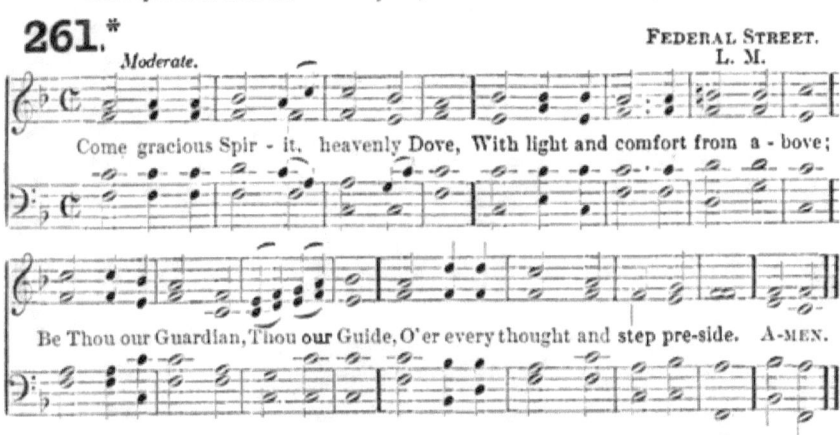

Come gracious Spirit, heavenly Dove, With light and comfort from above; Be Thou our Guardian, Thou our Guide, O'er every thought and step preside. A-MEN.

2 The light of truth to us display,
  And make us know and choose Thy way;
  Plant holy fear in every heart,
  That we from Thee may ne'er depart.

3 Lead us to Christ, the living way,
  Nor let us from His precepts stray;
  Lead us to holiness, the road
  That we must take to dwell with God.

4 Lead us to heaven, that we may share
  Fulness of joy for ever there;
  Lead us to God, our final rest
  To be with Him for ever blest.

* May be used at other seasons.

THE HOLY SPIRIT.

262.*

Moderate. CAPETOWN. 7s. 5.

Gra-cious Spir-it, Ho-ly Ghost, Taught by Thee we cov-et most, Of Thy gifts at Pen-te-cost, Ho-ly, heaven-ly Love. A-MEN.

2 Love is kind, and suffers long,
Love is meek, and thinks no wrong,
Love than death itself more strong;
   Therefore, give us Love.

3 **Prophecy** will fade away,
Melting in the light of day;
Love will ever with us stay;
   Therefore, give us Love.

4 Faith will vanish into sight;
Hope be emptied in delight;
Love in heaven will shine more bright;
   Therefore, give us Love.

5 Faith and Hope and Love we see
Joining hand in hand agree;
But the greatest of the three,
   And the best, **is Love.**

6 From the overshadowing
Of Thy gold and silver wing,
Shed on us who to Thee sing,
   Holy, heavenly Love.

263.*

Moderate. HOLY COMFORTER. 7s.

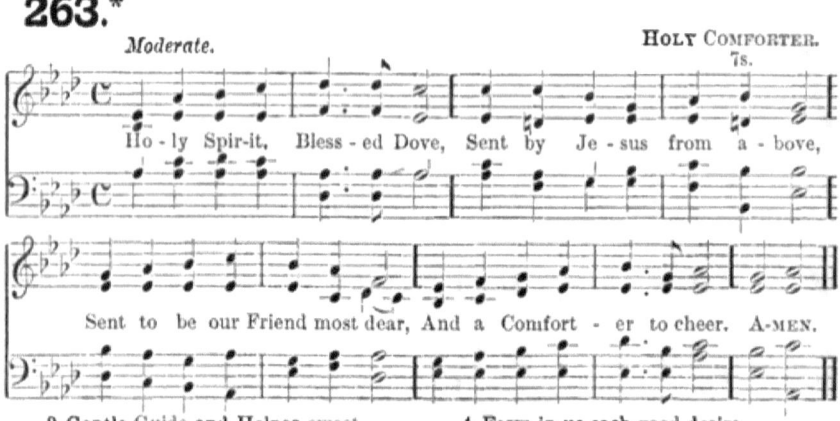

Ho-ly Spir-it, Bless-ed Dove, Sent by Je-sus from a-bove, Sent to be our Friend most dear, And a Comfort-er to cheer. A-MEN.

2 **Gentle** Guide and **Helper** sweet,
Lead our weary wayworn feet
Safely through this world of care,
Till they reach Thy dwelling fair.

3 **Tender** Friend, Companion blest,
Deign to be our constant Guest,
All that grieves Thee put away,
And with us for **ever** stay.

4 **Form in us each** good **desire,**
Quicken them with holy fire,
Till the life on love's strong wing
Upward soar, and soaring sing.

5 Holy Spirit, Blessèd Dove,
Comforter, Whose Name is Love,
Helper, Friend, Companion, Guide,
Evermore with us abide.

* *May be used at other seasons.*

THE HOLY SPIRIT.

264. PENTECOST.
Six 7s.
Moderate.

Gracious Spirit, dwell with me,—I myself would gracious be; And, with words that help and heal, Would Thy life in mine reveal; And, with actions bold and meek, Would for Christ, my Saviour, speak. A-MEN.

2 Truthful Spirit, dwell with me,—
I myself would truthful be;
And with wisdom kind and clear,
Let Thy life in mine appear;
And, with actions brotherly,
Speak my Lord's sincerity.

3 Tender Spirit, dwell with me,—
I myself would tender be;
Shut my heart up like a flower
At temptation's darksome hour;
Open it, when shines the sun,
And his love by fragrance own.

4 Holy Spirit, dwell with me,—
I myself would holy be;
Separate from sin, I would
Choose and cherish all things good;
And whatever I can be
Give to Him who gave me Thee.

265. WOLHAYES.
7s.
Cheerful.

Thou, who camest from above, Bringing light and breathing love, Teaching us Thy perfect way, Giving gifts to men to-day. A-MEN.

2 Thou, who once did change our state,
Making us regenerate,
Help us evermore to be
Faithful subjects unto Thee.

3 Often have we grieved Thee sore;
May we never grieve Thee more;
Thou the feeble canst protect,
Thou the wandering direct.

4 We are dark; be Thou our Light;
We are blind; be Thou our Sight;
Be our Comfort in distress;
Guide us through the wilderness.

5 Praise the blessèd Three in One,
Praise the Father and the Son;
To the Holy Ghost arise
Praise from all below the skies!

* *May be used at other seasons.*

266.* The Holy Trinity.

Earnestly. NICAEA. P M.

Holy, holy, holy! Lord God Almighty!
Early in the morning our song shall rise to Thee:
Holy, holy, holy! merciful and mighty!
God in Three Persons, Blessèd Trinity! A-MEN.

2 Holy, holy, holy! all the saints adore Thee,
   Casting down their golden crowns around the glassy sea,
   Cherubim and seraphim falling down before Thee,
   Which wert, and art, and evermore shalt be.

3 Holy, holy, holy! though the darkness hide Thee,
   Though the eye of sinful man Thy glory may not see,
   Only Thou art holy; there is none beside Thee
   Perfect in power, in love, and purity.

4 Holy, holy, holy! Lord God Almighty!
   All Thy works shall praise Thy Name, in earth, and sky, and sea:
   Holy, holy, holy! merciful and mighty!
   God in Three Persons, Blessèd Trinity.

(1) The small notes are intended for the second and third verses.

* *May also be sung at other seasons.*

TRINITY.

267. *Joyous.* CAPETOWN. 7s. 5.

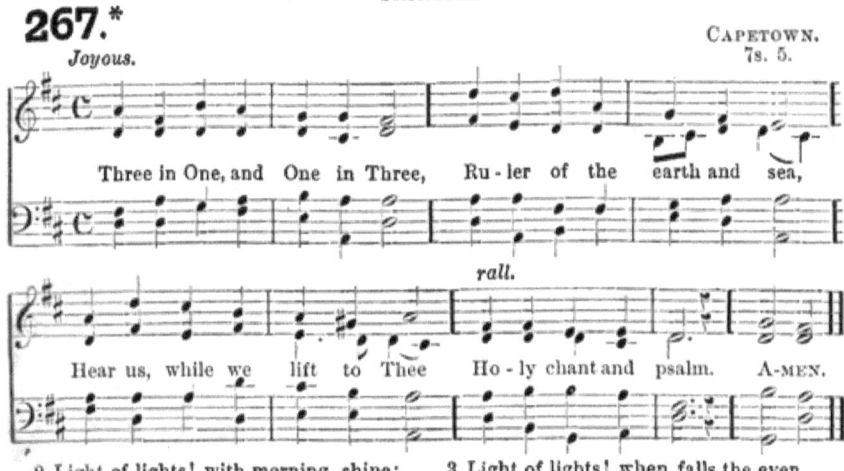

Three in One, and One in Three, Ru-ler of the earth and sea,
Hear us, while we lift to Thee Ho-ly chant and psalm. A-MEN.

2 Light of lights! with morning, shine:
Lift on us Thy light divine;
And let charity benign
Breathe on us her balm.

3 Light of lights! when falls the even,
Let it close on sins forgiven;
Fold us in the peace of heaven,
Shed a holy calm.

4 Three in One and One in Three,
Dimly here we worship Thee:
With the saints hereafter we
Hope to bear the palm.

268. *Joyous.* NUREMBERG. 7s.

Glo-ry to the Fa-ther give, God in whom we move and live:
Children's prayers He deigns to hear, Children's songs de-light His ear. A-MEN.

2 Glory to the Son we bring,
Christ our Prophet, Priest and King:
Children, raise your sweetest strain
To the Lamb, for He was slain.

3 Glory to the Holy Ghost,
He reclaims the sinner lost;
Children's minds may He inspire,
Touch their tongues with holy fire.

4 Glory in the highest be
To the Blessèd Trinity
For the Gospel from above,
For the word that " God is love."

* *May also be used at other seasons.*

Apostles and Saints.

269.

Moderate.

S. BARTHOLOMEW.
C. M. D.

How bright these glorious spirits shine! Whence all their white array?
How came they to the blissful seats Of everlasting day?
Lo, these are they, from sufferings great, Who came to realms of light;
And in the blood of Christ have wash'd Those robes which shine so bright. A-MEN.

2 Now with triumphal palms they stand
  Before the throne on high,
And serve the God they love amidst
  The glories of the sky.
His presence fills each heart with joy,
  Tunes every mouth to sing;
By day, by night, the sacred courts
  With glad hosannas ring.

3 The Lamb, which reigns upon the throne,
  Shall o'er them still preside;
Feed them with nourishment divine,
  And all their footsteps guide.
'Mong pastures green He'll lead His flock,
  Where living streams appear;
And God the Lord from every eye
  Shall wipe off every tear.

* *May also be used at other seasons.*

APOSTLES AND SAINTS.

270.*
MOULTRIE.
8s. 7s. D.

Joyous.

Hark! the sound of ho-ly voi-ces, Chanting o'er the crystal sea,
Al-le-lu-ia, Al-le-lu-ia, Al-le-lu-ia, Lord, to Thee;
Mul-ti-tude, which none can num-ber, Like the stars in glo-ry stands,
Clothed in white ap-par-el, hold-ing Palms of vic-tory in their hands. A-MEN.

2 Patriarch, and Holy Prophet,
  Who prepared the way of Christ,
King, Apostle. Saint. Confessor,
  Martyr and Evangelist,
Saintly Maiden. Godly Matron,
  Widows who have watched to prayer,
Joined in holy concert, singing
  To the Lord of all, are there.

3 They have come from tribulation,
  And have wash'd their robes in blood,
Wash'd them in the blood of Jesus;
  Tried they were, and firm they stood;
Mock'd, imprison'd, stoned, tormented,
  Sawn assunder, slain with sword,
They have conquer'd death and Satan
  By the might of Christ the Lord.

4 Marching with Thy Cross their banner,
  They have triumph'd, following
Thee, the Captain of salvation,
  Thee, their Saviour and their King;
Gladly, Lord, with Thee they suffer'd:
  Gladly, Lord, with Thee they died;
And by death to life immortal
  They were born and glorified.

5 Now they reign in heavenly glory,
  Now they walk in golden light,
Now they drink, as from a river,
  Holy bliss and infinite:
Love and peace they taste for ever,
  And all truth and knowledge see
In the beatific vision
  Of the Blessèd Trinity.

* *May also be used at other seasons.*

APOSTLES AND SAINTS.

271. *

With spirit.

LAMBETH.
C. M.

The Son of God goes forth to war, A king-ly crown to gain; His blood red ban-ner streams a-far; Who fol-lows in His train? A-MEN.

2 Who best can drink his cup of woe,
  Triumphant over pain;
  Who patient, bears his cross below,
  He follows in His train.

3 The martyr first, whose eagle eye
  Could pierce beyond the grave;
  Who saw his Master in the sky,
  And call'd on Him to save.

4 Like Him, with pardon on his tongue,
  In midst of mortal pain,
  He prayed for them that did the wrong:
  Who follows in His train.

5 A glorious band, the chosen few,
  On whom the spirit came:
  Twelve valiant saints, their hope they knew,
  And mock'd the cross and flame.

6 They met the tyrant's brandish'd steel,
  The lion's gory mane,
  They bow'd their necks the death to feel:
  Who follows in their train?

7 A noble army—men and boys,
  The matron and the maid;
  Around the Saviour's throne rejoice,
  In robes of light array'd.

8 They climb'd the steep ascent to heaven
  Through peril, toil and pain:
  O God, to us may grace be given
  To follow in their train.

272. Quietly.

MENDELSSOHN.
88. 6.

Come let us sing of those sweet babes, Whom Herod murdered long a-go, When all thro' Ramah's coast was heard A sound of bit-ter woe.... A sound of bit-ter woe. A-MEN.

2 They tore them from the cradle bed,
  They tore them from their mother's breast;
  But since they died for Jesu's sake,
  We call those babies blest.

3 They might have grown up wicked men,
  That heeded not God's holy word;
  They might have joined their cruel cry
  Who crucified the Lord.

4 But early called, they gave their lives
  For Him, who fleeing through the wild,
  Yet had a part in all their pangs,
  And loved each martyr child.

5 Safe from beneath the murderer's knife
  They passed to His eternal rest:
  And since they died for Jesu's sake,
  We call those babies blest.

* *May also be used at other seasons.*

APOSTLES AND SAINTS.

273.
Joyful.
CRAMER.
7s. 6s. D.

1. The Friend of little children We ever call to mind,
   That Friend so true and gentle, That Friend so won-drous kind,
   That Friend of youths and maidens, Of travellers by sea,
   And wand'rers over this world Wherever they may be. A-MEN.

2. We know the guardian Angels' Blest work and sweet employ
   Is aye to keep from evil, And fill with holy joy;
   The Saints all gone before us Must love and watch us still,
   And do for each redeemed one According to God's will.

3 But chief, they lead us onward,
  And heavenward point the way
  To every earth-born wand'rer,
  Lest he should go astray;
  They hold on high Christ's banner,
  With Holy Cross and shield,
  And bid us all, full bravely,
  Take now the battle-field.

4 And then, above us shining,
  They show the golden Crown,
  The palm branch and the lily,
  The streets with roses strown,
  The harping of the victors
  Upon the sea of glass;
  The gates for those all open
  Who into glory pass.

5 Then to the throne of Jesus,
  They lead our trembling feet,
  Until, with Him safe sheltered,
  We rest in pastures sweet;
  The pastures green of Eden
  Above the starry skies,
  The waters of the sheep-fold
  All still in Paradise.

6 O Shepherd dear, we thank Thee
  For all Thy Saints so blest,
  Who lead us ever onward
  To our dear Home of rest;
  O never, never leave us,
  But keep us in the way,
  Until at last we see Thee,
  In everlasting Day.

274.

The Church: Her Ordinances and Offices.

AUSTRIA.
8s. 7s. D.

Earnestly.

Glo-rious things of thee are spo-ken, Zi-on, cit-y of our God;
He, whose word can-not be bro-ken, Form'd thee for His own a-bode;
On the Rock of A-ges found-ed, What can shake thy sure re-pose?
With sal-va-tion's walls surrounded, Thou may'st smile at all thy foes. A-MEN.

2 See, the streams of living waters,
  Springing from eternal love,
Well supply thy sons and daughters,
  And all fear of want remove;
Who can faint, while such a river
  Ever flows their thirst t' assuage?
Grace, which like the Lord, the Giver,
  Never fails from age to age.

3 Round each habitation hovering,
  See the cloud and fire appear,
For a glory and a covering,
  Showing that the Lord is near.
Blest inhabitants of Zion,
  Wash'd in the Redeemer's blood!
Jesus, whom our souls rely on,
  Makes them kings and priests to God.

THE CHURCH: HER ORDINANCES AND OFFICES.

275.
Moderate.

AURELIA.
7s. 6s. D.

The Church's one foundation Is Jesus Christ her Lord;
She is His new creation By water and the word:
From heaven He came and sought her To be His holy bride;
With His own blood He bought her, And for her life He died. A-MEN.

2 Elect from every nation,
  Yet one o'er all the earth,
Her charter of salvation
  One Lord, one faith, one birth;
One Holy Name she blesses,
  Partakes one holy food,
And to one hope she presses,
  With every grace endued.

3 Though with a scornful wonder
  Men see her sore opprest,
By schisms rent asunder,
  By heresies distrest;
Yet saints their watch are keeping,
  Their cry goes up, "How long?"
And soon the night of weeping
  Shall be the morn of song.

4 'Mid toil and tribulation,
  And tumult of her war,
She waits the consummation
  Of peace for evermore;
Till with the vision glorious
  Her longing eyes are blest,
And the great Church victorious
  Shall be the Church at rest.

5 Yet she on earth hath union
  With God the Three in One,
And mystic sweet communion
  With those whose rest is won:
O happy ones and holy!
  Lord, give us grace that we
Like them, the meek and lowly,
  On high may dwell with Thee.

THE CHURCH: HER ORDINANCES AND OFFICES.

276.

MAIDSTONE.
7s. D.

Joyous.

Pleasant are Thy courts above, In the land of light and love;
Pleasant are Thy courts below, In this land of sin and woe.
O, my spirit longs and faints For the converse of Thy saints,
For the brightness of Thy face, King of Glory, God of grace! A-MEN.

2 Happy birds that sing and fly
Round Thy altars, O Most High!
Happier souls, that find a rest,
In a Heavenly Father's breast!
Like the wandering dove, that found
No repose on earth around,
They can to their ark repair,
And enjoy it ever there.

3 Happy souls! their praises flow,
Ever in this vale of woe;
Waters in the desert rise,
Manna feeds them from the skies;
On they go from strength to strength,
Till they reach Thy throne at length;
At Thy feet adoring fall,
Who hast led them safe through all.

4 Lord, be mine this prize to win;
Guide me through a world of sin,
Keep me by Thy saving grace,
Give me at Thy side a place;
Sun and shield alike Thou art,
Guide and guard my erring heart;
Grace and glory flow from Thee,
Shower, O shower them, Lord, on me.

THE CHURCH: HER ORDINANCES AND OFFICES.

277. *Earnestly.* S. THOMAS. S. M.

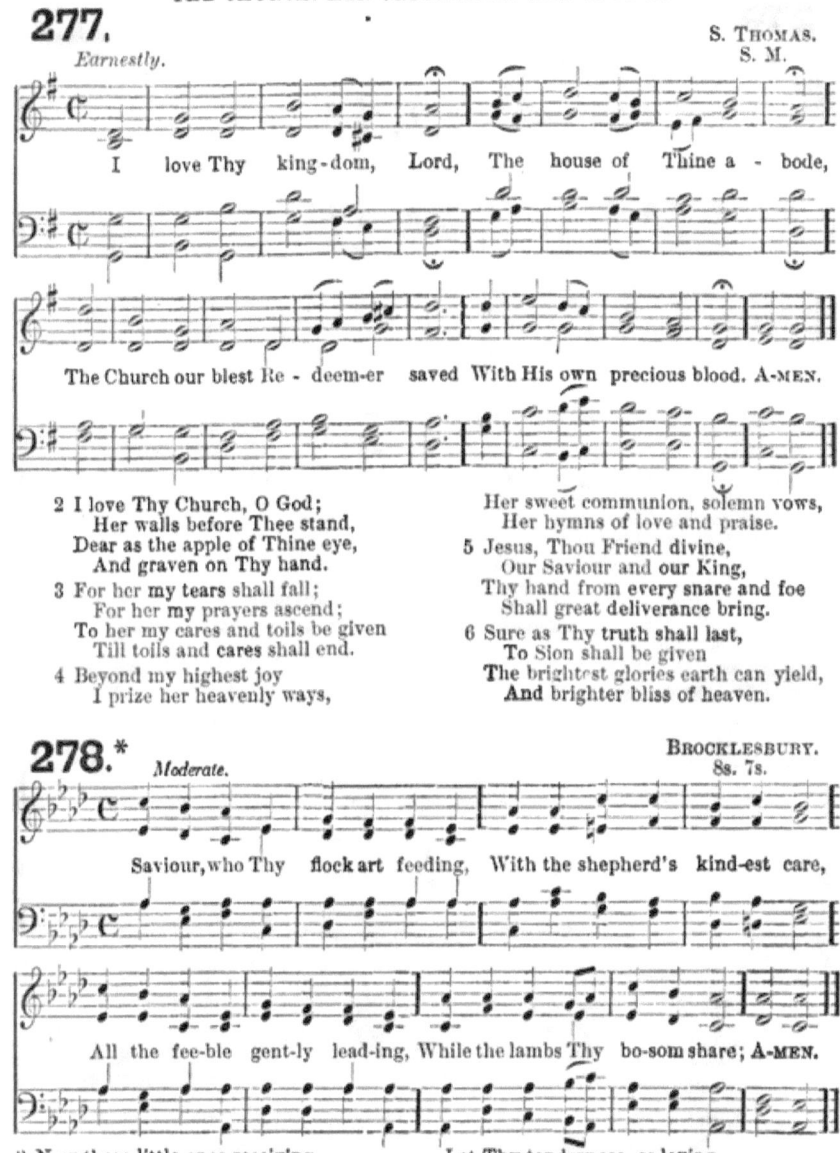

I love Thy king-dom, Lord, The house of Thine a-bode,
The Church our blest Re-deem-er saved With His own precious blood. A-MEN.

2 I love Thy Church, O God;
   Her walls before Thee stand,
Dear as the apple of Thine eye,
   And graven on Thy hand.

3 For her my tears shall fall;
   For her my prayers ascend;
To her my cares and toils be given
   Till toils and cares shall end.

4 Beyond my highest joy
   I prize her heavenly ways,
Her sweet communion, solemn vows,
   Her hymns of love and praise.

5 Jesus, Thou Friend divine,
   Our Saviour and our King,
Thy hand from every snare and foe
   Shall great deliverance bring.

6 Sure as Thy truth shall last,
   To Sion shall be given
The brightest glories earth can yield,
   And brighter bliss of heaven.

278.* *Moderate.* BROCKLESBURY. 8s. 7s.

Saviour, who Thy flock art feeding, With the shepherd's kind-est care,
All the fee-ble gent-ly lead-ing, While the lambs Thy bo-som share; A-MEN.

2 Now these little ones receiving,
   Fold them in Thy gracious arm;
There, we know, Thy word believing,
   Only there secure from harm.

3 Never from Thy pasture roving,
   Let them be the lion's prey;
Let Thy tenderness, so loving,
   Keep them all life's dangerous way;

4 Then, within Thy fold eternal,
   Let them find a resting-place;
Feed in pastures ever vernal,
   Drink the rivers of Thy grace.

* May be used on other occasions.

THE CHURCH: HER ORDINANCES AND OFFICES.

279. *Moderate.* S. STEPHEN. C. M.

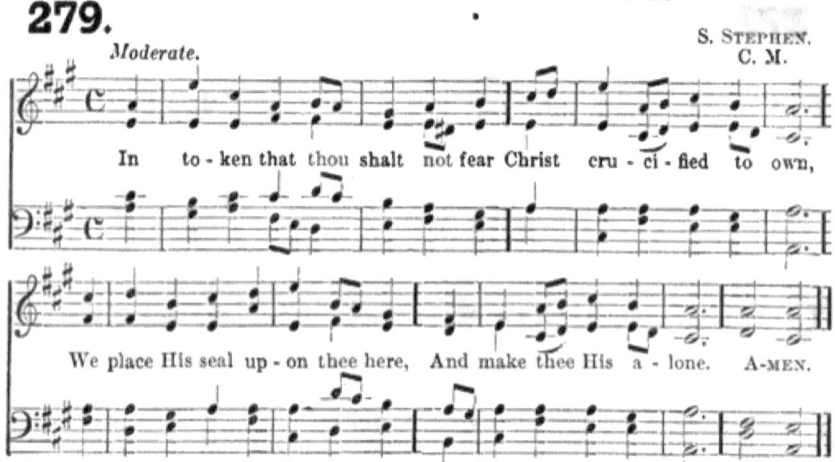

In token that thou shalt not fear Christ cru-ci-fied to own, We place His seal up-on thee here, And make thee His a-lone. A-MEN.

2 In token that thou shalt not blush
  To glory in His Name,
We blazon here upon thy front
  His glory and His shame.

3 In token that thou too shalt tread
  The path He travell'd by,
Endure the cross, despise the shame,
  And sit thee down on high;

4 Thus outwardly and visibly
  We seal thee for His own;
And may the brow that wears His seal
  Hereafter share His crown.

280. *Moderate.* HOLY CROSS. L. M.

Thy seal, O Lord, the ho-ly sign That we, here-af-ter, should be Thine, Was placed up-on our in-fant brow, And shall we fear to own it now? A-MEN.

2 O God, forbid; before the vain,
  The proud, the scoffing, the profane,
  We will, through grace, our Lord confess,
  His faint but faithful witnesses.

3 His strength in weakness He displays,
  From youthful lips He perfects praise,
  And we, His faithful soldiers, stand
  Strong in the might of His right hand.

4 Smile on us, Lord, and we will fear
  Nor scorn, nor shame, whilst Thou art near;
  Reproach is glory, suffering rest,
  If borne for Thee, if by Thee blest.

5 Great Judge of all, in that dread day,
  When heaven and earth shall flee away,
  Before the universe confess
  Thy faint but faithful witnesses.

* *May be used on other occasions.*

281.

Bold.

SILVER STREET.
S. M.

Soldiers of Christ, arise, And put your armour on; Strong in the strength which God supplies, Thro' His eternal Son. A-MEN.

2 Strong in the Lord of hosts,
And in His mighty power;
Who in the strength of Jesus trusts,
Is more than conqueror.

3 Stand then in His great might,
With all His strength endued:
And take, to arm you for the fight,
The panoply of God;

4 That having all things done,
And all your conflicts past,
Ye may behold your victory won,
And stand complete at last.

282.

Moderate.

EVERMORE.
7s.

Thine for ever:—God of love, Hear us from Thy throne above; Thine for ever may we be, Here and in eternity. A-MEN.

2 Thine for ever:—Lord of life,
Shield us through our earthly strife:
Thou the Life, the Truth, the Way,
Guide us to the realms of day.

3 Thine for ever—O how bless'd
They who find in Thee their rest!
Saviour, Guardian, heavenly Friend,
O defend us to the end.

4 Thine for ever:—Saviour, keep
These Thy frail and trembling sheep;
Safe alone beneath Thy care,
Let us all Thy goodness share.

5 Thine for ever:—Thou our Guide,
All our wants by Thee supplied,
All our sins by Thee forgiven,
Lead us, Lord, from earth to heaven.

* *May be used on other occasions.*

THE CHURCH: HER ORDINANCES AND OFFICES.

283.* DEERHURST. 8s. 7s. D.

Jesus, I my cross have taken, All to leave and follow Thee;
Destitute, despised, forsaken, Thou from hence my all shalt be:
Perish every fond ambition, All I've sought, or hoped, or known;
Yet how rich is my condition! God and heaven are all my own. A-MEN.

2 Man may trouble and distress me,
   'Twill but drive me to Thy breast;
Life with trials hard may press me,
   Heaven will bring me sweeter rest.
O 'tis not in grief to harm me,
   While Thy love is left to me;
O 'twere not in joy to charm me,
   Were that joy unmix'd with Thee.

3 Take, my soul, thy full salvation;
   Rise o'er sin, and fear, and care;
Joy to find in every station
   Something still to do or bear:
Think what Spirit dwells within Thee,
   What a Father's smile is thine;
What a Saviour died to win thee;
   Child of heaven, shouldst thou repine?

4 Haste then on from grace to glory,
   Arm'd by faith, and wing'd by prayer;
Heaven's eternal day's before thee,
   God's own hand shall guide thee there.
Soon shall close thy earthly mission,
   Swift shall pass thy pilgrim days;
Hope soon change to glad fruition,
   Faith to sight, and prayer to praise.

* *May be used on other occasions.*

Burial.

284. (ON THE DEATH OF A CHILD.) MEINHOLD. P. M.

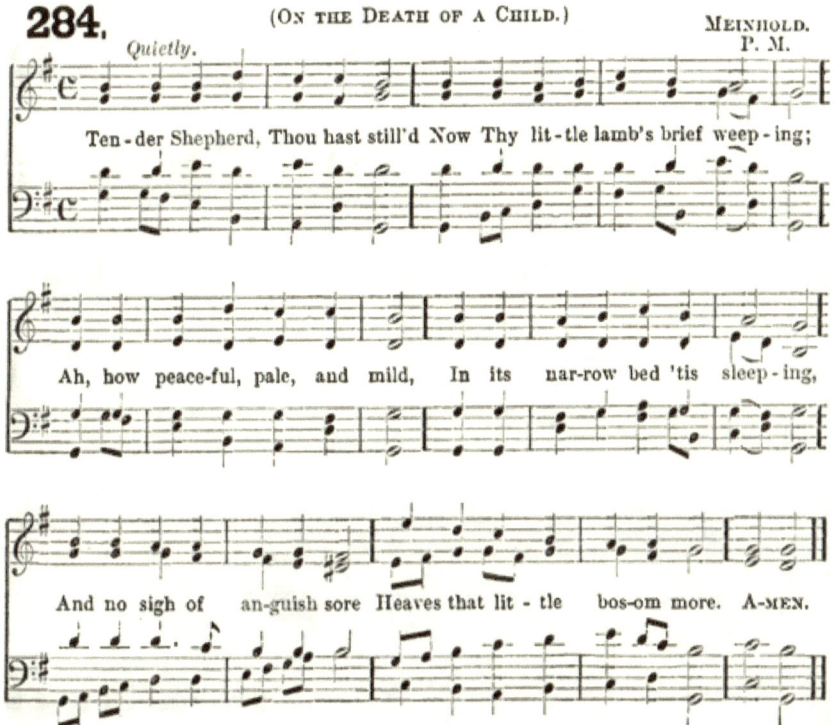

Tender Shepherd, Thou hast still'd Now Thy little lamb's brief weeping;
Ah, how peaceful, pale, and mild, In its narrow bed 'tis sleeping,
And no sigh of anguish sore Heaves that little bosom more. A-MEN.

2 In this world of care and pain,
    Lord, Thou wouldst no longer leave it;
To the sunny, heavenly plain
    Thou dost now with joy receive it;
      Clothed in robes of spotless white,
      Now it dwells with Thee in light.

3 Ah, Lord Jesus, grant that we
    Where it lives may soon be living,
And the lovely pastures see
    That its heavenly food are giving;
      Then the gain of death we prove,
      Tho' Thou take what most we love.

Also the following:

387. Hark! hark, my soul.
379. Jerusalem the golden.
252. Jesus lives, no longer now.
310. Jesus, Lover of my soul.
349. My God, my Father, while I stray.
388. O Paradise, O Paradise.
369. The King of love my Shepherd is.
381. There is a blessed Home.
385. We are but strangers here.
386. We speak of the realms of the blest.
383. Who are these like stars appearing.

285. Missions.

Joyful.   MISSIONARY HYMN. 7s. 6s. D.

From Greenland's icy mountains, From India's coral strand,
Where Afric's sunny fountains Roll down their golden sand;
From many an ancient river, From many a palmy plain,
They call us to deliver Their land from error's chain. A-MEN.

2 What though the spicy breezes
  Blow soft o'er Ceylon's isle;
Though every prospect pleases,
  And only man is vile:
In vain with lavish kindness
  The gifts of God are strewn;
The heathen in his blindness
  Bows down to wood and stone.

3 Shall we, whose souls are lighted
  With wisdom from on high;
Shall we to men benighted
  The lamp of life deny?
Salvation, O salvation,
  The joyful sound proclaim,
Till each remotest nation
  Has learnt Messiah's Name.

4 Waft, waft, ye winds, His story,
  And you, ye waters, roll,
Till, like a sea of glory,
  It spreads from pole to pole:
Till o'er our ransom'd nature
  The Lamb for sinners slain,
Redeemer, King, Creator,
  In bliss returns to reign.

MISSIONS.

286.*
Moderate.   WARRINGTON.   L. M.

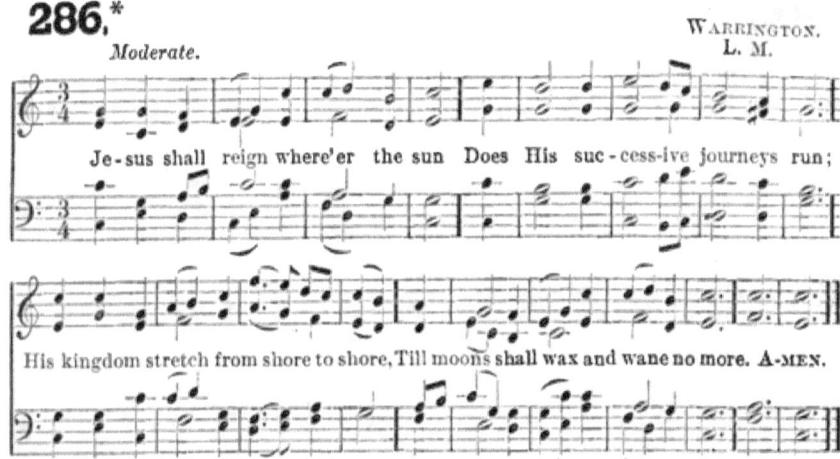

Jesus shall reign where'er the sun Does His successive journeys run; His kingdom stretch from shore to shore, Till moons shall wax and wane no more. A-MEN.

2 To Him shall endless prayer be made,
And praises throng to crown His head;
His Name like sweet perfume shall rise
With every morning sacrifice.

3 People and realms of every tongue
Dwell on His love with sweetest song;
And infant voices shall proclaim
Their early blessings on His Name.

4 Blessings abound where'er He reigns;
The prisoner leaps to burst his chains,
The weary find eternal rest,
And all the sons of want are blest.

5 Let every creature rise and bring
Peculiar honours to our King:
Angels descend with songs again,
And earth repeat the loud Amen.

287.*
Bold.   CALKIN.   L. M.

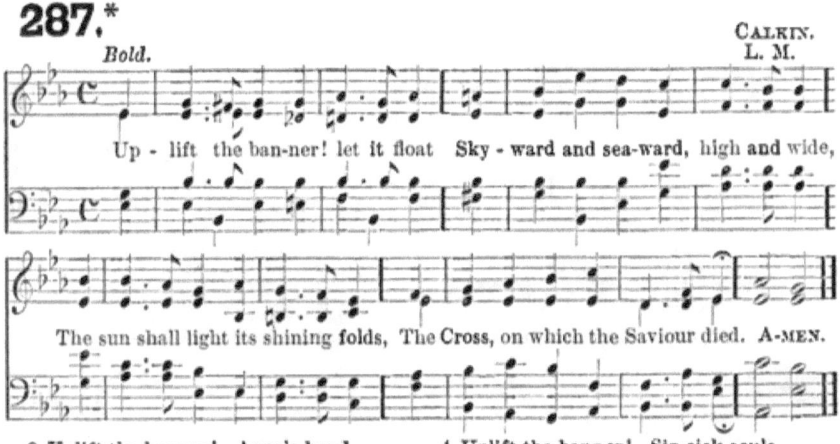

Uplift the banner! let it float Skyward and seaward, high and wide, The sun shall light its shining folds, The Cross, on which the Saviour died. A-MEN.

2 Uplift the banner! Angels bend
In anxious silence o'er the sign;
And vainly seek to comprehend
The wonder of the love divine.

3 Uplift the banner! Heathen lands
Shall see from far the glorious sight,
And nations, gathering at the call,
Their spirits kindle in its light.

4 Uplift the banner! Sin-sick souls,
That sink and perish in the strife,
Shall touch in faith its radiant hems,
And spring immortal into life.

5 Uplift the banner! Let it float
Skyward and seaward high and wide;
Our glory only in the Cross,
Our only hope the Crucified.

* May be used on other occasions.

MISSIONS.

288. *Moderate.* SHILOH. 7s, 6s. D.

With hearts in love a-bounding, Pre-pare we now to sing
A lof-ty theme, re-sound-ing Thy praise, Al-migh-ty King;
Whose love, rich gifts be-stow-ing, Re-deemed the hu-man race;
Whose lips, with zeal o'er-flow-ing, Breathe words of truth and grace. A-MEN.

2 So reign, O God, of Heaven,
  Eternally the same;
And endless praise be given
  To Thy Almighty Name.
Clothed in Thy dazzling brightness
Thy Church on earth behold,
In robe of purest whiteness,
  In raiment wrought in gold.

3 And let each Gentile nation
    Come gladly in her train,
  To share Thy great salvation,
    And join her grateful strain;
  Then ne'er shall note of sadness
  Awake the trembling string;
  One song of joy and gladness
    The ransomed world shall sing.

289. *Moderate.* BARTON. 8s. 7s.

Je-sus calls us; o'er the tu-mult Of our life's wild rest-less sea,

* *May be used on other occasions.*

MISSIONS.

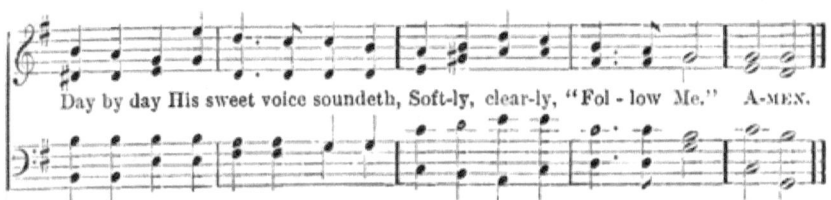

Day by day His sweet voice soundeth, Soft-ly, clear-ly, "Fol-low Me." A-MEN.

2 Jesus calls us, from the evil
  In a world we cannot flee,
From each idol that would keep us,
  Softly, clearly—"Follow Me."

3 Still in joy, and still in sadness,
  We discern His own decree;
Still He calls, in cares and pleasures,
  Softly, clearly—"Follow Me."

4 As Saint Andrew, heard Thee, Saviour,
  By the Lake of Galilee,
May we hear, and help each other
  Day by day to follow Thee.

5 Thou dost call us! May we ever
  To Thy call attentive be;
Give our hearts to Thine obedience,
  Rise, leave all, and follow Thee.

290.*

Earnestly.

POSTWICK.
P. M.

Come, la-bour on! Who dares stand i-dle on the har-vest plain, While all a-round him waves the gol-den grain? And to each ser-vant does the Mas-ter say, "Go, work to-day." A-MEN.

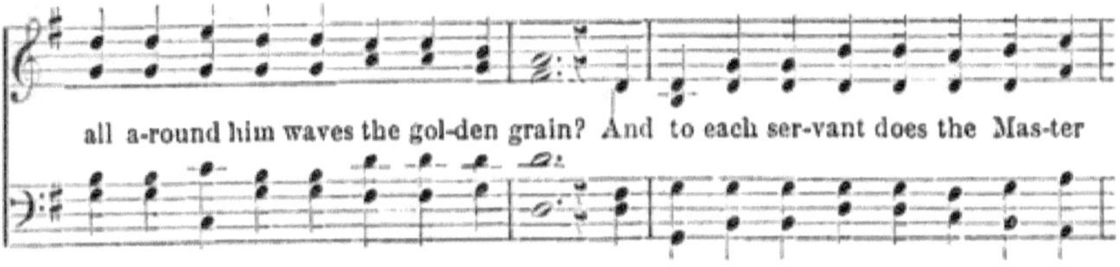

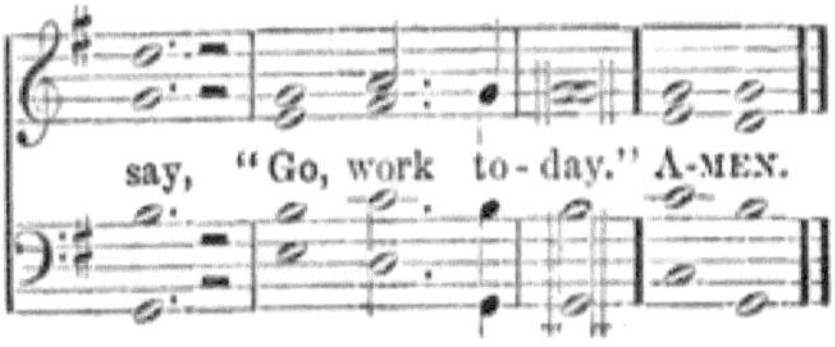

2 Come, labour on!
Claim the high calling angels cannot share,
To young and old the gospel glorious bear;
Redeem the time, its hours too swiftly fly,
  The night draws nigh.

3 Come, labour on!
Away with gloomy doubt and faithless fear!
No arm so weak but may do service here;
By feeblest agents can our God fulfil
  His righteous will.

4 Come, labour on!
The toil is pleasant, the reward is sure,
Blessèd are those who to the end endure;
How full their joy, how deep their rest shall be,
  O Lord, with Thee!

* *May be used on other occasions.*

2 Tell it out among the heathen that the Saviour
    Tell it out! Tell it out!   [reigns.
Tell it out among the nations, bid them burst their
    Tell it out! Tell it out!   [chains.
Tell it out among the weeping ones that Jesus lives;
Tell it out among the weary ones what rest He
    [gives;
Tell it out among the sinners that He came to save,
Tell it out among the dying that He triumphed
    [o'er the grave.

3 Tell it out among the heathen, Jesus reigns above!
    Tell it out! Tell it out!
Tell it out among the nations that His reign is
    Tell it out! Tell it out!   [love!
Tell it out among the highways and the lanes at
    [home;
Let it ring across the mountains and the ocean
    [foam;
Like the sound of many waters let the glad shout be,
Till it echo and re-echo from the islands of the sea.

* *May be used on other occasions.*

292. Offerings.

HOLY OFFERINGS.
P. M.

Moderate.

Ho-ly off'-rings rich and rare, Of-fer-ings of praise and prayer,
Pur-er life and pur-pose high, Clasp-ed hands, up-lift-ed eye,
Low-ly acts of a-do-ra-tion, To the God of our sal-va-tion—
On His al-tar laid we leave them; Christ, present them! God re-ceive them! A-MEN.

2 Vows and longings, hopes and fears,
Broken-hearted sighs and tears,
Dreams of what we yet might be,
Could we cling more close to Thee,
Which, despite of faults and failings,
Help Thy grace in its prevailings—
On Thine altar laid we leave them;
Christ, present them! God receive them!

3 Homage of each humble heart,
Ere we from Thy house depart;
Worship fervent, deep and high,
Adoration, ecstacy;
All that childlike love can render
Of devotion true and tender—
On Thine altar laid we leave them,
Christ, present them! God receive them!

4 To the Father, and the Son,
And the Spirit, Three in One,
Though our mortal weakness raise
Off'rings of imperfect praise,
Yet with hearts bowed down most lowly,
Crying, Holy! Holy! Holy!
On Thine altar laid we leave them;
Christ, present them! God receive them!

OFFERINGS.

293. GRATITUDE. 8s. 4.

O Lord of heaven, and earth, and sea, To Thee all praise and glo-ry be;
How shall we show our love to Thee, Giv-er of all. A-MEN.

2 The golden sunshine, vernal air,
Sweet flowers and fruits Thy love declare;
When harvests ripen, Thou art there,
  Giver of all.
3 For peaceful homes and healthful days,
For all the blessings earth displays,
We owe Thee thankfulness and praise,
  Giver of all.
4 For souls redeemed, for sins forgiven,
For means of grace and hopes of heaven,
What can to Thee, O Lord, be given,
  Who givest all?
5 We lose what on ourselves we spend,
We have as treasure without end,
Whatever, Lord, to Thee we lend,
  Who givest all.
6 Whatever, Lord, we lend to Thee,
Repaid a thousandfold will be;
Then gladly will we give to Thee,
  Giver of all.

294. TELLEFSEN. S. M.

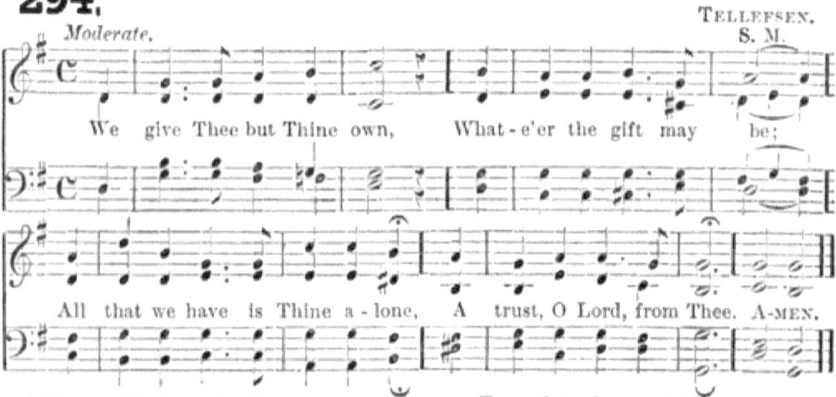

We give Thee but Thine own, What-e'er the gift may be;
All that we have is Thine a-lone, A trust, O Lord, from Thee. A-MEN.

2 May we Thy bounties thus
  As stewards true receive,
And gladly, as Thou blessest us,
  To Thee our first fruits give.
3 O! hearts are bruised and dead,
  And homes are bare and cold,
And lambs for whom the Shepherd bled,
  Are straying from the fold.
4 To comfort and to bless,
  To find a balm for woe,
To tend the lone and fatherless
  Is angel's work below.
5 The captive to release,
  To God the lost to bring,
To teach the way of life and peace,
  It is a Christ-like thing.
6 And we believe Thy word,
  Though dim our faith may be;
Whate'er for Thine we do, O Lord,
  We do it unto Thee.

Thanksgiving and Harvest Home.

295.

S. GEORGE'S WINDSOR.
7s. D.

Come, ye thankful people, come, Raise the song of Harvest-home;
All is safely gathered in, Ere the winter storms begin;
God, our Maker, doth provide For our wants to be supplied;
Come to God's own temple, come, Raise the song of Harvest home. A-MEN.

2 All the world is God's own field,
Fruit unto His praise to yield;
Wheat and tares together sown,
Unto joy or sorrow grown:
First the blade, and then the ear,
Then the full corn shall appear:
Lord of harvest, grant that we
Wholsome grain and pure may be.

3 For the Lord our God shall come,
And shall take His harvest home;
From His field shall in that day
All offences purge away;
Give His angels charge at last
In the fire the tares to cast,
But the fruitful ears to store
In His garner evermore.

4 Even so, Lord, quickly come
To Thy final Harvest-home:
Gather Thou Thy people in,
Free from sorrow, free from sin;
There for ever purified,
In Thy presence to abide:
Come with all Thine angels, come,
Raise the glorious Harvest-home.

THANKSGIVING AND HARVEST HOME.

296. *Joyful.* MONKLAND. 7s.

Praise, O praise our God and King! Hymns of a-dor-a-tion sing; For His mer-cies still en-dure, Ev-er faith-ful, ev-er sure. A-MEN.

2 Praise Him that He made the sun
Day by day his course to run;
  For His mercies still endure,
  Ever faithful, ever sure:

3 And the silver moon by night,
Shining with her gentle light;
  For His mercies still endure,
  Ever faithful, ever sure.

4 Praise Him that He gave the rain
To mature the swelling grain;
  For His mercies still endure,
  Ever faithful, ever sure.

5 And hath bid the fruitful field
Crops of precious increase yield;
  For His mercies still endure,
  Ever faithful, ever sure.

6 Praise Him for our harvest-store,
He hath fill'd the garner-floor;
  For His mercies still endure,
  Ever faithful, ever sure:

7 And for richer Food than this,
Pledge of everlasting bliss;
  For His mercies still endure,
  Ever faithful, ever sure.

8 Glory to our bounteous King!
Glory let creation sing!
  Glory to the Father, Son,
  And blest Spirit, Three in One.

297. *Cheerful.* FARMER. 7s. 6s. D.

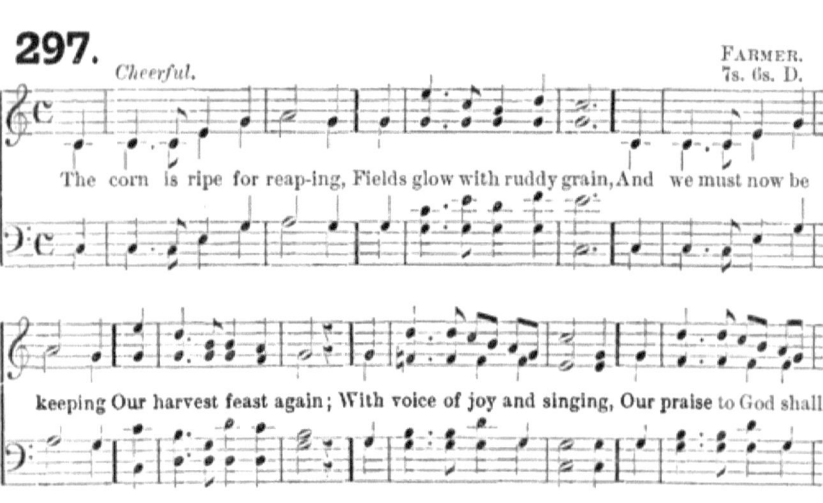

The corn is ripe for reap-ing, Fields glow with ruddy grain, And we must now be keeping Our harvest feast again; With voice of joy and singing, Our praise to God shall rise, Who, whilst the seed was springing, Rain'd blessings from the skies. A-MEN.

2 Thine, Father, is the river
 That maketh rich the earth;
Through Thee, O gracious Giver,
 The buried seed had birth:
Thou on the furrows raining,
 Didst make them soft with show'rs;
The thirsty crops maintaining
 Through silent summer hours.

3 The year, by Thee anointed,
 Is now with goodness crowned,
Robed in the robes appointed,
 With gladness girded round.
We thank Thee for the blessing
 Which meets us on our way,
And come, Thy love confessing,
 With happy hearts to-day.

4 But whilst our *lips* are praising,
 Our *lives* to Thee belong;
With them we would be raising
 A nobler, sweeter song;
One that may sound for ever,
 Whilst earth's great Harvest speeds,
A song of high endeavour
 Rung out in earnest deeds.

National Festivals.

298. Moderate.   AMERICA. 6s. 4s.

God bless our na-tive land! Firm may she ev-er stand, Thro' storm and night; When the wild tempests rave, Ru-ler of wind and wave, Do Thou our country save By Thy great might. A-MEN.

2 For her our prayer shall rise
 To God, above the skies;
  On Him we wait;
Thou who art ever nigh,
Guarding with watchful eye,
 To Thee aloud we cry,
  God save the State.

299. School Festivals.

EMMANUEL.
C. M.

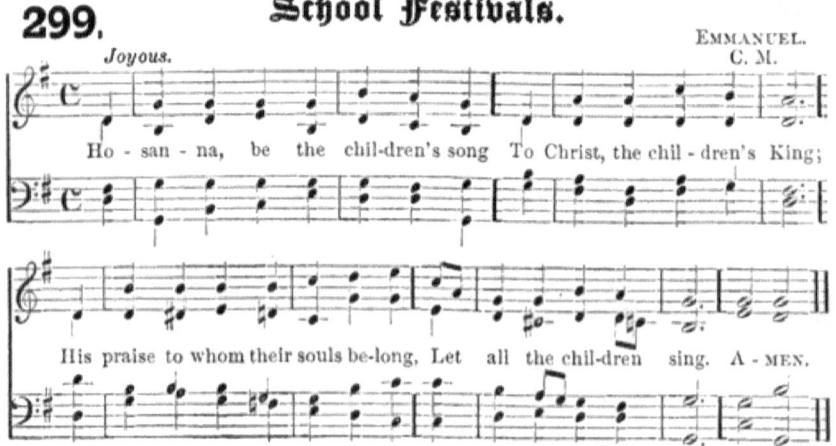

Ho-san-na, be the children's song To Christ, the children's King;
His praise to whom their souls be-long, Let all the children sing. A-MEN.

2 Hosanna, sound from hill to hill,
And spread from plain to plain:
While, louder, sweeter, clearer still,
Woods echo to the strain.

3 Hosanna, on the wings of light
O'er earth and ocean fly;
Till morn to eve, and noon to night,
And heaven to earth reply.

4 Hosanna, then, our song shall be,
Hosanna to our King;
This is the children's jubilee,
Let all the children sing.

300.

S. BEES.
7s.

Lord, this day Thy children meet, In Thy courts with willing feet;
Un-to Thee this day they raise, Grate-ful hearts in hymns of praise. A-MEN.

2 Not alone the day of rest
With Thy worship shall be blest;
In our pleasure and our glee
Lord, we would remember Thee.

3 Help us unto Thee to pray,
Hallowing our happy day;
From Thy presence thus to win
Hearts all pure and free from sin.

4 All our pleasures here below,
Saviour, from Thy mercy flow;
Little children Thou dost love;
Draw our hearts to Thee above.

5 Make, O Lord, our childhood shine
With all lowly grace, like Thine;
Then, through all eternity,
We shall live in heaven with Thee.

SCHOOL FESTIVALS.

301.*   Joyous.   SCHUMANN. C. M. with Chorus.

Let ev' ry heart rejoice and sing, Let cho-ral anthems rise; Let old and young to-ge-ther bring To God their sa-cri-fice.

CHORUS.

For He is good; the Lord is good, And kind are all His ways; With songs and honours sounding loud, The Lord Jehovah praise.

While the rocks and the rills, while the vales and the hills, A glo-rious an-them raise, Let all pro-long their grateful song, And the God of our fathers praise. A-MEN.

2 He bids the sun to rise and set;
In heaven His power is known;
And earth subdued to Him shall yet
Bow low before His throne.
   CHO.— For He is good, &c.

Also the following:

329. Above the clear blue sky   **327.** Come, praise your Lord and Saviour.
464. Brightly gleams our banner.   **324.** Come sing with holy gladness.
326. Hosanna we sing, like the children.   **406.** We plough the fields and scatter.

* *May be used on other occasions.*

General Hymns.

Holy Scriptures.

302.

Moderate.   ZOAN. 7s. 6s. D.

O word of God incarnate, O wisdom from on high,
O truth unchang'd, unchanging, O Light of our dark sky!
We praise Thee for the radiance That from the hallow'd page,
A lantern to our footsteps, Shines on from age to age. A-MEN.

2 The Church from her dear Master
  Received the gift divine,
And still that light she lifteth
  O'er all the earth to shine.
It is the golden casket
  Where gems of truth are **stored**,
It is the heaven-drawn picture
  Of Christ the living Word.

3 It floateth like a banner
  Before God's host unfurl'd,
It shineth like a beacon
  Above the darkling world;
It is the chart and compass
  That o'er life's surging sea,
Mid mists, and rocks, and quicksands
  Still guide, O Christ, to Thee.

4 O make Thy Church, dear **Saviour**
  A lamp of burnish'd gold,
To bear before the nations
  Thy true light as of old;
O teach Thy wandering pilgrims
  By this their path to trace,
Till, clouds and darkness ended,
  They see Thee face to face.

GENERAL HYMNS.

303.
Joyful.

CHESTERFIELD.
C. M.

Fa-ther of mer-cies! in Thy word What end-less glo-ry shines! For e - ver be Thy Name a-dored For these ce-les-tial lines. A-MEN.

2 Here the Redeemer's welcome voice,
Spreads heavenly peace around;
And life and everlasting joys
Attend the blissful sound.

3 O may these heavenly pages be
My ever dear delight;
And still new beauties may I see,
And still increasing light.

4 Divine Instructor, gracious Lord,
Be Thou for ever near:
Teach me to love Thy sacred word,
And view my Saviour there.

304.
Cheerful.

BATTISHILL.
7s.

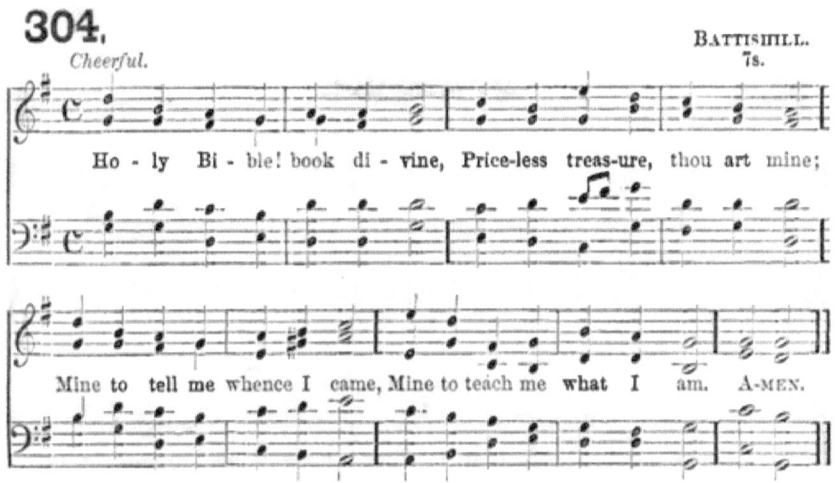

Ho - ly Bi - ble! book di - vine, Price-less treas-ure, thou art mine; Mine to tell me whence I came, Mine to teach me what I am. A-MEN.

2 Mine, to chide me when I rove;
Mine, to show a Saviour's love;
Mine art thou to guide my feet,
Mine, to judge, condemn, acquit.

3 Mine, to comfort in distress,
If the Holy Spirit bless;
Mine, to show by living faith
Man can triumph over death.

4 Mine to tell of joys to come,
Light and life beyond the **tomb**;
Holy Bible, book divine.
Priceless treasure, thou art mine.

305. (BEFORE CATECHISING.) S. CATHERINE. 8s. 7s.

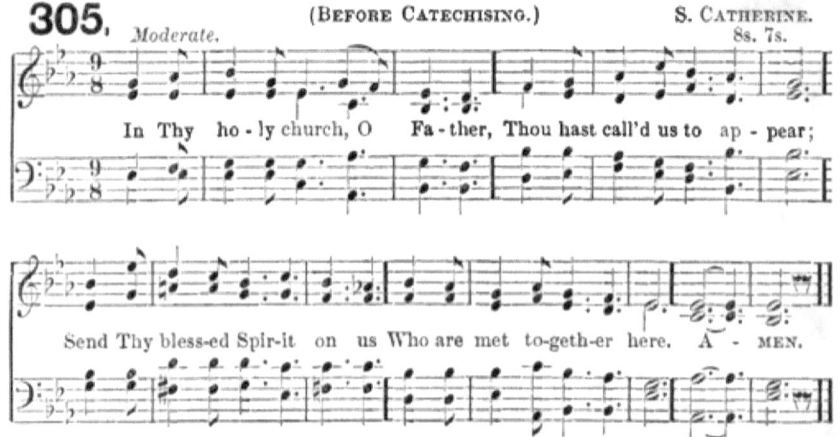

In Thy holy church, O Father, Thou hast call'd us to appear;
Send Thy blessed Spirit on us Who are met together here. A-MEN.

2 Much there is, far past our knowing,
   Written in Thy holy word,
May we here receive instruction
   In its meaning, Blessèd Lord!

3 Not for human praise or notice,
   Not our cleverness to show,
But because Thou, Lord, art honoured
   When Thy children serve Thee so.

4 We are daily growing older,
   Make us wiser day by day,
Daily knowing Jesus better,
   As the Life, the Truth, the Way!

5 Here, O Lord, we see Thee "darkly,"
   Here we know Thee but "in part;"
May we, gracious Lord, in Heaven,
   See Thee, know Thee, as Thou art!

306. Redemption. YARNDLEY. 7s.

Jesus Christ hath lived and died, What is all the world beside;
This to know is all I need, This to know is life indeed. A-MEN.

2 Other wisdom seek I none,
Teach me this and this alone,
Christ for me has lived and died,
Christ for me was crucified.

307.

Moderate. ADORATION. 6s. 5s. D.

Hail the Cross of Jesus; Lift it up on high: Hail the mighty Signal, Pointing to the sky! Hail the Guide of pilgrims, Through the desert drear! Hail the Sign of Jesus, Chasing far our fear! A-MEN.

2 God forbid we glory,
   Save in that blest Sign—
Sign of Him who saved us
   Through His love divine.
Hail the Cross of Jesus,
   Lifted up on high!
Hail the mighty Signal,
   Pointing to the sky!

3 Stands the Cross of Jesus
   Foremost in the fight,
Drawing ever all men
   By Its wondrous might.
Hail the Cross of Jesus,
   Lifted up on high!
Hail the mighty Standard,
   Pointing to the sky!

4 See! It moveth onward:
   Gladly follow we;
Wheresoe'er It goeth
   Should Christ's soldiers be.
Hail the Cross of Jesus,
   Lifted up on high!
Hail the mighty Standard,
   Pointing to the sky!

5 Lo! It reacheth Jordan,
   Cleaves the surging wave,
Lighteth up the portals
   Of the opening grave.
Hail the Cross of Jesus,
   Lift It up on high!
Hail the guide of pilgrims,
   Pointing to the sky!

6 Then, O then, what glory
   Shines upon our eyes,
From the sunny pastures
   Spread in Paradise!
Lo! the Cross of Jesus,
   Pointing to the sky,
Hath His children guided
   Home to victory.

308.

Moderate.

TRUST.
8s. 7s.

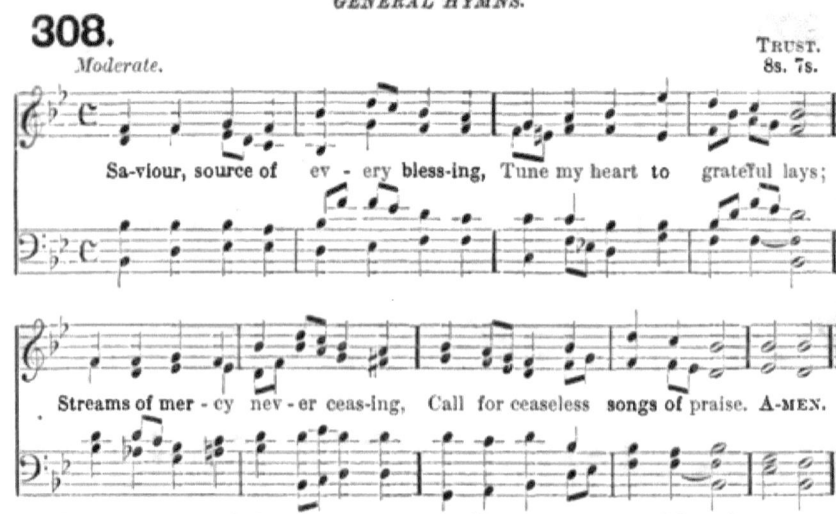

Saviour, source of every blessing, Tune my heart to grateful lays; Streams of mercy never ceasing, Call for ceaseless songs of praise. A-MEN.

2 Teach me some melodious measure,
   Sung by raptured saints above;
   Fill my soul with sacred pleasure,
   While I sing redeeming love.

3 Thou did'st seek me when a stranger,
   Wandering from the fold of God;
   Thou to save my soul from danger,
   Didst redeem me with Thy blood.

4 By Thy hand restored, defended,
   Safe through life thus far I've come;
   Safe, O Lord, when life is ended,
   Bring me to my heavenly home.

309.

Quietly.

S. RAPHAEL.
7s. 5.

Jesus, when He left the sky, And for sinners came to die, In His mercy passed not by Little ones like me. A-MEN.

2 Mothers then the Saviour sought
   In the places where He taught,
   And to Him their children brought—
      Little ones like me.

3 Did the Saviour say them nay?
   No, He kindly bade them stay;
   Suffered none to turn away
      Little ones like me.

4 'Twas for them His life He gave,
   To redeem them from the grave;
   Jesus able is to save
      Little ones like me.

5 Children, then, should love Him too,
   Strive His holy will to do,
   Pray to Him, and praise Him too—
      Little ones like me.

Faith.

310. *Moderate.* HOLLINGSIDE. 7s. D.

Je-sus, Lov-er of my soul, Let me to Thy bo-som fly,
While the near-er wa-ters roll, While the tem-pest still is high;
Hide me, O my Sa-viour, hide, Till the storm of life be past;
Safe in-to the ha-ven guide, O re-ceive my soul at last. A-MEN.

2 Other refuge have I none,
   Hangs my helpless soul on Thee;
Leave, ah! leave me not alone,
   Still support and comfort me:
All my trust on Thee is stay'd;
   All my help from Thee I bring;
Cover my defenceless head
   With the shadow of Thy wing.

3 Plenteous grace with Thee is found,
   Grace to cover all my sin;
Let the healing streams abound,
   Make and keep me pure within:
Thou of life the fountain art,
   Freely let me take of Thee:
Spring Thou up within my heart,
   Rise to all eternity.

311.

Quietly.

REDHEAD, No. 76.
Six 7s.

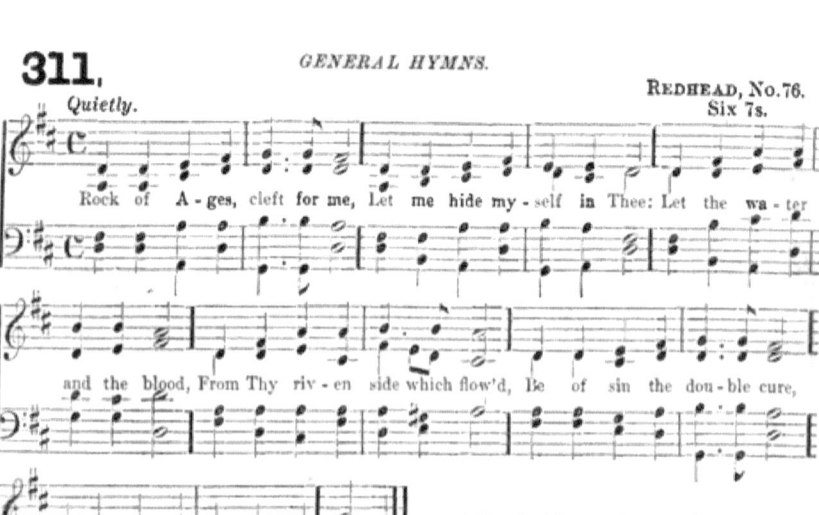

Rock of Ages, cleft for me, Let me hide myself in Thee: Let the water and the blood, From Thy riven side which flow'd, Be of sin the double cure,

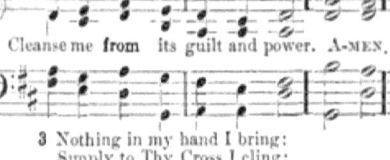

Cleanse me from its guilt and power. A-MEN.

2 Not the labours of my hands
Can fulfil Thy law's demands;
Could my zeal no respite know,
Could my tears for ever flow,
All for sin could not atone,
Thou must save, and Thou alone.

3 Nothing in my hand I bring:
Simply to Thy Cross I cling;
Naked, come to Thee for dress;
Helpless, look to Thee for grace:
Foul, I to the fountain fly;
Wash me, Saviour, or I die.

4 While I draw this fleeting breath,
When my eyelids close in death,
When I soar through tracts unknown,
See Thee on Thy judgment throne,
Rock of Ages, cleft for me,
Let me hide myself in Thee.

312.

Moderate.

S. PETER.
C. M.

How sweet the Name of Jesus sounds In a believer's ear! It soothes his sorrows, heals his wounds, And drives away his fear. A-MEN.

2 It makes the wounded spirit whole,
  And calms the troubled breast;
'Tis manna to the hungry soul,
  And to the weary rest.

3 Dear Name, the rock on which I build
  My shield and hiding-place,
My never-failing treasury, filled
  With boundless stores of grace.

4 Jesus! my Shepherd, Husband, Friend,
  My Prophet, Priest and King,
My Lord, my life, my way, my end,—
  Accept the praise I bring.

5 Weak is the effort of my heart,
  And cold my warmest thought;
But when I see Thee as Thou art,
  I'll praise Thee as I ought.

6 Till then I would Thy love proclaim
  With every fleeting breath;
And may the music of Thy Name
  Refresh my soul in death.

GENERAL HYMNS.

Prayer.

313. Moderate. GARDINER. 7s. 6s. D.

Go when the morn-ing shi-neth, Go when the moon is bright;
Go when the day de-cli-neth, Go in the hush of night;
Go with pure heart and feel-ing, Cast earth-ly thoughts a-way,
And in thy cham-ber kneel-ing, Do thou in se-cret pray. A-MEN.

2 Remember all who love thee;
  All who are loved by thee;
Pray, too, for those who hate thee,
  If any such there be.
Then for thyself in meekness,
  A blessing humbly claim;
And link with each petition
  Thy great Redeemer's Name.

3 But if 'tis e'er denied thee
    In solitude to pray,
  Should holy thoughts come o'er thee,
    When friends are round the way—
  E'en then, in silence breathing,
    The spirit, rais'd above,
  Will reach the throne of glory,
    Of mercy, truth, and love.

4 When'er thou pin'st in sickness
    Before His foot-stool fall;
  Remember in thy gladness,
    His love who gave thee all.
  Oh! not a joy or blessing
    With this we can compare,
  The power which He has given,
    To approach His throne in prayer.

314.

Moderate. EMMAUS. C. M.

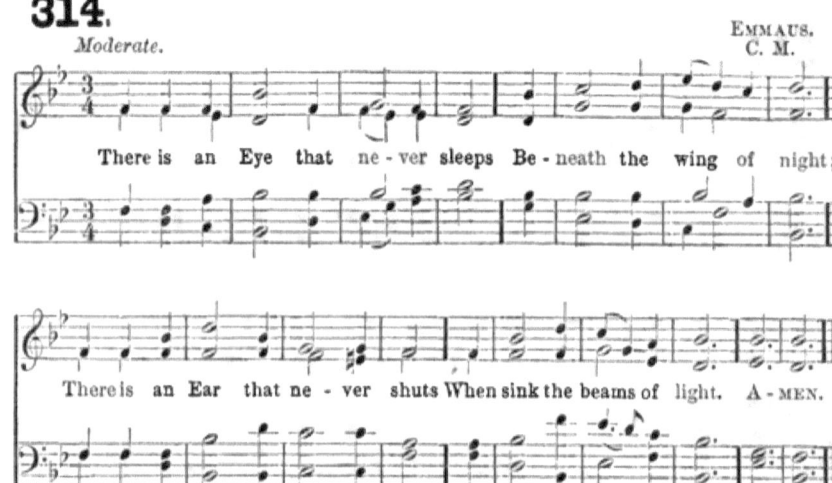

There is an Eye that ne-ver sleeps Be-neath the wing of night;
There is an Ear that ne-ver shuts When sink the beams of light. A-MEN.

2 There is an Arm that never tires
  When human strength gives way;
  There is a Love that never fails,
  When earthly loves decay.

3 That Eye is fixed on Seraph throngs;
  That Arm upholds the sky;
  That Ear is filled with Angel songs;
  That Love is throned on high.

4 But there's a power which man can wield,
  When mortal aid is vain,
  That Eye, that Arm, that Love to reach,
  That listening Ear to gain.

5 That power is Prayer, which soars on high
  Through Jesus to the throne,
  And moves the Hand which moves the world
  To bring salvation down.

315.

Moderate. PRAYER. 8s. 6s. 8s.

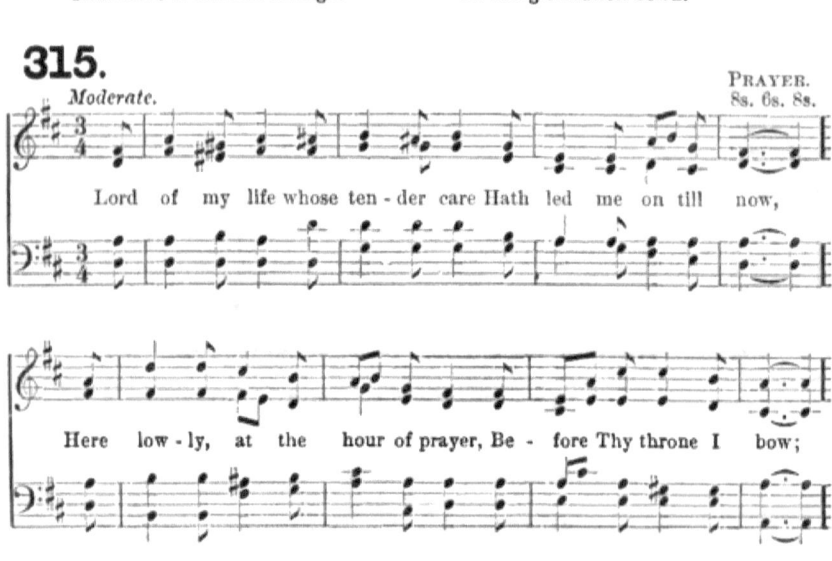

Lord of my life whose ten-der care Hath led me on till now,
Here low-ly, at the hour of prayer, Be-fore Thy throne I bow;

GENERAL HYMNS.

I bless Thy gracious hand, and pray For-giveness for an-oth-er day. A-MEN.

2 Oh, may I daily, hourly strive
 In heavenly grace to grow;
To Thee and to Thy glory live,
 Dead to all else below;
Tread in the path my Saviour trod,
Though thorny, yet the path of God.

3 With prayer, my humble praise I bring,
 For mercies day by day:
Lord, teach my heart, Thy love to sing,
 Lord, teach me how to pray.
All that I am and have, to Thee
I offer through eternity.

316.

SURSUM CORDA.
7s. 5s. 7s.

Moderate.

Fold thy hands in prayer, my child, Gent-ly bow thine head;
To our glo-rious God in heaven Chil-dren's prayers are said;
And the An-gels pure and fair Bow be-fore His pres-ence there. A-MEN.

The last two lines to be sung more slowly.

2 Close thine eyes in prayer, my child,
 Close thy roving eyes;
Wandering looks would fill thine heart
 With all vanities.
Kneeling to the King of kings,
Would thou gaze on earthly things?

3 Guard thine heart in prayer, my child,
 Closely guard thine heart,
Lest with holy, earnest thoughts
 Bad ones have their part:
When we to our Father pray
Let us mean the things we say.

317.

THE WHITE DOVE.
P. M.

Not too slowly.

There sitteth a Dove, so white and fair, Upon a lily spray; And she listens when to our Saviour dear The little children pray. Lightly she spreads her friendly wings, And speeds to heaven her way, And to the heavenly Father bears The prayers which the children say, The prayers which the children say. A-MEN.

2 And downward she comes from heaven's gate,
   And brings—that Dove so mild—
From the Father in heaven, who hears her speak,
   A grace for every child.
Children, lift up your faithful prayers,
   It hears whate'er you say,
That holy Dove, so white and fair,
   That sits on the lily spray,
   That sits on the lily spray.

318.

Praise.

Joyful.

VIENNA.
7s.

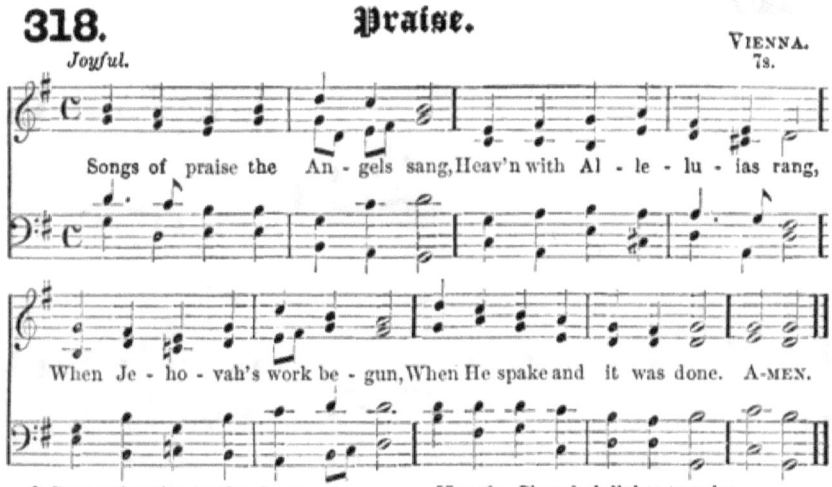

Songs of praise the Angels sang, Heav'n with Alleluias rang,
When Jehovah's work begun, When He spake and it was done. A-MEN.

2 Songs of praise awoke the morn,
When the Prince of Peace was born;
Songs of praise arose, when He
Captive led captivity.

3 Heaven and earth must pass away;
Songs of praise shall crown that day:
God will make new heavens and earth;
Songs of praise shall hail their birth.

4 And shall man alone be dumb
Till that glorious kingdom come?

No; the Church delights to raise
Psalms, and hymns, and songs of praise.

5 Saints below, with heart and voice,
Still in songs of praise rejoice;
Learning here, by faith and love,
Songs of praise to sing above.

6 Borne upon their latest breath,
Songs of praise shall conquer death;
Then, amidst eternal joy,
Songs of praise their powers employ.

319.

Moderate.

S. WINIFRED.
8s. 7s.

Humble praises, holy Jesus, Infant voices raise to Thee:
In Thy mercy O receive us! Suffer us Thy lambs to be. A-MEN.

2 Blessed Jesus! Thou hast bidden
Babes like us to come to Thee,
Though by Thy disciples chidden,
Thou didst tell them not to flee.

3 Saviour, condescend to feed us;
Richly let Thy mercy flow:
Send Thy Spirit, blessed Jesus!
Light and Life on us bestow.

320.

MILES LANE.
C. M.

Bold.

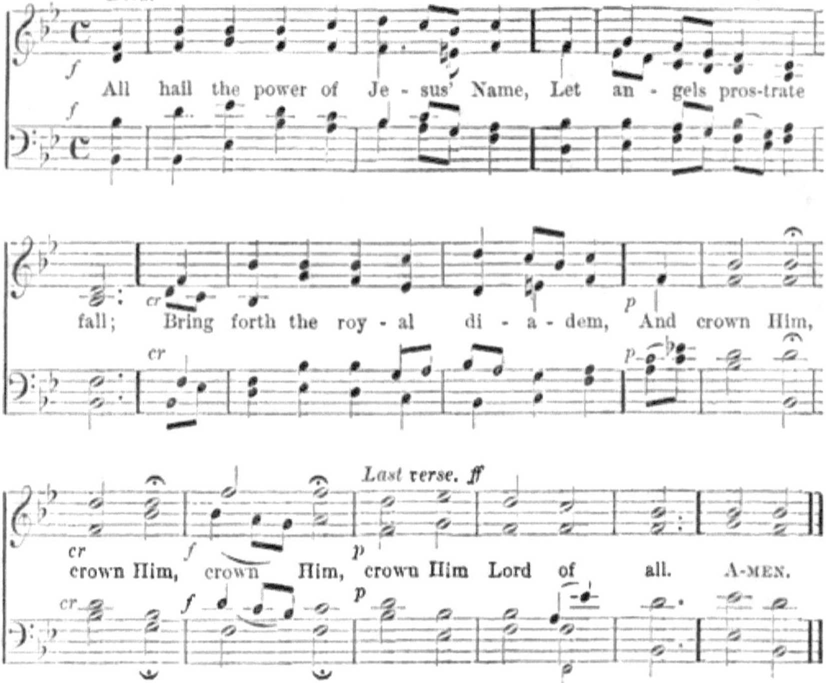
f
All hail the power of Je - sus' Name, Let an - gels pros-trate
fall; cr Bring forth the roy - al di - a - dem, p And crown Him,
Last verse. ff
cr crown Him, f crown Him, p crown Him Lord of all. A-MEN.

2 Crown Him, ye martyrs of our God,
Who from His altar call;
Extol the Stem of Jesse's rod,
And crown Him Lord of all.

3 Hail Him, the Heir of David's line,
Whom David, Lord did call;
The God Incarnate! Man divine,
And crown Him Lord of all!

4 Ye seed of Israel's chosen race,
Ye ransomed of the fall,
Hail Him who saves you by His grace,
And crown Him Lord of all.

5 Sinners, whose love can ne'er forget
The wormwood and the gall,
Go, spread your trophies at His feet,
And crown Him Lord of all.

6 Let every kindred, every tribe,
On this terrestrial ball,
To Him all Majesty ascribe,
And crown Him Lord of all.

321.

DULCE CARMEN.
8s. 7s. Six lines.

Bold.

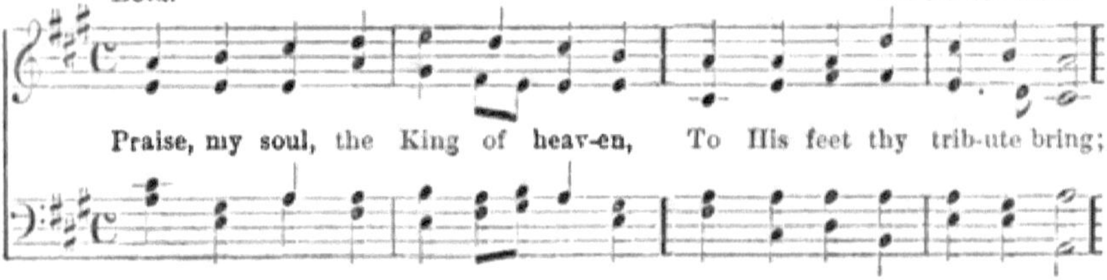
Praise, my soul, the King of heav-en, To His feet thy trib-ute bring;

GENERAL HYMNS.

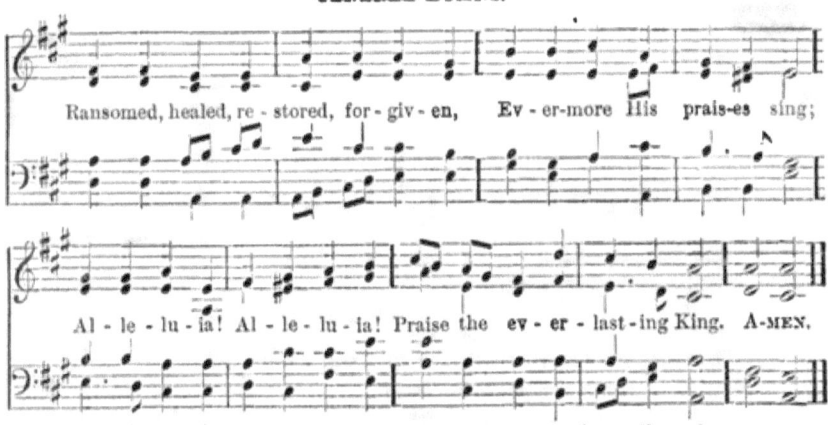

Ransomed, healed, restored, forgiven,
Evermore His praises sing;
Alleluia! Alleluia! Praise the everlasting King. A-MEN.

2 Praise Him for His grace and favour
   To our fathers in distress;
 Praise Him still the same as ever,
   Slow to chide, and swift to bless;
 Alleluia! Alleluia!
   Glorious in His faithfulness.

3 Father-like, He tends and spares us,
   Well our feeble frame He knows;
 In His hands He gently bears us,
   Rescues us from all our foes;
 Alleluia! Alleluia!
   Widely yet His mercy flows.

4 Angels in the height adore Him!
   Ye behold Him face to face;
 Saints triumphant bow before Him!
   Gathered in from every race:
 Alleluia! Alleluia!
   Praise with us the God of grace.

322.

CHESALON.
C. M.

Joyous.

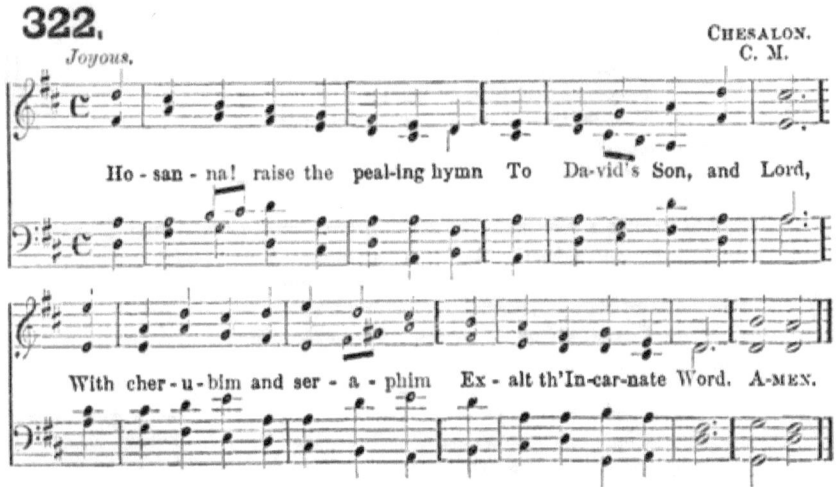

Hosanna! raise the pealing hymn
To David's Son, and Lord,
With cherubim and seraphim
Exalt th'Incarnate Word. A-MEN.

2 Hosanna! Lord, our feeble tongue
   No lofty strains can raise,
 But Thou wilt not despise the young
   Who feebly sing Thy praise.

3 Hosanna! Master, may we bring
   Our offerings to Thy throne:
 Not gold, nor myrrh, nor mortal thing,
   But hearts to be Thine own.

4 Hosanna! once Thy gracious ear
   Approved a youthful throng:
 Be gracious now, and deign to hear
   Our humble, grateful song.

5 O Saviour, if redeemed by Thee,
   Thy Temple we behold,
 Thy praises through eternity
   We'll sing to harps of gold.

323.

Joyful. TROYTE, NO. 2.

Al - le - lu - ia! Alle - lu - ia! A-MEN.

THE strain up*raise* of joy and *praise*, Alle | luia!
To the glory of their King
Shall the *ransom*'d | people sing, ‖ *A*lle- | luia! ‖ *A*lle- | luia!
And the *choirs* that | dwell on high,
Shall re-*echo* | through the sky, ‖ *A*lle- | luia! ‖ *A*lle- | luia!

They in the *rest* of | Paradise who dwell,
The blessèd ones with *joy* the | chorus swell, ‖ *A*lle- | luia! ‖ *A*lle- | luia!
The planets beaming *on* their | heavenly way,
The shining constella*tions*, | join and say, ‖ *A*lle- | luia! ‖ *A*lle- | luia!

    Ye clouds that onward sweep,
      Ye *winds* on | pinions light,
    Ye thunders, echoing loud and deep,
      Ye light*nings*, | wildly bright,
    In *sweet* con- | sent unite ‖ *your* Alle- | luia!

    Ye floods and ocean billows,
      Ye *storms* and | winter snow,
    Ye days of cloudless beauty,
      Hoar *frost* and | summer glow:
    Ye groves that wave in spring,
    And *glorious* | forests, sing, ‖ *A*lle- | luia!

First let the birds, with *painted* | plumage gay,
Exalt their great Crea*tor's* | praise, and say, ‖ *A*lle- | luia! ‖ *A*lle- | luia!
Then let the beasts of *earth*, with | varying strain,
Join in creation's *hymn* and | cry again, ‖ *A*lle- | luia! ‖ *A*lle- | luia!

Here let the mountains thunder *forth* so- | norous, ‖ *A*lle- | luia!
There let the valleys sing in *gentler* | chorus, ‖ *A*lle- | luia!
Thou jubilant a*byss* of | ocean, cry, ‖ *A*lle- | luia!
Ye tracts of earth and *conti*- | nents, reply ‖ *A*lle- | luia!

To God, who *all* cre- | ation made,
The frequent *hymn* be | duly paid: ‖ *A*lle- | luia! ‖ *A*lle- | luia!
This is the strain, the eternal strain, the **Lord** Al- | mighty loves: ‖ *A*lle- | luia!
This is the song, the heavenly song, that *Christ*, the | King, approves: ‖ *A*lle- | luia!
Wherefore we sing, both heart and *voice* a- | waking, ‖ *A*lle- | luia!
And children's voices echo, an*swer* | making, ‖ *A*lle- | luia!

    Now from all *men* | be outpoured
    Allelu*ia* | to the Lord;—
    With Allelu*ia* | evermore
    The Son and Sp*irit* | we adore.
    Praise be *done* to the | Three in One,
      *A*lle- | luia! ‖ *A*lle- | luia! ‖ *A*lle- | luia! ‖

324.

ELLACOMBE.
7s. 6s. D.

Joyous.

Come sing with ho-ly glad-ness, High al-le-lu-ias sing,
Up-lift your loud ho-san-nas, To Je-sus, Lord and King;
Sing, boys, in joy-ful cho-rus Your hymn of praise to-day,
And sing, ye gen-tle maid-ens, Your sweet re-sponsive lay. A-MEN.

2 'Tis good for boys and maidens
   Sweet hymns to Christ to sing,
'Tis meet that children's voices
   Should praise the children's King;
For Jesus is salvation,
   And glory, grace, and rest;
To babe and boy and maiden
   The one Redeemer blest.

3 O boys be strong in Jesus,
   To toil for Him is gain,
And Jesus wrought with Joseph,
   With chisel, saw, and plane;
O maidens live for Jesus,
   Who was a maiden's Son;
Be patient, pure and gentle,
   And perfect grace begun.

4 Soon in the golden City
   The boys and girls shall play,
And through the dazzling mansions
   Rejoice in endless day;
O Christ, prepare Thy children
   With that triumphant throng
To pass the burnished portals,
   And sing th' eternal song.

325.

TRISAGION.
6s. 5s. D.

Moderate.

Round the throne of glo - ry, Cir-cling che-ru - bim Raise their hal-low'd voi - ces, In the sa - cred hymn. True their notes are blend - ed, Loud the strains they raise, Through the courts e - ter - nal, Rolls the song of praise; Ho - ly, Ho - ly, Ho - ly, Bless-ed Tri - ni - ty, Heav'n and earth are fill - ed With Thy Ma-jes - ty! A-MEN.

2 Earth hath many voices
  Blended with the sea,
Pealing forth the anthem
  Of their praise to Thee;
Night and day it rises,
  Mingling with the song
Which these sacred singers
  Endlessly prolong.
    Holy, Holy, Holy, &c.

3 Where the city steeple
    And the village spire
  Point each faithful toiler
    To His soul's desire,
  There in faith we gather,
    There our homage pay,
  Prayer and praise we offer
    On each hallowed day.
      Holy, Holy, Holy, &c.

4 One our heavenly Father.
    Round whose throne we meet,
  One our great Redeemer,
    One our Paraclete;
  Bound in living union,
    By one holy tie,
  In Thy sacred presence,
    Triune God, we cry:
      Holy, Holy, Holy, &c.

5 Raise the hymn of triumph!
    Heaven and earth and sea,
  Roll your thousand voices
    Forth in harmony!
  Voices young and aged,
    Voices grand in song,
  Blend them, singers holy,
    Loud the strain prolong.
      Holy, Holy, Holy, &c.

GENERAL HYMNS.

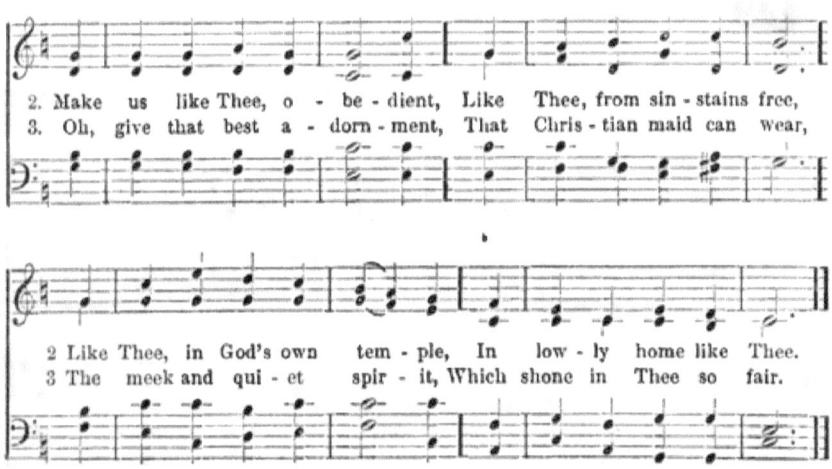

2. Make us like Thee, o-be-dient, Like Thee, from sin-stains free,
3. Oh, give that best a-dorn-ment, That Chris-tian maid can wear,

2 Like Thee, in God's own tem-ple, In low-ly home like Thee.
3 The meek and qui-et spir-it, Which shone in Thee so fair.

328.
Moderate. BERNARD. P. M.

Glo-ry to the Bless-ed Je-sus! Who for us was born, In the sta-ble, cold and poor, On glad Christ-mas morn. A-MEN.

2 Glory to the Blessèd Jesus!
  Who was crucified
 On Good Friday for our sins;
  Loving us He died.

3 Glory to the Blessèd Jesus!
  Who for sinners lay
 In the tomb, and rose upon
  Happy Easter Day.

4 Glory to the Blessèd Jesus!
  He who is our Way

Went up in a cloud to heaven
  On Ascension Day.

5 Glory to the Blessèd Jesus!
  Who at Whitsuntide
 Sent His Holy Spirit down
  With us to abide.

6 Glory to the Blessèd Jesus!
  We will praise His love,
 All our days on earth below,
  And for aye above.

2 But God from infant tongues
　On earth receiveth praise;
　We then our cheerful songs
　　In sweet accord will raise:
　　　Alleluia!
　　We too will sing
　　To God our King
　　　Alleluia!

3 O Blessed Lord, Thy Truth
　To us Thy babes impart,
　And teach us in our youth
　　To know Thee as Thou art.
　　　Alleluia!
　　Then shall we sing
　　To God our King
　　　Alleluia!

4 O may Thy holy Word
　Spread all the world around;
　And all with one accord
　　Uplift the joyful sound,
　　　Alleluia!
　　All then shall sing
　　To God their King
　　　Alleluia!

330.

RISEHOLME.
8s. 7s. D.

There is no name so sweet on earth, No name so dear in hea-ven,
As that be-fore His won-drous birth To Christ the Sa-viour giv-en.
We love to sing un-to our King, And hail Him bles-sed Je-sus!
For there's no word ear ev-er heard, So dear, so sweet as Je-sus. A-MEN.

2 'Twas Gabriel first that did proclaim
 To His most blessèd Mother
That Name which now and evermore
 We praise above all other.
  We love to sing unto our King,
   And hail Him blessèd Jesus!
  For there's no word ear ever heard,
   So dear, so sweet as Jesus!

3 And when He hung upon the Cross,
 They wrote this Name above Him,
That all might see the reason we
 For evermore must love Him.
  We love to sing unto our King,
   And hail Him blessèd Jesus!
  For there's no word ear ever heard,
   So dear, so sweet as Jesus!

4 So now upon His Father's throne
 Almighty to release us
From sin and pains, He ever reigns
 The Prince and Saviour Jesus!
  We love to sing unto our King,
   And hail Him blessèd Jesus!
  For there's no word ear ever heard,
   So dear, so sweet as Jesus.

331.

Joyous. INNOCENTS. 7s.

God eternal, mighty King, Unto Thee our praise we bring;
All the earth doth worship Thee, We amid the throng would be. A-MEN.

2 Holy, Holy, Holy! cry
  Angels round Thy Throne on high;
  Lord of all the heavenly powers,
  Be the same loud anthem ours.

3 Glorified Apostles raise
  Night and day continual praise;
  Hast Thou not a mission too
  For Thy children here to do?

4 With the Prophets' goodly line
  We in mystic bond combine;
  For Thou hast to babes revealed
  Things that to the wise were sealed.

5 Martyrs, in a noble host,
  Of the cross are heard to boast;
  O that we our cross may bear,
  And a crown of glory wear.

6 All Thy Church in heaven and earth,
  Jesus, hail Thy spotless birth;
  Own the God who all has made,
  And the Spirit's soothing aid.

332.

S. SAVIOUR. 6s. 5s.

Moderate.

Jesus, high in glory, Lend a listening ear,
When we bow before Thee, Children's praises hear. A-MEN.

2 Though Thou art so holy,
  Heaven's Almighty King,
  Thou wilt stoop to listen,
  When Thy praise we sing.

3 We are little children,
  Weak and apt to stray;
  Saviour, guide and keep us
  In the heavenly way.

4 Save us, Lord, from sinning,
  Watch us day by day;
  Help us now to love Thee;
  Take our sins away:

5 Then, when Jesus calls us
  To our heavenly Home,
  We would gladly answer,
  "Saviour, Lord, we come."

GENERAL HYMNS.

333. HENRY.
Joyous. 8s. 7s. D.

Alleluia! thanks and glory, High adoring praise we bring,
Hearts and voices both uplifted To our crown'd and conquering King!
Children in the temple prais'd Thee, Thou the children's praise didst own;
Now let children's praise accepted Reach Thee on Thy radiant throne. A-MEN.

2 Alleluia! King, Redeemer,
　Saviour of our Eden lost!
Though but children, sinful children,
　We are Thine by priceless cost;
Though but children, weak and wayward,
　Yet through Thy redeeming love
Washed, forgiven, sealed for glory,
　We shall reign with Thee above.

3 Alleluia! Oh! the mercy!
　Oh! the goodness, love, and grace!
Mercy rich, and free, and glorious,
　Passing bound of time and space!
Let Thy children sing Hosanna,
　Sing and say, in faith divine,
"Such a Saviour, such salvation,
　Such eternal joys are mine!"

4 Alleluia! O most holy,
　O most patient, O most true,
Ever faithful, all-forgiving,
　Still bestowing mercies new!
Day by day has mercy kept us,
　Soul and body kept from ill;
Night by night, in peace descending,
　Cometh mercy, mercy still.

5 Then to Him, the Fount of mercy,
　Jesus Christ, the children's King,
Blessing, honour, thanks, and glory,
　Let His children ever bring.
Let their mighty Alleluia
　Fill the earth from shore to shore,
Till with that new song it mingles,
　Sung in heaven for evermore!

334.

TINTERN ABBEY.
7s. 6s. D.

God, who hath made the daisies
And ev'ry lovely thing;
He will accept our praises,
And hearken while we sing.
He says, though we are simple,
Though ignorant we be,
"Suffer the little children,
And let them come to Me." A-MEN.

2 Though we are young and simple,
    In praise we may be bold;
  The children in the temple
    He heard in days of old.
  And if our hearts are humble,
    He says to you and me,
  "Suffer the little children,
    And let them come to Me."

3 He sees the bird that wingeth
    Its way o'er earth and sky;
  He hears the lark that singeth
    Up in the heaven so high;
  He sees the heart's low breathings,
    And says (well pleased to see),
  "Suffer the little children.
    And let them come to Me."

4 Therefore we will come near Him,
    And joyfully we'll sing;
  No cause to shrink or fear Him,
    We'll make our voices ring:
  For in our temple speaking,
    He says to you and me,
  "Suffer the little children.
    And let them come to Me."

GENERAL HYMNS.

335.

Moderate.

HOMAGE.
8s. 8s. 7.

Upward where the stars are burn-ing, Si-lent, si-lent in their turning, Round the nev-er changing pole; Up-ward where the sky is bright-est, Upward where the blue is light-est,— Lift I now my long-ing soul. A-MEN.

2 Far beyond that arch of gladness,
  Far beyond these clouds of sadness,
    Are the many mansions fair:
  Far from pain and sin and folly,
  In that palace of the holy—
    I would find my mansion there.

3 Where the Lamb on high is seated,
  By ten thousand voices greeted:
    Lord of lords, and King of kings!
  Son of man, they crown, they crown Him,
  Son of God, they own, they own Him,
    With His Name the palace rings.

4 Blessing, honour, without measure,
  Heavenly riches, earthly treasure,
    Lay we at His blessèd feet:
  Poor the praise that now we render,
  Loud shall be our voices yonder,
    When before His throne we meet.

336.

Cheerful.

PENTECOST.
Six 7s.

For the beau-ty of the earth, For the glo-ry of the skies,
For the love which from our birth O-ver and a-round us lies;
Christ, our Lord, to Thee we raise This our hymn of grate-ful praise. A-MEN.

2 For the wonder of each hour
  Of the day and of the night;
  Hill and vale, and tree and flower,
  Sun and moon, and stars of light;
  Christ, our Lord, to Thee we raise
  This our hymn of grateful praise.

3 For the joy of human love,
  Brother, sister, parent, child;
  Friends on earth, and friends above,
  Pleasures pure and undefiled;
  Christ, our Lord, to Thee we raise
  This our hymn of grateful praise.

4 For Thy Church that evermore
  Lifts her holy hands above,
  Offering up on every shore
  Her pure sacrifice of love;
  Christ, our Lord, to Thee we raise
  This our hymn of grateful praise.

337.

Joyous.

HOSANNA.
7s. 6s. D.

Ho-san-na! loud ho-san-na! From Heav'nly choirs peal, And from the earth's glad

GENERAL HYMNS.

bo-som The echoes upward steal, From sacred fanes upspringing, From aisles mid leafy grove, From in-fant voi-ces tell-ing The mys-te-ry of love. A-MEN.

2 Hosanna! loud Hosannas
To Mary's Holy Child.
Emmanuel! to dwell with us
The sinless, undefiled.
Come, kneel in adoration
While angels hymn His praise,
The Lord of our salvation!
To Him an anthem raise.

3 Hosanna! loud Hosannas
Unto the Prince of Peace,
The Wonderful, the Counsellor,
Who maketh strife to cease.
Now may our joy triumphant
Unite with songs on high;
And earth in strains exultant
Her noblest praise employ.

338.

CARTER.
8s. 7s.

Joyful.

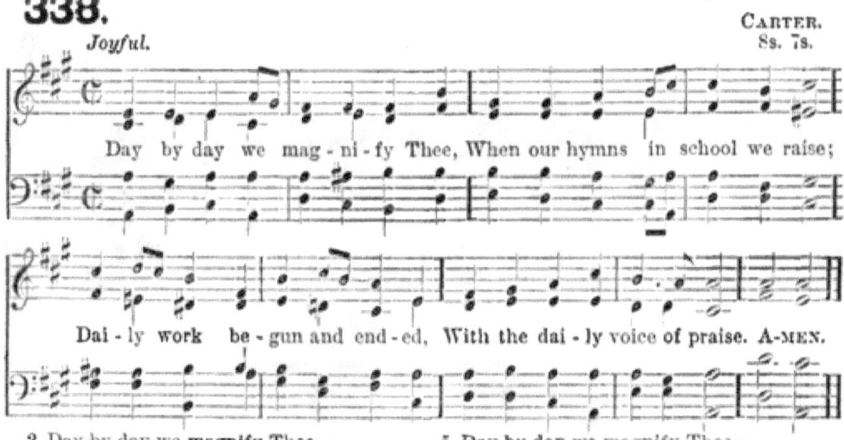

Day by day we mag-ni-fy Thee, When our hymns in school we raise; Dai-ly work be-gun and end-ed, With the dai-ly voice of praise. A-MEN.

2 Day by day we **magnify Thee**—
When as each new **day is born**,
On our knees at home **we bless Thee**
For the mercies of the morn.

3 Day by **day we magnify Thee**—
In our hymns before we sleep;
Angels hear them, watching by us,
Christ's dear lambs all night to keep.

4 Day by day we magnify Thee
Not in words of praise alone;
Truthful lips and meek obedience
Show Thy glory in Thine own.

5 Day by day we magnify Thee—
When, for Jesus' sake, we try
Every wrong to bear with patience,
Every sin to mortify.

6 Day by day we magnify Thee—
Till our days on earth shall cease,
Till we rest from these our labours,
Waiting for Thy Day in peace!

7 Then, on that eternal morning,
With Thy great redeemèd host,
May we fully magnify Thee—
Father, Son and Holy Ghost!

O Saviour, precious Saviour, Whom yet unseen we love,
O Name of might and favour, All other names above;
We worship Thee, we bless Thee, To Thee alone we sing;
We praise Thee and confess Thee, Our holy Lord and King. A-MEN.

2 O Bringer of salvation,
  Who wondrously hast **wrought**,
 Thyself the revelation
  Of love beyond our thought;
 We worship Thee, we bless Thee,
  To Thee alone we sing;
 We praise Thee and confess Thee,
  Our gracious Lord and King.

3 In Thee all fulness dwelleth,
  All grace and power divine;
 The glory that excelleth,
  O Son of God, is Thine;
 We worship Thee, we bless Thee,
  To Thee alone we sing;
 We praise Thee and confess Thee,
  Our glorious Lord and King.

4 Oh, grant the consummation
  Of this our song above,
 In endless adoration
  And everlasting love;
 Then shall we praise and bless **Thee**,
  Where perfect praises ring,
 And evermore confess Thee,
  Our Saviour and our King.

GENERAL HYMNS.

340.

ALLHALLOWS.
C. M. D.

Come, Christian children, come and raise Your voice with one accord;
Come, sing in joyful songs of praise The glories of your Lord.
Sing of the wonders of His Love, And loudest praises give,
To Him who left His throne above, And died that you might live. A-MEN.

2 Sing of the wonders of His Truth,
   And read in every page
The promise made to earliest youth
   Fulfilled to latest age.
Sing of the wonders of His Power,
   Who with His own right arm
Upholds and keeps you hour by hour,
   And shields from every harm.

3 Sing of the wonders of His Grace,
   Who made and keeps you His,
And guides you to the appointed place
   At His right hand in bliss.
Sing of the wonders of His Name,
   And Jesus Christ adore;
Him for your Lord and God proclaim,
   And praise Him evermore.

341. GENERAL HYMNS. LINDAU. 11s. 10s. with Refrain.

2 When stooping to earth from the brightness of heaven,
Thy blood for our ransom so freely was given,
Thou deignedst to listen while children adored,
With joyful hosannas the Bless'd of the Lord.
                    Hallelujah, &c.

3 Those arms which embraced little children of old,
Still love to encircle the lambs of the fold,
That grace which inviteth the wandering home,
Hath never forbidden the youngest to come.
                    Hallelujah, &c.

4 Hosanna! Hosanna! Great Teacher, we raise
Our hearts and our voices in hymning Thy praise
For precept and promise so graciously given,
For blessings of earth, and the glories of heaven.
                    Hallelujah, &c.

GENERAL HYMNS.

342.
Joyful.

MEHUL.
7s. 6s. D., with Refrain.

When, His salvation bringing, To Zion Jesus came,
The children all stood singing Hosanna to His Name.
Nor did their zeal offend Him, But, as He rode along,
He let them still attend Him, And smiled to hear their song:
Hosanna, Hosanna, to Jesus they sang. A-MEN.

2 And since the Lord retaineth
His love for children still:
Though now as King He reigneth
On Zion's heavenly hill;
We'll flock around His banner,
Who sits upon the throne,
And cry aloud, Hosanna
To David's royal Son:
Hosanna to Jesus we'll sing.

3 For should we fail proclaiming
Our great Redeemer's praise,
The stones, our silence shaming,
Would their Hosannas raise.
But shall we only render
The tribute of our words?
No, while our hearts are tender,
They too shall be the Lord's.
Hosanna to Jesus, our King.

GENERAL HYMNS.

343. Consecration.

Earnestly. S. EDMUND. 6s. 4s.

Near-er, my God, to Thee, Near-er to Thee,
E'en though it be a cross That rais-eth me;
Still all my song shall be, Near-er, my God, to Thee,
Near-er, my God, to Thee, Near-er to Thee. A-MEN.

2 Though like a wanderer,
  Weary and lone,
Darkness comes over me,
  My rest a stone;
Yet in my dreams I'd be
Nearer, my God, to Thee,
  Nearer to Thee.

3 There let my way appear
  Steps unto heaven;
All that Thou sendest me
  In mercy given;
Angels to beckon me
Nearer, my God, to Thee,
  Nearer to Thee.

4 Then, with my waking thoughts
  Bright with Thy praise,
Out of my stony griefs
  Altars I'll raise;
So by my woes to be
Nearer, my God, to Thee,
  Nearer to Thee.

5 Or, if on joyful wing,
  Cleaving the sky,
Sun, moon, and stars forgot,
  Upward I fly,
Still all my song shall be
Nearer, my God, to Thee,
  Nearer to Thee.

Trust.

344.

As help-less as a child who clings, Fast to his father's arm,
And casts his weakness on the strength That keeps him safe from harm;
So I, my Father, cling to Thee, And every passing hour
Would link my earthly feebleness To Thine Almighty power. A-MEN.

2 As trustful as a child who looks
  Up in his mother's face,
And all his little griefs and fears
  Forgets in her embrace;
So I to Thee, my Saviour, look,
  And in Thy face Divine,
Can read the love that will sustain
  As weak a faith as mine.

3 As loving as a child who sits
  Close by his parent's knee,
And knows no want while it can have
  That sweet society;
So, sitting at Thy feet, my heart
  Would all its love outpour,
And pray that Thou wouldst teach me, Lord,
  To love Thee more and more.

GENERAL HYMNS.

345.
Moderate.

THE DIVINE FRIEND.
8s. 7s. D.

There's no oth-er friend like Je-sus, None so faith-ful, none so true; Though the waves break wildly o'er us, He will guide us safe-ly through; Storms and tempests shrink be-fore Him, He can calm them at His will: Je-sus, calm our stormy passions With Thy wondrous "Peace, be still." A-MEN.

2 There's no other friend like Jesus,
   He who died our souls to save;
He who dwelt on earth in meekness,
   Healed, and pitied, and forgave.
Still He pities, still He loves us,
   In His holy, happy home,
And with voice of gracious mercy,
   Bids the wandering sinner, come.

3 There's no other friend like Jesus,
   Holy angels, chant the song;
Sing His love and wondrous mercy;
   Children, join the heavenly throng.

Raise the joyful, happy chorus,
   Thank Him for His loving grace,
Let it be your happy portion
   To proclaim the Saviour's praise.

346.
Joyful.

BUCKLAND.
7s.

Lov-ing Shep-herd of Thy sheep, Keep Thy lamb, in safe-ty keep;

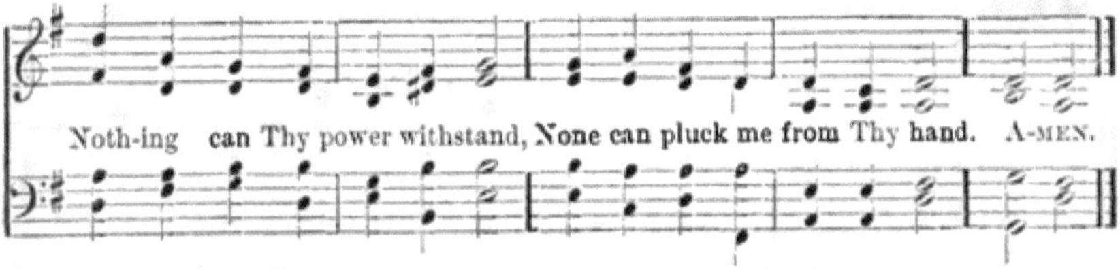

[Music notation]

Noth-ing can Thy power withstand, None can pluck me from Thy hand. A-MEN.

2 Loving Saviour, Thou did'st give
    Thine own life that we might live,
  And the Hands outstretched to bless
    Bear the cruel nails' impress.

3 I would praise Thee every day,
    Gladly all Thy will obey,
  Like Thy blessèd ones above,
    Happy in Thy precious love.

4 Loving Shepherd, ever near,
    Teach Thy lamb Thy voice to hear,
  Suffer not my steps to stray,
    From the straight and narrow way.

5 Where Thou leadest I would go,
    Walking in Thy steps below,
  Till before my Father's Throne
    I shall know as I am known.

347.

PRINCETHORPE.
6s. 5s. D.

Moderate.

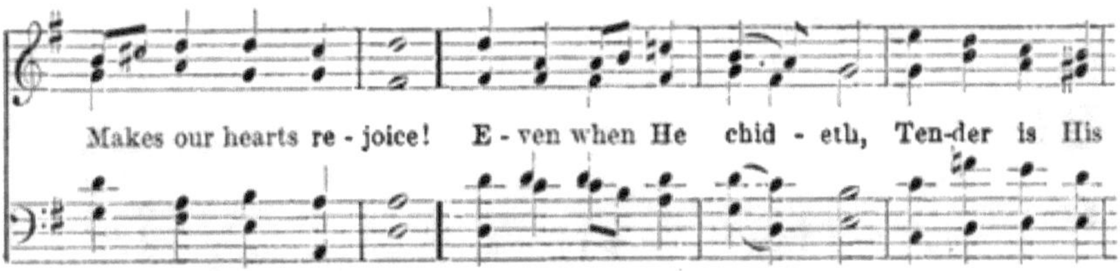

[Music notation]

Je-sus is our Shepherd, Well we know His voice; How the gentlest whis-per, Makes our hearts re-joice! E-ven when He chid-eth, Ten-der is His tone; None but He shall guide us; We are His a-lone. A-MEN.

2 Jesus is our Shepherd;
    Guided by His Arm,
  Though the wolves may raven,
    None can do us harm;
  When we tread death's valley,
    Dark with fearful gloom,
  We will fear no evil,
    Victors o'er the tomb.

3 Jesus is our Shepherd;
    With His goodness now
  And His tender mercy,
    He doth us endow!
  Let us sing His praises
    With a gladsome heart,
  Till in heaven we meet Him,
    Never more to part.

348.

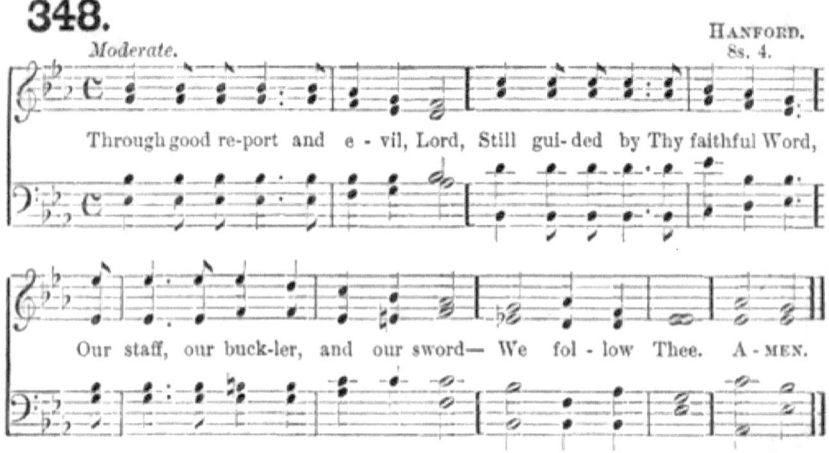

Hanford.
8s. 4.

Moderate.

Through good report and evil, Lord, Still guided by Thy faithful Word, Our staff, our buckler, and our sword— We follow Thee. A-MEN.

2 In silence of the lonely night,
In the full glow of day's clear light,
Through life's strange wanderings, dark or bright,
    We follow Thee.

3 Strengthened by Thee we forward go,
'Mid smile or scoff of friend or foe,
Through pain or ease, through joy or woe,
    We follow Thee.

4 With enemies on every side,
We lean on Thee, the Crucified,
Forsaking all on earth beside,
    We follow Thee.

5 O Master, point Thou out the way,
Nor suffer Thou our steps to stray;
Then in the path that leads to Day,
    We follow Thee.

6 Thou hast passed on before our face;
Thy footsteps on the way we trace;
Oh, keep us, aid us by Thy grace:
    We follow Thee.

7 Whom have we in the heaven above,
Whom on this earth, save Thee, to love?
Still in Thy light we onward move;
    We follow Thee.

349.

Troyte, No. 1.

Calmly.

1 My God, my Father, while I stray
Far from my home, on life's rough way,
O teach me from my heart to say,
    "Thy will be done."

2 Though dark my path, and sad my lot,
Let me be still and murmur not,
And breathe the prayer divinely taught,
    "Thy will be done."

3 What though in lonely grief I sigh
For friends beloved no longer nigh,
Submissive still would I reply,
    "Thy will be done."

4 If Thou should'st call me to resign
What most I prize—it ne'er was mine;
I only yield Thee what is Thine—
    "Thy will be done."

5 Renew my will from day to day,
Blend it with Thine, and take away
All that now makes it hard to say,
    "Thy will be done."

6 Let but my fainting heart be blest
With Thy sweet Spirit for its Guest,
My God, to Thee I leave the rest;
    "Thy will be done."

350.

THE SHEPHERD'S FOLD.
8s. 7s. D.

2 But night and day He went His way
    In sorrow till He found it;
  And when He saw it fainting lie
    He clasped His arms around it.
  Then, safely folded to His breast,
    From every ill to save it,
  He brought it to His home of rest,
    And pitied and forgave it.

3 And thus the Saviour will receive
    The little ones who love Him,
  Their pains remove, their sins forgive,
    And draw them gently near Him.
  Blest while they live and when they die,
    When flesh and spirit sever—
  Conduct them to His home on high,
    To dwell with Him for ever.

GENERAL HYMNS.

351.

Moderate.   PASTOR BONUS.
                                         6s. 5s. D.

Christ, who once amongst us As a child did dwell, Is the children's Saviour, And He loves us well; If we keep our promise Made Him at the Font, He will be our Shepherd, And we shall not want. A-MEN.

2 Then it was they laid us
    In those tender Arms,
  Where the lambs are carried
    Safe from all alarms;
  If we trust His promise,
    He will let us rest
  In His Arms forever,
    Leaning on His Breast.

3 Though we may not see Him
    For a little while,
  We shall know He holds us,
    Often feel His smile;
  Death will be to slumber
    In that sweet embrace,
  And we shall awaken
    To behold His Face.

4 He will be our Shepherd
    After as before,
  By still heavenly waters
    Lead us evermore;
  Make us lie in pastures
    Beautiful and green,
  Where none thirst or hunger,
    And no tears are seen.

5 Jesus, our good Shepherd,
    Laying down Thy life,
  Lest Thy sheep should perish
    In the cruel strife,
  Help us to remember
    All Thy love and care,
  Trust in Thee, and love Thee,
    Always, everywhere.

352.

Tenderly.   PALMER.
                                         5s. 4s. D.

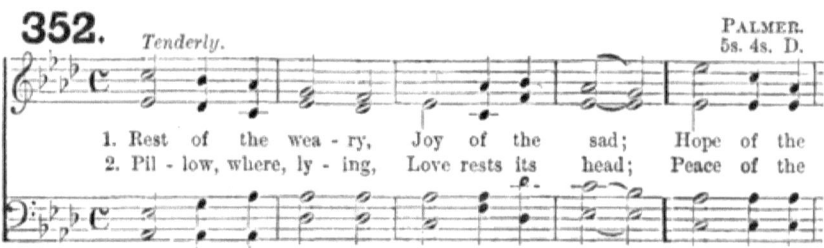

1. Rest of the weary, Joy of the sad; Hope of the
2. Pillow, where, lying, Love rests its head; Peace of the

drea - ry, Light of the glad; Home of the stran - ger, Strength to the end; Re - fuge from dan - ger, Sa - viour and Friend.
dy - ing, Life of the dead; Path of the low - ly, Prize at the end; Breath of the ho - ly, Sa - viour and Friend. A - MEN.

3 When my feet stumble, I'll to Thee cry;
Crown of the humble, cross of the high:
When my steps wander, over me bend,
Truer and fonder, Saviour and Friend.

4 Ever confessing Thee, I will raise
Unto Thee blessing, glory, and praise:—
All my endeavour, world without end,
Thine to be ever, Saviour and Friend.

353.

S. OSWALD.
8s. 7s.

Moderate.

Ho - ly Fa - ther, Thou hast taught me I should live to Thee a - lone;
Year by year Thy hand hath brought me On through dangers oft un-known. A-MEN.

2 When I wandered, Thou hast found me;
When I doubted, sent me light;
Still Thine Arm has been around me,
All my paths were in Thy sight.

In the world will foes assail me,
Craftier, stronger far than I,
And the strife may never fail me,
Well I know, before I die.

4 Therefore, Lord, I come believing
Thou canst give the power I need;
Through the prayer of faith, receiving
Strength—the Spirit's strength indeed.

5 I would trust in Thy protection,
Wholly rest upon Thine Arm,
Follow wholly Thy direction,
Thou mine only Guard from harm.

6 Keep me from mine own undoing;
Let me turn to Thee when tried,
Still my footsteps, Father, viewing,
Keep me ever at Thy side.

354. Hope.

PILGRIM BAND.
7s. 6s. D.

Joyful.

O happy band of pilgrims, If onward ye will tread,
With Jesus as your fellow, To Jesus as your Head;
O happy if ye labour As Jesus did for men;
O happy if ye hunger As Jesus hungered then. A-MEN.

2 The Cross that Jesus carried
  Was carried as your due;
The Crown that Jesus weareth
  He weareth it for you.
The trials that beset you,
  The sorrows ye endure,
The manifold temptations,
  That death alone can cure;

3 What are they but His jewels
  Of right celestial worth?
What are they but the ladder
  Set up to heaven on earth?
O happy band of pilgrims,
  Look upward to the skies,
Where such a light affliction
  Shall win so great a prize.

355.

Joyous.   PLEYEL'S HYMN. 7s.

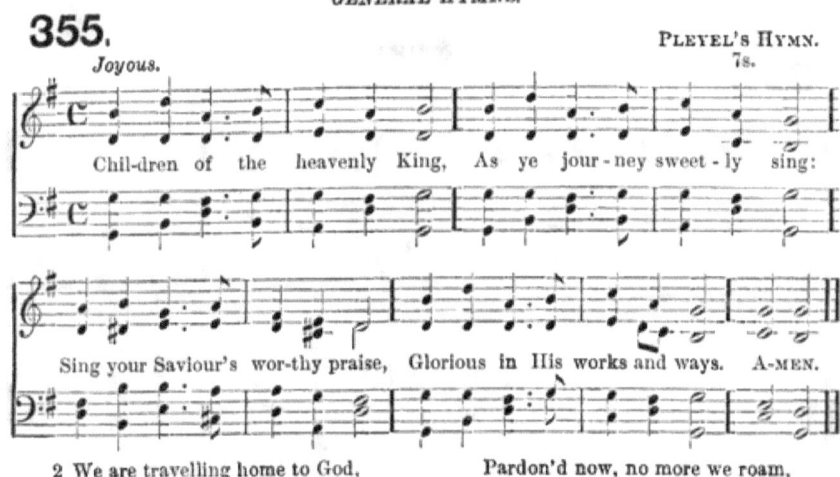

Chil-dren of the heavenly King, As ye jour-ney sweet-ly sing: Sing your Saviour's wor-thy praise, Glorious in His works and ways. A-MEN.

2 We are travelling home to God,
In the way the fathers trod:
They are happy now, and we
Soon their happiness shall see.

3 Banish'd once, by sin betray'd,
Christ our Advocate was made;

Pardon'd now, no more we roam,
Christ conducts us to our home.

4 Lord, obediently we go,
Gladly leaving all below;
Only Thou our Leader be,
And we still will follow Thee.

356.

Joyful.   HULLAH. 6s. 5s. D.

We are lit-tle pilgrims, We are strangers here, We are hast'ning onward

Harmony.   *rall.*   *a tempo.*

To our Home most dear; All that stays our progress We will cast aside, Sinful lusts and

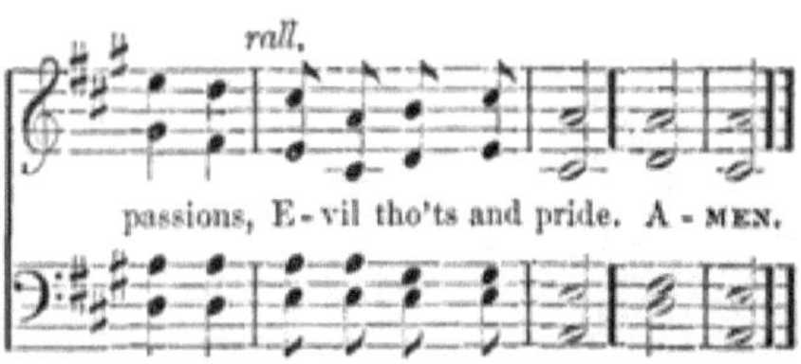

rall.

passions, E-vil tho'ts and pride. A-MEN.

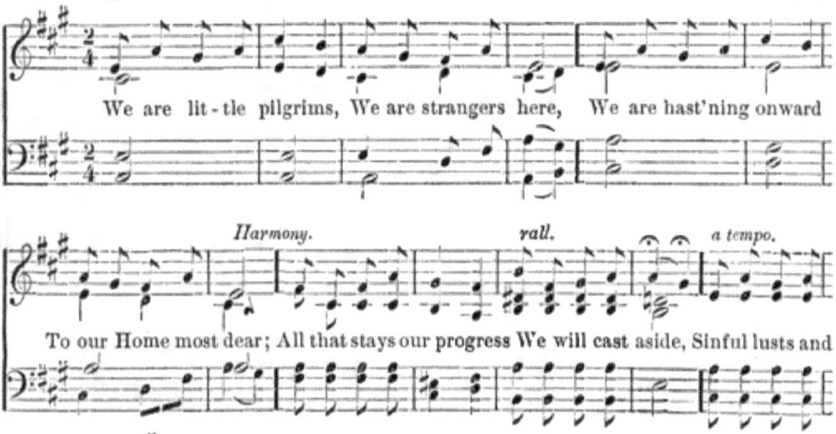

2 Ofttimes we are weary,
Oftentimes in pain;
But the hope of Heaven
Cheers our souls again.
Grief will there be rapture,
Toil will there be rest;
Each day brings us nearer
To our Home most blest.

Love.

357.

WESTON.
8s. 7s. D.

Moderate.

Love di-vine, all love ex-cel-ling, Joy of heaven, to earth come down!
Fix in us Thy hum-ble dwell-ing, All Thy faith-ful mer-cies crown.
Je-sus, Thou art all com-pas-sion, Pure un-bound-ed love Thou art;
Vis-it us with Thy sal-va-tion, En-ter ev-ery trembling heart. A-MEN.

2 Breathe, O breathe Thy loving Spirit
　Into every troubled breast;
Let us all in Thee inherit,
　Let us find Thy promised rest;
Take away the love of sinning,
　Alpha and Omega be,—
End of faith, as its beginning,
　Set our hearts at liberty.

3 Come, Almighty to deliver,
　Let us all Thy grace receive;
Suddenly return, and never,
　Never more Thy temples leave.
Thee we would be always blessing;
　Serve Thee as Thy hosts above;
Pray, and praise Thee without ceasing;
　Glory in Thy perfect love.

4 Finish then Thy new creation,
　Pure and spotless let us be:
Let us see Thy great salvation,
　Perfectly restored in Thee.
Changed from glory into glory,
　Till in heaven we take our place:
Till we cast our crowns before Thee,
　Lost in wonder, love, and praise.

GENERAL HYMNS

358.

Angel Voices.
7s. 6s. D.

Joyously.

I love to hear the story Which angel voices tell,
How once the King of glory Came down on earth to dwell. A-MEN.
I am both weak and sinful, But this I surely know,
The Lord came down to save me, Because He loved me so.

2 I'm glad my Blessed Saviour
　Was once a child like me,
To show how pure and holy
　His little ones might be;
And if I try to follow
　His footsteps here below,
He never will forget me,
　Because He loves me so.
　　I love to hear the story
　　　Which Angel voices tell,
　　How once the King of glory
　　　Came down on earth to dwell.

3 To sing His love and mercy
　My sweetest songs I'll raise;
And though I cannot see Him,
　I know He hears my praise;
For He has kindly promised
　That even I may go
To sing among His Angels,
　Because He loves me so.
　　I love to hear the story
　　　Which Angel voices tell,
　　How once the King of glory
　　　Came down on earth to dwell.

GENERAL HYMNS.

359.

Moderate.

AMOR.
7s. 6s. D.

How dear-ly God must love us, And this poor world of ours,
To spread blue skies a-bove us, And deck the earth with flowers!
There's not a weed so low-ly, Nor bird that cleaves the air,
But tells, in ac-cents ho-ly, His kind-ness and His care. A-MEN.

2 He bids the sun to warm us,
  And light the path we tread;
At night, lest aught should harm us,
  He guards our welcome bed:
He gives our needful clothing,
  And sends our daily food;
His love denies us nothing
  His wisdom deemeth good.

3 The Bible, too, He sends us,
  That tells how Jesus came,
Whose word can save and cleanse us
  From guilt and sin and shame.
O may God's mercies move us
  To serve Him with our powers,
For O how He must love us,
  And this poor world of ours!

360.

Smoothly.

S. SALVADOR.
7s.

All things beau-ti-ful and fair, Earth and sky and balm-y air;

GENERAL HYMNS.

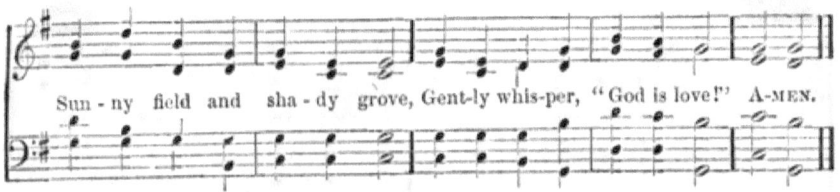

2 Every tree and flower we pass,
  Every tuft of waving grass,
  Every leaf and opening bud,
  Seem to tell us "God is good".
3 Little streams that glide along,
  Verdant, mossy banks among,
  Shadowing forth the clouds above,
  Softly murmur, "God is love."
4 He who dwelleth high in heaven,
  Unto us has all things given;
  Let us, as through life we move,
  Ever feel that "God is love".

361.

SHERBROOKE.
8s. 7s. 7.

ORG.

2 Which of all our friends, to save us,
    Could, or would, have shed His blood?
  Christ the Saviour died to have us
    Reconciled in Him to God:
      This was boundless love indeed!
      Jesus is a Friend in need.
3 When He lived on earth abased,
    Friend of sinners was His name;
  Now above all glory raised,
    He rejoices in the same.
      Still He calls them brethren, friends;
      And to all their wants attends.
4 Oh, for grace our hearts to soften!
    Teach us, Lord, at length to love;
  We, alas! forget too often
    What a Friend we have above;
      But, when home our souls are brought,
      We will love Thee as we ought.

362. Moderate. CARITAS. 8s. 4s.

One there is above all others, O how He loves! His is love beyond a brother's, O how He loves! Earthly friends may fail or leave us, One day soothe, the next day grieve us, But this Friend will ne'er deceive us, O how He loves! A-MEN.

2 'Tis eternal life to know Him,
  O how He loves!
 Think, O think how much we owe Him,
  O how He loves!
 With His precious blood He bought us,
 In the wilderness He sought us,
 To His fold He safely brought us,
  O how He loves!

3 We have found a friend in Jesus,
  O how He loves!
 'Tis His great delight to bless us,
  O how He loves!
 How our hearts delight to hear Him—
 Bid us dwell in safety near Him:
 Why should we distrust or fear Him?
  O how He loves!

4 Through His Name we are forgiven,
  O how He loves!
 Backward shall our foes be driven,
  O how He loves!
 Best of blessings He'll provide us,
 Nought but good shall e'er betide us,
 Safe to glory He will guide us,
  O how He loves!

363. Moderate. PERRY. 8s. 7s.

God is love; His mercy brightens All the path in which we rove;

2 Lord, Thy guardian presence ever,
   Meekly bending, we implore:
  We have found Thee, and would never,
   Never wander from Thee more.
  Heavenly Shepherd, Heavenly Shepherd,
   Thou hast loved us, Thine we are.

2 With a childlike heart of love,
At Thy bidding may I move;
Prompt to serve and follow Thee,
Loving Him who first loved me.

3 Teach me all Thy steps to trace,
Strong to follow in Thy grace,
Learning how to love from Thee,
Loving Him who first loved me.

4 Love in loving finds employ,
In obedience all her joy;
Ever new that joy will be
Loving Him who first loved me.

5 Thus may I rejoice to show
That I feel the love I owe;
Singing, till Thy face I see,
Of His love who first loved me.

367.

CLAUGHTON.
8s. 7s.

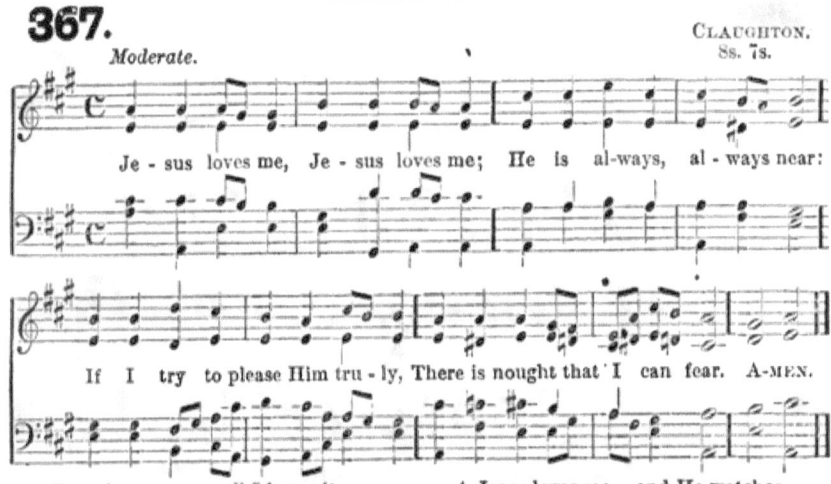

Je-sus loves me, Je-sus loves me; He is al-ways, al-ways near:
If I try to please Him tru-ly, There is nought that I can fear. A-MEN.

2 Jesus loves me,—well I know it,
  For to save my soul He died:
  He for me bore pain and, sorrow,
  Nailed hands and piercèd side.

3 Jesus loves me,—night and morning
  Jesus hears the prayers I pray;
  And He never, never leaves me,
  When I work or when I play.

4 Jesus loves me,—and He watches
  Over me with loving eye,
  And He sends His Holy Angels,
  Safe to keep me, till I die.

5 Jesus loves me,—O Lord Jesus,
  Now I pray Thee by Thy love,
  Keep me ever pure and holy,
  Till I come to Thee above!

368.

HART.
7s.

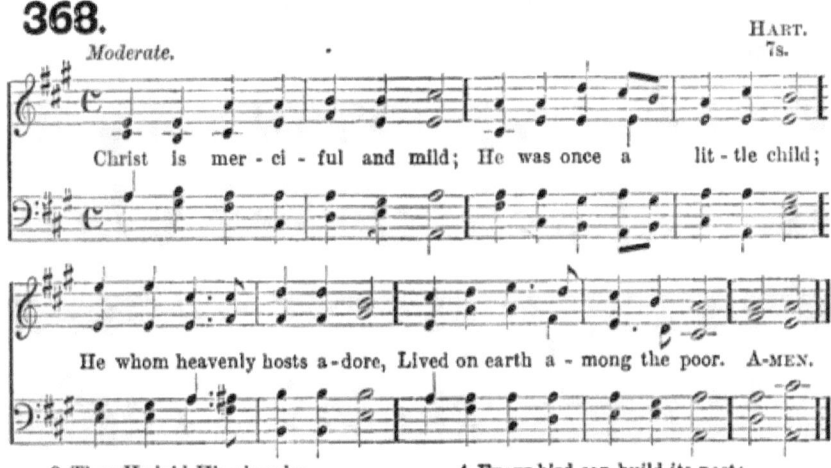

Christ is mer-ci-ful and mild; He was once a lit-tle child;
He whom heavenly hosts a-dore, Lived on earth a-mong the poor. A-MEN.

2 Thus He laid His glory by,
  When for us He stooped to die;
  How I wonder, when I see
  His unbounded love to me.

3 He the sick to health restored,
  To the poor He preached the word;
  Even children had a share
  Of His love and tender care.

4 Every bird can build its nest;
  Foxes have their place of rest;
  He, by whom the world was made,
  Had not where to lay His head.

5 He who is the Lord most high,
  Then was poorer far than I,
  That I might hereafter be
  Rich to all eternity.

GENERAL HYMNS.

369.
DOMINUS REGIT ME.
8s. 7s.

Joyful.

The King of love my Shepherd is, Whose goodness faileth never;
I nothing lack if I am His, And He is mine for ever. A-MEN.

2 Where streams of living water flow
My ransom'd soul He leadeth,
And, where the verdant pastures grow,
With food celestial feedeth.

3 Perverse and foolish, oft I stray'd,
But yet in love He sought me,
And on His shoulder gently laid,
And home, rejoicing brought me.

4 In death's dark vale I fear no ill
With Thee, dear Lord, beside me;
Thy rod and staff my comfort still,
Thy Cross before to guide me.

5 Thou spreadst a table in my sight,
Thy unction grace bestoweth,
And O the transport of delight
With which my cup o'erfloweth.

6 And so, through all the length of days,
Thy goodness faileth never;
Good Shepherd, may I sing Thy praise
Within Thy house forever!

370.
BROCKLESBURY.
8s. 7s.

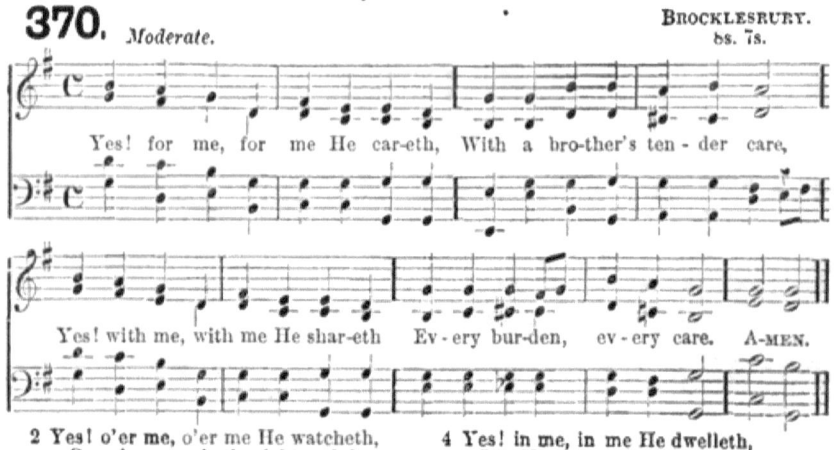

Moderate.

Yes! for me, for me He careth, With a brother's tender care,
Yes! with me, with me He shareth Every burden, every care. A-MEN.

2 Yes! o'er me, o'er me He watcheth,
Ceaseless watcheth night and day;
Yes! e'en me, e'en me He snatcheth
From the perils of the way.

3 Yes! for me He standeth pleading
At the mercy-seat above;
Ever for me interceding,
Constant in untiring love.

4 Yes! in me, in me He dwelleth,
I in Him, and He in me;
And my empty soul He filleth,
Here, and through eternity.

5 Thus I wait for His returning,
Singing all the way to heaven;
Such the joyful song of morning,
Such the joyful song of even.

371. Courage.

Boldly. S. Asaph.
8s. 7s. D.

Through the night of doubt and sorrow, Onward goes the pilgrim band,
Singing songs of expectation, Marching to the Promised Land.
Clear before us through the darkness Gleams and burns the guiding Light;
Brother clasps the hand of brother, Stepping fearless through the night. A-MEN.

2 One the Light of God's own Presence,
  O'er His ransom'd people shed,
 Chasing far the gloom and terror,
  Brightening all the path we tread;
 One the object of our journey,
  One the faith which never tires,
 One the earnest looking forward,
  One the hope our God inspires.

3 One the strain the lips of thousands
  Lift as from the heart of one;
 One the conflict, one the peril,
  One the march in God begun;
 One the gladness of rejoicing
  On the far eternal shore.
 Where the one Almighty Father
  Reigns in love for evermore.

4 Onward, therefore, pilgrim brothers,
  Onward, with the Cross our aid!
 Bear its shame, and fight its battle,
  Till we rest beneath its shade!
 Soon shall come the great awaking;
  Soon the rending of the tomb;
 Then, the scattering of all shadows,
  And the end of toil and gloom!

GENERAL HYMNS.

372.

UNIVERSITY COLLEGE. 7s.

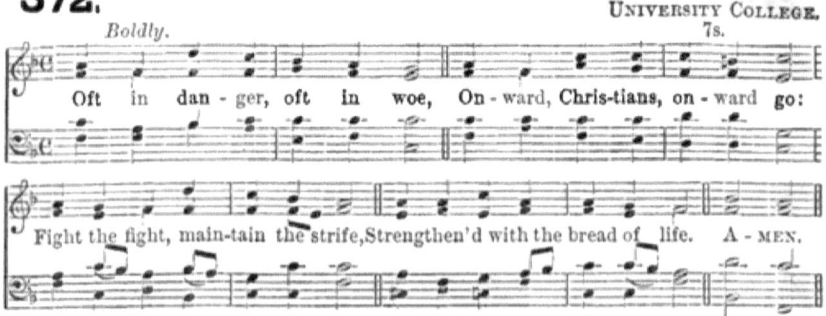

Oft in danger, oft in woe, Onward, Christians, onward go: Fight the fight, maintain the strife, Strengthen'd with the bread of life. A-MEN.

2 Onward, Christians, onward go,
Join the war and face the foe:
Will ye flee in danger's hour?
Know ye not your Captain's power?

3 Let your drooping hearts be glad;
March in heavenly armor clad:
Fight, nor think the battle long,
Victory soon shall tune your song.

4 Let not sorrow dim your eye,
Soon shall every tear be dry;
Let not fears your course impede,
Great your strength, if great your need.

5 Onward then in battle move,
More than conquerors ye shall prove:
Though opposed by many a foe,
Christian soldiers, onward go.

373.

VICTORY. 7s. 6s. D.

Go forward, Christian soldier! Beneath His banner true;
The Lord Himself thy Leader, Shall all thy foes subdue:
His love foretells thy trials; He knows thine hourly need;
He can with bread of heaven Thy fainting spirit feed. A-MEN.

2 Go forward, Christian soldier!
Fear not the secret foe;
Far more o'er thee are watching
Than human eyes can know;
Trust only Christ, thy Captain;
Cease not to watch and pray;
Heed not the treacherous voices
That lure thy soul astray.

3 Go forward, Christian soldier!
Nor dream of peaceful rest,
'Till Satan's host is vanquished,
And heaven is all possessed;
'Till Christ Himself shall call thee
To lay thine armor by,
And wear in endless glory
The crown of victory.

4 Go forward, Christian soldier!
Fear not the gathering night,
The Lord has been thy Shelter,
The Lord will be thy Light.
When morn His face revealeth,
Thy dangers all are past;
Oh, pray that faith and virtue
May keep thee to the last!

374. Action.

Earnestly. CHRISTMAS. C. M.

A-wake, my soul, stretch every nerve, And press with vigour on; A heavenly race demands thy zeal, And an immor-tal crown, And an immortal crown. A-MEN.

2 A cloud of witnesses around
Hold thee in full survey;
Forget the steps already trod,
And onward urge thy way.

3 'Tis God's all animating voice
That calls thee from on high,
'Tis His own hand presents the prize
To thine uplifted eye.

4 Then wake, my soul, stretch every nerve,
And press with vigour on;
A heavenly race demands thy zeal,
And an immortal crown.

375.

Moderate. MABEL. 8s. 7s. 4.

In the vine-yard of our Fa-ther, Dai-ly work we find to do; Scattered gleanings we may gather, Though we are but young and few; Lit-tle clusters, Lit-tle clusters Help to fill the garners too. A-MEN.

2 Toiling early in the morning,
Catching moments through the day,
Nothing small or lowly scorning
While we work, and watch, and pray;
Gathering gladly
Free-will offerings by the way.

3 Not for selfish praise or glory,
Not for objects nothing worth,
But to send the blessèd story
Of the Gospel o'er the earth,
Telling mortals
Of our Lord and Saviour's birth.

4 Steadfast, then, in our endeavour,
Heavenly Father, may we be;
And for ever, and for ever,
We will give the praise to Thee;
Hallelujah
Singing, all eternity.

376.

Moderate.

ALSTONE.
L. M.

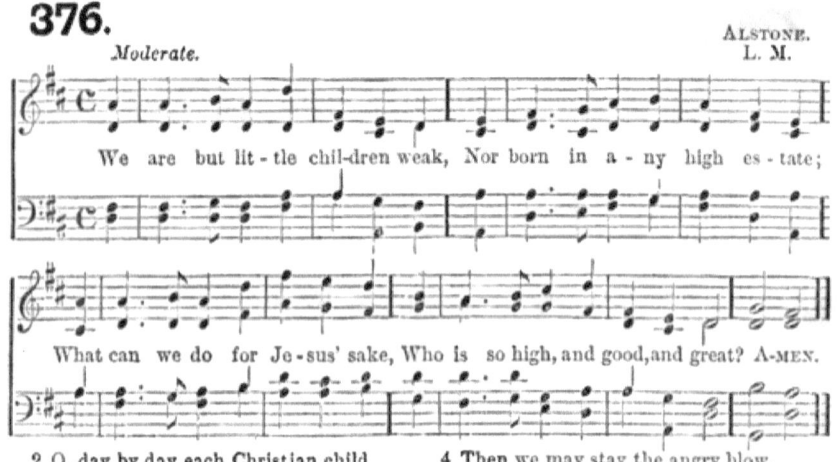

We are but lit-tle chil-dren weak, Nor born in a-ny high es-tate;
What can we do for Je-sus' sake, Who is so high, and good, and great? A-MEN.

2 O, day by day each Christian child
Has much to do, without, within;
A death to die for Jesus' sake,
A weary war to wage with sin.

3 When deep within our swelling hearts
The thoughts of pride and anger rise,
When bitter words are on our tongues,
And tears of passion in our eyes;

4 Then we may stay the angry blow,
Then we may check the hasty word,
Give gentle answers back again,
And fight a battle for our Lord.

5 There's not a child so small and weak
But has his little cross to take,
His little work of love and praise
That he may do for Jesus' sake.

377. *Joyous.* Heaven.

JERUSALEM.
C. M.

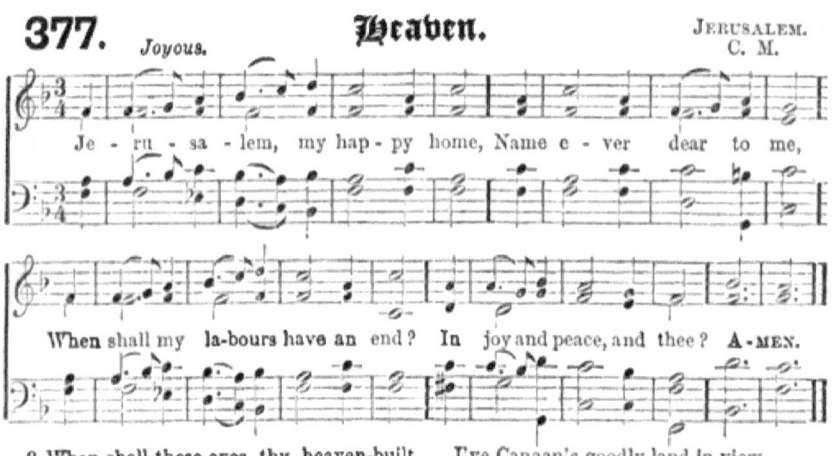

Je-ru-sa-lem, my hap-py home, Name e-ver dear to me,
When shall my la-bours have an end? In joy and peace, and thee? A-MEN.

2 When shall these eyes thy heaven-built walls,
And pearly gates behold?
Thy bulwarks with salvation strong,
And streets of shining gold?

3 There happier bowers than Eden's bloom,
Nor sin nor sorrow know:
Blest seats! through rude and stormy scenes
I onward press to you.

4 Why should I shrink from pain or woe,
Or feel at death dismay?
I've Canaan's goodly land in view,
And realms of endless day.

5 Apostles, martyrs, prophets, there
Around my Saviour stand:
And soon my friends in Christ below
Will join the glorious band.

6 Jerusalem, my happy home,
My soul still pants for thee;
Then shall my labours have an end,
When I thy joys shall see.

378.

HEAVENLY CITY.
8s. 7s. *with Refrain.*

2 All the walls of that dear City
   Are of bright and burnished gold;
 It is matchless in its beauty,
   And its treasures are untold.
     Oh that I had, &c.

3 In the midst of that dear City
   Christ is reigning on His seat,
 And the Angels swing their censers
   In a ring about His feet.
     Oh that I had, &c.

4 From the throne a river issues
   Clear as crystal, passing bright,
 And it traverses the City
   Like a sudden beam of light.
     Oh that I had, &c.

5 Where it waters leafy Eden,
   Rolling over silver sands,
 Sit the Angels, softly chiming
   On the harps between their hands.
     Oh that I had, &c.

6 There the wind is sweetly fragrant,
   And is laden with the song
 Of the Seraphs and the Elders,
   And the great redeemèd throng.
     Oh that I had, &c.

7 Oh I would my ears were open
   Here to catch that happy strain!
 Oh I would my eyes some vision
   Of that Eden could attain!
     Oh that I had, &c.

GENERAL HYMNS.

379.

Cheerful.   EWING.   7s. 6s. D.

Jerusalem the golden, With milk and honey blest,
Beneath thy contemplation Sink heart and voice oprest.
I know not, O I know not What joys await us there,
What radiancy of glory, What bliss beyond compare. A-MEN.

2 They stand, those halls of Zion,
  All jubilant with song,
And bright with many an angel,
  And all the martyr throng.
The Prince is ever in them,
  The daylight is serene;
The pastures of the blessèd
  Are decked in glorious sheen.

3 There is the throne of David;
  And there, from care released,
The shout of them that triumph,
  The song of them that feast.
And they, who with their Leader,
  Have conquered in the fight,
For ever and for ever
  Are clad in robes of white.

4 O sweet and blessèd country,
  The home of God's elect!
O sweet and blessèd country,
  That eager hearts expect!
Jesus, in mercy bring us
  To that dear land of rest;
Who art, with God the Father,
  And Spirit, ever blest.

380.

O BONA PATRIA.
7s. 6s. D.

Cheerful.

For thee, O dear, dear country, Mine eyes their vigils keep;
For very love beholding Thy happy name, they weep,
The mention of thy glory, Is unction to the breast,
And medicine in sickness, And love, and life, and rest. A-MEN.

2 O one, O only mansion;
  O Paradise of joy!
Where tears are ever banished,
  And smiles have no alloy;
The Lamb is all thy splendour,
  The Crucified thy praise;
His laud and benediction
  Thy ransomed people raise.

3 With jasper glow thy bulwarks,
  Thy streets with emeralds blaze;
The sardius and the topaz
  Unite in thee their rays;
Thine ageless walls are bonded
  With amethyst unpriced:
The saints build up its fabric,
  And the corner-stone is Christ.

4 Thou hast no shore, fair ocean!
  Thou hast no time, bright day!
Dear fountain of refreshment
  To pilgrims far away!
Upon the Rock of Ages
  They raise thy holy tower;
Thine is the victor's laurel,
  And thine the golden dower.

5 O sweet and blessèd country,
  The home of God's elect!
O sweet and blessèd country,
  That eager hearts expect!
Jesus, in mercy bring us
  To that dear land of rest;
Who art, with God the Father,
  And Spirit, ever blest.

381.

2 There is a land of peace,
  Good angels know it well;
Glad songs that never cease
  Within its portals swell;
Around its glorious throne
  Ten thousand saints adore
Christ, with the Father One,
  And Spirit, **evermore**.

3 O joy all joys beyond,
  To see the Lamb who died,
And count each sacred wound
  In hands and feet and side;
To give to Him the praise
  Of every triumph won,
And sing through endless days
  The great things He hath done.

4 Look up, ye **saints of** God,
  Nor fear to tread below
The path your Saviour trod
  Of daily toil and **woe**;
Wait but a little **while**
  In uncomplaining **love**,
His own most gracious **smile**
  Shall welcome **you above**.

382.

2 There's a rest for little children,
　　Above the bright blue sky,
　Who love the blessèd Saviour,
　　And to the Father cry,—
　A rest from every trouble,
　　From sin and danger free;
　There every little pilgrim
　　Shall rest eternally.

3 There's a home for little children,
　　Above the bright blue sky,
　Where Jesus reigns in glory,
　　A home of peace and joy;
　No home on earth is like it,
　　Nor can with it compare,
　For every one is happy,
　　Nor can be happier there.

4 There are crowns for little children,
　　Above the bright blue sky,
　And all who look to Jesus
　　Shall wear them by-and-by;
　Yea, crowns of brightest glory
　　Which He shall sure bestow,
　On all who loved the Saviour,
　　And walked with Him below.

5 There are songs for little children,
　　Above the bright blue sky,
　And harps of sweetest music
　　For their hymn of victory:
　And all above is pleasure,
　　And found in Christ alone;
　Lord, grant Thy little children,
　　To know Thee as their own.

GENERAL HYMNS.

383.
HULLAH.
8s. 7s. 7.

Joyous.

Who are these, like stars appearing, These before God's throne who stand? Each a gold-en crown is wearing, Who are all this glorious band? Al-le-lu-ia, Hark, they sing—Praising loud their heavenly King, Praising loud their heavenly King. A-MEN.

2 These are they, who have contended
   For their Saviour's honour long,
Wrestling on till life was ended,
   Following not the sinful throng.
These, who well the fight sustained,
Triumph by the Lamb have gained.

3 These are they whose hearts were riven,
   Sore with woe and anguish tried,
Who in prayer full oft have striven,
   With the God they glorified:
Now, their painful conflict o'er,
God has bid them weep no more.

384.
S. MONICA.
L. M.

Moderate.

O come, dear child, a-long with me, And look on yon-der clear blue sky, The moon is shining bright, you see, And stars are twinkling up on high. A-MEN.

2 'Tis there, my child, far, far above,
   That Heaven's eternal Kingdom lies,
There holy Angels dwell in love,
   And tears are wiped from off all eyes.

3 It is a happy, happy place,
   Without a sorrow, pain, or care,
There you may see the Saviour's face,
   Who loves to take good children there.

4 O pray each night that God may bless,
   And keep you while on earth you stay,
And give you endless happiness,
   When from the earth you pass away.

GENERAL HYMNS.

385. Moderate.
S. EDMUND.
6s. 4s.

We are but strangers here, Heaven is our Home; Earth is a desert drear,
Heaven is our Home. Danger and sorrow stand Round us on every hand, Heaven is our Father-land, Heaven is our Home. A-MEN.

2 What though the tempests rage?
　Heaven is our Home;
Short is our pilgrimage,
　Heaven is our Home.
And Time's wild wintry blast
Soon shall be overpast,
We shall reach home at last;
　Heaven is our Home.

3 There at our Saviour's side,
　Heaven is our Home:
May we be glorified;
　Heaven is our Home:
There are the good and blest,
Those we love most and best,
Grant us with them to rest;
　Heaven is our Home.

4 Grant us to murmur not,
　Heaven is our Home;
Whate'er our earthly lot,
　Heaven is our Home.
Grant us at last to stand
There at Thine own Right Hand
Jesus, in Fatherland;
　Heaven is our Home!

386. Moderate.
REALMS OF THE BLEST.
P. M.

We speak of the realms of the blest, Of that country so bright and so fair;
And oft are its glories confess'd; But what must it be to be there? A-MEN.

2 We speak of its pathways of gold,
　Of its walls deck'd with jewels most rare,
Its wonders and pleasures untold—
　But what must it be to be there?

3 We speak of its freedom from sin,
　From sorrow, temptation, and care,
From trials without and within—
　But what must it be to be there?

4 We speak of its service of love,
　The robes which the glorified wear
The Church of the First-born above—
　But what must it be to be there?

5 Do Thou, Lord, 'midst pleasure or woe,
　For heaven our spirits prepare;
Then soon shall we joyfully know
　And feel what it is to be there.

GENERAL HYMNS.

387. Moderate. Vox Angelica. P. M.

Hark! hark, my soul; Angelic songs are swelling O'er earth's green fields, and ocean's wave-beat shore:
How sweet the truth those blessed strains are telling Of that new life when sin shall be no more!
Angels of Jesus, Angels of light, Singing to welcome the pilgrims of the night,
Singing to welcome the pilgrims, the pilgrims of the night. A-men, A-men.

2 Onward we go, for still we hear them singing,
"Come, weary souls, for Jesus bids you come;"
And through the dark, its echoes sweetly ringing,
The music of the Gospel leads us home.
Angels of Jesus, &c.

3 Far, far away, like bells at evening pealing,
The voice of Jesus sounds o'er land and sea,
And laden souls by thousands meekly stealing,
Kind Shepherd, turn their weary steps to Thee.
Angels of Jesus, &c.

4 Rest comes at length, though life be long and dreary,
The day must dawn, and darksome night be past;
All journeys end in welcome to the weary,
And heaven, the heart's true home, will come at last.
Angels of Jesus, &c.

5 Angels, sing on! your faithful watches keeping;
Sing us sweet fragments of the songs above;
Till morning's joy shall end the night of weeping,
And life's long shadows break in cloudless love.
Angels of Jesus, &c.

GENERAL HYMNS.

388.

PARADISE.
P. M.

Moderate.

O Par-a-dise! O Par-a-dise! Who doth not crave for rest? Who would not seek the hap-py land Where they that loved are blest? Where loy-al hearts and true Stand ev-er in the light; All rap-ture thro' and thro' In God's most ho-ly sight. A-MEN.

2 O Paradise, O Paradise,
  The world is growing old;
Who would not be at rest and free
  Where love is never cold?
    Where loyal hearts and true, &c.

3 O Paradise, O Paradise,
  'Tis weary waiting here;
I long to be where Jesus is,
  To feel, to see Him near;
    Where loyal hearts and true, &c.

4 O Paradise, O Paradise,
  I want to sin no more,
I want to be as pure on earth
  As on thy spotless shore;
    Where loyal hearts and true, &c.

5 O Paradise, O Paradise,
  I greatly long to see
The special place my dearest Lord
  In love prepares for me;
    Where loyal hearts and true, &c.

6 Lord Jesus, King of Paradise,
    O keep me in Thy love,
  And guide me to that happy land
    Of perfect rest above;
      Where loyal hearts and true,
      Stand ever in the light,
      All rapture through and through,
      In God's most holy sight.

389.

Parry. 8s. 7s. D.

Listen to the wondrous story. Jesus left His throne on high;
He, the Lord of life and glory, Came to dwell on earth and die.
Prophets thro' the long past ages, From Creation's early dawn,
Christ foretold in sacred pages, Shadowing forth a glorious morn. A-MEN.

2 Like a vein of metal golden,
  Through the Holy books it ran;
  First obscured in language olden,
  Then a promise clear to man.
  "Unto us a child is given,"
  Formed like us in mortal mould;
  Sinless as the hosts of heaven,
  Jesus, Shepherd of the fold.

3 Seraphs bright on high adore Him
  In the crystal paven street;
  Cast their glittering crowns before Him
  At the blessèd Saviour's feet.

  He has closed hell's yawning portals,
  Opening wide the gates of heaven;
  He has won for sinful mortals
  Peace, the peace of the forgiven.

390.

Regent Square. 8s. 7s. Six lines.

Joyous.

Light's abode, celestial Salem, Vision whence true peace doth spring;

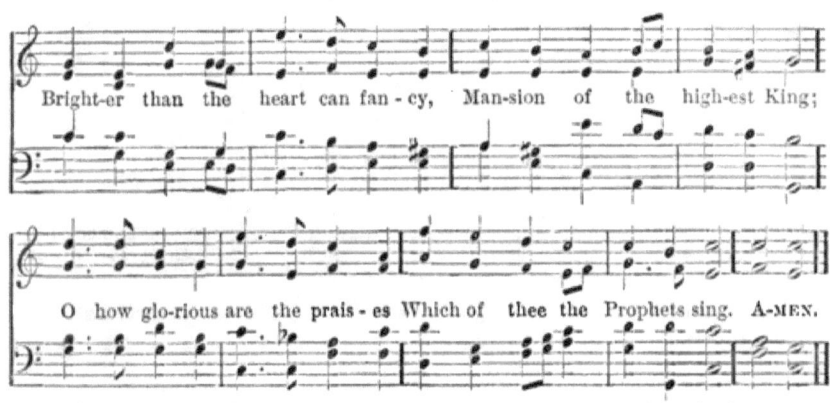

Bright-er than the heart can fan-cy, Man-sion of the high-est King;

O how glo-rious are the prais-es Which of thee the Prophets sing. A-MEN.

2 There for ever and for ever
   Alleluia is outpoured;
For unending, for unbroken,
   Is the feast-day of the Lord;
All is pure and all is holy
   That within thy walls is stored.

3 There no cloud nor passing vapour
   Dims the brightness of the air;
Endless noonday, glorious noonday,
   From the Sun of suns is there;
There no night brings rest from labour,
   There unknown are toil and care.

4 O how glorious and resplendent,
   Fragile body, shalt thou be,
When endued with so much beauty,
   Full of health, and strong and free;
Full of vigour, full of pleasure,
   That shall last eternally.

5 Now with gladness, now with courage,
   Bear the burden on thee laid,
That hereafter these thy labours
   May with endless gifts be paid,
And in everlasting glory
   Thou with brightness be arrayed.

Miscellaneous.

391. Moderate.   CRUSADERS' HYMN. P. M.

Beau-ti-ful Saviour, King of cre-a-tion, Son of God and Son of Man!

Tru-ly I'd love Thee, Tru-ly I'd serve Thee, Light of my soul, my Joy, my Crown. AMEN.

2 Fair are the meadows,
   Fairer the woodlands,
Robed in flowers of blooming spring;
   Jesus is fairer,
   Jesus is purer,
He makes our sorrowing spirits sing.

3 Fair is the sunshine,
   Fairer the moonlight,
And the sparkling stars on high;
   Jesus shines brighter,
   Jesus shines purer,
Than all the angels in the sky.

4 Beautiful Saviour,
   Lord of the nations,
Son of God and Son of man!
   Glory and honour,
   Praise, adoration,
Now and for evermore be Thine.

GENERAL HYMNS.

392. Moderate. S. LUCY. D. C. M.

When Je-sus left His Father's throne, He chose an humble birth; Like us, un-hon-our'd and unknown, He came to dwell on earth, Like Him may we be found be-low, In wisdom's path of peace; Like Him in grace and knowledge grow, As years and strength increase. A-MEN.

2 Sweet were His words and kind His look,
    When mothers round Him press'd;
  Their infants in His arms He took,
    And on His bosom bless'd.
  Safe from the world's alluring harms,
    Beneath His watchful eye,
  Thus in the circle of His arms
    May we for ever lie.

3 When Jesus into Salem rode,
    The children sang around;
  For joy they pluck'd the palms, and
    Their garments on the ground. [strow'd
  Hosanna our glad voices raise,
    Hosanna to our King!
  Should we forget our Saviour's praise,
    The stones themselves would sing.

393. Quietly. MERIEL. 6s. 5s.

Je-sus, meek and gen-tle, Son of God Most High, Pity-ing, lov-ing Sa-viour, Hear Thy children's cry. A-MEN.

2 Pardon our offences,
    Loose our captive chains,
  Break down every idol
    Which our soul detains.

3 Give us holy freedom,
    Fill our hearts with love;
  Draw us, Holy Jesus,
    To the realms above.

4 Lead us on our journey,
    Be Thyself the Way,
  Through terrestrial darkness,
    To celestial day.

5 Jesus, meek and gentle,
    Son of God Most High,
  Pitying, loving Saviour,
    Hear Thy children's cry.

GENERAL HYMNS.

394. *Quietly.*
S. AGATHA.
8s. 7s. Six lines.

Gra-cious Saviour, gentle Shepherd, Lit-tle ones are dear to Thee; Gathered with Thine arms, and car-ried In Thy bos-om may we be; Sweetly, fond-ly, safely tend-ed, From all want and an-ger free. A-MEN.

2 Tender Shepherd, never leave us
From Thy fold to go astray;
By Thy look of love directed
May we walk the narrow way;
Thus direct us, and protect us,
Lest we fall an easy prey.

3 Let Thy holy Word instruct us;
Fill our minds with heavenly light,
Let Thy love and grace constrain us
To approve whate'er is right,
Take Thine easy yoke and wear it,
And to prove Thy burden light.

4 Taught to lisp the holy praises
Which on earth Thy children sing,
Both with lips and hearts unfeigned
May we our thank-offerings bring;
Then, with all the saints in glory,
Join to praise our Lord and King.

395. *Moderate.*
HOLYROOD.
S. M.

Fair waved the gold-en corn In Ca-naan's pleas-ant land, When full of joy some shi-ning morn, Went forth the rea-per-band. A-MEN.

2 To God so good and great
Their cheerful thanks they pour;
Then carry to His temple-gate
The choicest of their store.

3 Like Israel, Lord, we give
Our earliest fruits to Thee,
And pray that, long as we shall live,
We may Thy children be.

4 Thine is our youthful prime,
And life and all its powers;
Be with us in our morning time,
And bless our evening hours.

5 In wisdom let us grow,
As years and strength are given,
That we may serve Thy Church below,
And join Thy saints in heaven.

396.

BEATITUDE.
C. M.

Thou art the Way; to Thee alone From sin and death we flee:
And he who would the Father seek, Must seek Him, Lord, by Thee. A-MEN.

2 Thou art the Truth; Thy word alone
True wisdom can impart;
Thou only canst inform the mind,
And purify the heart.

3 Thou art the Life; the rending tomb
Proclaims Thy conquering arm;
And those who put their trust in Thee
Nor death nor hell shall harm.

4 Thou art the Way, the Truth, the Life,
Grant us that Way to know,
That Truth to keep, that Life to win,
Whose joys eternal flow.

397.

SILOAM.
C. M.

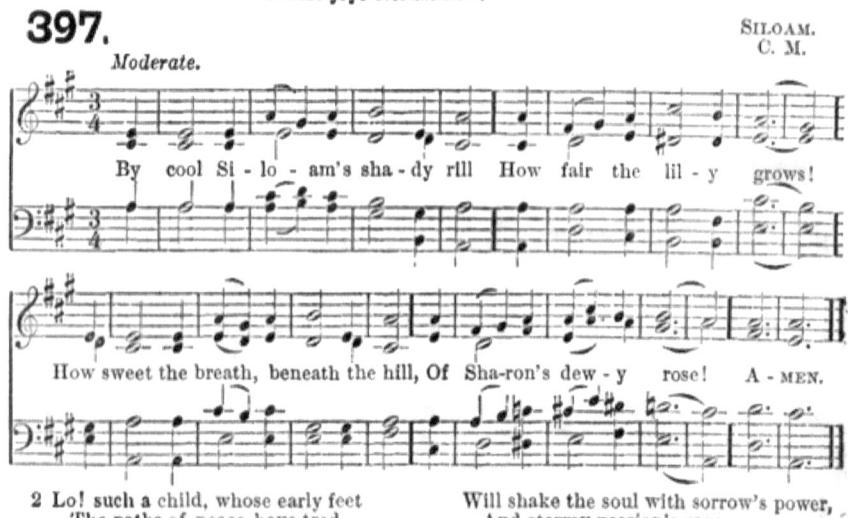

By cool Siloam's shady rill How fair the lily grows!
How sweet the breath, beneath the hill, Of Sharon's dewy rose! A-MEN.

2 Lo! such a child, whose early feet
The paths of peace have trod,
Whose secret heart, with influence sweet,
Is upward drawn to God.

3 By cool Siloam's shady rill
The lily must decay;
The rose that blooms beneath the hill
Must shortly fade away.

4 And soon, too soon, the wintry hour
Of man's maturer age
Will shake the soul with sorrow's power,
And stormy passion's rage.

5 O Thou, whose infant feet were found
Within Thy Father's shrine,
Whose years, with changeless virtue
Were all alike divine: [crown'd,

6 Dependent on Thy bounteous breath,
We seek Thy grace alone,
In childhood, manhood, age, and death,
To keep us still Thine own.

GENERAL HYMNS.

398.
Quietly.

FLOWERS.
P. M.

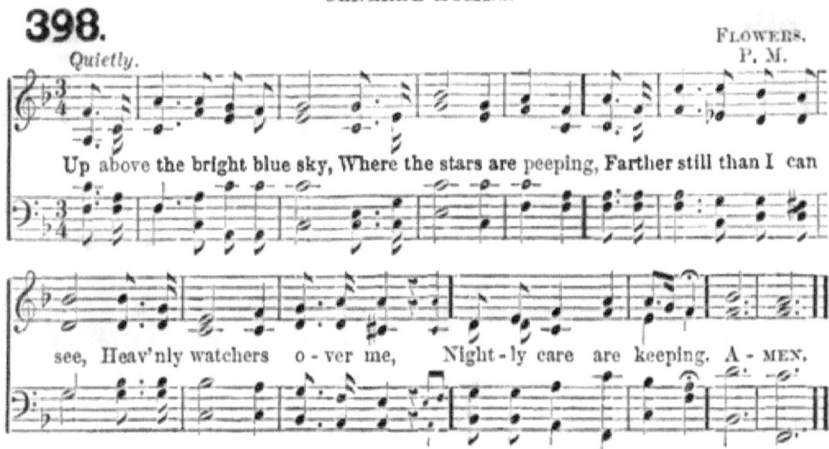

Up above the bright blue sky, Where the stars are peeping, Farther still than I can see, Heav'nly watchers o-ver me, Night-ly care are keeping. A-MEN.

2 And, if like the Angels, I
   Could behold around me,
   I should see them come and go,
   Pass from Heaven to earth below;
   And their hosts surround me.
3 All day long, and all night too,
   While I'm safely sleeping,
   Busy on their task of love,
   They are sent from Heaven above
   Faithful vigil keeping.
4 And whilst us, from evil things
   Angels are defending,
   Little children robed in white

Sing before the throne of light,
   In daylight never ending.
5 Jesus took them for His own,
   Made them pure and holy,
   And on earth His gentle love
   Trained them for their Home above,
   Safe from sin and folly.
6 Blessèd Jesus take me too,
   Though I'm weak and lowly,
   Let Thy gentle grace within
   Make my garments white and clean,
   And my spirit holy.

399.
Quietly.

GUARDIAN ANGELS.
L. M.

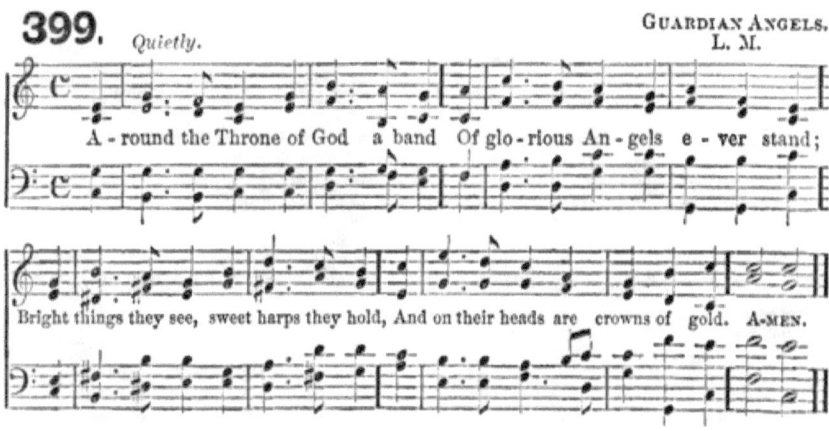

A-round the Throne of God a band Of glo-rious An-gels e-ver stand; Bright things they see, sweet harps they hold, And on their heads are crowns of gold. A-MEN.

2 Some wait around Him, ready still
   To sing His praise and do His will;
   And some, when He commands them, go
   To guard His servants here below.
3 Lord give Thy Angels every day
   Command to guide us on our way,

And bid them every evening keep
   Their watch around us while we sleep.
4 So shall no wicked thing draw near,
   To do us harm or cause us fear;
   And we shall dwell, when life is past,
   With Angels round Thy Throne at last.

400.

Moderate.   Bost. 8s. 7s. D.

All Thy works, O Heavenly Fa-ther, What Thou biddest them, ful-fil,
Shall not I, Thy child, much ra-ther Sing Thy praise and do Thy will?
Hith-er-to Thy hand hath led me, And hath brought me on my way;
Thou hast clothed me, Thou hast fed me, Thou hast blest me ev-ery day. A-MEN.

2 Lord, 'tis of Thy loving kindness
   That Thy Gospel I have known;
Else I might have sat in blindness,
   Bowing down to wood and stone.
To Thy Font my parents brought me,
   Ere Thy tender love I knew;
And Thy minister has taught me
   What to flee, and what to do.

3 Since my time is like an arrow,
   Hast'ning on without delay:
And Thy gate is straight and narrow,
   Very narrow is the way;
Thou who gav'st Thy Son to save me,
   Send Thy Holy Spirit down,
Make me do as Thou wouldst have me,
   Make me more and more Thine own.

401.

Moderate.   ELEANOR. 7s.

God of mer-cy throned on high, Lis-ten from Thy lof-ty seat;

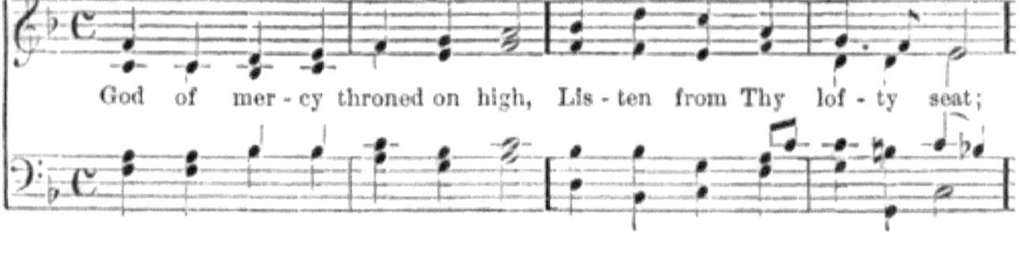

Hear, O hear our humble cry, Guide, O guide our wand'ring feet. A-MEN.

2 Young and erring travellers, we
All our dangers do not know;
Scarcely fear the stormy sea,
Hardly feel the tempest blow.

3 Jesus, Lover of the young,
Cleanse us with Thy blood divine;
Ere the tide of sin grow strong,
Save us, keep us, make us Thine!

4 Let us ever hear Thy voice;
Ask Thy counsel every day;
Saints and angels will rejoice,
If we walk in Wisdom's way.

5 Saviour, give us faith, and pour
Hope and love on every soul.
Hope, till time shall be no more;
Love, while endless ages roll.

402.

ANGEL VOICES.
P. M.

Moderate.

An-gel voi-ces e-ver sing-ing Round Thy throne of light,

An-gel harps, for e-ver ring-ing, Rest not day nor night;

Thousands on-ly live to bless Thee, And confess Thee, Lord of might! A-MEN.

2 Thou, who art beyond the farthest
Mental eye can scan,
Can it be that Thou regardest
Songs of sinful man?
Can we feel that Thou art near us
And wilt hear us? Yea, we can.

3 Yea, we know Thy love rejoices
O'er each work of Thine!
Thou didst ears and hands and voices
For Thy praise combine!
Craftsman's art and music's measure
For Thy pleasure, didst design.

4 Here, Great God, to-day we offer
Of Thine own to Thee;
And for Thine acceptance proffer
All unworthily,
Hearts and minds, and hands and voices,
In our choicest melody.

GENERAL HYMNS.

403.

Moderate.   ROSSLYN. P. M.

I think when I read that sweet story of old, When Jesus was here among men, How He call'd little children as lambs to His fold, I should like to have been with them then. A-MEN.

2 I wish that His hands had been placed on my head,
   That His arm had been thrown around me,
And that I might have seen His kind look when He said,
   Let the little ones come unto Me.

3 Yet still to His footstool in prayer I may go,
   And ask for a share in His love:
And if I thus earnestly seek Him below,
   I shall see Him and hear Him above.

4 In that beautiful place He has gone to prepare
   For all who are washed and forgiven;
And many dear children shall be with Him there,
   For of such is the kingdom of heaven.

5 But thousands and thousands who wander and fall,
   Never heard of that heavenly home;
I wish they could know there is room for them all,
   And that Jesus has bid them to come.

404.

Moderate.   HOPKINS. P. M.

God hath made the moon, whose beam Shimmers soft o'er hill and stream, Lighting with her

sil-v'ry gleam All our lone-ly way: Glides she, with companions bright, Thro' the si-lent hours of night; Then fades in o-ver-whelming light, Lost in per-fect day. A-MEN.

2 God hath made the glorious sun,
Through his daily course to run;
From the dawn till day is done
Brightly shineth he.
When his circling round is o'er,
And we see him here no more,
He rises on a brighter shore,
Far beyond the sea.

3 God hath sent me here below,
In my daily life to show,
Constant love to friend and foe,
As He showed for me.
When we here have closed our eyes,
Sunk where death's dark ocean lies,
To worlds of glory may we rise,
Lighted, Lord, by Thee!

405.

Moderate.

WILFRED.
7s.

Gen-tle Je-sus, meek and mild, Look up-on a lit-tle child; Pit-y my sim-plic-i-ty; Suf-fer me to come to Thee. A-MEN.

2 Hold me fast in Thine embrace;
Let me see Thy smiling face;
Give me, Lord, Thy blessing give;
Pray for me, and I shall live.

3 Lamb of God, I look to Thee,
Thou shalt my example be;
Thou art gentle, meek, and mild;
Thou wast once a little child.

4 Let me, above all, fulfil
God my Heavenly Father's will;
Never His good Spirit grieve,
Only to His glory live.

5 Loving Jesus, gentle Lamb,
In Thy gracious hands I am;
Make me, Saviour, what Thou art,
Live Thyself within my heart.

6 I shall then show forth Thy praise,
Serve Thee all my happy days;
Then the world shall always see
Christ, the holy Child, in me.

GENERAL HYMNS.

406.

Cheerful.

HOLY INNOCENTS.
8s. 7s. D.

Heaven-ly Fa-ther, send Thy bless-ing On Thy chil-dren gath-ered here,

May they all, Thy Name con-fess-ing, Be to Thee for e-ver dear:

May they be like Jo-seph, lov-ing, Du-ti-ful, and chaste, and pure;

And their faith like Da-vid, prov-ing, Steadfast un-to death en-dure. A-MEN.

2 Holy Saviour, who in meekness
  Didst vouchsafe a child to be,
Guide their steps and help their weakness,
  Bless and make them like to Thee;
Bear Thy lambs when they are weary
  In Thine arms and at Thy breast,
Through life's desert dry and dreary,
  Bring them **to** Thy heavenly **rest.**

3 Spread Thy golden pinions o'er them,
  Holy Spirit from above,
Guide them, lead them, go before them,
  Give them peace, and joy, and love:
Thy true temples, Holy Spirit,
  May they with Thy glory shine,
And immortal bliss inherit,
  And for evermore be Thine.

407.

Moderate.

CECIL.
8s. 7s. 4.

Fa-ther, though Thy Name be ho-ly, High and lift-ed up Thy throne,

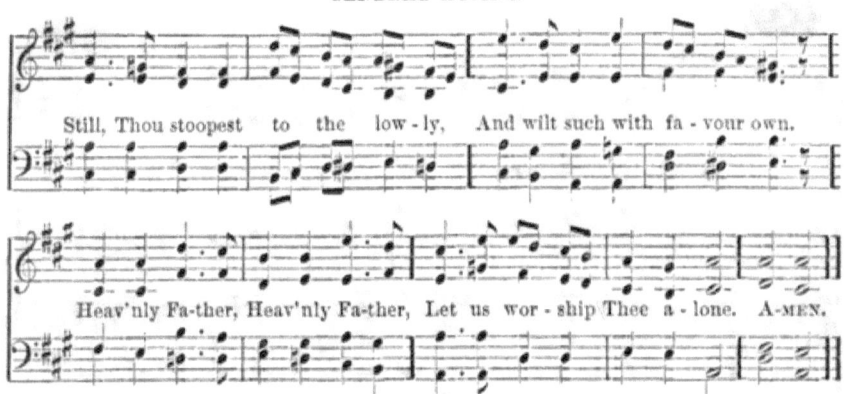

Still, Thou stoopest to the lowly, And wilt such with favour own.
Heav'nly Father, Heav'nly Father, Let us worship Thee alone. A-MEN.

2 Heaven itself cannot contain Thee,
   Bright and glorious as Thou art;
   Yet a little child may claim Thee
   As a dweller in his heart.
     Heavenly Father,
   Let me not from Thee depart.

3 With Thy gracious presence cheer me,
   Keep me in Thy perfect love;
   All my journey be Thou near me,
   Bring me to Thy home above.
     Heavenly Father,
   May I all Thy fulness prove!

408.

Joyous. BREIDDEN. 7s. 6s.

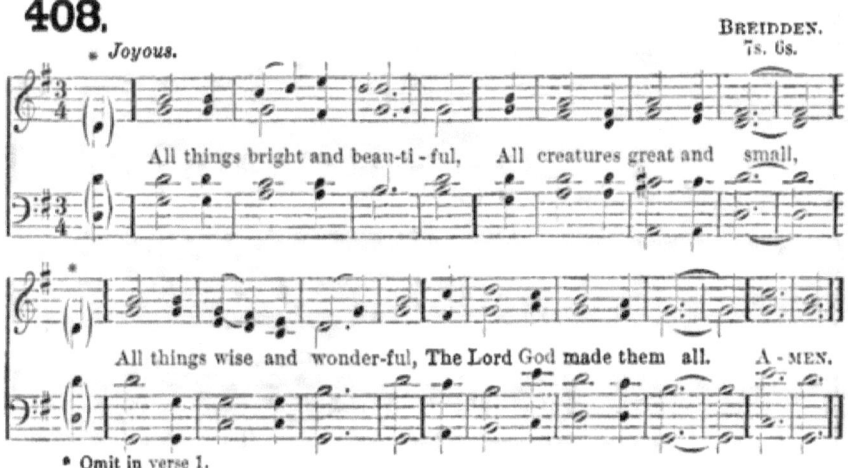

All things bright and beautiful, All creatures great and small,
All things wise and wonderful, The Lord God made them all. A-MEN.

* Omit in verse 1.

2 Each little flower that opens,
   Each little bird that sings,
   He made their glowing colours,
   He made their tiny wings.

3 The rich man in his castle,
   The poor man at his gate,
   He made them, high and lowly,
   And ordered their estate.

4 The purple-headed mountain,
   The river running by,
   The sunset, and the morning
   That brightens up the sky.

5 The cold wind in the winter,
   The pleasant summer sun,
   The ripe fruits in the garden,
   He made them every one.

6 The tall trees in the greenwood,
   The meadows where we play,
   The rushes by the water,
   We gather every day;

7 He gave us eyes to see them,
   And lips that we might tell
   How great is God Almighty,
   Who has made all things well.

2 He only is the Maker
　Of all things near and far;
　He paints the wayside flower,
　He lights the evening star;
　The winds and waves obey Him,
　By Him the birds are fed;
　Much more to us, His children,
　He gives our daily bread.
　　Cho.—All good gifts, &c.

3 We thank Thee, then, O Father,
　For all things bright and good,
　The seed-time and the harvest,
　Our life, our health, our food;
　Accept the gifts we offer,
　For all Thy love imparts,
　And, what Thou most desirest
　Our humble, thankful hearts.
　　Cho.—All good gifts &c.

410. 7s. 6s. D.

Moderate. — STAINER.

I love the Ho-ly An-gels, So beau-ti-ful and bright;
And though I can-not see them, They're with me day and night:
They watch a-round my bed-side, They see me at my play;
They know my eve-ry ac-tion, They hear the words I say. A-MEN.

2 'Tis God our Heavenly Father,
  Who doth the Angels send,
To guard His little children
  Until their life shall end.
When we are cross and naughty,
  The Holy Angels grieve,
For they are sad when children
  The way of goodness leave.

3 And when I die, the Angels
  Will bear my soul away,
While here my body resteth
  Until the Judgment Day.
They'll bear me gently, softly,
  With loving care most sweet,
And lay me down in safety
  At my Redeemer's feet.

4 There with the Holy Angels,
  And holy men of old,
And all good friends who loved me,
  Too many to be told,
Shall I be with the Angels,
  And all that people bright,
For ever and for ever,
  In God's most glorious light,

5 Among the flowers of Heaven
  That never die or fade,
And far more lovely music,
  Than here on earth is made,
For ever, ever happy
  Together we shall be,
For there our Lord and Saviour
  For ever we shall see!

411.

Moderate. S. HELIER. 7s. 6s. D.

The wise may bring their learning, The rich may bring their wealth,
And some may bring their greatness, And some bring strength and health;
We, too, would bring our treasures, To offer to the King;
We have no wealth or learning, What shall we children bring? A-MEN.

2 We'll bring Him hearts that love Him,
  We'll bring Him thankful praise;
  And young souls meekly striving
    To walk in holy ways.
  And these shall be the treasures
    We offer to the King,
  And these are gifts that ever
    The poorest child may bring.

3 We'll bring the little duties
    We have to do each day,
  We'll try our best to please Him
    At home, at school, at play.
  And better are these treasures
    To offer to our King,
  Than richest gifts without them;
    Yet these a child may bring.

412.

Moderate. CALKIN. 6s. 5s. D

Jesus Christ, our Saviour, Once for us a child, In Thy whole behaviour,

Meek, obedient, mild; In Thy footsteps treading We Thy lambs will be, Foe nor danger dread-ing, While we follow Thee. A-MEN.

2 For all Thou bestowest,
All Thou dost withhold,
Whatsoe'er Thou knowest
Best for us, Thy fold.
For all gifts and graces
While we live below,
Till in heavenly places
We Thy face shall know.

3 We, Thy children, raising
Unto Thee our hearts,
In Thy constant praising
Bear our duteous parts.
As Thy love hath won us
From the world away,
Still Thy hands put on us;
Bless us day by day.

4 Let Thine Angels guide us;
Let Thine Arms enfold;
In Thy Bosom hide us,
Sheltered from the cold;
To Thyself us gather,
'Mid the ransomed host,
Praising Thee, the Father,
And the Holy Ghost.

413.

S. MONICA.
7s.

Brightly.

Sweet it is for child like me, Bless-ed Lord, to think of Thee, For our sake so low-ly made, And in Bethlehem's manger laid. A-MEN.

2 Of the Virgin Mary born,
Thou wilt not an infant scorn,
Wrapped in swaddling clothes wast Thou,
Throned in highest glory now.

3 Laid in helplessness to rest,
Pillowed upon Mary's breast,
Thou, whose everlasting Arms
Fold us all secure from harms.

4 What can little ones like me
Find to offer unto Thee?
Only of Thy bounty fed,
Suppliants for our daily bread.

5 Saviour, from Thy Word I learn
There are gifts Thou wilt not spurn—
Gifts that little ones may bring
To their Brother and their King.

6 Childlike heart of truth shall be
Dearer gift than gold to Thee,
And its prayer and psalm shall rise
Like sweet incense to the skies.

7 Teach me then Thy steps to trace,
Jesus, full of truth and grace,
All Thy footsteps as a child,
Holy, harmless, undefiled.

GENERAL HYMNS.

2 Forbear with all our sins,
  Our wayward selfish will;
  Our penitence accept,
  And guide and bless us still.
"Heirs of Salvation" made
  Within His Holy Place,
The Angels now behold
  Our Heavenly Father's Face!

3 They worship, evermore
  On His Eternal Throne,
The perfect God and Man,
  The sole Begotten One.
Yet, day and night they guard
  His little ones from ill,
And by their works of love,
  They do His perfect will.

4 O gracious Father! grant
  That we, so loved and blest,
Like them, from praise and love
  May never, never rest.
Now to the Lamb, once slain,
  Blessing and thanks be given,
By Angels and by men,
  On earth, as, aye, in Heaven!

415.

Joyful.

IRBY.
8s. 7s. 7.

Once in royal David's city Stood a lowly cattle shed,
Where a mother laid her Baby, In a manger for His bed:
Mary was that mother mild, Jesus Christ her little Child. A-MEN.

2 He came down to earth from heaven,
   Who is God and Lord of all,
And His shelter was a stable,
   And His cradle was a stall;
With the poor, the mean, and lowly,
Lived on earth our Saviour Holy.

3 And, through all His wondrous childhood,
   He would honour, and obey,
Love, and watch the lowly maiden
   In whose gentle arms He lay;
Christian children all must be
Mild, obedient, good as He.

4 For He is our childhood's Pattern,
   Day by day like us He grew,
He was little, weak, and helpless,
   Tears and smiles like us He knew;
And He feeleth for our sadness,
And He shareth in our gladness.

5 And our eyes at last shall see Him,
   Through His own redeeming love,
For that Child so dear and gentle
   Is our Lord in heaven above;
And He leads His children on
To the place where He is gone.

6 Not in that poor lowly stable,
   With the oxen standing by,
We shall see Him; but in heaven,
   Set at God's right hand on high;
When like stars His children crowned
All in white shall wait around.

416. Moderate.   PURITAS.   L. M. D.

Bless-ed are the pure in heart; They have loved the bet-ter part;
When life's jour-ney they have trod, They shall go to see their God.
Till in glo-ry they ap-pear They shall oft-en see Him here;
And His grace shall learn to know In His glorious works be-low. A-MEN.

2 When the sun begins to rise,
Spreading brightness through the skies,
They will love to praise and bless,
Christ, the Sun of Righteousness.
In the watches of the night,
When the stars are clear and bright,
"Thus the just shall shine," they say,
"In the Resurrection-day."

3 When the leaves in Autumn die,
Falling fast and silently, [dead,
"These," they think, "that now seem
Shall in Spring lift up their head."
God in everything they see;
First in all their thoughts is He:
They had loved the better part:—
Blessèd are the pure in heart.

417. Moderate.   ALLEN.   8s. 7s. 7.

Bless-ed Je-sus, wilt Thou hear us, Lit-tle children though we be?

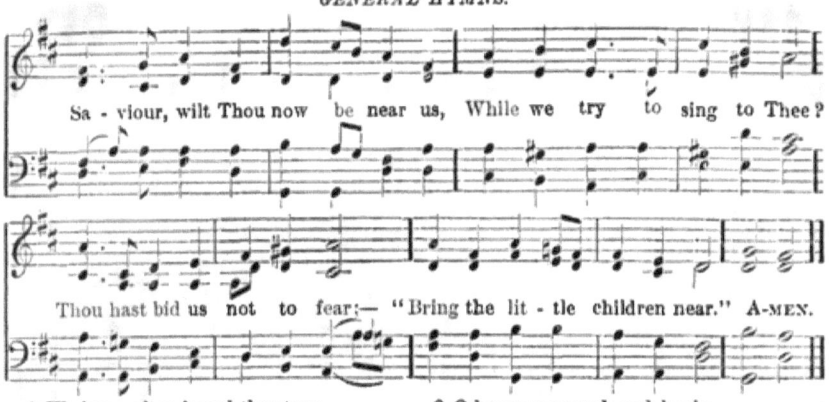

Saviour, wilt Thou now be near us, While we try to sing to Thee? Thou hast bid us not to fear:— "Bring the little children near." A-MEN.

2 We have often heard the story
    Of Thy great and wondrous love;
  How Thou left the world of glory,
    And Thy Father's house above,
  Here to suffer and to die
  For such little ones as I.

3 O how very meek and lowly
    Little children then should be,
  When the Son of God most holy
    Came a little child like me:—
  Thou didst suffer grief and shame
  Like a meek and quiet lamb.

4 May our sins be all forgiven,
    Take our naughty hearts away;
  Bring us all at last to heaven,
    Ever there with Thee to stay;
  There may we, Thy children, raise
  Hymns of joy and perfect praise.

418. *Moderate.* VENABLES. L. M.

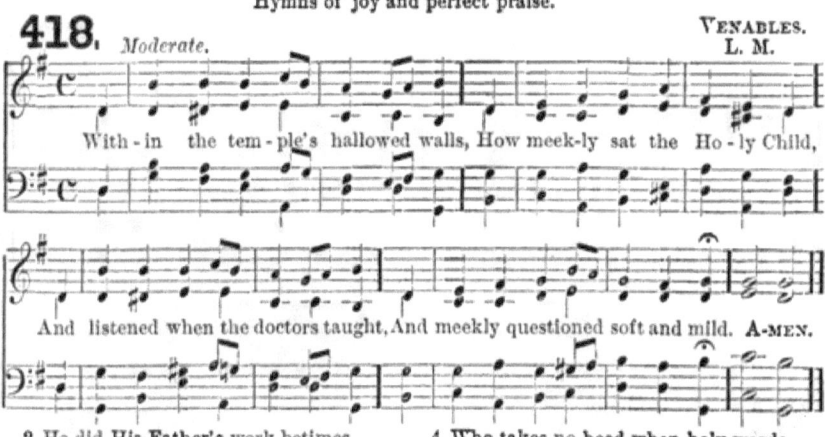

Within the temple's hallowed walls, How meekly sat the Holy Child, And listened when the doctors taught, And meekly questioned soft and mild. A-MEN.

2 He did His Father's work betimes,
    He loved within His courts to stay,
  While three long days the Mother trod
    Alone her weary homeward way.

3 Oh! shame on any Christian child
    Who does not love the house of prayer;
  Who goes with cold, unwilling heart,
    To serve his Heavenly Father there:

4 Who takes no heed when holy words
    Are spoken to his listless ears,
  Nor ever questions in his heart,
    What mean the sacred things he hears.

5 Come let him learn what Jesus did,
    And love to trace, with wondering eyes,
  His perfect works, His holy ways,
    Who was in early years so wise.

6 And let him ask of God in heaven,
    A spirit teachable and mild,
  A simple heart to learn and love,
    Like Jesus, that sweet, Holy Child.

GENERAL HYMNS.

419. *Moderate. Voices in unison.* THANET. 7s. 6s. D.

We sing a loving Jesus Who left His throne above,
And came on earth to ransom The children of His love;
It is an oft-told story, And yet we love to tell
How Christ, the King of glory, Once deigned with man to dwell. A-MEN.

2 We sing a holy Jesus;
　No taint of sin defiled
The Babe of David's city,
　The pure and stainless child:
O teach us, blessèd Saviour,
　Thy heavenly grace to seek,
And let our whole behaviour,
　Like Thine, be mild and meek.

3 We sing a lowly Jesus,
　No Kingly crown He had:
His heart was bowed with anguish,
　His face was marred and sad;
In deep humiliation
　He came, His work to do;
O Lord of our salvation,
　Let us be humble too.

4 We sing a mighty Jesus,
　Whose voice could raise the dead,
The sightless eyes He opened,
　The famished souls He fed.
Thou camest to deliver
　Mankind from sin and shame;
Redeemer and life giver,
　We praise Thy holy Name!

5 We sing a coming Jesus;
　The time is drawing near,
When Christ with all His Angels
　In glory shall appear;
Lord, save us, we entreat Thee,
　In this Thy day of grace,
That we may gladly meet Thee,
　And see Thee face to face.

GENERAL HYMNS.

420.
Moderate.

S. JOHN'S.
8s. 7s. D.

Who is this, so weak and help-less, Child of low-ly He-brew maid? Rude-ly in a sta-ble shel-ter'd, Cold-ly in a man-ger laid? 'Tis the Lord of all cre-a-tion, Who this won-drous path hath trod; He is God from e-ver-last-ing, And to e-ver-last-ing, God. A-MEN.

2 Who is this, a Man of sorrows,
   Walking sadly life's hard way,
Homeless, weary, sighing, weeping
   Over sin and Satan's sway?
'Tis our God, our glorious Saviour,
   Who above the starry sky
Now prepares the many mansions,
   Where no tear can dim the eye.

3 Who is this—behold Him shedding
   Drops of blood upon the ground?
Who is this—despised, rejected,
   Mock'd, insulted, beaten, bound?
'Tis our God, who gifts and graces
   On His Church now poureth down;
Who shall smite in holy vengeance
   All His foes beneath His throne.

4 Who is this that hangeth dying,
   While the rude world scoffs and scorns,
On the cross with sinners number'd,
   Pierced by nails and crown'd with thorns?
'Tis the God who ever liveth
   'Mid the shining ones on high,
In the glorious golden city
   Reigning everlastingly.

GENERAL HYMNS.

421.

Moderate. CHEDDAR.
8s. 7s. D.

Lord, a lit-tle band and low-ly, We are come to sing to Thee,
Thou art great, and high, and ho-ly, Oh! how sol-emn we should be.
Fill our hearts with thoughts of Je-sus, And of heav'n where He is gone,
And let nothing e-ver please us, He would grieve to look up-on. A-MEN.

2 For we know the Lord of glory
  Always sees what children do,
And is writing now the story
  Of our thoughts and actions too.

Let our sins be all forgiven,
  Make us fear whate'er is wrong;
Lead us on our way to heaven,
  There to sing a nobler song.

422.

Moderate. SAMUEL.
6s. 8s.

Hushed was the eve-ning hymn, The tem-ple courts were dark,

GENERAL HYMNS.

The lamp was burning dim, Before the sacred ark: When suddenly a voice divine Rang thro' the silence of the shrine. A-MEN.

2 The old man, meek and mild,
　The priest of Israel, slept;
His watch the temple-child,
　The little Levite, kept;
And what from Eli's sense was sealed,
The LORD to Hannah's son revealed.

3 Oh! give me Samuel's ear,
　The open ear, O Lord,
Alive and quick to hear
　Each whisper of Thy word,
Like him to answer at Thy call,
And to obey Thee first of all.

4 Oh! give me Samuel's heart,
　A lowly heart, that waits
Where in Thy House Thou art,
　Or watches at Thy gates,
By day and night, a heart that still
Moves at the breathing of Thy will.

5 Oh! give me Samuel's mind,
　A sweet, unmurmuring faith,
Obedient and resigned
　To Thee in life and death,
That I may read with childlike eyes
Truths that are hidden from the wise.

423. *Brightly.*

HAPPY LAND.
P. M.

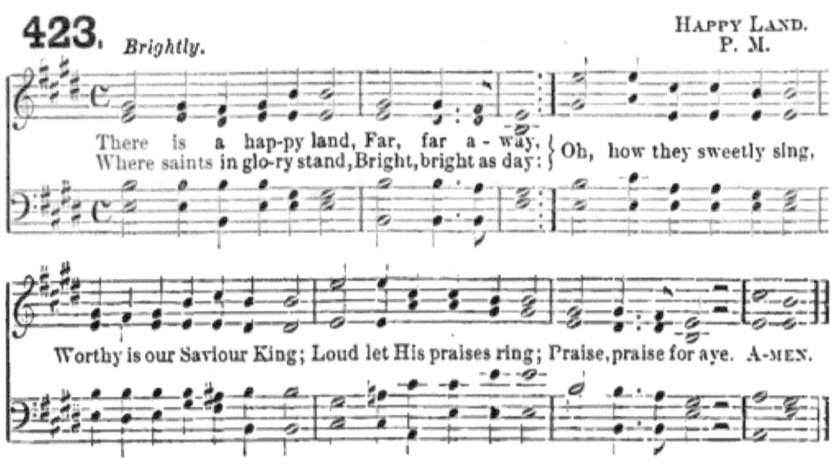

There is a happy land, Far, far away, } Oh, how they sweetly sing,
Where saints in glory stand, Bright, bright as day: }
Worthy is our Saviour King; Loud let His praises ring; Praise, praise for aye. A-MEN.

2 Come to this happy land,
　Come, come away:
Why will ye doubting stand?
　Why still delay?
Oh, we shall happy be,
When from sin and sorrow free;
Lord, we shall live with Thee,
　Blest, blest for aye.

3 Bright in that happy land
　Beams every eye;
Kept by a Father's hand,
　Love cannot die.
On then to glory run,
Be a crown and kingdom won;
And bright above the sun
　Reign, reign for aye.

GENERAL HYMNS.

424. *Cheerful.*

RUGBY.
8s. 7s. D.

We are lit-tle Chris-tian chil-dren, We can run, and talk, and play;
The great God of earth and heav-en, Made and keeps us eve-ry day.

2. We are lit-tle Chris-tian chil-dren; Christ, the Son of God most high,
With His precious Blood redeem'd us, Dy-ing that we might not die. A-MEN.

3 We are little Christian children,
 God, the Holy Ghost, is here;
Dwelling in our hearts, to make us
 Kind and holy, good and dear.

4 We are little Christian children,
 Sav'd by Him who lov'd us most,
We believe in God Almighty,
 Father, Son, and Holy Ghost.

425.

Cheerful. WESTLAKE. 7s. D.

In our work, and in our play, Jesus, be Thou ever near;
Guarding, guiding all the day, Keeping in Thy holy fear.

2. Thou didst toil, a lowly Child, In the far off Holy Land,
Blessing labour undefiled, Pure and honest of the hand. A-MEN.

3 Thou wilt bless our playhour too,
  If we ask Thy succour strong;
Watch o'er all we say and do,
  Hold us back from guilt and wrong.

4 Oh! how happy thus to spend,
  Work and playtime in His sight,
Till the Rest which shall not end,
  Till the Day which knows not night.

GENERAL HYMNS.

426.
Moderate. SILKSWORTH. 7s. 5s. 7.

Eve-ry morning the red sun Ris-es warm and bright; But the evening com-eth on, And the dark, cold night: There's a bright land far a-way, Where is nev-er end-ing day. A—MEN.

2 Every spring the sweet young flowers
　Open fresh and gay;
　Till the chilly autumn hours
　　Wither them away:
　There's a land we have not seen
　Where the trees are always green.

3 Little birds sing songs of praise
　All the summer long;
　But in colder, shorter days
　　They forget their song:
　There's a place where Angels sing
　Ceaseless praises to their King.

4 Christ our Lord is ever near
　Those who follow Him!
　But we cannot see Him here,
　　For our eyes are dim:
　There is a most happy place,
　Where men always see His Face.

5 Who shall go to that **bright** land?
　All who do the right:
　Holy children there shall **stand**,
　　In their **robes** of white,
　For that Heaven so bright and blest,
　Is our everlasting rest.

427.
Moderate. JESU, BONE PASTOR. 8s. 7s. 4.

Sa-viour, like a shep-herd lead us, Much we need Thy ten-der care;

GENERAL HYMNS.

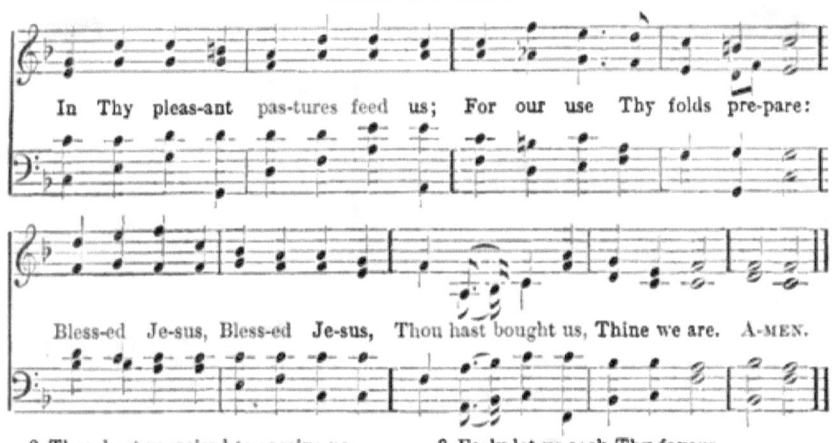

In Thy pleas-ant pas-tures feed us; For our use Thy folds pre-pare:
Bless-ed Je-sus, Bless-ed Je-sus, Thou hast bought us, Thine we are. A-MEN.

2 Thou hast promised to receive us,
    Poor and sinful though we be;
  Thou hast mercy to relieve us;
    Grace to cleanse and power to free:
        Blessèd Jesus!
  Let us early turn to Thee.

3 Early let us seek Thy favour,
    Early let us learn Thy will;
  Do Thou, Lord, our only Saviour,
    With Thy love our bosoms fill:
        Blessèd Jesus!
  Thou hast loved us,—love us still.

428.

Moderate. BERNE.
7s. 6s.

Where is the Ho-ly Je-sus? He lives in Heav'n a-bove.
He looks up-on good chil-dren, With ten-der-ness and love. A-MEN.

2 Where is the Holy Jesus?
    His home is everywhere,
  He loves that little children
    Should speak to Him in prayer.

3 Once He came down from Heavèn;
    He came a little child;
  He was so good and gentle,
        Obedient, meek, and mild.

4 He had no naughty temper,
    He said no angry word;
  And all good little children
    Should be like Christ their Lord.

5 For He will make them holy,
    And teachable and mild,
  And has sent His Blessèd Spirit
    To every Christian child.

6 Then every night and morning
    When I kneel down to pray,
  I will ask the Holy Jesus,
    To help me day by day.

GENERAL HYMNS.

429.

HERZOG.
C. M. D.

The ro-seate hues of ear ly dawn, The brightness of the day;
The crim-son of the sun-set sky, How fast they fade a-way.
O for the pear-ly gates of Heaven, O for the gold-en floor,
O for the Sun of Righteousness, That set-teth ne-ver-more. A-MEN.

2 The highest hopes we cherish here,
  How fast they tire and faint;
  How many a spot defiles the robe
  That wraps an earthly saint:
  O for a heart that never sins;
  O for a soul wash'd white;
  O for a voice to praise our King,
  Nor weary day or night.

3 Here faith is ours, and heavenly hope,
  And grace to lead us higher;
  But there are perfectness and peace
  Beyond our best desire.
  O by Thy love and anguish, Lord,
  O by Thy life laid down,
  O that we fall not from Thy grace,
  Nor cast away our crown.

GENERAL HYMNS.

430.

Cheerful.

CORINTH.
8s. 7s. D.

What a strange and wondrous sto-ry From the book of God is read,
How the Lord of life and glo-ry Had not where to lay His head;
How He left His throne in heav-en, Here to suf-fer, bleed, and die,
That my soul might be for-gi-ven, And as-cend to God on high. A-MEN.

2 While I bless the Hand which gave me
   Life and health and all things here,
O may He who died to save me,
   To my soul be very dear.
Jesus Christ, my Lord, and Saviour,
   Let me not ungrateful be;
Let my words and my behaviour
   Prove I love and honour Thee.

3 Father, let Thy Holy Spirit
   Still reveal a Saviour's love,
And prepare me to inherit
   Glory, where He reigns above.
There with saints and Angels dwelling,
   May I that great love proclaim,
And with them be ever telling
   All the wonders of His Name.

GENERAL HYMNS.

431.
Joyously.

BONCHURCH.
7s. 6s. D

'Twas God that made the ocean, And laid its sandy bed;
He gave the stars their motion, And built the mountain's head;
He made the rolling thunder, The lightning's forked flame;
His works are full of wonder, All glorious is His Name. A-MEN.

2 And must it not surprise us
　That One, so high and great,
Should see and not despise us,
　Poor sinners, at His feet?
Yet day by day He gives us
　Our raiment and our food;
In sickness He relieves us,
　And is in all things good.

3 But things that are far greater
　His mighty hand hath done;
And sent us blessings sweeter
　Through Christ His only Son;
Who, when He saw us dying
　In sin and sorrow's night,
On wings of mercy flying,
　Came down with life and light.

4 He gives His Word to teach us
　Our danger and our wants;
And kindly doth beseech us
　To take the life He grants.
His Holy Spirit frees us
　From Satan's deadly power;
Leads us by faith to Jesus,
　And makes His glory ours!

432.

RUDSTONE.
C. M. D.

In the soft sea-son of thy youth, In nature's smiling bloom, Ere age ar-rives, and, trembling, wait Its summons to the tomb. 2. Re-mem-ber thy Cre-a-tor, God; For Him thy powers em-ploy. Make Him thy fear, thy love, thy hope, Thy con-fi-dence, thy joy. A-MEN.

3 He shall defend and guide thy course
 Through life's uncertain sea,
 Till thou art landed on the shore
 Of blest eternity.

4 Then seek the Lord betimes, and choose
 The path of heavenly truth;
 The earth affords no lovelier sight
 Than a religious youth.

433.

Moderate.   CANTERBURY. Six 7s.

Lord, Thy children guide and keep, As with feeble steps they press On the pathway, rough and steep, Through this weary wilderness. Holy Jesus, day by day Lead us in the narrow way. A-MEN.

2 There are stony ways to tread;
   Give the strength we sorely lack:
There are tangled paths to thread;
   Light us, lest we miss the track.
Holy Jesus, day by day
Lead us in the narrow way.

3 There are sandy wastes that lie
   Cold and sunless, vast and drear,
Where the feeble faint and die;
   Grant us grace to persevere.
Holy Jesus, day by day
Lead us in the narrow way.

4 There are soft and flowery glades
   Deck'd with golden-fruited trees;
Sunny slopes and scented shades;
   Keep us, Lord, from slothful ease.
Holy Jesus, day by day
Lead us in the narrow way.

5 Upward still to purer heights,
   Onward yet to scenes more blest,
Calmer regions, clearer lights,
   Till we reach the promised rest.
Holy Jesus, day by day
Lead us in the narrow way.

434.

Moderate.   PASTORAL. Six 6s.

Great Shepherd of the sheep, Who all Thy flock dost keep,

Leading by waters calm; Do Thou my foot-steps guide, To follow by Thy side; Make me Thy little lamb, Make me Thy little lamb. A-MEN.

2 But when the road is long,
Thy tender arm and strong
The weary one will bear;
And Thou wilt wash me clean,
And lead to pastures green,
Where all the flowers are fair.

3 Till from the soil of sin,
Cleansed and made pure within,
Dear Saviour, whose I am;
Thou bringest me in love
To Thy safe fold above,
A little snow-white lamb.

435.

Moderate. FRANCES. C. M.

I love to think, though I am young, My Saviour was a child; That Jesus walked this earth along, With feet all un-de-filed. A-MEN.

2 He kept His Father's word of truth,
  As I am taught to do;
And while He walked the paths of youth,
  He walked in wisdom too.

3 I love to think that He who spake,
  And made the blind to see,
And called the sleeping dead to wake,
  Was once a child like me.

4 That He who wore the thorny crown,
  And tasted death's despair,
Had a kind mother like my own,
  And knew her love and care.

5 I know 'twas all for love of me
  That He became a child,
And left the heavens, so fair to see,
  And trod earth's pathway wild.

6 Then, Saviour, who wast once a child,
  A child may come to Thee;
And oh! in all Thy mercy mild,
  Dear Saviour, come to me.

436.

Moderate. BETHLEHEM. 8s. 7s.

Youth-ful days are pass-ing o'er us, Childhood's years will soon be gone;
Cares and sorrows lie before us, Hidden dangers, snares unknown. A-MEN.

2 Oh! may He, who meek and lowly
Visited this world below,
Make us His, and make us holy,
Guard and guide us, where we go.

3 Hark! it is the Saviour calling,
"Come, ye children, come to Me."
Jesus, keep our feet from falling,
Teach us all to follow Thee.

4 Soon we part; it may be, never,
Never here to meet again;
May we meet in heaven for ever,
And the crown eternal gain.

437.

Moderate. FROME. C. M.

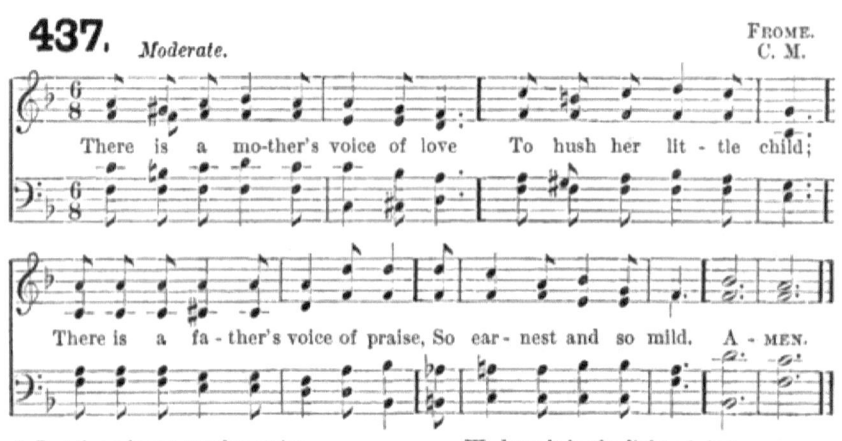

There is a mother's voice of love To hush her little child;
There is a father's voice of praise, So earnest and so mild. A-MEN.

2 But there is yet another voice,
That speaks in gentlest tone—
I think that we can hear it best
When we are quite alone.

3 It is a still, small, holy voice,
The voice of God most high,
That whispers always in our heart,
And says that He is by.

4 The voice will blame us when we're wrong,
And praise us when we're right;

We hear it in the light of day,
And in the quiet night.

5 And even they whose ears are deaf
To every other sound—
When they have listened in their hearts
The still small voice have found.

6 And they have felt that God is good,
And thanked Him for the voice
That told them what was right and true,
And made their hearts rejoice.

GENERAL HYMNS.

438.

NORWOOD.
7s. 6s.

2 Christ smiled on little children,
  And drew them to His breast;
  "Of such is Heaven's kingdom,"
  Of love, and joy, and rest.
3 They trust, and fear no evil,
  Confiding, gentle, kind;
  In simple faith, as children,
  We happiness may find.
4 They sing their joyous carols,
  With lips and hearts as free

As winds, and waves, and sunshine,
  Or birds upon the tree.
5 They love the fields and flowers,
  The fragrance, and the light;
  And all this world of ours
  For them is ever bright.
6 They love the name of Jesus,
  They trust His tender care,
  And all they know of Heaven,
  Is—Christ Himself is there.

439.

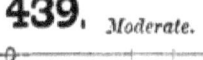

HERBERT.
8s. 7s.

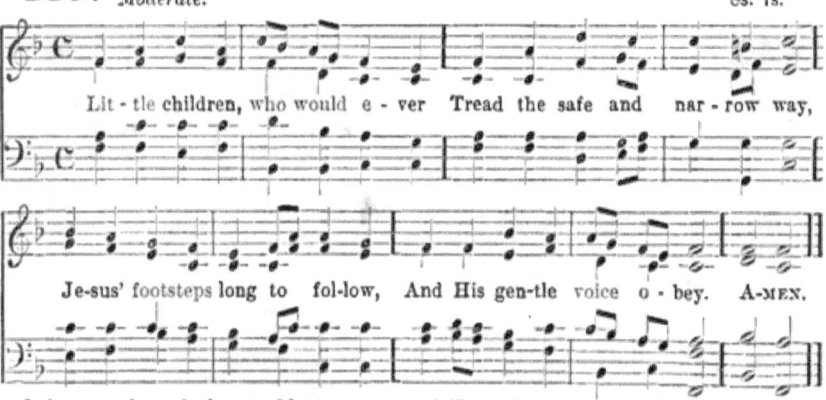

2 As a rough road often trodden,
  Smooth and easy doth become,
  So the straight and narrow pathway
  Widens, brightens nearer Home.
3 Eye ne'er saw, nor ear hath heard it,
  Neither can the heart conceive,
  Of the joy which God prepareth,
  For His children who believe.
4 Yet the Spirit doth reveal it,
  Here we have our bliss in part,
  Since, our heritage for ever,
  God abideth in our heart.

GENERAL HYMNS.

440. *Quietly.* HEATHLANDS.
8s. 7s. Six lines.

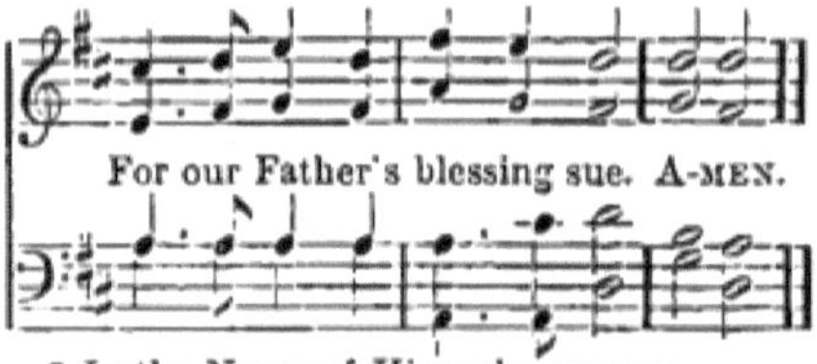

In the Name of Him who loves us With a love for e-ver true, Kind and patient while He proves us, Noting what our hearts will do; We poor children, all un-wor-thy, For our Father's blessing sue. A-MEN.

2 In the Name of Him who bought us
With His own atoning Blood,
To His fold in childhood brought us,
He our shelter, He our food;
We poor lambs upon the mountain
Gather round our Shepherd good.

3 In the Name of Him who gave us
All our childhood's guiding light,
Ready now to help and save us,
And to rule our lives aright;
We poor sinners, weak and helpless,
Here implore the Spirit's might.

4 Heavenly Father, bless Thy children;
Saviour, bind us fast to Thee;
Holy Spirit, teach us, save us,
Make us strong and truly free;
Lord of love, in truth and goodness
Thine for ever may we be.

441. *Cheerful.* GOD IS GOOD.
6s. 5s.

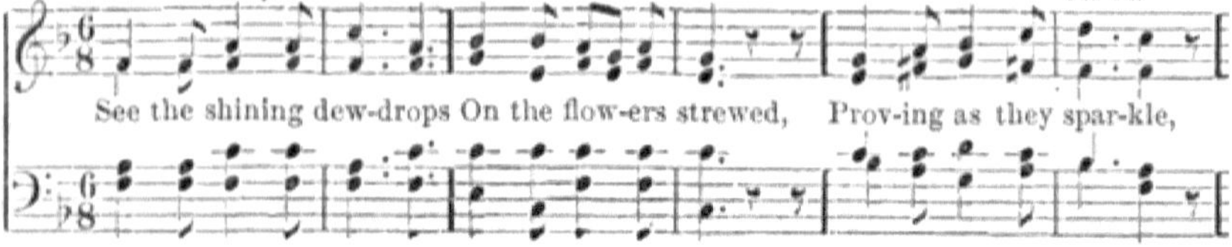

See the shining dew-drops On the flow-ers strewed, Prov-ing as they spar-kle, "God is e-ver good." A-MEN.

2 See the morning sunbeams
Lighting up the wood,
Silently proclaiming
"God is ever good."

3 Hear the mountain streamlet,
In its solitude,
With its ripple saying
"God is ever good."

4 In the leafy tree-tops,
Where no fears intrude,
Merry birds are singing
"God is ever good."

5 He who came to save us,
Shed His precious blood;

Better things it speaketh
"God is ever good."

6 Bring, my heart, thy **tribute**,
Songs of gratitude;
All things join to **tell us**
"God is ever good."

442.

GENERAL HYMNS.

MARGARET.
P. M.

*Earnestly

Thou didst leave Thy throne and Thy Kingly crown When Thou camest to earth for me; But in Bethlehem's home was there found no room For Thy holy nativity. Oh, come to my heart, Lord Jesus! There is room in my heart for Thee! AMEN.

* The ties and slurs are to be used as the syllables require.

2 Heaven's arches rang when the Angels sang,
   Proclaiming Thy Royal degree;
   But in lowly birth didst Thou come to earth,
   And in great humility.
      Oh, come to my heart, Lord Jesus!
      There is room in my heart for Thee!

3 The foxes found rest, and the bird had its nest
   In the shade of the cedar tree:
   But Thy couch was the sod, O Thou Son of God,
   In the desert of Galilee.
      Oh, come to my heart, Lord Jesus!
      There is room in my heart for Thee!

4 Thou camest, O Lord, with the living word
   That should set Thy people free;
   But with mocking scorn, and with crown of thorn,
   They bore Thee to Calvary.
      Oh, come to my heart, Lord Jesus!
      There is room in my heart for Thee!

5 When the heavens shall ring and the Angels sing
   At Thy coming to victory,
   Let Thy voice call me home saying "Yet there is room,
   There is room at My side for Thee."
      Oh, come to my heart, Lord Jesus!
      There is room in my heart for Thee!

443.

S. Helier.
P. M.

I was wandering and weary When my Saviour came unto me, For the ways of sin grew dreary, And the world had ceased to woo me; And I thought I heard Him say, As He came along His way—"O silly souls come near me, My sheep shall never fear Me, I am the Shepherd true. Amen.

2 At first I would not hearken,
　And put off till the morrow;
　But life began to darken,
　And I was sick with sorrow;
　　And I thought I heard Him say,
　　As He came along His way—
　　　"O silly souls," &c.

3 At last I stopped to listen,
　His voice could not deceive me;
　I saw His kind eyes glisten,
　So anxious to relieve me;
　　And I thought I heard Him say,
　　As He came along His way—
　　　"O silly souls," &c.

4 He took me on His shoulder,
　And tenderly He kissed me;
　He bade my love grow bolder,
　And said how He had missed me.
　　And I'm sure I heard Him say,
　　As He went along His way—
　　　"O silly souls," &c.

5 I thought His love would weaken
　As more and more He knew me,
　But it burneth like a beacon,
　And its light and heat go through me.
　　And I ever hear Him say,
　　As He goes along His way—
　　　"O silly souls," &c.

6 Let us do then, dearest brothers,
　What will best and longest please us,
　Follow not the way of others,
　But trust ourselves to Jesus,
　　We shall ever hear Him say,
　　As He goes along His way—
　　　"O silly souls," &c.

444.

QUEST. 2 You will soon be weary, pilgrims of a day,
   Trials are before you, dangers in your way;
 ANS. Still by faith we'll journey on, tho' our path be drear,
   If the Saviour lead us, what have we to fear?
   CHO:—Onward, ever onward, &c.

QUEST. 3 Pilgrims, are you going, where the Angels' song,
   O'er the fields of glory, gently flows along?
 ANS. Yes, we seek the better land, lovely, pure and fair,
   Where no grief can enter—will you meet us there?
   CHO:—Onward, ever, onward, &c.

QUEST. 4 May we journey with you, pilgrims of a day?
   Will you help us onward in the heavenly way?
 ANS. Come, we gladly bid you come, day is waning fast,
   We must reach the haven, ere the light is past.
   CHO:—Onward, ever onward, &c.

GENERAL HYMNS.

445.

Moderate. ALSTONE. L. M.

Yes, God is good: in earth and sky, From ocean's depths and spreading wood, Ten thousand voi-ces seem to cry, God made us all, and God is good. A-MEN.

2 The sun that keeps his trackless way,
And downward pours his golden flood,
Night's sparkling hosts, all seem to say,
In accents clear, that God is good.

3 The merry birds prolong the strain,
Their song with ev'ry spring renewed;
And balmy air, and falling rain,
Each softly whispers, God is good.

4 Yes, God is good, all nature says,
By God's own hand with speech endued
And man, in louder notes of praise,
Should sing for joy that God is good.

5 For all Thy gifts we bless Thee, Lord,
But chiefly for our heavenly food;
Thy pard'ning grace, Thy quick'ning word,
These prompt our song that God is good.

446.

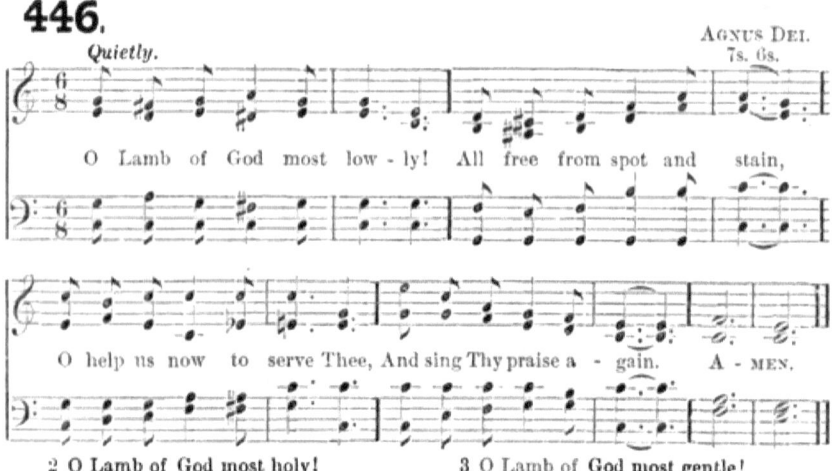

Quietly. AGNUS DEI. 7s. 6s.

O Lamb of God most low-ly! All free from spot and stain, O help us now to serve Thee, And sing Thy praise a-gain. A-MEN.

2 O Lamb of God most holy!
So great, and yet so meek;
May we, when pride allures us,
Thy lowly spirit seek.

3 O Lamb of God most gentle!
So kind, and good, and true;
May we, when passion tempts us,
Thy gentleness pursue.

4 O Lamb of God most lovely!
To Thee our faith would flee;
Reveal to us Thy beauty,
And win our hearts to Thee.

447.

Cheerful.

PEACE.
8s. 7s.

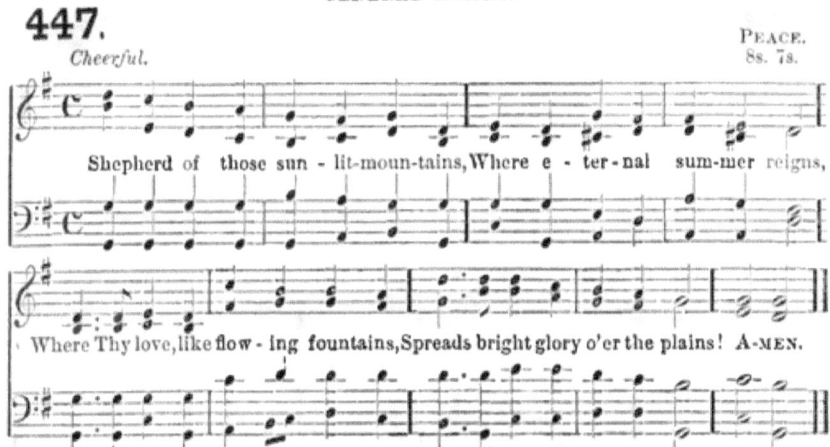

Shepherd of those sun-lit-moun-tains, Where e-ter-nal sum-mer reigns,
Where Thy love, like flow-ing fountains, Spreads bright glory o'er the plains! A-MEN.

2 In this wilderness of sorrow,
  May Thy crook now guide our feet;
  Through Thy words, oh, feed and guide us
  To Thy truth most pure and sweet.

3 From Thy love like sheep we wander,
  We have erred from Thy way;
  Let Thy loving voice reclaim us,
  Never let us from Thee stray.

4 Thou didst give Thy life to save us,
  Loving Shepherd of Thy sheep;
  To Thy fold again restore us,
  All our hearts now claim and keep.

448.

Moderate.

BAYSWATER.
7s.

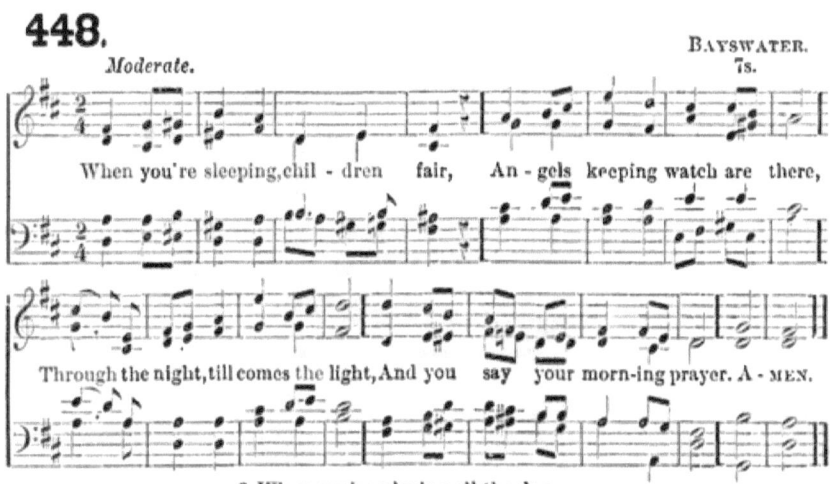

When you're sleeping, chil-dren fair, An-gels keeping watch are there,
Through the night, till comes the light, And you say your morn-ing prayer. A-MEN.

2 When you're playing all the day,
  When you wander far away,
  By your side an angel guide
  Watches, lest you go astray.

3 When, heart weary, each has trod
  Life's great journey all the road,
  Angel hands, to other lands,
  Carry back the soul to God.

GENERAL HYMNS.

449.
Moderate.

Lux.
P. M.

Sunny days of childhood, Beautiful ye seem,
Fair as spring-tide flowers, Bright as summer's beam.
Days with joy o'erflowing, Care nor sadness knowing, Must ye pass away? A-MEN.

2 Precious days of childhood!
   Days of promise fair;
If bedewed with wisdom,
   Rich the fruits ye bear.
Jesus' footsteps keeping,
Blest shall be our reaping
   In life's harvest day.

3 Happy days of childhood,
   Swiftly moving on;
Into manhood changing
   Ye will soon be gone,
Like a streamlet flowing,
Pause nor stillness knowing,
   Thus ye pass away!

4 Sunny days of childhood!
   We no tear will shed
When, like spring-tide flowers,
   Youth and health are fled.
Earthly scenes forsaking,
We shall hail the breaking
   Of an endless day.

450.
Moderate.

Benison.
Six 8s.

1 praised the earth in beauty seen, With garlands gay of various green;

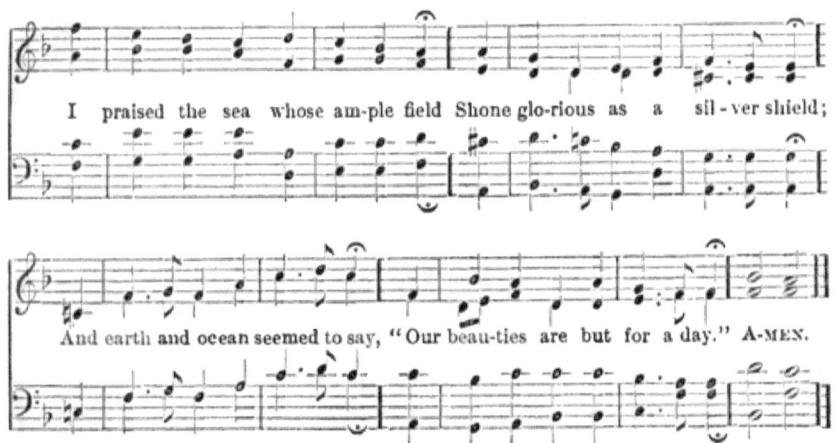

2 I praised the sun, whose chariot rolled
  On wheels of amber and of gold;
  I praised the moon, whose softer eye
  Gleamed sweetly through the summer sky;
  And moon and sun in answer said,
  "Our days of light are numbered."

3 O God! O Good beyond compare!
  If thus Thy meaner works are fair,
  If thus Thy bounties gild the span
  Of ruined earth and sinful man,
  How glorious must the mansion be,
  Where Thy redeemed shall dwell with Thee!

451. *Moderate.* CHILDHOOD. L. M.

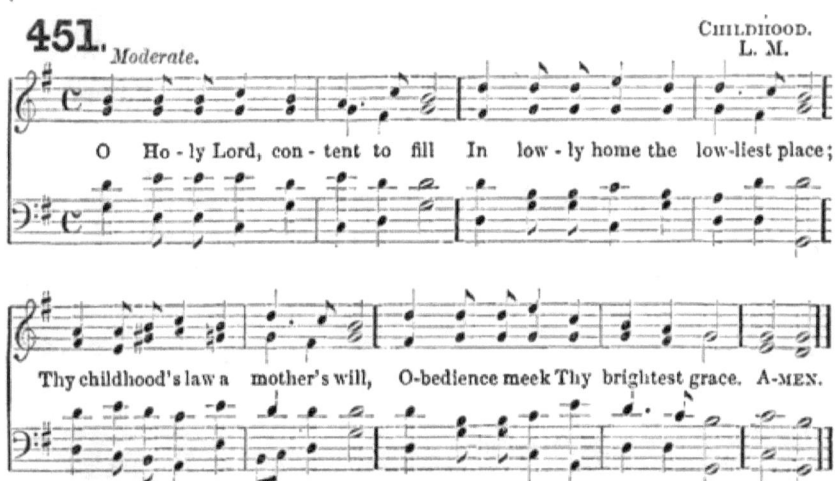

2 Lead every child that bears Thy Name
  To walk in Thine own guileless way,
  To dread the touch of sin and shame,
  And humbly, like Thyself, obey.

3 Oh! let not this world's scorching glow
  Thy Spirit's quickening dew efface,
  Nor blast of sin too rudely blow,
  And quench the trembling flame of grace.

4 Gather Thy lambs within Thine arm,
  And gently in Thy bosom bear;
  Keep them, O Lord, from hurt and harm,
  And bid them rest for ever there!

452.

Quietly. KEBLE. 7s.

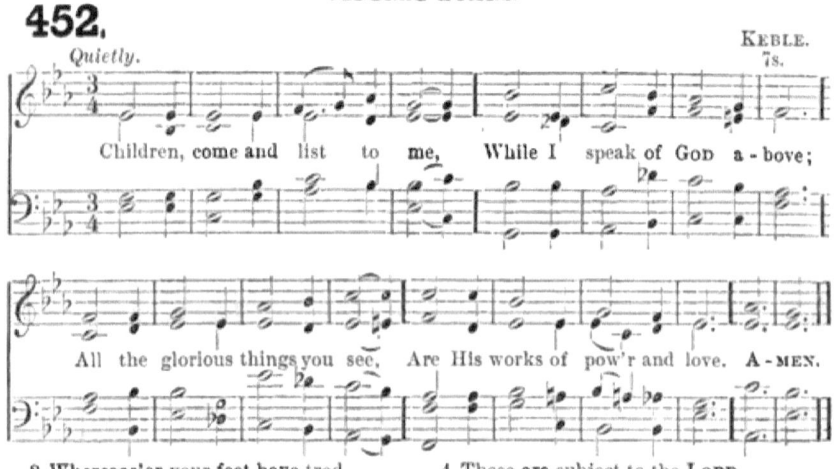

Children, come and list to me, While I speak of GOD above; All the glorious things you see, Are His works of pow'r and love. A-MEN.

2 Wheresoe'er your feet have trod,
  Scattered blessings round you lie,
  All by God's kind love bestowed,
  Who has made both earth and sky.

3 When you hear the loud winds howling,
  Tearing by with sudden crash,
  Or the thunder's fearful growling,
  Mingled with the lightning's flash:

4 These are subject to the LORD,
  All created by His will,
  And with one Almighty word,
  He can make the storm be still.

5 O dear children, you should try,
  This Almighty GOD to love,
  That when your frail bodies die,
  Your may see His face above.

453.

Cheerful. CLARABELLA. C. M.

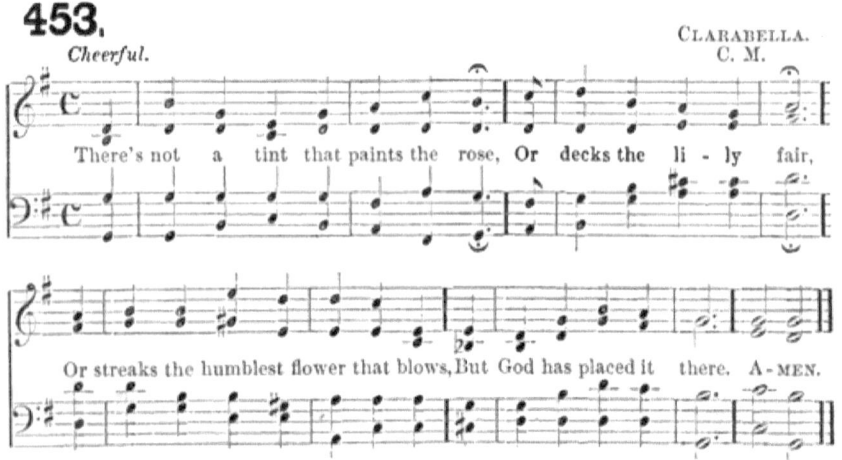

There's not a tint that paints the rose, Or decks the li-ly fair, Or streaks the humblest flower that blows, But God has placed it there. A-MEN.

2 At early dawn there's not a gale
  Across the landscape driven,
  And not a breeze that sweeps the vale,
  That is not sent by Heaven.

3 There's not of grass a single blade,
  Or leaf of loveliest green,
  Where heavenly skill is not displayed,
  And heavenly wisdom seen.

4 Around, beneath, below, above,
  Wherever space extends,
  There God displays His boundless love,
  And power with mercy blends.

2 He who gladly barters
    All on earthly ground;
He who, like the martyrs,
    Says, "I will be crowned:"
He, whose one oblation
    Is a life of love;
Clinging to the nation
    Of the blest above.

3 Shame upon you, legions
    Of the heavenly King,
Citizens of regions
    Past imagining!
What! with pipe and tabor
    Dream away the light,
When He bids you labour—
    When He tells you, "Fight?"

4 Jesu, Lord of Glory,
    As we breast the tide,
Whisper Thou of beauty
    On the other side!
What though sad the story
    Of this life's distress;
Oh, the future glory!
    Oh, the loveliness!

Responsive Prayers.

[These Hymns may be sung by the clergyman, or any other person, the school singing the Response to every verse: or the verses may be taken alternately by the boys and girls, all joining in the Response.]

455.   THE HOLY CHILD JESUS.

VERSE.

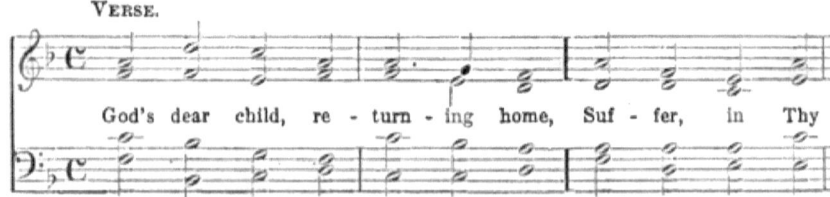

God's dear child, re-turn-ing home, Suf-fer, in Thy

RESPONSE.

love, to come, Ho-ly Child,...... to THEE. A-MEN.

2 And Thy gentle hands to bless,
Lay in brotherly caress,
    Holy Child, on me.

3 Let my joy be in the thought
That I was in childhood brought
    Holy Child, to Thee:

4 Let my hope be in the grace
That will never turn Thy face,
    Holy Child, from me.

5 All my work, with all my might,
Let me do as in Thy sight,
    Holy Child, for Thee;

6 And before the Father's throne,
O, present it as Thine own,
    Holy Child, for me.

7 In my pleasant hours of play
Be not ever far away,
    Holy Child, from me.

8 Let me, all the happy while,
Have the comfort of a smile,
    Holy Child, from Thee.

9 All my sins, repented sore,
Let them be a grief no more,
    Holy Child, to Thee.

10 Put the pure and seamless dress
Of Thy perfect righteousness,
    Holy Child, on me.

11 Turn my heart, when sins surprise,
And temptations in me rise,
    Holy Child, to Thee;

12 And with Thy dear Word of might
Satan put again to flight,
    Holy Child, from me.

13 Fix my thoughts, and rest my heart,
(Choosing thus the better part,)
    Holy Child, on Thee.

14 Never let my footsteps stray,
Nor Thy Spirit take away,
    Holy Child, from me.

15 Thy dear will my will control,
Be the sunshine of my soul.
    Holy Child, in Thee;

16 And my only shade or night,
When Thou dost not shed Thy light,
    Holy Child, on me.

17 By Thy Father's love divine,
Fill with love this soul of mine,
    Holy Child, for Thee.

18 By Thy Mother's tears and grief,
In my sorrows bring relief,
    Holy Child, to me.

19 For the blessing of the Dove
That hath settled from above,
    Holy Child, on me.

20 To the Father laud and praise,
Offered be, through all my days,
    Holy Child, by Thee.

RESPONSIVE PRAYERS.

456. VERSE.   THE HOLY CHILDHOOD, No. 1.

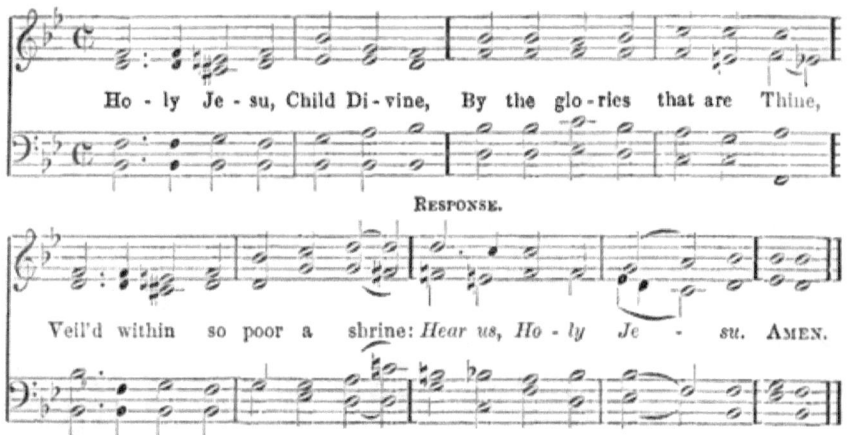

Ho-ly Je-su, Child Di-vine, By the glo-ries that are Thine,

RESPONSE.

Veil'd within so poor a shrine: *Hear us, Ho-ly Je - su.* AMEN.

2 By Thy form so weak and small,
  By Thy plaintive infant call,
  By Thy childish tears that fall:
        Hear us, Holy Jesu.

3 By the Angels' holy song,
  As around they wondering throng,
  Owning Thee Their Ruler strong:
        Hear us, Holy Jesu.

4 By the **lowly** cattle shed,
  By the narrow manger-bed,
  By the rough **clothes** o'er Thee spread:
        Hear us, Holy Jesu.

5 By the solemn praise and prayer,
  By the gifts and offerings rare
  Laid in lowly manger there:
        Hear us, Holy Jesu.

6 By Thy blessèd mother's woes,
  By Thy fleeing from Thy foes,
  By Thy grief that no man knows:
        Hear us, Holy Jesu.

7 By Thy growing, day by day,
  By Thy zeal in wisdom's way,
  Quick to learn and to obey:
        Hear us, Holy Jesu.

8 By Thy life, so lone and still,
  By Thy waiting to fulfil
  In its time Thy Father's will:
        Hear us, Holy Jesu.

9 By the care that weighed on **Thee**,
  By Thy toil and poverty,
  By Thy sorrows yet to be:
        Hear us, Holy Jesu.

10 Jesu, Holy Child Divine,
   On our darkened nature shine,
   Give us virtues like to Thine:
        Hear us, Holy Jesu.

11 Make us pure and undefiled,
   Gentle, patient, loving, mild,
   Trustful as a little child:
        Hear us, Holy Jesu.

12 Make us ever long to know
   Where our God would have us go,
   Shrinking not from toil or woe:
        Hear us, Holy Jesu.

13 May we mark the pattern fair
   Of Thy life of work and prayer,
   And for truth all perils dare:
        Hear us, Holy Jesu.

14 May we **calmly** suffer blame,
   Bear the cross, despise the shame,
   In Thy strength and in Thy Name.
        Hear us, Holy Jesu.

15 As we live, from year to year,
   Jesu, be Thou ever near;
   Make us like Thee, Saviour dear;
        Hear us, Holy Jesu.

16 Bid us come at last to **Thee**,
   And for ever perfect be,
   When Thy glory we shall see:
        Hear us, Holy Jesu.

RESPONSIVE PRAYERS.

THE HOLY CHILDHOOD, No. 2.

457. Music for Parts I and III.

God the Father, God the Son, God the Spirit, Three in One,
Hear us from Thy heavenly Throne, Spare us, Holy Trinity. A-MEN.

2 Jesu, Saviour ever mild,
Born for us a little Child
Of the Virgin undefiled:
  Hear us, Holy Jesu.

3 Jesu, by the Mother-Maid
In Thy swaddling-clothes arrayed,
And within a manger laid:
  Hear us, Holy Jesu.

4 Jesu, at whose infant feet
Shepherds, coming Thee to greet,
Knelt to pay their worship meet:
  Hear us, Holy Jesu.

5 Jesu, unto whom of yore
Wise men, hastening to adore,
Gold and myrrh and incense bore:
  Hear us, Holy Jesu.

6 Jesu, to Thy temple brought,
Whom, by Thy good Spirit taught,
Simeon and Anna sought:
  Hear us, Holy Jesu.

7 Jesu, who didst deign to flee
From King Herod's cruelty
In Thy earliest infancy:
  Hear us, Holy Jesu.

8 Jesu, whom Thy Mother found,
'Midst the doctors sitting round,
Marvelling at Thy words profound:
  Hear us, Holy Jesu.

Part II. VERSE.

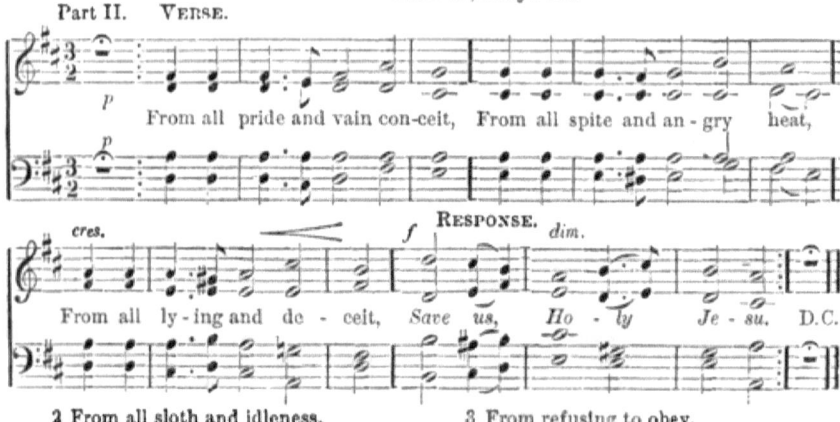

From all pride and vain conceit, From all spite and angry heat,
From all lying and deceit, Save us, Holy Jesu. D.C.

2 From all sloth and idleness,
From not caring for distress,
From all lust and greediness:
  Save us, Holy Jesu.

3 From refusing to obey,
From the love of our own way,
From forgetfulness to pray:
  Save us, Holy Jesu.

RESPONSIVE PRAYERS.

Part III.   (For Tune, see preceding page.

1 By Thy Birth and early years,
By Thine Infant wants and fears,
By Thy sorrows and Thy tears;
    Save us, Holy Jesu.

2 By Thy Pattern bright and pure,
By the pains Thou didst endure
Our salvation to procure,
    Save us, Holy Jesu.

3 By Thy wounds and thorn-crowned head,
By Thy blood for sinners shed,
By Thy rising from the dead
    Save us, Holy Jesu.

4 By the Name we bow before,
Human Name, which evermore
All the hosts of heaven adore,
    Save us, Holy Jesu.

5 By Thine own unconquered might,
By Thy glory in the height,
By Thy mercies infinite:
    Save us, Holy Jesu.

458.

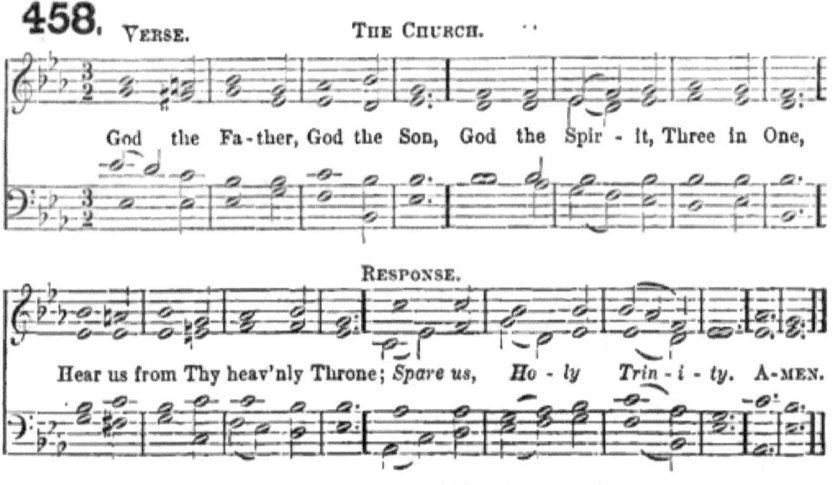

THE CHURCH.

Verse: God the Father, God the Son, God the Spirit, Three in One,
Response: Hear us from Thy heav'nly Throne; Spare us, Holy Trinity. A-MEN.

2 Jesus, with Thy Church abide,
Be her Saviour, Lord, and Guide,
While on earth her faith is tried,
    We beseech Thee, hear us.

3 Arms of love around her throw,
Shield her safe from every foe,
Comfort her in time of woe:
    We beseech Thee, hear us.

4 Keep her life and doctrine pure,
Grant her patience to endure,
Trusting in Thy promise sure:
    We beseech Thee, hear us.

5 May she one in doctrine be,
One in truth and charity,
Winning all to faith in Thee:
    We beseech Thee, hear us.

6 May she guide the poor and bind:
Seek the lost until she find,
And the broken-hearted blind:
    We beseech Thee, hear us.

7 May her lamp of truth be bright,
Bid her bear aloft its light
Through the realms of heathen night:
    We beseech Thee, hear us.

8 May her scattered children be
From reproach of evil free,
Blameless witnesses for Thee:
    We beseech Thee, hear us.

9 May she soon all glorious be,
Spotless and from wrinkle free,
Pure, and bright, and worthy Thee:
    We beseech Thee, hear us.

10 Fit her all Thy joy to share
In the home Thou dost prepare,
And be ever blessèd there:
    We beseech Thee, hear us.

FESTIVALS.

2 The bands of the Alien flee away
  When our chant goes up like thunder,
  And the van of the Lord in serried array,
  Cleaves Satan's ranks asunder.
    We march, we march, &c.

3 Our sword is the Spirit of God on High,
  Our helmet His Salvation;
  Our banner the Cross of Calvary,
  Our watchword—THE IN-CAR-NA-TION.
    We march, we march, &c.

4 He marches in front of His banner unfurl'd,
  Which He raised that His own might find
    Him;
  And the Holy Church throughout all the world
  Fall into rank behind Him.
    We march, we march, &c,

5 And the choir of Angels with songs awaits
  Our march to the golden Sion;
  For our Captain has broken the brazen gates,
  And burst the bars of iron.
    We march, we march, &c.

6 Then onward we march, our arms to prove,
  With the banner of Christ before us,
  With His eye of love looking down from above,
  And His Holy Arm spread o'er us.
    We march, we march, &c.

460.

LICHFIELD.
7s.

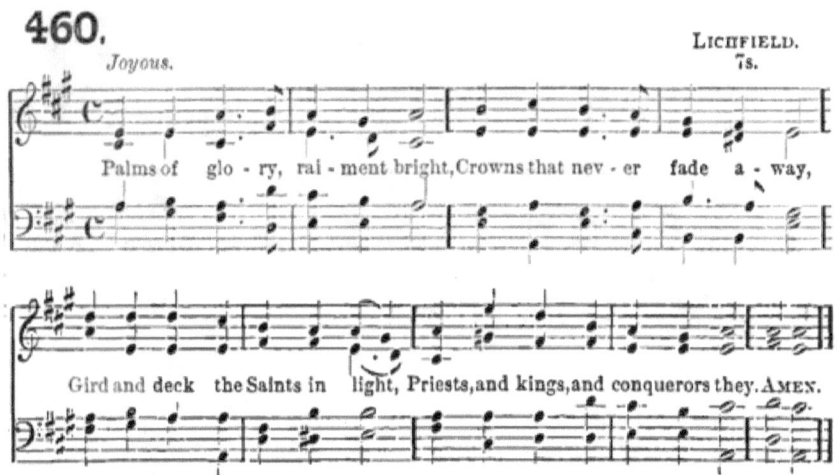

2 Yet the conquerors bring their palms
  To the LAMB amidst the Throne,
  And proclaim in joyful psalms
  Victory through His Cross alone.

3 Kings their crowns for harps resign,
  Crying as they strike the chords,
  "Take the Kingdom, it is Thine,
  King of kings, and LORD of lords."

4 Round the Altar Priests confess,
  If their robes are white as snow,
  'Twas the Saviour's Righteousness,
  And His Blood, that made them so.

5 They were mortal too like us:
  O, when we like them must die,
  May our souls translated thus
  Triumph, reign, and shine on high.

3 Great and ever greater
   Are Thy mercies here,
   True and everlasting
   Are the glories there.
   Where no pain or sorrow,
   Toil, or care is known,
   Where the Angel-legions
   Circle round Thy Throne.

4 Brighter still and brighter
   Glows the western sun,
   Shedding all its gladness
   O'er our work that's done;
   Time will soon be over,
   Toil and sorrows past,
   May we, Blessèd Saviour,
   Find a rest at last.

5 Onward, ever onward,
   Journeying o'er the road,
   Worn by saints before us,
   Journeying on to God:
   Leaving all behind us,
   May we hasten on.
   Backward never looking
   Till the prize is won.

6 Bliss, all bliss excelling,
   When the ransomed soul
   Earthly toil forgetting
   Finds its promise goal;
   Where in joys unheard of
   Saints with angels sing,
   Never weary raising
   Praises to their King.

FESTIVALS.

462.
Earnestly.   ALFORD.
                                                        P. M.

Ten thou-sand times ten thou-sand, In sparkling rai-ment bright,
The ar-mies of the ransomed saints Throng up the steeps of light.
'Tis fin-ished! all is fin-ished, Their fight with death and sin;
Fling o-pen wide the gold-en gates, And let the vic-tors in. A-MEN.

2 What rush of Alleluias
  Fills all the earth and sky!
  What ringing of a thousand harps
  Bespeaks the triumph nigh!
  O day, for which creation
  And all its tribes were made!
  O joy for all its former woes
  A thousand-fold repaid.

3 Oh, then what raptured greetings
  On Canaan's happy shore.
  What knitting severed friendships up,
  Where partings are no more!
  Then eyes with joy shall sparkle
  That brimmed with tears of late;
  Orphans no longer fatherless,
  Nor widows desolate.

4 Bring near the great salvation,
  Thou Lamb for sinners slain,
  Fill up the roll of Thine elect;
  Then take Thy power and reign:
  Appear, Desire of nations,
  Thine exiles long for home:
  Show in the heavens Thy promised sign;
  Thou Prince and Saviour, come.

FESTIVALS.

463.
Joyous.

HERMAS.
11s.
with Chorus.

2 If with honest-hearted love for God and man,
   Day by day Thou find us doing what we can,
   Thou who giv'st the seed-time wilt give large increase,
   Crown the head with blessings, fill the heart with peace.
      Cho:— On our way rejoicing, &c.

3 On our way rejoicing gladly let us go;
   Conquered hath our Leader, vanquished is our foe!
   Christ without, our safety, Christ within, our joy;
   Who, if we be faithful, can our hope destroy?
      Cho:— On our way rejoicing, &c.

4 Unto God the Father joyful songs we sing;
   Unto God the Saviour thankful hearts we bring;
   Unto God the Spirit bow we and adore,
   On our way rejoicing now and evermore!
      Cho:— On our way rejoicing, &c.

FESTIVALS.

464.
With spirit.

S. ALBAN.
6s. 5s. D. with Refrain.

Brightly gleams our banner, Pointing to the sky, Waving wanderers onward To their home on high. Journey-ing o'er the des-ert, Glad-ly thus we pray, And with hearts u-ni-ted Take our heavenward way. Brightly gleams our banner, Pointing to the sky, Waving wanderers on-ward To their home on high. A-MEN.

2 Jesus, Lord and Master,
At Thy sacred feet,
Here with hearts rejoicing
See Thy children meet;
Often have we left Thee,
Often gone astray,
Keep us mighty Saviour,
In the narrow way.
Brightly gleams, &c.

3 All our days direct us
In the way we go,
Lead us on victorious
Over every foe;
Bid Thine angels shield us
When the storm-clouds lour,
Pardon Thou and save us
In the last dread hour.
Brightly gleams, &c.

4 Then with Saints and Angels
May we join above,
Offering prayers and praises
At Thy Throne of love;
When the toil is over,
Then comes rest and peace,
Jesus, in His Beauty,
Songs that never cease.
Brightly gleams, &c.

FESTIVALS.

465.

With spirit.

S. GERTRUDE.
6s. 5s. D. *with Refrain.*

Onward, Christian soldiers, Marching as to war, With the Cross of Jesus Going on before. Christ, the Royal Master, Leads against the foe, Forward into battle See, His banners go. Onward, Christian soldiers, Marching as to war, With the Cross of Jesus Going on before. A-MEN.

2 At the sign of triumph
   Satan's host doth flee;
On, then, Christian soldiers,
   On to victory.
Hell's foundations quiver,
   At the shout of praise;
Brothers, lift your voices,
   Loud your anthems raise.
      Onward, Christian soldiers, &c.

3 Like a mighty army
   Moves the Church of God;
Brothers, we are treading
   Where the Saints have trod;
We are not divided,
   All one body we,
One in hope and doctrine,
   One in charity.
      Onward, Christian soldiers, &c.

4 Crowns and thrones may perish,
   Kingdoms rise and wane,
But the Church of Jesus
   Constant will remain;
Gates of hell can never
   'Gainst that Church prevail;
We have Christ's own promise,
   And that cannot fail.
      Onward, Christian soldiers, &c.

5 Onward, then, ye people,
   Join our happy throng,
Blend with ours your voices,
   In the triumph song—
Glory, laud and honour,
   Unto Christ the King,
This through countless ages
   Men and Angels sing.
      Onward, Christian soldiers, &c.

FESTIVALS.

466.

2 Fear not the din of battle,
  Follow where He has trod
  Perfecting strength in weakness—
  JESUS, INCARNATE GOD.
    Lift ye, &c.

Trebles and Altos in Unison.

3 Angels around us hover,
  Succour in time of need,
  Ever at hand to strengthen,
  Guardians they indeed.
    Lift ye, &c.

Tenors and Basses in Unison.

4 Arm ye against the battle,
  Watch ye, and fast, and pray,
  Peace shall succeed the warfare,
  Night shall be changed to day.
    Lift ye, &c.

5 Fight, for the Lord is o'er you,
  Fight, for He bids you fight:
  There where the fray is thickest
  Close with the hosts of night.
    Lift ye, &c.

FESTIVALS.

467. S. BOTOLPH.
6s. 5s. Twelve lines.

Forward! be our watchword, Step and voices joined, Seek the things before us, Not a look behind; Burns the fiery pillar At our army's head; Who shall dream of shrinking, By our Captain led? Forward thro' the desert, Thro' the toil and fight, Jordan flows before us, Sion beams with light. A-MEN.

2 Forward when in childhood
  Buds the infant mind;
All through youth and manhood,
  Not a thought behind:
Speed through realms of nature,
  Climb the steps of grace;
Faint not, till in glory
  Gleams our Father's face.
    Forward, all the life-time
      Climb from height to height:
    Till the head be hoary,
    Till the eve be light!

3 Forward, flock of Jesus,
  Salt of all the earth,
Till each yearning purpose
  Spring to glorious birth;
Sick, they ask for healing,
  Blind, they grope for day;

Pour upon the nations
  Wisdom's loving ray.
    Forward, out of error,
      Leave behind the night;
    Forward through the darkness,
      Forward into light.

4 Glories upon glories,
  Hath our God prepared,
By the souls that love Him
  One day to be shared,
Eye hath not beheld them,
  Ear hath never heard;
Nor of these hath uttered
  Thought or speech or word.
    Forward, marching eastward
      Where the heaven is bright,
    Till the veil be lifted,
    Till our faith be sight!

FESTIVALS.

468.

Earnestly.

S. BONIFACE.
6s. 5s. Twelve lines.

Far o'er yon hor-i-zon Rise the cit-y towers; Where our God a-bid-eth;
That fair Home is ours: Flash the streets with jas-per, Shine the gates with gold;
Flows the gladdening riv-er, Shedding joys un-told. Thither, on-ward thith-er,
In the Spi-rit's might; Pilgrims to your coun-try, For-ward in-to light. A-MEN.

2 Into God's high temple
  Onward as we press,
Beauty spreads around us,
  Born of holiness;
Arch, and vault, and carving,
  Lights of varied tone,
Softened words and holy,
  Prayer and praise alone:
Every thought upraising
  To our city bright,
Where the tribes assemble
  Round the Throne of light.

3 Nought that city needeth
  Of these aisles of stone:
Where the GODHEAD dwelleth,
  Temple there is none:
All the Saints, that ever
  In these courts have stood,
Are but babes, and feeding
  On the children's food.
On through sign and token,
  Stars amid the night,
Forward through the darkness,
  Forward into light.

4 To the eternal FATHER
  Loudest anthems raise;
To the SON and SPIRIT
  Echo songs of praise;
To the Lord of glory,
  Blessed THREE in ONE,
Be by men and Angels
  Endless honours done:
Weak are earthly praises;
  Dull the songs of night;
Forward into triumph,
  Forward into light!

FESTIVALS.

469.

CONQUEST.
6s. 5s. D. *with refrain.*
With spirit.

Sol-diers of the Captain! Stand, for Him, and fight, Hardness glad en-dur-ing, Armour'd in His might! He is that great Vic-tor Praised in Angels' songs, Glo-ry of each sol-dier Who to Him be-longs. Sol-diers of the Cap-tain! Stand, for Him, and fight, Hardness glad en-dur-ing, Armour'd in His might! Might! A-MEN.

2 Leader never vanquished—
  More than conquerors too,
Through Himself, He maketh
  All His soldiers true;
O'er the foe, triumphant,
  He must still prevail—
So, His soldiers faithful,
  With Him cannot fail.
    Soldiers of the Captain! &c.

3 Take ye, then, the Helmet,
  Breastplate, Shield, and Sword—
Thus equipped, for battle
  Ready at His word:
Fierce though be the warfare,
  Sure is the renown—
And, though dark the conflict,
  Bright the promised crown.
    Soldiers of the Captain! &c.

4 Jesus! Captain! help us
  Soldiers good to be—
Living, dying, ever,
  Fighting Lord, for Thee:
Eager to march forward,
  In those ranks of Thine—
Waiting but the order
  From Thy voice divine!
    Soldiers of the Captain! &c.

FESTIVALS.

470. WELCOME, HAPPY MORNING.
Joyous. Five 11s.

2 Earth with joy confesses, clothing her for Spring,
All good gifts returned with her returning King:
Bloom in every meadow, leaves on every bough,
Speak His sorrows ended, hail His triumph now.
Hell to-day is vanquished; Heaven is won to-day.

3 Months in due succession, days of lengthening light,
Hours and passing moments praise Thee in their flight;
Brightness of the morning, sky and fields and sea,
Vanquisher of darkness, bring their praise to Thee.
"Welcome, happy morning!" age to age shall say.

4 Maker and Redeemer, Life and Health to all,
Thou from Heaven beholding human nature's fall,
Of the Father's Godhead true and only Son,
Manhood to deliver, manhood didst put on.
Hell to-day is vanquished: Heaven is won to-day!

5 Thou, of Life the Author, death didst undergo,
Tread the path of darkness, saving strength to show;
Come, then, True and Faithful, now fulfil Thy word,
'Tis Thine own Third Morning! Rise, O buried Lord!
"Welcome, happy morning!" age to age shall say.

6 Loose the souls long prisoned, bound with Satan's chain;
All that now is fallen raise to life again;
Show Thy Face in brightness, bid the nations see;
Bring again our day-light; day returns with Thee!
Hell to-day is vanquished; Heaven is won to-day.

FESTIVALS.

471. Boldly. S. EDWARD, CONFESSOR. P. M.

Advance! advance! the day is come To sing our Maker's praises: Each thankful heart in faith and hope, The strain of joy upraises: In robes all pure and white We chase the shades of night, The gloom shall pass away Before the dawn of day; The Lord of Hosts is with us. A-MEN.

2 Advance! Advance! though sore the strife,
Though timid hearts are quailing,
The Lord of Hosts doth lead our van,
And He is all availing:
    With His blest Presence near,
    No mortal foe we fear;
    Our Captain goes before,
    'Mid strife of battle sore;
The Lord of Hosts is with us.

3 Advance! Advance! nor gaze behind,
Nor deem the pathway weary;
The Leader's footsteps print the track,
Through all that region dreary:
    In faith we follow on,
    We tread where He has gone;
    The stormy wind may rave,
    The stormy wind we brave;
The Lord of Hosts is with us.

4 Advance! Advance! lift up your hearts!
The sky above doth lighten;
Most dark around the shadows fall,
Ere rays of dawn may brighten:
    The night is dark and chill,
    The dawn is on the hill,
    We reck not of the night,
    'Twill soon be warm and bright;
The Lord of Hosts is with us.

5 Advance! Advance! ah, dearest Lord,
'Tis Thou, 'tis Thou dost lead us;
'Tis Thou dost point the narrow way,
'Tis Thou dost tend, dost feed us:
    No power, no might have we,
    Our strength is all of Thee;
    At morn, at eventide,
    Our aid, our hope, our guide,
Great Lord of Hosts be with us.

FESTIVALS.

472. *Earnestly.*

S. THOMAS À BECKET.
8s. 7s.

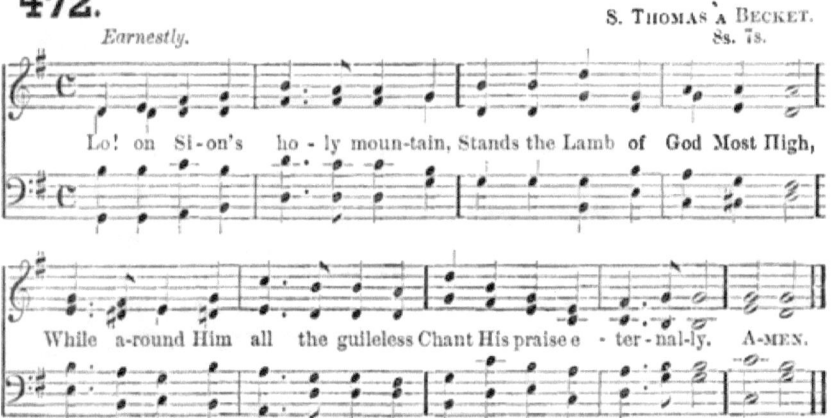

Lo! on Sion's holy mountain, Stands the Lamb of God Most High, While around Him all the guileless Chant His praise eternally. A-MEN.

2 On their foreheads, pure and spotless,
   Shines the Father's awful Name;
 And these Saints, so bright and glorious,
   Out of tribulation came.

3 Onward, onward, ever onward!
   Follow they the Lamb Most High,
 Wheresoever Jesus goeth,
   Nigh to Him, for ever nigh.

4 Shepherd kind, we too would follow;
   We are Thine, our Leader be,
 Give us holy perseverance,
   That Thy Glory we may see.

5 So on Sion's holy mountain,
   In the dear Land far away,
 With all pure and guileless spirits
   We may dwell in endless day.

6 Onward, onward, ever onward,
   Following Thee, O Christ Most High,
 Wheresoever, Lord, Thou goest,
   Nigh to Thee, for ever nigh.

473. *Boldly.*

S. FABIAN.
7s.

Soldiers who to Christ belong, Trust ye in His word, be strong; For His promises are sure, His rewards for aye endure. A-MEN.

2 His no crowns that pass away;
   His no palm that sees decay;
   His the joy that shall not fade:
   His the light that knows no shade.

3 His the Home for spirits blest,
   Where He gives them peaceful rest,
   Far above the starry skies,
   In the bliss of Paradise.

4 Here on earth ye can but clasp
   Things that perish in the grasp;
   Lift your hearts then to the skies;
   God Himself shall be your prize.

5 Praise we now with saints at rest,
   Father, Son and Spirit blest;
   For His promises are sure,
   His rewards shall aye endure.

The following Hymns are also suitable in marching.

ADVENT.
206. Behold! behold He cometh.
210. Hark! the glad sound, the Saviour comes.
207. Lift up the Advent strain.

CHRISTMAS.
220. Angels from the realms of glory.
219. Hail! Thou long expected Jesus.
213. Hark! the herald Angels sing.
217. Hark! what mean those holy voices.
212. O come, all ye faithful.
224. Sing with joy, 'tis Christmas morn.

MANIFESTATION.
232. As with gladness men of old.

229. Bethlehem! of noblest cities.

TRIUMPHAL ENTRY.
239. All glory, laud, and honour.
238. Sion, Sion, haste to meet Him.

EASTER.
251. Angels, roll the rock away.
256. Come, ye faithful, raise the strain.
249. Jesus Christ is risen to-day.

THANKSGIVING.
295. Come, ye thankful people, come.
296. Praise, O praise our God and King.

ANY SEASON.

179. Abide with me : fast falls the eventide.
195. Again the morn of gladness.
320. All hail the power of Jesus' Name.
333. Alleluia! thanks and glory.
402. Angel voices ever singing.
355. Children of the Heavenly King.
373. Go forward, Christian soldier.
331. God eternal, Mighty King.
307. Hail the Cross of Jesus.
387. Hark! hark, my soul, angelic songs.
270. Hark! the sound of holy voices.
266. Holy! holy! holy! Lord God Almighty.
299. Hosanna be the children's song.
377. Jerusalem, my happy home.
379. Jerusalem, the golden.
393. Jesus, meek and gentle.
390. Light's abode, celestial Salem.

343. Nearer, my God to Thee.
191. Now the day is over.
196. O Day of rest and gladness.
354. O happy band of pilgrims.
388. O Paradise, O Paradise.
372. Oft in danger, oft in woe.
276. Pleasant are Thy courts above.
321. Praise, my soul, the King of Heaven.
318. Songs of praise the Angels sang.
180. Sun of my soul, Thou Saviour dear.
181. Sweet Saviour, bless us ere we go.
275. The Church's one foundation.
369. The King of love my Shepherd is.
271. The Sun of God goes forth to war.
454. Those eternal bowers.
371. Through the night of doubt and sorrow.
385. We are but strangers here.

The following Hymns are specially suitable for little children.

329. Above the clear blue sky.
417. Blessèd Jesus, wilt Thou hear us.
405. Gentle Jesus, meek and mild.
394. Gracious Saviour, gentle Shepherd.
434. Great Shepherd of the sheep.
319. Humble praises, holy Jesus.
435. I love to think, though I am young.
403. I think when I read that sweet story.
332. Jesus, high in glory.
175. Jesus, holy, undefiled.
192. Jesus, tender Shepherd, hear me.

309. Jesus, when He left the sky.
439. Little children, who would ever.
346. Loving Shepherd of Thy sheep.
184. Now the light has gone away.
413. Sweet it is for child like me.
174. The morning bright.
423. There is a happy land.
209. Up in heaven, up in heaven.
376. We are but little children weak.
424. We are little Christian soldiers.
356. We are little pilgrims.

428. Where is the Holy Jesus.

Carols.

Sleep, Holy Babe!

474. *Tenderly.*

pp — *cres.* — *mf*

Sleep, Ho-ly Babe! up-on Thy Mo-ther's breast; Great Lord of earth and sea and sky, How sweet it is to see Thee lie

dim. — *pp*

In such a place of rest, In such a place of rest...... *Accomp.*

2 Sleep! Holy Babe! Thine Angels watch around,
All bending low with folded wings,
Before the Incarnate King of kings,
In reverent awe profound.

3 Sleep! Holy Babe! while I with Mary gaze
In joy upon that Face awhile,
Upon the loving infant smile
Which there Divinely plays.

4 Sleep! Holy Babe! ah! take Thy brief repose;
Too quickly will Thy slumbers break,
And Thou to lengthened pains awake
That Death alone shall close.

GENERAL FESTIVALS.

The following Hymns are also suitable in marching.

ADVENT.
206. Behold! behold He cometh.
210. Hark! the glad sound, the Saviour comes.
207. Lift up the Advent strain.

CHRISTMAS.
220. Angels from the realms of glory.
219. Hail! Thou long expected Jesus.
213. Hark! the herald Angels sing.
217. Hark! what mean those holy voices.
212. O come, all ye faithful.
224. Sing with joy, 'tis Christmas morn.

MANIFESTATION.
232. As with gladness men of old.

229. Bethlehem! of noblest cities.

TRIUMPHAL ENTRY.
239. All glory, laud, and honour.
238. Sion, Sion, haste to meet Him.

EASTER.
251. Angels, roll the rock away.
256. Come, ye faithful, raise the strain.
249. Jesus Christ is risen to-day.

THANKSGIVING.
295. Come, ye thankful people, come.
296. Praise, O praise our God and King.

ANY SEASON.

179. Abide with me : fast falls the eventide.
195. Again the morn of gladness.
320. All hail the power of Jesus' Name.
333. Alleluia! thanks and glory.
402. Angel voices ever singing.
355. Children of the Heavenly King.
373. Go forward, Christian soldier.
331. God eternal, Mighty King.
307. Hail the Cross of Jesus.
387. Hark! hark, my soul, angelic songs.
270. Hark! the sound of holy voices.
266. Holy! holy! holy! Lord God Almighty.
299. Hosanna be the children's song.
377. Jerusalem, my happy home.
379. Jerusalem, the golden.
393. Jesus, meek and gentle.
390. Light's abode, celestial Salem.

343. Nearer, my God to Thee.
191. Now the day is over.
196. O Day of rest and gladness.
354. O happy band of pilgrims.
388. O Paradise, O Paradise.
372. Oft in danger, oft in woe.
276. Pleasant are Thy courts above.
321. Praise, my soul, the King of Heaven.
318. Songs of praise the Angels sang.
180. Sun of my soul, Thou Saviour dear.
181. Sweet Saviour, bless us ere we go.
275. The Church's one foundation.
369. The King of love my Shepherd is.
271. The Sun of God goes forth to war.
454. Those eternal bowers.
371. Through the night of doubt and sorrow.
385. We are but strangers here.

The following Hymns are specially suitable for little children.

329. Above the clear blue sky.
417. Blessèd Jesus, wilt Thou hear us.
405. Gentle Jesus, meek and mild.
394. Gracious Saviour, gentle Shepherd
434. Great Shepherd of the sheep.
319. Humble praises, holy Jesus.
435. I love to think, though I am young.
403. I think when I read that sweet story.
332. Jesus, high in glory
175. Jesus, holy, undefiled.
192. Jesus, tender Shepherd, hear me.

309. Jesus, when He left the sky.
439. Little children, who would ever.
346. Loving Shepherd of Thy sheep.
184. Now the light has gone away.
413. Sweet it is for child like me.
174. The morning bright.
423. There is a happy land.
209. Up in heaven, up in heaven.
376. We are but little children weak.
424. We are little Christian soldiers.
356. We are little pilgrims.

428. Where is the Holy Jesus.

Carols.

Sleep, Holy Babe!

474. *Tenderly.*

Sleep, Ho-ly Babe! up-on Thy Mo-ther's breast; Great Lord of earth and sea and sky, How sweet it is to see Thee lie In such a place of rest, In such a place of rest....... *Accomp.*

2 Sleep! Holy Babe! Thine Angels watch around,
  All bending low with folded wings,
  Before the Incarnate King of kings,
In reverent awe profound.

3 Sleep! Holy Babe! while I with Mary gaze
  In joy upon that Face awhile,
  Upon the loving infant smile
Which there Divinely plays.

4 Sleep! Holy Babe! ah! take Thy brief repose;
  Too quickly will Thy slumbers break,
  And Thou to lengthened pains awake
That Death alone shall close.

CAROLS.

475. Once again, O blessed time.

Smoothly.

Once again, O bless-ed time, Thankful hearts em-brace thee; If we lost thy festal chime, What could e'er re-place...... thee? What could e'er...... re-place thee? Change will darken many a day, Many a bond dis-sev-er; Many a joy shall pass away, But the "Great Joy" nev-er! But the "Great Joy" nev- - -er...... But the "Great Joy" nev - - - er!

2 Once again the Holy Night
   Breathes its blessing tender;
   Once again the Manger Light
   Sheds its gentle splendour;
   O could tongues by Angels taught
   Speak our exultation
   In the Virgin's Child that brought
   All mankind Salvation!

3 Welcome Thou to souls athirst,
   Fount of endless pleasure;
   Gates of Hell may do their worst,
   While we clasp our Treasure:
   Welcome, though an age like this
   Puts Thy Name on trial,
   And the Truth that makes our bliss
   Pleads against denial!

4 Yea, if others stand apart,
   We will press the nearer;
   Yea, O best fraternal Heart,
   We will hold Thee dearer;
   Faithful lips shall answer thus
   To all faithless scorning,
   "Jesus Christ is God with us,
   Born on Christmas morning."

5 So we yield Thee all we can,
   Worship, thanks, and blessing;
   Thee true God, and Thee true Man,
   On our knees confessing;
   While Thy Birth-day morn we greet
   With our best devotion,
   Bathe us, O most true and sweet!
   In Thy Mercy's ocean.

476. Stars all bright are beaming.

CAROLS.

Brightly. VERSE.

Stars all bright are beaming, From the skies above, Nature's face all gleaming, Shines with Heav'n's own love.

CHORUS.

Wake and sing, good Christians, On this Birth-day Morn, Heaven and Earth are telling God for man is born.

2 Here for us abiding,
  Cradled in a Stall,
All His glory hiding,
  See the Lord of all! CHO.

3 Born that He might lead us,
  From this desert home,
Guide our way, and feed us,
  Till the end shall come. CHO.

4 Thousand thousand blessings
  Sing we for His Love,
Choral Hymns addressing
  To our Lord above. CHO.

5 Glory in the Highest,
  For this wondrous Birth;
Choir of Heaven! thou criest
  Peace to all the Earth! CHO.

477. Sleep, my Saviour, sleep.

Softly.

1. Sleep, my Saviour, sleep, On Thy bed of hay, An-gels in the spangled Heaven Sing their glad-some Christmas car-ols Till the dawn of day,
2. Sleep, my Saviour, sleep, On Thy bed of hay, Ere the mourning An-gel com-eth To the moon-lit o-live gar-den, Wip-ing tears a-way.

3 Sleep, my Saviour, sleep,
  Sweet on Mary's breast:
Now the shepherds kneel adoring,
Now the mother's heart is joyous,
  Take a happy rest.

4 Sleep, my Saviour, sleep,
  Sweet on Mary's breast;
Crucified, with wounds and bruises,
Bleeding, purple, stained, disfigured,
  One day Thou wilt rest.

CAROLS.

480. *With spirit.* **Sing ye the songs of praise.**

1. Sing ye the songs of praise; Jesus is come! High your glad voices raise; Jesus is come Cast worldly cares away, Worship and homage pay, Welcome the blessed day, Jesus is come!
2. This day in Bethlehem, Jesus was born! King of Jerusalem, Jesus was born! Sun of all righteousness, Shining with blessedness, Healing our wretchedness, Jesus was born!

3 Cleanse us from all our sin,
    Saviour Divine!
Make our thoughts pure within,
    Saviour Divine!
Lo! now the herald sound
Carols the love profound,
Telling of Jesus found,
    Saviour Divine!

4 Save through Thy merit,
    Great Prince of Peace!
Give Thy good Spirit,
    Great Prince of Peace!
Let not Thy love depart,
But holy gifts impart,
Born into every heart,
    Great Prince of Peace!

481. *Moderate.* **Christ is born of maiden fair.**

Christ is born of maiden fair; Hark the heralds in the air, Thus adoring descant there, "In excelsis gloria."

2 Shepherds saw those Angels bright,
    Carolling in glorious light;
"God, His Son is born to-night,
    In excelsis gloria."

3 Christ is come to save mankind,
    As in holy page we find,
Therefore this song bear in mind,
    "In excelsis gloria."

CAROLS.

482. *Moderate.* **From far away we come to you.**

From far away we come to you; The snow under foot and the moon in the sky, To tell of great tidings, strange and true, Christian men all, salvation is nigh! Salvation is nigh. From far away we come to you; To tell of great tidings, strange and true; From far away we come to you, To tell of great tidings strange........... and true...........

2 Out on a field where the night was deep,
   The snow under foot, &c.   [sheep,
   There lay three shepherds tending their
   Christian men all, &c.

3 "O ye shepherds what did you see?
   The snow under foot, &c.
   To make you so full of joy and glee?"
   Christian men all, &c.

4 "In an oxstall this night we saw,
   The snow under foot, &c.
   A Babe in a manger, laid on straw,
   Christian men all, &c.

5 And as we gazed this sight upon,
   The snow under foot, &c.
   The angels called Him, the Holy ONE,
   Christian men all, &c.

6 And a marvellous song we straight heard
   The snow under foot, &c.   [then,
   Of Peace on Earth, Good will towards
   Christian men all, &c.   [men,"

7 News of a fair and marvellous thing!
   The snow under foot, &c.
   Nowell, Nowell, Nowell, we sing!
   Christian men all, &c.

N. B.—In the 2nd, 3rd, 4th and 9th verses, the melody in the first bar will need a slight modification, in order to fit it to the accent of the words.
And a corresponding change must be made in the subsequent parts of the melody where the same words recur.

CAROLS.

483. Angel hosts in bright array.

VERSE. *Joyous.*

An-gel hosts in bright ar - ray, Stars their night-watch keeping,— Earthward wend their si-lent way, While the world lies sleep-ing. Through the wintry clouds they glide, On through por-tal hoa - ry, Where, the ox and ass be - side, Lies the Babe of Glo - ry.

CHORUS.

Ring the bells, and sound the horn! Shout with ex - ul - ta - tion! Christ the Lord to - day is born For the world's sal - va - tion!

2 All unseen by mortal eye,
  Reverent and lowly;
Prostrate there, they laud **on high**
  Him, the Infant Holy;
From their lips celestial rise
  Sounds, with joy o'erflowing,
Strains upborne beyond the skies,
  Hymns with **rapture** glowing.
Cho.— Ring the bells, &c.

3 Hark the news the Angel tells;—
  Lo! an Infant Stranger,
God's dear Son among you dwells,
  Born in Bethlehem's manger!
Bursts a chorus from the sky,
  Loud from Heaven's portal:—
Glory be to God on High,
  Peace, good will to mortal!
Cho.— Ring the bells, &c.

4 Angel spirits **earthward led**,
  With a hope endearing,
First to worship, first to spread,
  News of Christ's Appearing!
Trace we out your footfalls light,
  Praise we Christ in glory,
Then waft ye the tidings bright
  Of the Gospel story!
Cho.—Ring the bells, &c.

Carol, brothers, Carol.

2 At the merry table,
  Think of those who've none,
The orphan and the widow,
  Hungry and alone.
Bountiful your offerings
  To the altar bring;
Let the poor and needy
  Christmas carols sing.
CHORUS. Carol, brothers, carol, &c.

3 Listening angel music,
  Discord sure must cease—
Who dare hate his brother
  On this day of peace?
While the heavens are telling
  To mankind good will,
Only love and kindness
  Every bosom fill.
CHORUS. Carol, brothers, carol, &c.

4 Let our hearts responding
  To the seraph band,
With this morning's sunshine
  Bright in every land:
Word, and deed, and prayer
  Speak the grateful sound,
Telling "Merry Christmas"
  All the world around,
CHORUS. Carol, brothers, carol, &c.

CAROLS.

485. Lo! a Star.

Moderate.

Lo! a star, ye sages hoary; Lo! a wondrous star above,
He is born, the King of glory, He, our wondrous star of love.
Lord of Life, Redeemer, Master, Loud the shepherds' welcome rolls,
He is born the peoples' pastor, He the Shepherd of our souls.

2 When from Thee we fain would borrow
  Peace for heart and soul opprest,
  Child of sorrows, heal our sorrow;
  Spirit, give our spirits rest.

  Let all evil past behaviour
  In Thy love forgotten be,
  Let our spirits, gentle Saviour,
  Be this day new-born with Thee.

486. Gently falls the winter snow.

VERSE. *Softly.*

Gently falls the winter snow, Earth lies silently below, While the tender

CAROLS.

Plant appears, Promis'd long by ho-ly seers. Hail the e-ver bless-ed morn, Hail the day that Christ was born; Tell it thro' Je-ru-sa-lem, Christ is born in Beth-le-hem.

2 He who built the starry skies
Low within a manger lies,
Stooping from His Throne sublime,
High above the cherubim.
  CHO.—Hail, &c.

3 Say, ye wand'ring shepherds, say
What your joyful news to-day;
Wherefore have ye left your sheep?—
Wherefore fail your watch to keep?
  CHO.—Hail, &c.

4 "As we watched at dead of night,
Lo! we saw a wondrous sight,—
Angels singing Peace on Earth,
Telling of the Saviour's Birth."
  CHO.—Hail, &c.

5 Haste we now to greet God's Child,
Watch His Face so meek and mild;
Learn the Love of Heaven to see
In our Lord's Humility.
  CHO.—Hail, &c.

487. A shepherd band their flocks.

A shepherd band their flocks are keeping, And gentle lambs are sweetly sleeping; When sudden-ly they all be-hold An an-gel in bright robes with harp of gold.

2 Glad tidings of great joy he bringeth,
The azure vault with anthems ringeth;
"Emmanuel" awakes the song, [prolong.
And countless hosts the glorious theme

3 "To you this day is born a Saviour,
Your Prophet, Priest, and King for ever;"
"All glory be to God," they cry:
"All glory be to God," let earth reply.

4 "On earth be peace with mercy blending,
Good-will to men, and love unending;"
Thus sweetly sing the angel throng,
And all the heavenly host rehearse the song.

5 Thro' field and wood the song resoundeth,
O'er hill and vale the chorus boundeth;
Exultingly the echoes roll, [pole.
And hymns of triumph spread from pole to

6 The shepherds view the host returning,
Their hearts with holy ardour burning;
To Bethlehem they wend their way,
Repeating with glad tongues th' angelic lay.

7 In haste they seek the heavenly Stranger;
They find the Babe laid in a manger;
With wonder and with awe they fall,
And joyfully adore Him, Lord of all!

8 Now every voice with rapture swelleth,
For Christ the Lord with mortals dwelleth;
Let men and angels Him adore,
And shout their glad Hosannas evermore.

CAROLS.

488. Gather around the Christmas Tree.

Brightly. [I. *To be sung before the Distribution of Gifts.*]

|: Gather around the Christmas tree! :| Evergreen Have its branches been, It is king of all the woodland scene; For Christ, our King, is born to-day! His reign shall nev-er pass a-way,

CHORUS.

Ho-san-na, Ho-san-na, Ho-san-na in the high-est!

[II. *To be sung after the Distribution of gifts.*]

2 |: Gather around the Christmas tree! :|
 Once the pride
 Of the mountain side,
Now cut down to grace our Christmas-tide:
For Christ from heaven to earth came down,
To gain, through death, a nobler crown.
 Hosanna, &c.

3 |: Gather around the Christmas tree! :|
 Every bough
 Bears a burden now,—
They are gifts of love for us, we trow:
For Christ is born, His love to show,
And give good gifts to men below.
 Hosanna, &c.

4 |: Farewell to Thee, O Christmas tree! :|
 Thy part is done,
 And Thy gifts are gone,
And thy lights are dying one by one:
For earthly pleasures die to-day,
But heavenly joys shall last alway.
 Hosanna, &c.

5 |: Farewell to thee, O Christmas tree! :|
 Twelve months o'er,
 We shall meet once more,
Merry welcome singing, as of yore:
For Christ now reigns, our Saviour dear,
And gives us Christmas every year!
 Hosanna, &c.

489. *Moderate.* Good Christian men rejoice.

Good Christian men, re-joice With heart and soul and voice, Give ye heed to

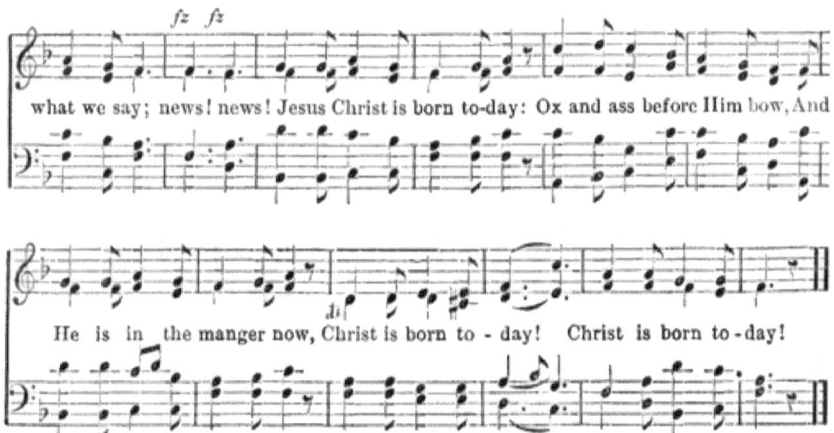

what we say; news! news! Jesus Christ is born to-day: Ox and ass before Him bow, And He is in the manger now, Christ is born to-day! Christ is born to-day!

2 Good Christian men, rejoice
With heart, and soul, and voice;
Now ye hear of endless bliss:
Joy! Joy!
Jesus Christ was born for this!
He hath oped the heav'nly door,
And man is blessèd evermore.
Christ was born for this!

3 Good Christian men, rejoice
With heart, and soul, and voice;
Now ye need not fear the grave;
Peace! Peace!
Jesus Christ was born to save!
Calls you one and calls you all,
To gain His everlasting hall:
Christ was born to save.

Hark! what sounds.

490. *Moderate.*

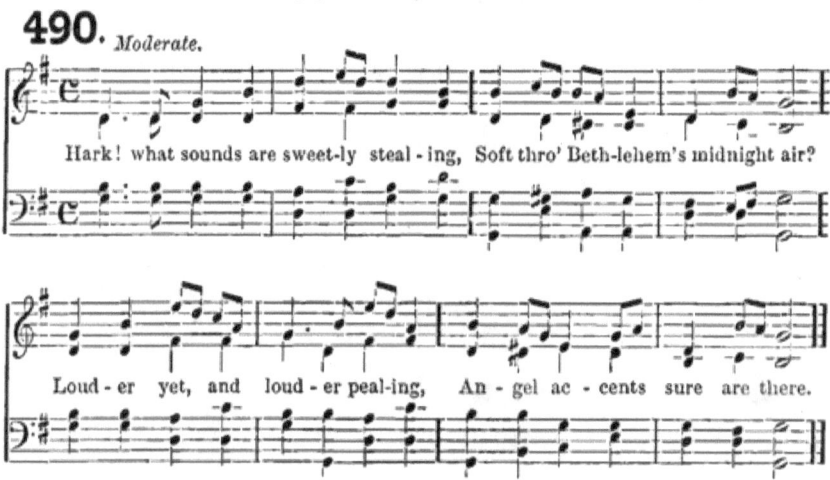

Hark! what sounds are sweet-ly steal-ing, Soft thro' Beth-lehem's midnight air? Loud-er yet, and loud-er peal-ing, An-gel ac-cents sure are there.

2 See! a light from heaven is streaming,
Night and darkness quit the plain;
See! an angel brightly beaming,
Followed by a radiant train.

3 "Fear not, shepherds! glad my story,
Tidings of the greatest joy:
Christ is born, the Lord of glory!
I proclaim a Saviour nigh."

4 Thus the angel, then ascending,
Seeks again the realms of light;
Now the chorus faintly ending,
All is silence, all is night.

CAROLS.

491. Now lift the Carol.

Moderate. VERSE.

Now lift the car-ol, men and maids, Now wake ex-ult-ant sing-ing; This day the Well of Life first sprang, Who shall declare His springing? It is the Birth-day of our Peace; This day for man the wea-ry, The E-ver-lasting Son of God was born of bless-ed Ma-ry.

CHORUS.

No-el! No-el! Proclaim the Saviour's Birth; He rais-es us to Heaven, O hail His com-ing down to earth.

2 He was not born in such sweet days,
    As we of yore remember:
'Twas not the sunny summer time,
    Oh! 'twas the cold December:
As shines the sun above the snows,
    When nature's life is lying
Fast bound in winter's icy chain,
    So came He to the dying.
CHO.— Noel, Noel, &c.

3 There were poor shepherds in the field,
    Their flocks at midnight tending:
Then Heaven came down and brought the
    A rapture never ending: [news,
So they went swift to Bethlehem,
    And saw—and told the story
Of Christ the Lord, a little Child,
    And Angels singing "Glory"
CHO.— Noel, Noel, &c.

4 Not in the manger lies He now;
    Far o'er the sapphire portal
At God's right Hand of power He sits
    Who was this day made mortal:
All in the highest, holiest place,
    Where there may dwell none other,
There our own Manhood sits enthroned,
    There is our Elder Brother.
CHO.— Noel, Noel, &c.

5 The Birthday of our God and King—
    Lo! we are called to greet Him;
The Everlasting Bridegroom comes,
    Oh, go ye out to meet Him.
This is the end of all below,
    The crown of Love's best story;
Christ stands and knocks—oh, happy souls,
    Receive the King of Glory.
CHO.— Noel, Noel, &c.

2 Lo, within a manger lies
He who built the starry skies:
He, who throned in height sublime,
Sits amid the Cherubim!
CHO.— Hail! Thou ever-blessèd, &c.

3 Say, ye holy shepherds, say,
What your joyful news to-day;
Wherefore have ye left your sheep
On the lonely mountain steep?
CHO.— Hail! Thou ever-blessèd, &c.

4 "As we watched at dead of night,
— Lo, we saw a wondrous light;

Angels singing peace on earth,
Told us of the Saviour's Birth."
CHO.— Hail! Thou ever-blessèd, &c.

5 Sacred Infant, all Divine,
What a tender love was Thine;
Thus to come from highest bliss
Down to such a world as this!
CHO.— Hail! Thou ever-blessèd, &c.

6 Teach, O teach us, Holy Child,
By Thy Face so meek and mild,
Teach us to resemble Thee,
In Thy sweet humility!
CHO.— Hail! Thou ever-blessèd, &c.

In the early morning.

493. *Joyously.*

In the ear-ly morn-ing, ear-ly, Ere the dawn was e-ven nigh—
Glo-ri-a in ex-cel-sis De-o! Glo-ry be to God on high.
When the crown-like stars were lus-trous; When the dew was on the sod,
Sang the An-gels to the shepherds, Sang the chor-is-ters of God.

2 To the humble Bethlehem shepherds,
  On the first glad Christmas morn,
Sang the choir of God Angelic,—
  Christ the Son of God is born!
When the dew was white and pearly,
  Flashed a light across the sky,
In the early morning, early,
  Glory be to God on high.

3 Glory in the heavens eternal,
  Upon earth be glory, too,
For the day of grace hath broken,
  And a King is born to you.
In the early morning, early,
  Glory be to God on high:
Rang the sound of Angels harping,
  Through the stilly list'uing sky.

2 Why lies He in such mean estate,
   Where ox and ass are feeding?
 Good Christian, fear: for sinners here
   The silent Word is pleading:
 Nails, spear, shall pierce Him through,
   The Cross be borne, for me, for you;
 Hail! Hail! the Word made flesh,
   The Babe, the Son of Mary!

3 So bring Him incense, gold and myrrh,
   Come peasant, King, to own Him;
 The King of kings salvation brings;
   Let loving hearts enthrone Him.
 Raise, raise the song on high,
   The Virgin sings her lullaby:
 Joy! joy! for Christ is born,
   The Babe, the Son of Mary!

CAROLS.

495. Holy night! peaceful night!

Moderate. *pp*   *mf*   *pp*

Ho-ly night! peace-ful night! All is dark, save the light,

Yon-der where they sweet vi-gil keep O'er the Babe who in si-lent sleep,

pp

Rests in hea-ven-ly peace, Rests in hea-ven-ly peace.

2 Holy night! peaceful night!
　Only for shepherds' sight,
　Came blest visions of Angel throngs,
　With their loud Alleluia songs,
　　Saying, JESUS is come,
　　Saying, JESUS is come.

3 Holy night! peaceful night!
　Child of heav'n! O! how bright
　Thou didst smile on us when Thou wast [born;
　Blest indeed was that happy morn,
　　Full of heavenly joy,
　　Full of heavenly joy.

496. Waken, Christian children.

Brightly.

Waken, Christian children, Up, and let us sing, With glad hearts and voi-ces,

Of our new-born King. Up! 'tis meet to wel-come With a joyous lay

CAROLS.

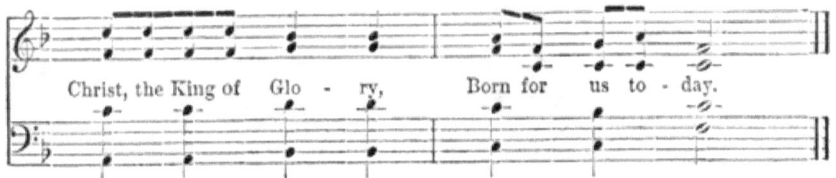

Christ, the King of Glo-ry, Born for us to-day.

2 In a manger lowly
  Sleeps the heavenly Child,
  O'er Him fondly bendeth
  Mary, Mother mild.
  Far above that stable,
  Up in heaven so high,
  One bright star outshineth,
  Watching silently.

3 Fear not, then, to enter,
  Though we cannot bring
  Gold, or myrrh, or incense,
  Fitting for a King.

Gifts He asketh richer,
Offerings costlier still,
Yet may Christian children
Bring them if they will.

4 Brighter than all jewels
  Shines the modest eye;
  Best of gifts, He loveth
  Infant purity.
  Haste we, then, to welcome
  With a joyous lay
  Christ, the King of Glory,
  Born for us to-day.

497. Christians, Carol sweetly.

Christians, car-ol sweet-ly, Up to-day and sing! 'Tis the hap-py birth-day Of our Ho-ly King: Haste we then to greet Him, Hum-bly fall-ing down, While our hands entwine Him, Dearest Babe, a crown.

2 Crowds of snow-white Angels
  Throng the golden stair;
  All things are resplendent,
  All things passing fair:
  Bells, clear music making,
  Peal the news o'er earth;
  Chimes within make answer,
  All is glee and mirth.

3 Michael, at the manger,
  Bows his royal face;
  Gabriel, with lily,
  Hides transcendent Grace;
  For, dear friends, the glory
  Of that lowly bed
  Overpowers the beauty
  On Archangels shed.

4 Shall I tell of **Joseph**,
  Who, with rapt surprise,
  Sees the light from Godhead
  Fill those infant eyes?
  Shall I sing of Mary,
  Who, upon her breast,
  Cradles her **Creator**,
  Soothes Him to **His** rest?

5 Angels, Mary, Joseph,
  Yes, I greet you all!
  Falling down in worship
  At the manger stall!
  For you hail our Monarch,
  Born a Child to-day;
  So, with you I worship,
  And my homage pay.

2 "To you in the City of **David**,
  A **Saviour is born** to-day!"
And sudden a host of **the heav'nly ones
  Flash'd forth** to join **the lay!**
O never hath sweeter message
  Thrill'd home to **the** souls of men,
And the Heav'ns themselves had never
  A gladder choir till then,— [heard
For they sang that Christmas Carol,
  That never on earth shall cease, &c.

3 And the shepherds came to the Manger,
  And gaz'd on the Holy Child;
And calmly o'er that rude cradle
  The Virgin Mother smil'd;
And the sky, in the star-lit silence,
  Seem'd full of the angel lay;
"To you in the City of David
  A Saviour is born to-day;"
Oh they sang—and I ween that never
  The carol on earth shall cease, &c.

CAROLS.

499. *Softly.*

Silent night! peaceful night!

Si-lent night! peaceful night! Through the darkness beams a light;
Si-lent night! peace-ful night; Through the darkness beams a light,
Through the dark-ness beams a light! Yonder, where they sweet vig-ils keep

Rallentando.

O'er the Babe, who, in si-lent sleep, Rests in heavenly peace, Rests in heavenly peace.

2 Silent night! holiest night!
  Darkness flies and all is light!
Shepherds hear the angels sing—
  "Hallelujah! hail the King!
    Jesus Christ is here!"

3 Silent night! peaceful night!
  Child of heaven! O how bright
Thou didst smile when Thou wast born;
  Blessèd was that happy morn,
    Full of heavenly joy.

4 Silent night! holiest night!
  Guiding Star, O, lend thy light!
See the eastern wise men bring
Gifts and homage to our King!
    Jesus Christ is here!

5 Silent night! holiest night!
  Wondrous Star! O, lend thy light!
With the angels let us sing
Hallelujah to our King!
    Jesus Christ is here!

2 Lifting our voices
    In worship and praise,
  To Christ our Redeemer
    An anthem we raise.
  Angels no longer
    Appear upon earth,
  To tell the glad tidings
    Of joy at His birth.

3 Visions of glory
    No more on our sight
  Will burst on the darkness
    With heavenly light.
  Welcome the morning
    Whose beams round us shine;
  Our sun is the Saviour,
    The light is Divine.

CAROLS.

501. Moderate. **Tune your harps for holy song.**

Tune your harps for ho-ly song, E-choes soft the notes pro-long,
Heav'n-ly joy thy soul pos-sess, Christ is born a world to bless;
Joy - ful strains of tri - umph wake, Stil - ly night's rapt si-lence break;
Sound the trump with loud ac-claim, Christ is born in Beth-le-hem!

2 See! the heavens open wide,
Glory streams a golden tide;
Seraphs throng the shining stairs,
Morn her fragrant incense bears.
Angel fingers sweep the lyres,
Earth relights her altar fires;
Sing loud anthems to His Name,
Christ is born in Bethlehem!

3 Alleluia! greet the dawn,
"Unto us a Child is born,"
Songs on high, and praise on earth
Wait upon the Saviour's birth;
Stars of morn in chorus sing,
Earth and sky with rapture ring;
Promised Branch of Jesse's stem,
Hail the Babe of Bethlehem!

4 With the Angel's welcome bring
Endless praise to Christ our King;
Carol songs around the earth,
Triumph in a Sovereign's birth.
Glad the Star to men of old,
Bright the Light we now behold;
Strike your harps, this day proclaim
Christ is born in Bethlehem!

502. Star of Glory! brightly streaming.

And lo! the Star, which they saw in the East went before them, till it came and stood o-ver where the young Child was.

CHORUS.
Star of Glo-ry! brightly streaming, Welcome, oh! thou bless-ed Star!
Star that erst se-rene-ly beaming, Led the wise men from a-far.
Thou their wand'ring foot-steps led-dest, Star of Glo-ry, plan-et mild!
Till thy heav'nly light thou sheddest O'er the ho-ly, bless-ed Child.

2 Holy Father! Thou who gavest
Them that light and grace to see!
Holy Son! O Christ, who savest
All that look for light to Thee!
Holy Spirit, ever pouring
Grace on them that seek aright!
Grant us, Lord, with hearts adoring,
Still to walk with Thee in light.

503. Deep the gloom.

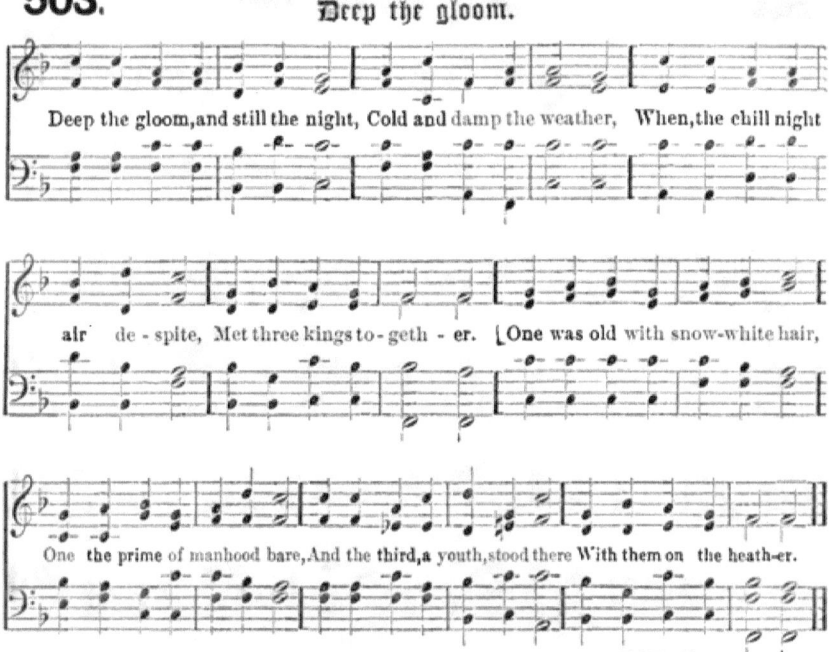

Deep the gloom, and still the night, Cold and damp the weather, When, the chill night air despite, Met three kings to-geth-er. One was old with snow-white hair, One the prime of manhood bare, And the third, a youth, stood there With them on the heath-er.

2 Looking for the promised King,
   Who, in Eastern quarters,
  Soon should spring to life, to rule
   O'er earth's sons and daughters,
  Them this eve, while rapt in sleep,
  One had roused in accents deep,
  " Haste ye; watch ye; vigil keep
   By Euphrates' waters!"

3 Up they spring, and quickly hie,
   Each his pathway bending,
  Through the chilly mist and gloom,
   O'er the earth depending,
  How the world in darkness lay,
  Till the Day-Star shed Its ray,
  Nature thus would fain display;
   Mystic emblems lending.

4 Then the kings with solemn gaze
   Looked on high beholding;
  For the marvel yet to come,
   Heav'n their spirits moulding,
  When behold, with silent awe,
  Suddenly the clouds they saw
  Like a darkened veil withdraw,
   Wonders more unfolding.

5 In a trice a star shone forth,
   O! so brightly shining!—
  Nearer, nearer yet it came,
   Still towards earth inclining!
  And 'twas shaped—O wondrous sight!
  Like a child enthroned in light,
  Crown'd, though yet, with sceptre bright.
   Victor—cross combining! *

6 Then one cried, "Behold the star
   Of which seers have spoken,
  Beaming on the land afar,
   And of life the token!
  Haste we, brothers! let us speed;
  See, it moves! It comes to lead
  To the Christ, of Judah's seed
   Born of line unbroken!"

7 Up they rise, and bend their way,
   Toil nor labour sparing,
  Over mountain, hill, and plain,
   Costly treasures bearing.—
  So do ye your off'rings make,
  Fear no pain for Jesu's sake,
  Ever strive heaven's road to take,
   For your Lord preparing!

* An allusion to a legend, preserved in an ancient Commentary on St. Matthew, that the star, on its first appearance to the Magi, had the form of a radiant child, bearing a sceptre or cross.

CAROLS.

504. We three Kings of Orient.

Moderate. *[See note below.]*

We three Kings of O-ri-ent are, Bearing gifts we traverse a-far, Field and fountain, Moor and mountain, Following yon-der Star.

CHORUS.

O Star of Wonder, Star of Night, Star with Royal Beau-ty bright, West-ward lead-ing, Still pro-ceed-ing, Guide us to thy per-fect light.

GASPARD.
2 **Born** a king on Bethlehem plain,
  Gold I bring to crown Him again;
    King forever,
    Ceasing never
  Over us all to reign.
    Cho.—O Star, &c.

MELCHIOR.
3 Frankincense to offer have I,
  Incense owns a Deity nigh:
    Prayer and praising
    All men raising,
  Worship Him God on high.
    Cho.—O Star, &c.

BALTHAZAR.
4 Myrrh is mine; its bitter perfume
  Breathes a life of gathering gloom;—
    Sorrowing, sighing,
    Bleeding, dying,
  Sealed in the stone-cold tomb.
    Cho.—O Star, &c.

5 Glorious now **behold Him arise,**
  King, and God, and **Sacrifice;**
    Heaven sings
    Alleluia:
  Alleluia the earth **replies.**
    Cho.—O Star, &c.

* *Verses 1 and 5 are sung as a trio. Verses 2, 3 and 4, are sung as a solo, to the same music, the chorus being the same throughout.*

505. In the wintry heaven.

Bold.
Two Sopr. and Alto (or a high Tenor.)

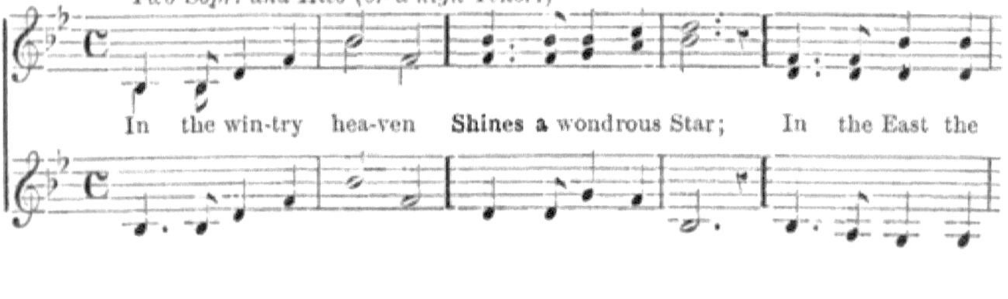

In the win-try hea-ven **Shines a** wondrous Star; In the East the

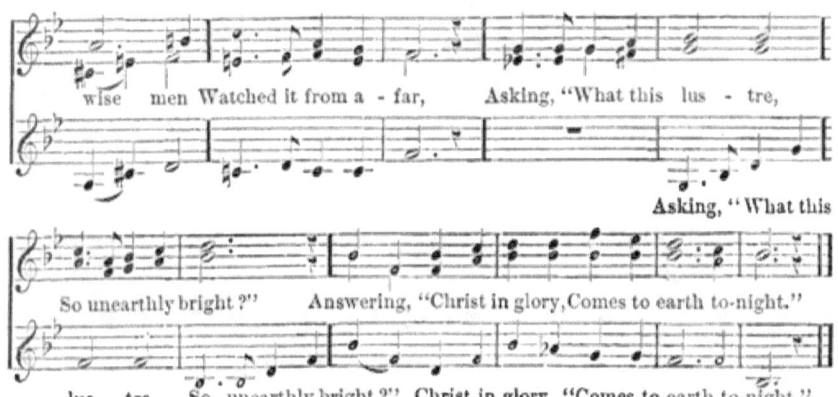

2 O'er the dusty highway,
O'er the desert drear,
From the East, the wise men,
Watch it shining clear;
Asking, "Shall we follow
In this starlight way?"
Answering, "Yes, 'twill lead us
To the perfect day."
3 In a lowly Manger,
Lies an Infant weak;
Is it He whom wise men
Come so far to seek?

Asking, "Where the monarch?
Where Judea's King?"
Saying, "Gifts and worship
To His throne we bring."
4 In our hearts, we children,
See this Star once more;
Not as wise men saw it,
In the days of yore;
Asking, "May we bring Him
Childhood's love to-day?"
Answering, "Come, dear children,
Jesus says we may."

506. Now to Bethlehem haste we.

2 They would ne'er have known Him,
In their country far,
Had not God, in mercy,
Placed in heaven a star.
3 Blessèd Star! outshining
Through the darkest night,
Leading up to Jesus,
Who is Light of Light!

4 Sing we now, rejoicing,
For to us as well
That bright Star so glorious
Doth glad tidings tell.
5 With them let us worship,
For our Light has come:
Star of Bethlehem! lead us
Safe to Heaven our Home.

Easter.

507. *With spirit.* **The Easter Sunshine breaks again.**

The Eas-ter sun-shine breaks a-gain On all the sin-ful earth,
More glo-rious than the star-lit morn, We've sang at Je-sus' Birth!
We've watch'd be-side our Sa-viour's Cross, We've sorrowed at His Grave;
But now He's broken Death's dark bands, Our Jesus, strong to save! Way! Sing
Last verse only.
on ye hap-py Chris-tian hearts, The Lord is risen to-day!

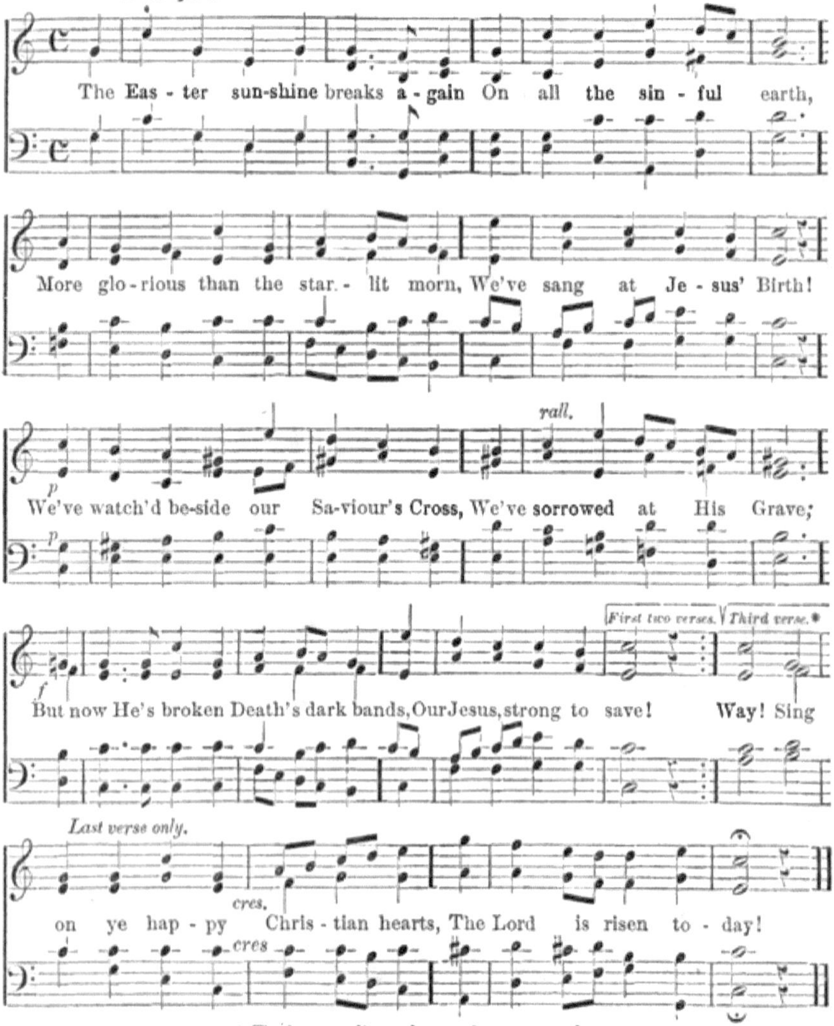

* The last two lines of verse 3 are repeated.

2 Fair blossoms on the Easter morn
   Fling forth their fragrance sweet,
  And tell of Resurrection-joy,
   And Jesus' work complete!
  But fairer still the offering
   Each loving heart should bring,
  Of faith and love and penitence,
   To Christ, its risen King.

3 So on this glorious Easter-day
   Our gladsome songs we raise,
  And echo e'en to Heaven's own gates
   Our happy notes of praise!
  For He who died is risen again,
   "The Life, the Truth, the Way!"
  Sing on, ye happy Christian hearts,
   The Lord is risen to-day.

509. God hath sent His Angels.

God hath sent His Angels to the earth again, Bringing joyful tidings to the sons of men. They who first at Christmas, throng'd the heav'nly way, Now beside the tomb-door, sit on Easter Day. Angels sing His triumph, as you sang His birth, "Christ the Lord is ris-en," "Peace, good-will on earth."

2 In the dreadful desert, where the Lord was tried,
There the faithful Angels gathered at His side.
And when in the garden, grief and pain and care
Bowed Him down with anguish, they were with Him there.
Cho.—Angels, sing, &c.

3 Yet the Christ they honour, is the same **Christ still**,
Who, in light and darkness, did His Father's will.
And the tomb deserted, shineth like the sky,
Since He passed out from it, **into** victory.
Cho.—Angels, sing, &c.

4 God has still His Angels, helping, at His word,
All His faithful children, like their faithful Lord;
Soothing them in sorrow, arming them in strife,
Opening wide the tomb-doors, leading into Life.
Cho.—Angels, sing, &c.

5 Father, send Thine Angels unto us, **we pray**;
Leave us not to wander, all along our way.
Let them guard and guide us, wheresoe'er we be,
Till our resurrection brings **us** home to Thee.
Cho.—Angels, sing, &c.

CAROLS.

510. The world itself keeps Easter Day.
Moderate.

The world itself keeps Easter Day, And Easter larks are singing:
And Easter flowers are blooming gay, And Easter buds are springing:
Alleluia! Alleluia! The Lord of all things lives anew, And all His works are rising too. Alleluia! Alleluia! Alleluia!

2 There stood three Maries by the tomb
  On Easter morning early,
When day had scarcely chased the gloom,
  And dew was white and pearly;
    Alleluia! Alleluia!
With loving but with erring mind
They came the Prince of Life to find:
    Alleluia! Alleluia! Alleluia!

3 But earlier still the Angel sped
    His news of comfort giving;
  And "why," he said, "among the dead
    "Thus seek ye for the living?"
        Alleluia! Alleluia!
  "Go tell them all and make them blest,
  "Tell Peter first, and then the rest."
        Alleluia! Alleluia! Alleluia!

4 But one, and one alone, remained
    With love that could not vary;
  And thus a joy past joy she gained,
    That sometime sinner Mary:
        Alleluia! Alleluia!
  The first the dear, dear form to see
  Of Him who hung upon the tree:
        Alleluia! Alleluia! Alleluia!

5 The Church is keeping Easter Day,
    And Easter hymns are sounding,
  And Easter flowers are blooming gay,
    The holy Font surrounding;
        Alleluia! Alleluia!
  The Lord hath risen, as all things tell,
  Good Christians, see ye rise as well:
        Alleluia! Alleluia! Alleluia!

CAROLS.

511. *Brightly.* **Easter flowers, Easter Carols.**

Eas-ter flow-ers, Eas-ter car-ols Deck the al-tar, fill the air;
Glo-rious dawns the hap-py morn-ing O'er a world so bright and fair.
Al-le-lu-ia let us sing, Al-le-lu-ia to the King!

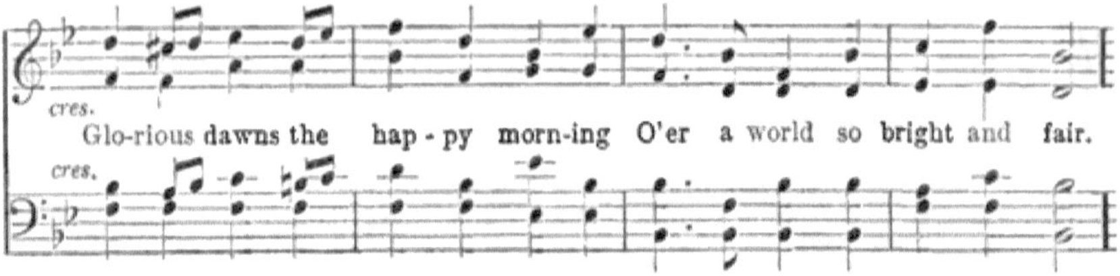

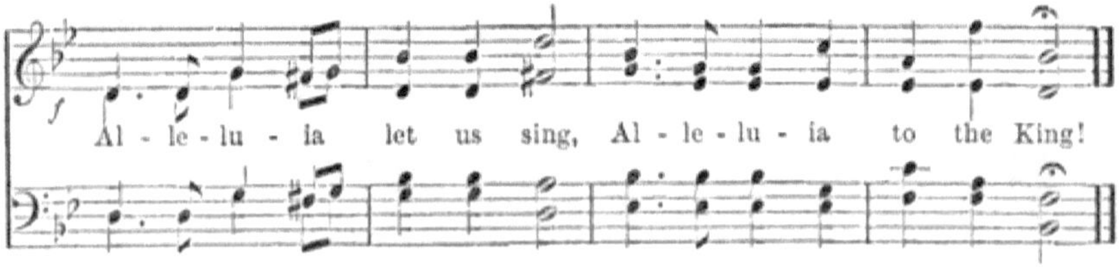

2 When the clouds of night were broken,
　Angels rolled the stone away,
　And on this bright Easter morning
　Sing we now the triumph lay.
　　Alleluia let us sing,
　　Alleluia to the King!

3 In the mists of early morning,
　Came the faithful to the tomb,
　Angel guardians clad in white robes,
　Sat there in the breaking gloom.
　　Alleluia let us sing,
　　Alleluia to the King!

4 "He is risen!" thus the Angel
　Spake unto the faithful three,
　"He is risen," wondrous story,
　"He has gone to Galilee."
　　Alleluia let us sing,
　　Alleluia to the King!

5 Now the clouds of night are broken,
　Mortals now the story tell,
　"He is risen! Alleluia!"
　Let the joyful anthem swell.
　　Alleluia let us sing,
　　Alleluia to the King.

512. *Joyous.* **Smile praises, O sky!**

Smile prais-es, O sky! Soft breathe them, O air! Be-low and on

CAROLS.

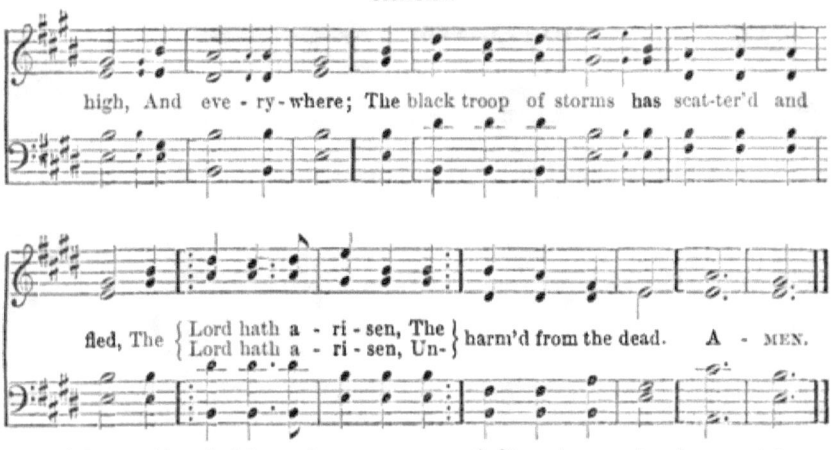

2 Sweep tides of rich music
  The new world along,
And pour in full measure
  Sweet lyres, your song,
Sing, sing, for He liveth,
  He lives, as He said;
The Lord hath arisen
  Unharmed from the dead.

3 Clap, clap your hands, mountains;
   Ye valleys, resound;
Leap, leap for joy, fountains;
   Ye hills, catch the sound;
All triumph! He liveth,
   He lives, as He said;
The Lord hath arisen
   Unharmed from the dead.

513. *Earnestly.*   The Lord is risen!

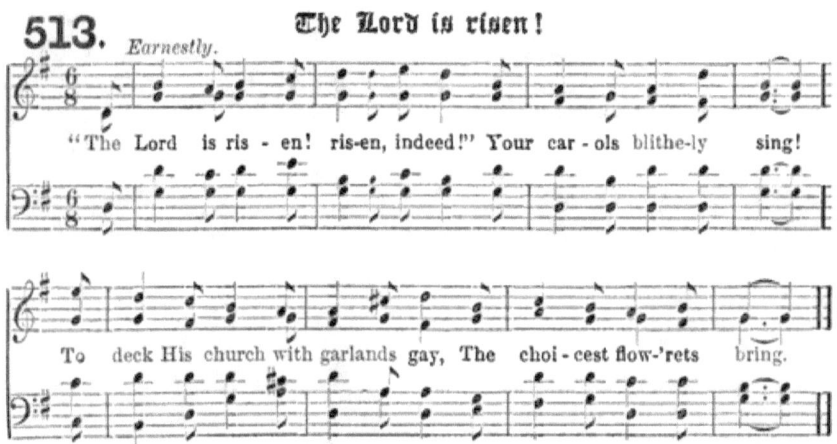

2 Come sing His praises loud and high,
    Ere yet appears the dawn—
  The birth-day of our Christian hope!
    The glorious Easter Morn.

3 For when the light of Easter dawned,
    Victorious in the strife,
  The Saviour burst the bands of death,
    And won our endless life.

4 He rose, and took the sting from death,
    Took from the grave its might;
  He led the way from earth to heaven,
    Through darkness into light.

5 "The Lord is risen." Let each voice
    Sing carols glad and gay,
  From morn till eve each heart repeat
    "The Lord is risen to-day!"

514. Ye happy bells of Easter Day.

2 Ye carol-bells of Easter Day!
  The teeming earth,
  That saw His birth
When lying 'neath the sword,
Upspringeth now in joy, to show
  The rising of the Lord!

3 Ye glory-bells of Easter Day!
  The hills that rise
  Against the skies,
Re-echo with the word—
The victor-breath that conquers death—
  The rising of the Lord!

4 Ye passion-bells of Easter Day!
  The bitter cup
  He lifted up,
Salvation to afford.
Ye saintly bells! your passion tells
  The rising of the Lord!

5 Ye mercy-bells of Easter Day!
  His tender side
  Was riven wide,
Where floods of mercy poured:
Redeemed clay doth sing to-day
  The rising of the Lord!

6 Ye victor-bells of Easter Day!
  The thorny crown
  He layeth down:
Ring! ring! with strong accord—
The mighty strain of love and pain,
  The rising of the Lord!

CAROLS.

515. Shine, O Sun, in splendour bright.

Brightly.

Shine, O Sun, in splendour bright, Em-blem of the Lord of light,
Who this day rose from the dead, And cap-tiv'-ty cap-tive led.

CHORUS.

Sing joy-ous-ly, ye mor-tals, For Christ hath op'd the por-tals Of life to all a-gain. Al-le-lu-ia, Al-le-lu-ia, Al-le-lu-ia, A-men! Al-le-lu-ia! Al-le-lu-ia, Al-le-lu-ia! A-men!

2 Now the flowers budding sweet,
In the soil beneath our feet,
Raise themselves from sleep like death,
Praising God with fragrant breath.
  CHO.—Sing joyously, &c.

3 All the trees and plants in spring
To the Resurrection bring
Signal offerings, and declare
Christ is ris'n, ev'ry where.
  CHO.—Sing joyously, &c.

CAROLS.

516. *Joyous.* **Christ, the Lord is risen again.**

Christ, the Lord, is ris'n again, Christ hath broken ev'ry chain; Hark! Angelic voices cry, Singing evermore on high. He who gave for us His life, Who for us endured the strife, Is our Paschal Lamb to-day: We too sing for joy, and aye.

2 He who **bore** all pain and loss
Comfortless upon the Cross,
Lives in glory now on high,
Pleads **for** us and hears our cry:
He who slumbered in the grave
Is exalted now to save;
Now through Christendom it rings
That the Lamb is King of kings.

3 Now He bids us tell abroad
How the lost may be restored,
How the penitent forgiven,
How we too may enter heaven.
Thou, our Paschal Lamb indeed,
Christ, Thy ransomed people feed:
Take our sins and guilt away,
Let us sing by night and day.

517. *Moderate.* **Near the Tomb where Jesus slept.**

Near the Tomb where Jesus slept, Roman guards their night watch kept, Pacing to and fro alone, By the closely sealed stone. *f* CHORUS. Christ! Thou Conqueror! All hail!

Guard and stone can nought avail! Death is slain in mortal strife; Hail the Prince and Lord of Life!

2 In the **darksome** midnight, lo!
  Hark! an earthquake rolls below!
  Sign of deadly conflict o'er,
  Death despoiled for evermore!
    Cho.—Christ, Thou Conqueror, &c.

3 That which by the cave-mouth lay,
  Angel hands have rolled away;
  And the Lord, His three days sped,
  Comes triumphant from the dead!
    Cho.—Christ, Thou Conqueror, &c.

4 Christ! Thou Victor o'er the tomb,
  Take us in the Day of Doom,
  Take us to Thine own dear side,
  At the last great Easter-tide!
    Chorus after 4th verse.
  Christ! Thou Conqueror! all hail!
  Let not Death o'er us prevail;
  Help us in our mortal strife,
  Bring us to the Land of Life.

518. *Joyous.* Christ is risen!

Christ is ris-en! Christ is ris-en! O let the joyful sounds Thro' ev'-ry land re-ech-o, To earth's re-motest bounds, Christ is ris-en! Christ is ris-en!

2 Christ is risen! **Christ is risen!**
  Bright Angels **join the cry;**
  Alleluias ever singing
  Before the Throne on high.
    Christ is risen! Christ is risen!

3 Christ is risen! Christ is risen!
  Ere earliest morning ray,
  Wake, slumb'ring hearts, awake! **arise!**
  And speed **you** on your way.
    Christ **is risen! Christ is risen!**

4 Christ is risen! Christ is risen!
  To all the words repeat,
  Till ev'ry knee before Him bow
  In adoration meet.
    Christ is risen! Christ is risen!

5 Christ is risen! Christ is risen!
  Bid all His praises sing;
  Praise Him, the God of earth and heaven,
  Redeemer, Lord and King.
    Christ is risen! Christ is risen!

CAROLS.

519. Now all the bells are ringing.

Fast.

Alleluia! Alleluia! Alleluia!

Now all the bells are ringing To welcome Easter Day, And we with joy are singing Our carol sweet and gay; For Jesus hath a-risen From Joseph's rocky cave, Hath burst His three days' prison, And triumph'd o'er the Grave.

Alleluia! Alleluia! Alleluia! A-MEN.

2 Alleluia! Alleluia! Alleluia!
  O hasten we to meet Him,
    With our companions dear,
  With love and awe to greet Him,
    As He is drawing near;
  Of old His friends were bidden
    To haste to Galilee:
  Still in His Church, all glorious,
    Our risen Lord will be.
      Alleluia! Alleluia! Alleluia!

3 Alleluia! Alleluia! Alleluia!
  Still, Jesus! we adore Thee
    With faith which may not fail,
  Still, as we kneel before Thee,
    We hear Thee say "All hail"!
  Thou, who art now descending
    To raise us up to Thee,
  An Easter-tide unending
    Grant us in Heaven to see.
      Alleluia! Alleluia! Alleluia!

*Note.—The Roman Soldier's part is set in the G-clef for the convenience of children; but it is much better when sung by a man, an octave below.

Child. 3 Roman Soldier, if you were
    All fast asleep, as you declare,
    How could you know, or see, or say,
    Who 'twas that stole the Lord away?
Sol. Old Annas and Caiphas told me so:
    The truth they wished that none
      should know;
    They gave me, therefore, silver and
      gold,
    To tell the story I have told.
Child. Fie, old Roman, why tell a lie! For
    Cho.—Christ is risen, &c.

Child. 4 Roman Soldier, tell no more
    The stories you have told before—
    Too foolish to deceive our youth;
    But tell us now the simple truth.

Sol. An earthquake rolled the stone away;
    Half dead with fear we Romans lay;
    While, like full sunrise at midnight,
    Christ rose, and glided from our sight.
Child. Aye, Old Roman, why tell a lie! For
    Cho.—Christ is risen, &c.

Child. 5 Roman Soldier, your own eyes
    Have seen our Lord and God arise;
    How can you, now that He is known,
    Still worship gods of wood and stone?
Sol. We Romans conquer where we come,
    But Christ hath power to vanquish
      Rome;
    My idols all I cast away,
    Christ's soldier till my dying day.
Child. Right, Old Roman, fight for the Light.
    Cho.—Christ is risen, &c.   [For

522. *'Twas at the matin hour.*

1. 'Twas at the matin hour, Before the early dawn;
The prison doors flew open, The bolts of death were drawn.

2. 'Twas at the matin hour, When pray'rs of saints are strong;
When two short days ago He bore The spitting, wounds, and wrong.

3 From realms unseen, an unseen way,
    Th' Almighty Saviour came,
    And following on His silent steps,
    An Angel armed in flame.

4 The stone is rolled away,
    The keepers fainting fall,
    Satan and Pilate's watchmen,
    The day has scared them all.

5 The Angel came full early,
    But Christ had gone before,
    Not for Himself, but for His Saints,
    Is burst the prison door.

6 When all His Saints assemble,
    Make haste ere twilight cease,
    His Easter blessing to receive,
    And so lie down in peace.

CAROLS.

523. Let the merry Church bells ring!

Let the mer-ry Church bells ring! Hence with tears and sighing! Frost and cold have fled from Spring, Life hath con-quered dy-ing. Flow'rs are smil-ing, fields are gay, Sun-ny is the weath-er; With our ris-ing Lord to-day, All things rise to-geth-er. Let the mer-ry Church bells ring! Ring! Ring! Ring! Let the mer-ry Church bells ring! Ring! Ring! Ring!

2 Let the birds sing out again
   From their leafy chapel,
Praising Him, with whom in vain
   Satan sought to grapple;
Sounds of joy come fast and thick,
   As the breezes flutter;
Resurrexit, non est hic,
   Is the strain they utter.
      Let the merry, &c.

3 Let the past of grief be past;
   This our comfort giveth,
He was slain on Friday last,
   But to-day He liveth:
Mourning heart must needs be gay,
   Nor let sorrow vex it,
Since the very grave can say,
   Christus Resurrexit.
      Let the merry, &c.

524. Sing your carols to-day.

Earnestly.

Sing your carols to-day, And your gladsomest lay,
To the Paraclete pay— Now to mortals given;
Now sent down from heaven, Sing, of joy, joy, joy; And to-day,
raise the lay, TE DEUM LAUDAMUS, DOMINUM.

2 Death and hell overcome,
　Easter morn, from the tomb
　Jesus chased all the gloom,—
　　Ope'd the prison portals—
　　Freedom brought to mortals.
　Sing, of life, life, life,
　　And the strain, raise again,
　TE DEUM LAUDAMUS, DOMINUM.

3 Forty days more with men
　Did the Lord live again,
　Blessed rites to ordain,
　　And His Kingdom founded
　　By the round world bounded.
　Sing of joy, joy, joy,
　　Till it rise to the skies,
　TE DEUM LAUDAMUS, DOMINUM.

4 Risen, never to die,
　Having gone up on high
　To His Throne in the sky,
　　He sent His Spirit Holy,
　　To bless His people solely.
　Sing of joy, joy, joy,
　　Praise His Name with acclaim,
　TE DEUM LAUDAMUS, DOMINUM.

5 With bright tongues as of flame,
　Then the Comforter came,
　In the Blessed One's Name
　　Dissipating sadness,—
　　Bringing joy and gladness,—
　Sing of joy, life, and peace:
　　Him adore, ever more,
　TE DEUM LAUDAMUS, DOMINUM.

Index of First Lines.

First Line	NUMBER
A little lamb one afternoon	350
Abide with me: fast falls the eventide	179
Above the clear blue sky	329
Advance! Advance! the day is come	471
Again the morn of gladness	195
All glory, laud, and honour	239
All hail the power of Jesus' Name	320
All is bright and cheerful round us	202
All praise to Thee, my God, this night	183
All things beautiful and fair	360
All things bright and beautiful	408
All Thy works, O heavenly Father	400
Alleluia! Fairest morning	198
Alleluia! Thanks and glory	333
Angel voices, ever singing	402
Angels from the realms of glory	230
Angels, roll the rock away	251
Around the Throne of God, a band	399
As helpless as a child who clings	344
As, with gladness, men of old	232
Awake, my soul, and with the sun	171
Awake, my soul, stretch every nerve	374
Beautiful Saviour	391
Behold a little Child	225
Behold, behold He cometh	206
Bethlehem, of noblest cities	229
Blessèd are the pure in heart	418
Blessèd Jesus, wilt Thou hear us	417
Brightest and best of the sons of the morning	231
Brightly gleams our banner	464
By cool Siloam's shady rill	397
Children, come and list to me	452
Children of the Heavenly King	355
Christ is merciful and mild	368
Christ the Lord is risen to-day	250
Christ, who once amongst us	351
Christians, awake, salute the happy morn	214
Christian children must be holy	227
Come, Christian children, come and raise	340
Come, gracious Spirit, heavenly Dove	261
Come, labour on	290
Come, let us sing of those sweet babes	272
Come praise your Lord and Saviour	327
Come sing with holy gladness	324
Come, ye faithful, raise the strain	256
Come, ye thankful people, come	295
Cradled in a manger	211
Daily, daily sing the praises	378
Day is past and gone	181
Day by day we magnify Thee	338
Dear children, evermore	208
Dear Saviour, we gather, our tribute to bring	341
Early, with blush of dawn	248
Easter Day hath dawned again	253
Every morning, the red sun	426
Fair waved the golden corn	395
Far o'er yon horizon	468
Father, lead me day by day	365
Father of mercies, in Thy word	303
Father, though Thy Name be holy	407
Fold thy hands in prayer, my child	316
For the beauty of the earth	336
For thee, O dear, dear country	380
For Thy mercy and Thy grace	228
Forth to the fight, ye ransomed	466
Forty days on earth He spent	259
Forward! be our watchword	467
From Greenland's icy mountains	285
Gentle Jesus, meek and mild	406
Give heed, my heart, lift up thine eyes	221
Glorious things of thee are spoken	274
Glory to the Blessèd Jesus	328
Glory to the Father give	268
Go forward, Christian soldier	373
Go when the morning shineth	313
God bless our native land	298
God eternal, mighty King	331
God hath made the moon, whose beam	404
God is Love — His mercy brightens	363
God of mercy, throned on high	401
God, that madest earth and heaven	185
God, who hath made the daisies	334
Golden harps are sounding	257
Gracious Saviour, gentle Shepherd	394
Gracious Spirit, dwell with me	264
Gracious Spirit, Holy Ghost	262
Great Shepherd of the sheep	434
Hail the Cross of Jesus	307
Hail the day that sees Him rise	258
Hail! Thou long-expected Jesus	219
Hail to the Lord's Anointed	230
Happy, happy Sunday	197
Hark! hark, my soul: angelic songs are swelling	387
Hark! the glad sound, the Saviour comes	210
Hark! the Heaven's sweet melody	216
Hark! the herald angels sing	213
Hark! the sound of holy voices	270
Hark! what mean those holy voices	217
Hear Thy children, gentle Jesus, Hear	246
Hear Thy children, gentle Jesus, While	187
Heavenly Father, send Thy blessing	406
Heavenly Shepherd, guide and feed us	364
Holy Bible! book divine	304
Holy Father, Thou hast taught me	353
Holy, Holy, Holy! Lord God Almighty	266
Holy offerings, rich and rare	292
Holy Spirit, Blessèd Dove	263
Hosanna, be the children's song	299
Hosanna! loud hosanna! From	337
Hosanna! loud hosanna! The	240
Hosanna! raise the pealing hymn	322
Hosanna we sing, like the children dear	326

INDEX OF FIRST LINES.

First Line	Number
How bright these glorious spirits shine	269
How dearly God must love us	359
How sweet the Name of Jesus sounds	312
Humble praises, Holy Jesus	319
Hushed was the evening hymn	422
I hear the children's voices	438
I love the holy Angels	410
I love Thy kingdom, Lord	277
I love to hear the story	358
I love to think, though I am young	435
I praised the earth, in beauty seen	450
I think, when I read that sweet story of old	403
I was wandering and weary	443
In His own raiment clad	233
In our work and in our play	425
In the Name of Him who loves us	440
In the soft season of thy youth	432
In the vineyard of our Father	375
In Thy holy church, O Father	305
In token that thou shalt not fear	279
It came upon the midnight clear	215
Jerusalem, my happy home	377
Jerusalem the golden	379
Jesus calls us: o'er the tumult	289
Jesus Christ hath lived and died	306
Jesus Christ is risen to-day	249
Jesus Christ, our Saviour	412
Jesus, high in glory	332
Jesus, holy, undefiled	175
Jesus, I my cross have taken	283
Jesus is our Shepherd	347
Jesus lives! no longer now	252
Jesus, Lover of my soul	310
Jesus loves me, Jesus loves me	367
Jesus, meek and gentle	393
Jesus! Name of wondrous love	226
Jesus, Royal Jesus	241
Jesus shall reign, where'er the sun	286
Jesus, tender Shepherd, hear me	192
Jesus, when He left the sky	309
Just as I am, without one plea	237
Let every heart rejoice and sing	301
Lift up the Advent strain	207
Light's abode, celestial Salem	390
Listen to the wondrous story	389
Little children, who would ever	459
Lo! on Sion's holy mountain	472
Lord, a little band and lowly	421
Lord, in this Thy mercy's day	236
Lord of my life, whose tender care	315
Lord, this day Thy children meet	300
Lord, Thy children guide and keep	433
Love divine, all love excelling	357
Loving Shepherd of Thy sheep	346
My God, my Father, while I stray	349
Nearer, my God, to Thee	343
New every morning is the love	172
Now the day is over	191
Now the dreary night is done	173
Now the light has gone away	184
O come, all ye faithful	212
O come, dear child, along with me	384
O day of rest and gladness	196
O God, who, when the night was deep	177
O happy band of pilgrims	354
O holy Lord, content to fill	451
O Lamb of God, most lowly	446
O little town of Bethlehem	223
O Lord of heaven, and earth, and sea	293
O Paradise! O Paradise!	388
O Saviour, precious Saviour	339
O sweet Sabbath bells	200
O Thou, to whose all-searching sight	235
O Word of God incarnate	302
Oft in danger, oft in woe	372
On our way rejoicing	463
Once in Bethlehem of Judah	222
Once in royal David's city	415
Once was heard the song of children	242
One there is above all others, O how	362
One there is above all others, Well	361
Onward, Christian soldiers	465
Our blest Redeemer, ere He breathed	260
Palms of glory, raiment bright	460
Pleasant are Thy courts above	276
Praise, my soul, the King of Heaven	321
Praise, O praise our God and King	296
Rest of the weary	352
Resting from His work to-day	247
Rise, the risen Saviour saith	255
Rock of Ages, cleft for me	311
Round the throne of glory	325
Saviour, abide with us	190
Saviour, again to Thy dear Name we raise	201
Saviour, Blessed Saviour	461
Saviour, breathe an evening blessing	188
Saviour, like a shepherd lead us	427
Saviour, source of every blessing	308
Saviour, teach me, day by day	366
Saviour, when in dust to Thee	234
Saviour, who Thy flock art feeding	278
See the shining dew-drops	441
Shepherd of those sunlit mountains	447
Sing with joy, 'tis Christmas morn	224
Sion, Sion, haste to meet Him	238
Soldiers of Christ, arise	281
Soldiers of the Captain	469
Soldiers who to Christ belong	473
Songs of praise the angels sang	318
Summer suns are glowing	203
Sun of my soul, Thou Saviour dear	180
Sunny days of childhood	449
Sweet it is for child like me	413
Sweet Saviour, bless us ere we go	182
Sweet the moments, rich in blessing	245
Tell it out among the heathen	291
Ten thousand times ten thousand	462
Tender Shepherd, Thou hast stilled	284
The breaking morn comes back to bless	176
The Church's one foundation	275
The corn is ripe for reaping	297
The day is past and over	186
The Day of Resurrection	254
The holy Angels sing	414
The hours of day are over	193
The King of love my Shepherd is	360
The morning bright, with rosy light	174
The morning light flingeth	178
The roseate hues of early dawn	429
The Friend of little children	273
The Son of God goes forth to war	271
The strain upraise of joy and praise	323
The wise may bring their learning	411
The year is swiftly waning	204
There is a blessed Home	381
There is a green hill far away	243
There is a happy land	425
There is a mother's voice of love	437
There is an eye that never sleeps	314
There is no name so sweet on earth	330
There's a Friend for little children	382
There's no other friend like Jesus	345
There's not a tint that paints the rose	453
There sitteth a Dove, so white and fair	317
Thine for ever, God of love	282
This is the day of light	194
Those eternal bowers	454

	NUMBER
Thou art the Way: to Thee alone	396
Thou didst leave Thy Throne and Thy kingly crown	442
Thou who camest from above	265
Three in One, and One in Three	267
Through good report, and evil, Lord	348
Through the night of doubt and sorrow	371
Thy seal, O Lord, the holy sign	280
'Twas God that made the ocean	431
Up above the bright blue sky	398
Up in heaven, up in heaven	209
Uplift the banner, let it float	287
Upward where the stars are burning	335
We are but little children weak	376
We are but strangers here	385
We are little Christian children	424
We are little pilgrims	356
We come, Lord, to Thy feet	199
We give Thee but Thine own	294
We march, we march to victory	459

	NUMBER
We plough the fields, and scatter	409
We sing a loving Jesus	419
We speak of the realms of the blest	386
Welcome, happy morning! age to age shall say	470
What a strange and wondrous story	430
When evening shadows gather	189
When, His salvation bringing	342
When I survey the wondrous Cross	244
When Jesus left His Father's throne	392
When you're sleeping, children fair	448
Where is the Holy Jesus	428
While shepherds watched their flocks by night	218
Whither are you going, pilgrims of a day	444
Who are these like stars appearing	383
Who is this, so weak and helpless	420
Winter reigneth o'er the land	205
With hearts in love abounding	288
Within the temple's hallowed walls	418
Yes, for me, for me He careth	370
Yes, God is good; in earth and sky	445
Youthful days are passing o'er us	436

Responsive Prayers.

OF THE HOLY CHILD JESUS	455	OF THE HOLY CHILDHOOD, No. 2	457
OF THE HOLY CHILDHOOD, No. 1	456	OF THE CHURCH	458

Carols.

A shepherd band their flocks are keeping	487
All this night bright Angels sing	478
Angel hosts in bright array	483
Bright Easter skies! Fair Easter skies	508
Carol, brothers, carol	484
Carol, sweetly carol	479
Christ is born of maiden fair	481
Christ is risen! Christ is risen! He hath	520
Christ is risen! Christ is risen! O let	518
Christ, the Lord, is risen again	516
Christians, carol sweetly	497
Deep the gloom, and still the night	503
Easter flowers, Easter carols	511
From far away we come to you	482
Gather around the Christmas Tree	488
Gently falls the winter snow	486
God hath sent His Angels	509
Good Christian men, rejoice	489
Hark! what sounds are sweetly stealing	490
Holy night! peaceful night!	495
In the early morning, early	493
In the field with their flocks abiding	498
In the wintry heaven	505
Let the merry Church bells ring	523
Lo! a star, ye sages hoary	485

Morning is breaking	500
Near the Tomb where Jesus slept	517
Now all the bells are ringing	519
Now lift the carol, men and maids	491
Now to Bethlehem haste we	506
Once again, O blessed time	475
Roman soldier, tell us true	521
See amid the winter's snow	492
Shine, O Sun, in splendour bright	515
Silent night! peaceful night	499
Sing ye the songs of praise	480
Sing your carols to-day	524
Sleep, Holy Babe	474
Sleep, my Saviour, sleep	477
Smile praises, O sky	512
Star of Glory! brightly streaming	502
Stars all bright are beaming	476
The Easter sunshine breaks again	507
The Lord is risen, risen indeed	513
The world itself keeps Easter Day	510
Tune your harps for holy song	501
'Twas at the matin hour	522
Waken, Christian children	496
We three kings of Orient are	504
What child is this, who laid to rest	494
Ye happy bells of Easter Day	514

THE
SUNDAY-SCHOOL HYMNAL.

Four editions are published, as follows:—

Edition A. Contains Morning and Evening Prayer, and Litany, arranged for Choral Service; all the Morning and Evening Canticles, with four single and double chants for each, and *blank staves* for the *insertion of other chants;* Four Short Services (to be read) for Sunday-schools; a Short Choral Service, for the same purpose; all the Collects of the Prayer Book with Marginal notes; the Selections of Psalms, pointed for Chanting, and having *two Anglican* and *one Gregorian* Chant for each Psalm; in all, there are one hundred and seventy Chants; nearly three hundred Hymns for the different seasons of the Christian year, and for children's use; five Litany Hymns; twelve Processional Hymns; and more than fifty Carols. This edition has 352 pages (of the size of the pages of the "Church Hymnal"), with hymns and music, most conveniently arranged for use.

Edition B. Has all that Edition A contains, *except the music.* That is, it is of such a size and shape, and sold at such a price, as to be adapted to the use of scholars who do not need the music. For convenience, the different portions of the Liturgical services are paged the same as in Edition A.

Edition C. Contains a large number of Psalms and Canticles from the Old and New Testaments, arranged and pointed for chanting, with accompanying Chants (in all one hundred and seventy single and double Chants), and all the Hymns and Carols contained in Edition A. The liturgical portions are omitted. This edition has been prepared at the request of ministers and others not belonging to the Episcopal Church.

Edition D. Is the same as Edition C, but in smaller form, and *without music.*

PRICES OF THE DIFFERENT EDITIONS POSTPAID.

Edition A . . . . . { Paper boards, 50 cents.
{ Cloth boards, 75 cents.

Edition B . . . . . { Paper boards, 25 cents.
{ Cloth limp, 25 cents.

Edition C . . . . . { Paper boards, 50 cents.
{ Cloth boards, 75 cents.

Edition D . . . . . { Paper boards, 25 cents.
{ Cloth limp, 25 cents.

A discount of 20 per cent from the above prices, when ordered (with accompanying remittance) in quantities, and sent by express. No discount when sent by mail.

PERSONS ORDERING MUST STATE WHICH EDITION THEY WISH.

ADDRESS

REV. CHARLES L. HUTCHINS,

MEDFORD, MASS.

This Hymnal, immediately on its first publication, seemed to supply a widely-felt need of the Church, and it has rapidly passed through many editions. The demand for it has steadily increased, and it is constantly being adopted in parishes where other Hymnals have heretofore been used. Larger than any other of the Hymnals of the Church (containing 624 pages), it has the following features, some of which are peculiar to it, and, it is believed, add not a little to its value:—

Many old Tunes, with which choirs and congregations are acquainted, are used. With most of these a second Tune of modern composition is also given. The use of open notes, which gives a clearer appearance to the page. The insertion of the first verse of each Hymn between the staves of the corresponding Tune. The Tune and Hymn are invariably printed on the same page. The Time, or metronomic mark, is given with every Tune. The marks of musical expression are given with every Hymn. The Metre, name of Tune, and composer's name are given with every Tune. The name of the author is given with every Hymn. At the end of the Hymns for each season, a list of Hymns in other parts of the book suitable for that season is given. Marks indicating that Hymns appointed for special seasons are suitable also for other times. Several blank music pages are given for the insertion of Tunes which may be favorites with any choir or congregation. A list of all the Scripture Texts in the book, with their references. This is a great convenience to the clergy. Other indexes of the most complete character.

All copies of the Book have marbled edges, to prevent soiling. And the price of Hymnal and Chant Book, elegantly bound in one volume,

IS BUT $1.25, POSTPAID,

with a discount of 20 per cent when sent in quantities, by express.

THE CHANT BOOK

Contains the largest number of Chants that has ever appeared in any collection published in this country. The selection is of great variety, and is very conveniently arranged.

With each Canticle from two to six blank staves are left for the insertion of chants, as choirs may desire.
The Chant Book contains 542 Chants, Glorias, Kyries, etc.
The Choral Service (Tallis's Festival Responses) for Morning and Evening Prayer, and Litany, is given.
The Ten Selections of Psalms are given, with one Gregorian and two Anglican Chants for each Psalm.
Price, in paper, postpaid, 30 cents in cloth, boards, 50 cents.

NOTICE: That this Hymnal is not published without the Chant Book.
That bound with the Chant Book its price is but $1.25.

By the use of guards made for the purpose, the Church Hymnal can be sent through the mails without injury, and will reach its destination in as good condition as if obtained at a bookstore. Many parishes in the most distant States and Territories have been supplied in this way.

REMITTANCES MUST ACCOMPANY ORDERS.

ADDRESS

REV. CHARLES L. HUTCHINS,

MEDFORD, MASS.

SERVICES

OF

SACRED SONG

For Sunday-school and Choir use on Christmas, Easter, and other festival or anniversary occasions. Each Service contains from twenty to thirty pages of Carols, Hymns, Anthems, etc. (with music for each), and Scripture Readings.

The price, which is the same for all the Services, is as follows: Single copy, 25 cents; ten copies, 20 cents each; twenty copies, 15 cents each; fifty copies, 12 cents each; one hundred copies, 10 cents each.

ADDRESS THE

REV. C. L. HUTCHINS,

MEDFORD, MASS.

No. 1.

THE CHILD JESUS.

Illustrating the Birth and early years of our Lord.

FOURTH EDITION.

No. 2.

THE DIVINE TEACHER.

Illustrating the sayings of our Master.

(IN PREPARATION.)

No. 3.

THE SUFFERING SAVIOUR.

Illustrating the Passion and Death of our Lord.

(IN PREPARATION.)

No. 4.

THE RISEN LORD.

Illustrating the Resurrection of Christ.

SECOND EDITION.

No. 5.

THE HEAVENLY KING.

Illustrating the post-Resurrection life, and the Ascension of our Lord.

(IN PREPARATION.)

No. 6.

HARVEST HOME.

For Thanksgiving Services, or Harvest Home Festivals.

FIRST EDITION.

THE PARISH CHOIR.

A MONTHLY PUBLICATION OF CHURCH MUSIC.

The publication of the "Parish Choir" was undertaken by the undersigned, for the purpose of furnishing to individuals and choirs a thoroughly good class of Church Music, at the lowest possible price. It contains Anthems, Hymns, Carols, settings of the Te Deum, Canticles, and Offertories, and other music suitable for Church Services. It is used in all kinds of choirs, and has met with a steadily increasing circulation. Twelve numbers, each containing four octavo pages of music, are guaranteed to subscribers; but, as pecuniary profit is not the object of the editor, he has annually given to subscribers several extra numbers, without additional charge. Choirs subscribing for five or more copies get them at a reduced price, and are thus enabled to provide themselves with a collection of the best music at trifling expense. Or, if but a single copy is taken by the choir leader or organist, additional copies may afterwards be ordered.

RATES OF SUBSCRIPTION TO THE "PARISH CHOIR."

Single subscription, 50 cents a year. Five copies for one year, 45 cents each. Ten or more copies, 40 cents each.

ALL SUBSCRIPTIONS BEGIN AND END WITH THE CURRENT YEAR.

Back numbers supplied. Less than twenty-five copies, 5 cents each. From twenty-five to one hundred copies, 4 cents each. Double numbers, 10 cents each.

CATALOGUES WILL BE SENT, ON APPLICATION, FREE OF CHARGE.

It is the publisher's invariable rule that all subscriptions and orders must be accompanied by Money, Draft, or Post-Office Order drawn on Medford.

ADDRESS

REV. CHARLES L. HUTCHINS,

MEDFORD, MASS.

www.ingramcontent.com/pod-product-compliance
Lightning Source LLC
Chambersburg PA
CBHW030749230426
43667CB00007B/897